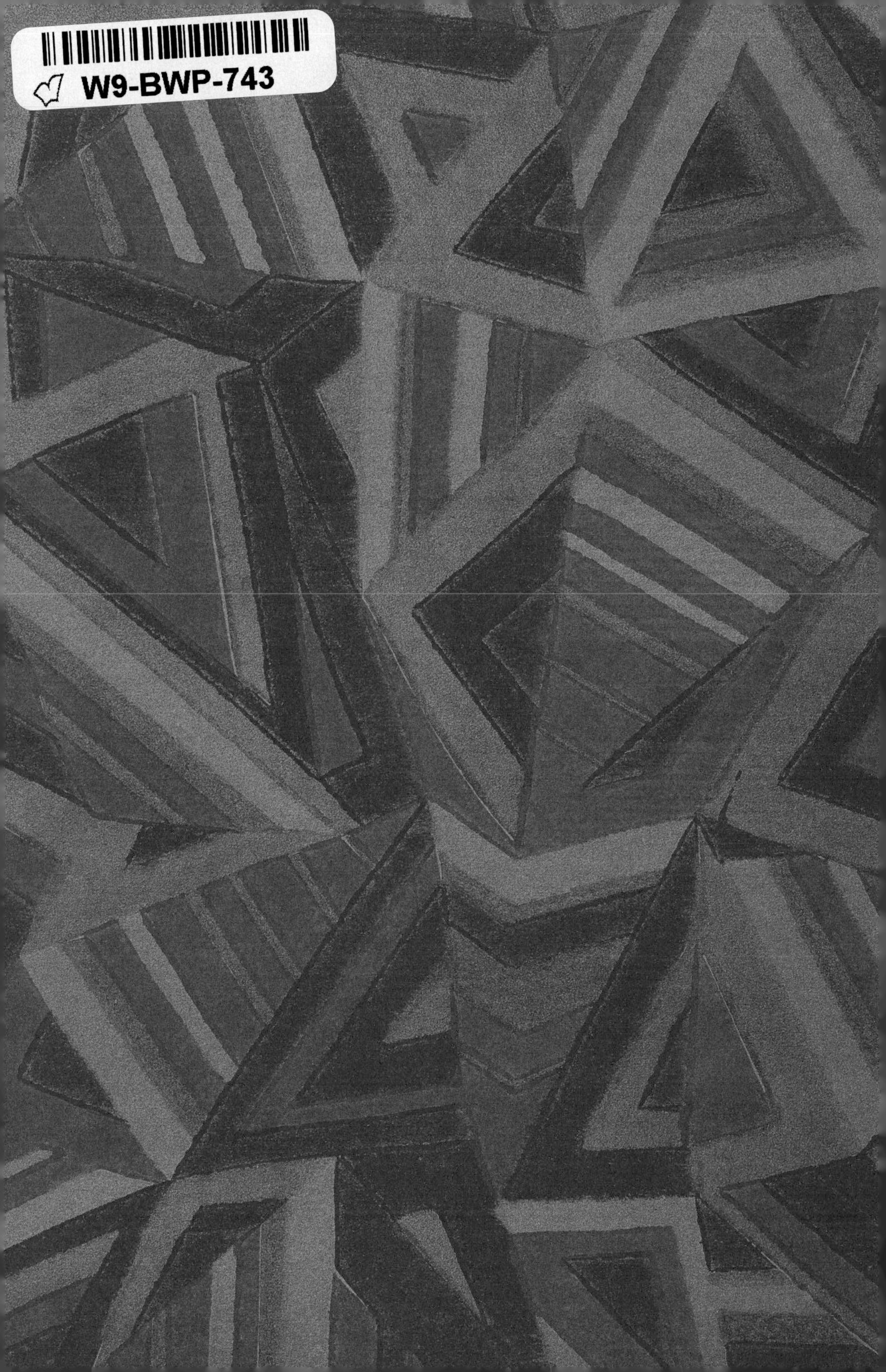

NATSUME ONO made her professional debut in 2003 with the webcomic *La Quinta Camera*. Her subsequent works *not simple, Ristorante Paradiso, Gente* and *House of Five Leaves* (*Saraiya Goyou*) met with both critical and popular acclaim. Both *Ristorante Paradiso* and *House of Five Leaves* have been adapted into TV anime series.

House of Five Leaves

3 第三集

NATSUME ONO

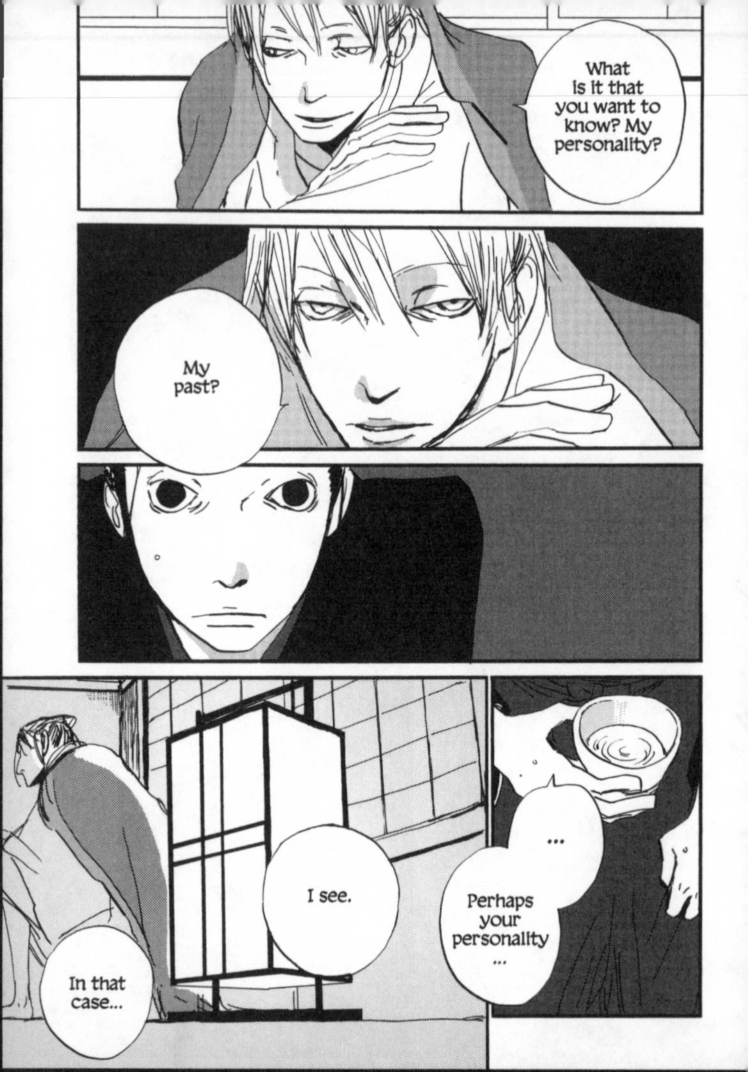
What is it that you want to know? My personality?
My past?
...
Perhaps your personality...
I see.
In that case...

MASANOSUKE, who became a *ronin* after being dismissed by his lord, joins gang of kidnappers calling themselves the "FIVE LEAVES." Though conflicte about his decision, he finds himself becoming increasingly involved with th gang members: UMEZO, OTAKE, MATSUKICHI, and the ever mysterious YAICH

A figure from Ume's past visits the home of GOINKYO—a man who aids th Five Leaves from time to time—in order to blackmail him. Masa, despit suffering from an illness, exerts himself and successfully protects Goinky and the others. However, upon returning to Edo, he flees from a duel wit a fellow ronin and once again loses his confidence. Afterwards, a chanc acquaintance named YAGI offers to train Masa, and while doing so mention

秋津政之助 AKITSU MASANOSUKE

A skilled swordsman without a position, he's striving to become a samurai retainer again. In need of money to service his brother's debt back home. Currently employed as a yojimbo at Katsuraya, a house of ill repute.

弥一 YAICHI

The leader of the Five Leaves, he makes his living through ransom. He takes a liking to Masa, inducting him into the crew and securing him a position at Katsuraya. May have once been part of the Bakuro no Kuhei gang.

おたけ OTAKE

A member of the Five Leaves, she's known Yaichi for a long time. Currently renting Masa's room in the rowhouse. She has a fondness for sake.

梅造 UMEZO

A member of the Five Leaves and owner of the *izakaya* where the crew gathers. An ex-thief, he loves his daughter and has feelings for Otake.

松吉 MATSUKICHI

A member of the Five Leaves, he's a silent man who serves as the gang's spy. An ornament craftsman, he used to work solo as a thief.

お絹 OKINU

Ume's daughter. One of the few people who know about the existence of the Five Leaves.

ご隠居 GOINKYO (Soji the Saint)

A long-time acquaintance of Ume's, he was once the head of an infamous gang.

八木 YAGI

A samurai whom Masa runs into occasionally in Edo. Has a deceased friend named "Yaichi."

House of Five Leaves

TABLE OF
CONTENTS

第三集

CHAPTER FIFTEEN ——————— INDEBTED (PART ONE) ——————— PAGE 7

CHAPTER SIXTEEN ——————— INDEBTED (PART TWO) —————— PAGE 35

CHAPTER SEVENTEEN —————— INDEBTED (PART THREE) ————— PAGE 67

CHAPTER EIGHTEEN ————— INDEBTED (PART FOUR) ————— PAGE 101

CHAPTER NINETEEN————— FROM BACK HOME (PART ONE) ——— PAGE 129

CHAPTER TWENTY ————— FROM BACK HOME (PART TWO) ——— PAGE 155

CHAPTER TWENTY-ONE —— FRIENDS ————————— PAGE 181

SIDE STORY—————————— WARMTH ——————————— PAGE 214

GLOSSARY ————————— PAGE 220

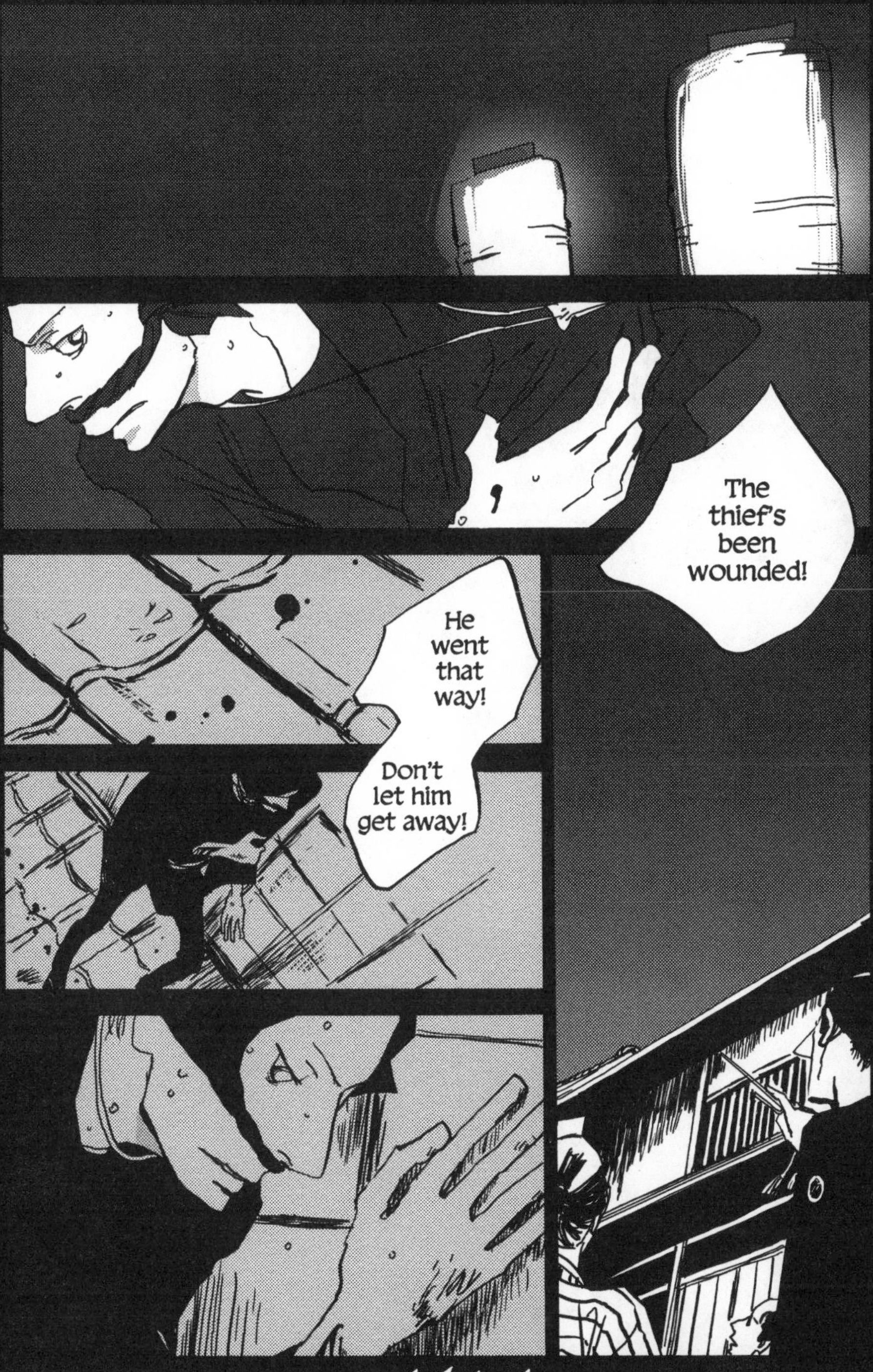
The thief's been wounded!
He went that way!
Don't let him get away!

Chapter Fifteen **Indebted** (Part One)

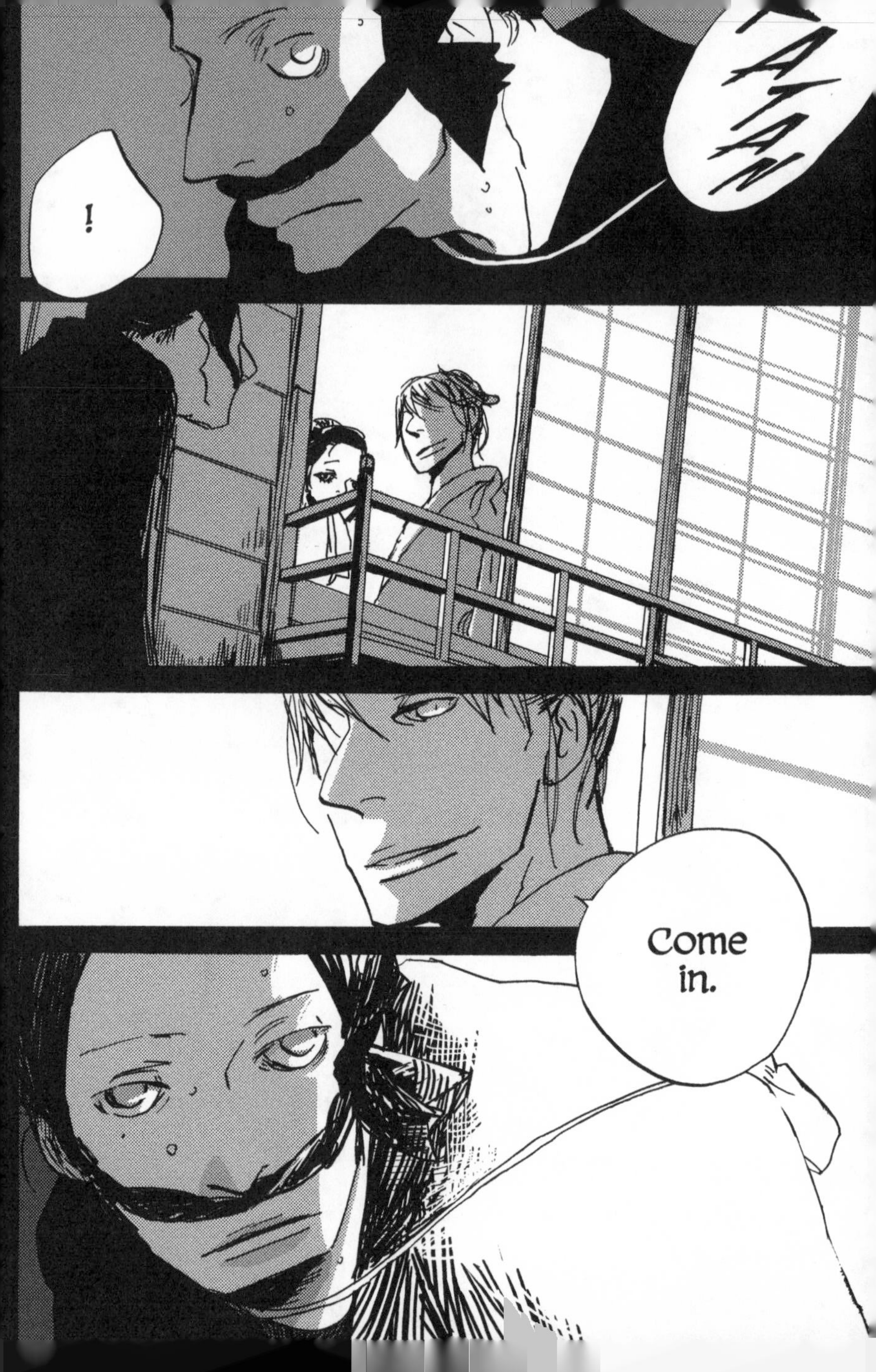
ATAN
!
Come in.

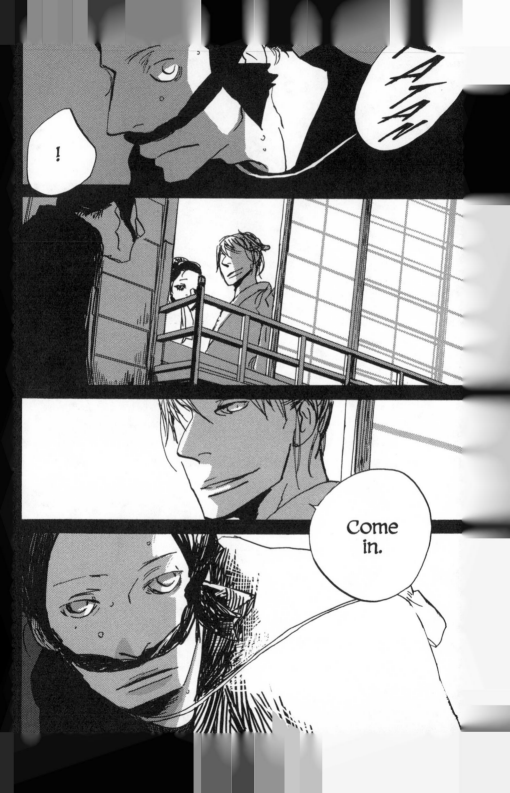

Chapter Fifteen Indebted (Part One)

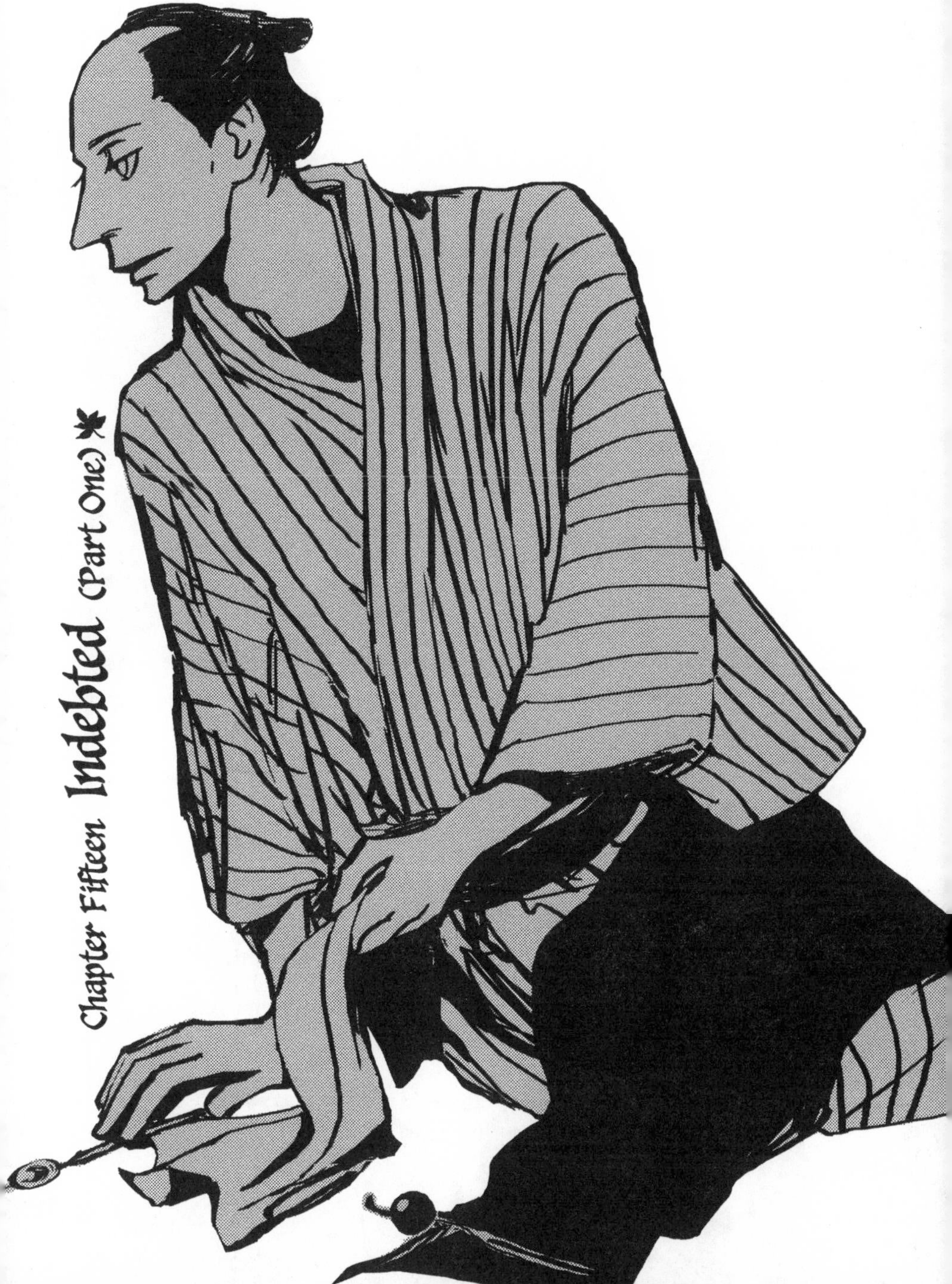

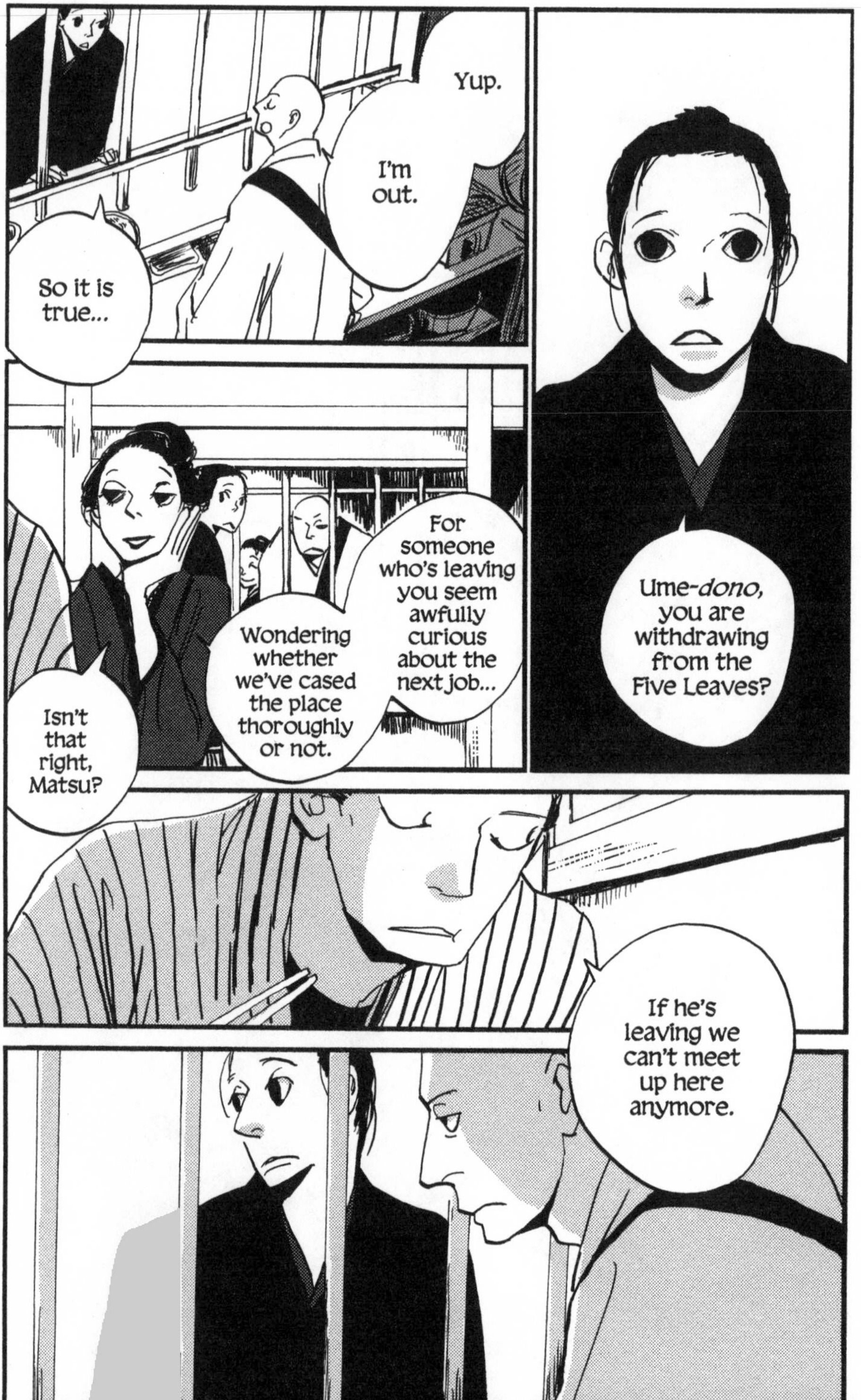
Ume-*dono*, you are withdrawing from the Five Leaves?
Yup.
I'm out.
So it is true...
For someone who's leaving you seem awfully curious about the next job...
Wondering whether we've cased the place thoroughly or not.
Isn't that right, Matsu?
If he's leaving we can't meet up here anymore.

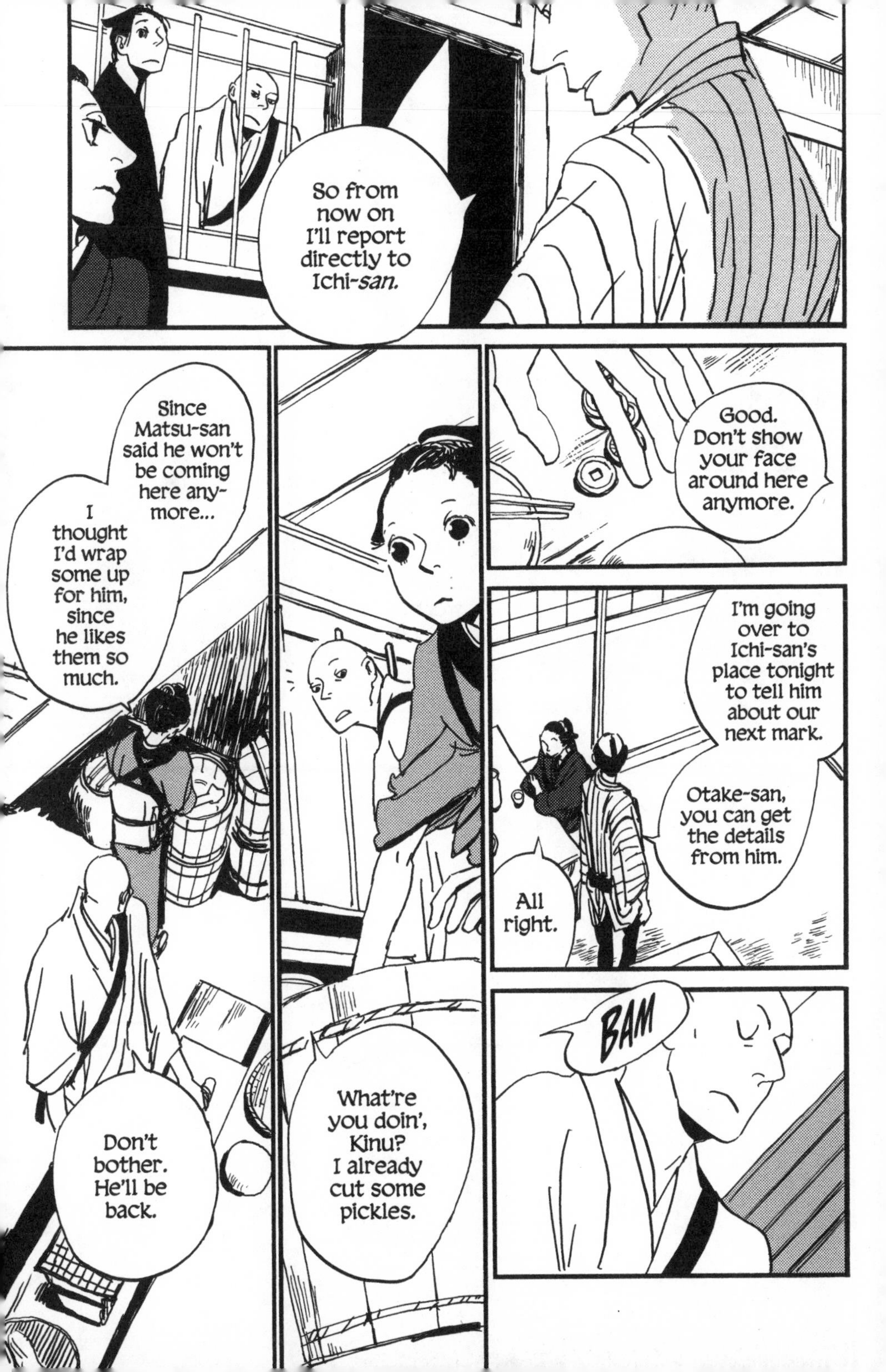
So from now on I'll report directly to Ichi-*san.*
Good. Don't show your face around here anymore.
I'm going over to Ichi-san's place tonight to tell him about our next mark.
Otake-san, you can get the details from him.
All right.
BAM
What're you doin', Kinu? I already cut some pickles.
Since Matsu-san said he won't be coming here anymore...
I thought I'd wrap some up for him, since he likes them so much.
Don't bother. He'll be back.

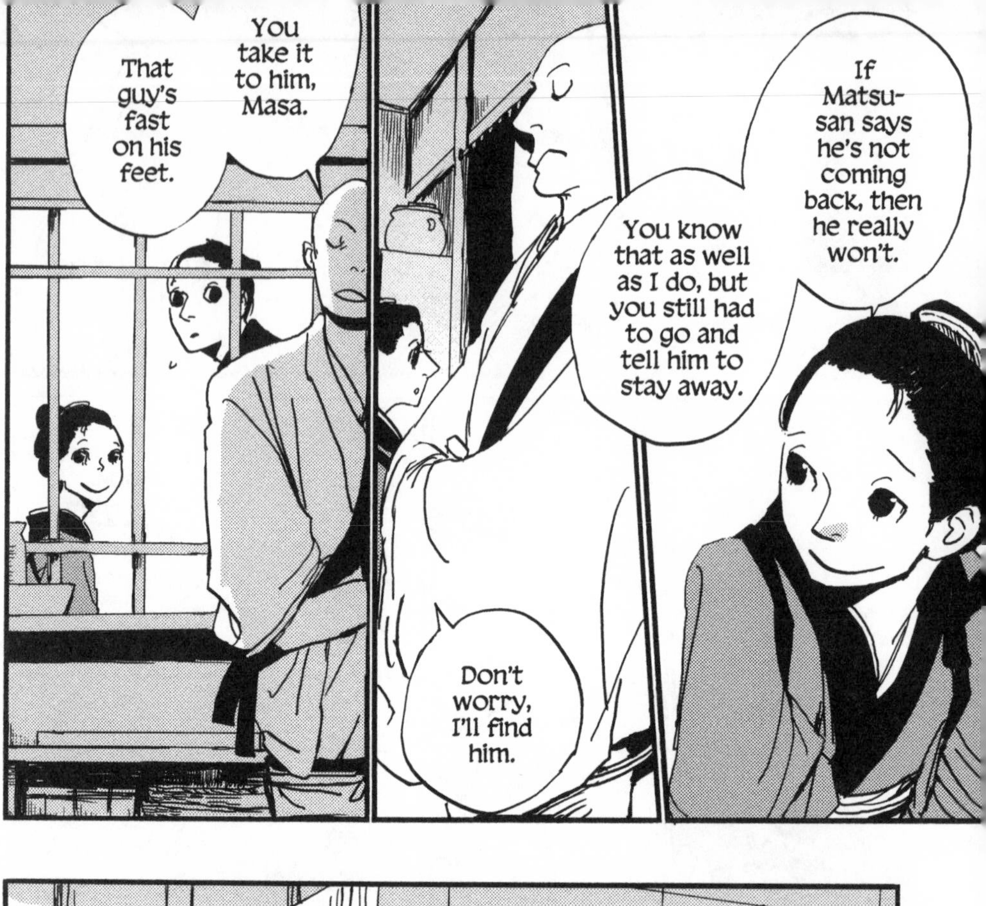
If Matsu-san says he's not coming back, then he really won't.
You know that as well as I do, but you still had to go and tell him to stay away.
Don't worry, I'll find him.
You take it to him, Masa.
That guy's fast on his feet.

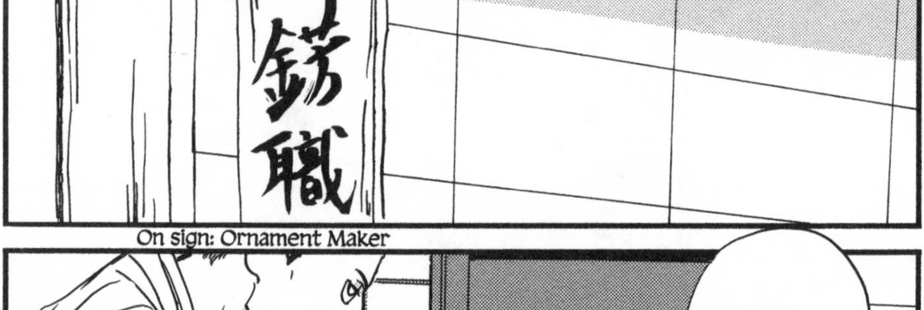
錺職

On sign: Ornament Maker

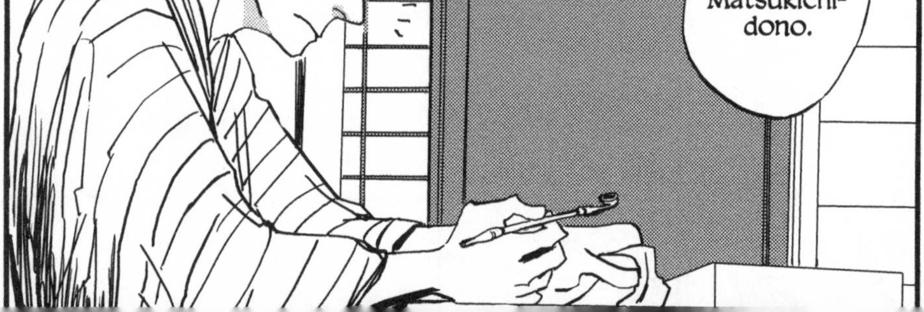
Matsukichi-dono.

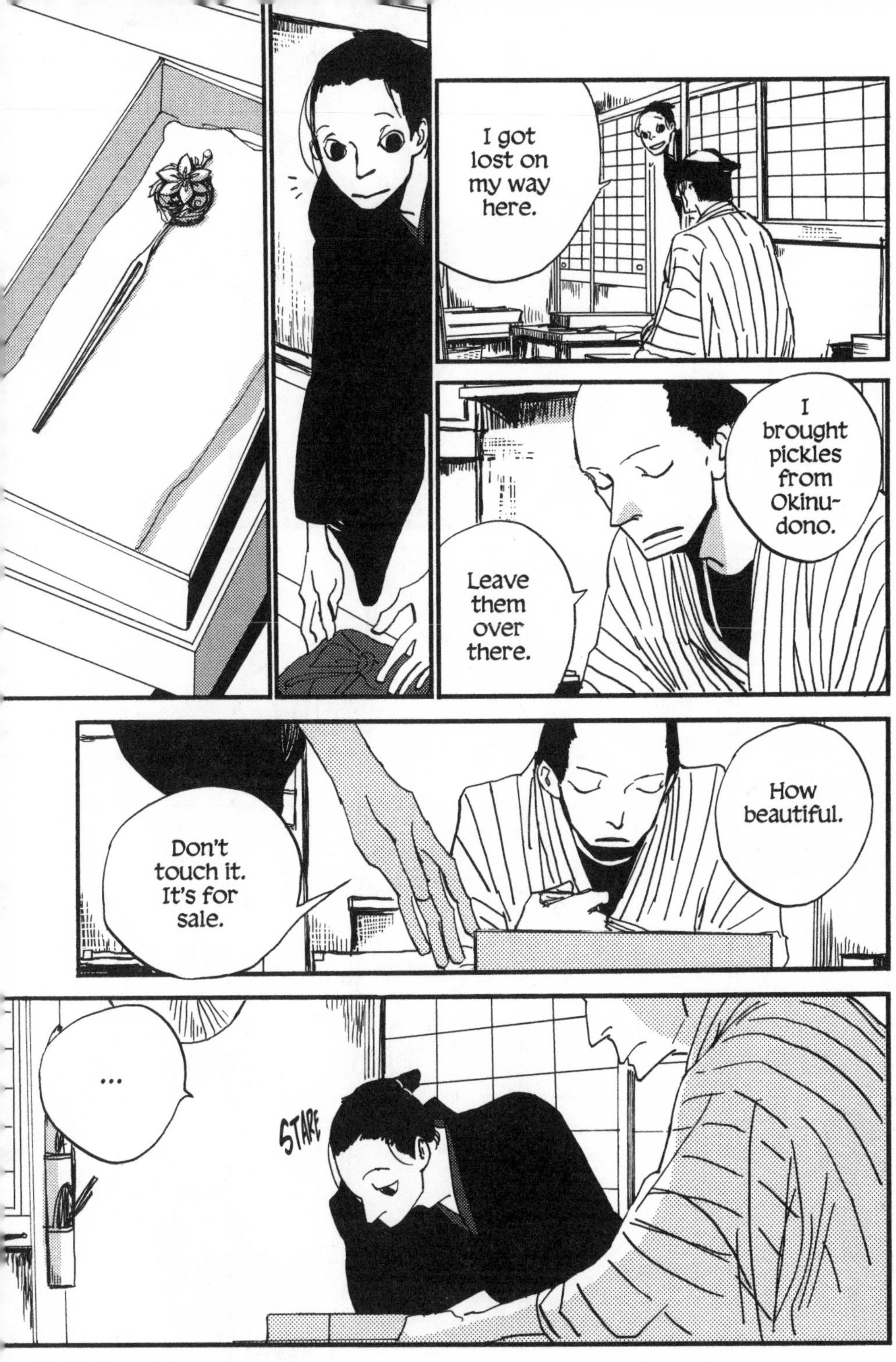
I got lost on my way here.
I brought pickles from Okinu-dono.
Leave them over there.
How beautiful.
Don't touch it. It's for sale.
...
STARE

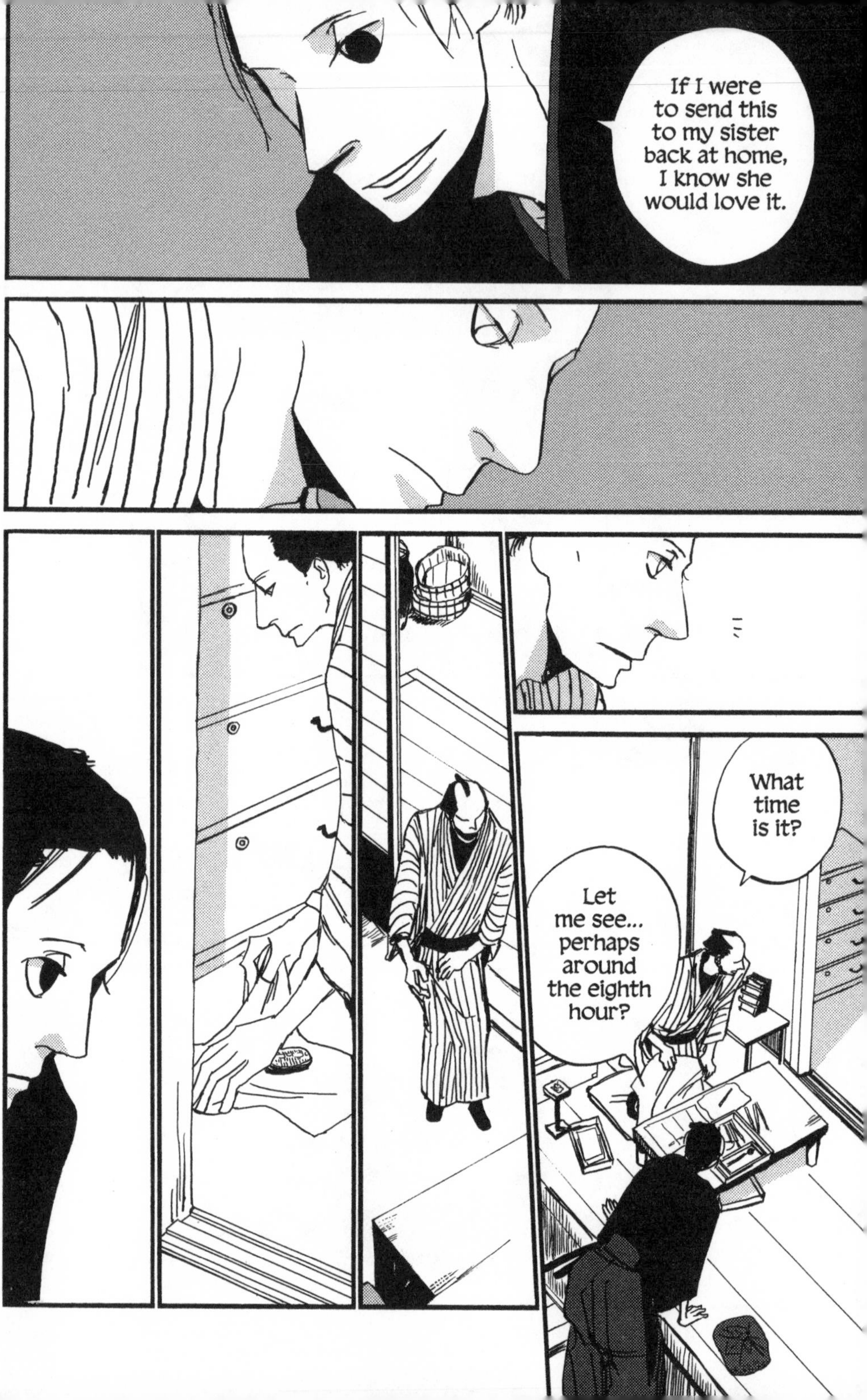
If I were to send this to my sister back at home, I know she would love it.
What time is it?
Let me see... perhaps around the eighth hour?

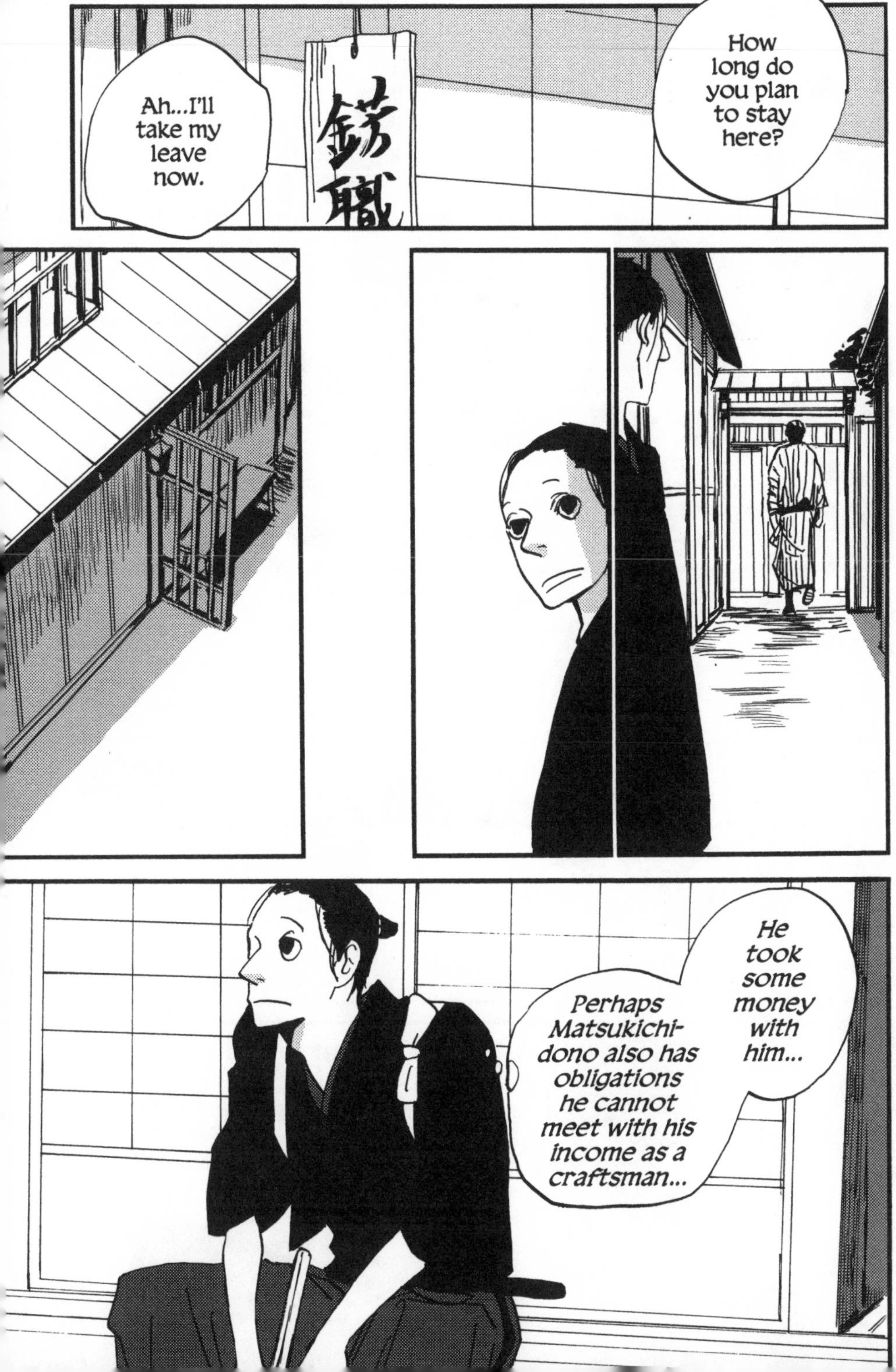
How long do you plan to stay here?
錺職
Ah...I'll take my leave now.
He took some money with him...
Perhaps Matsukichi-dono also has obligations he cannot meet with his income as a craftsman...

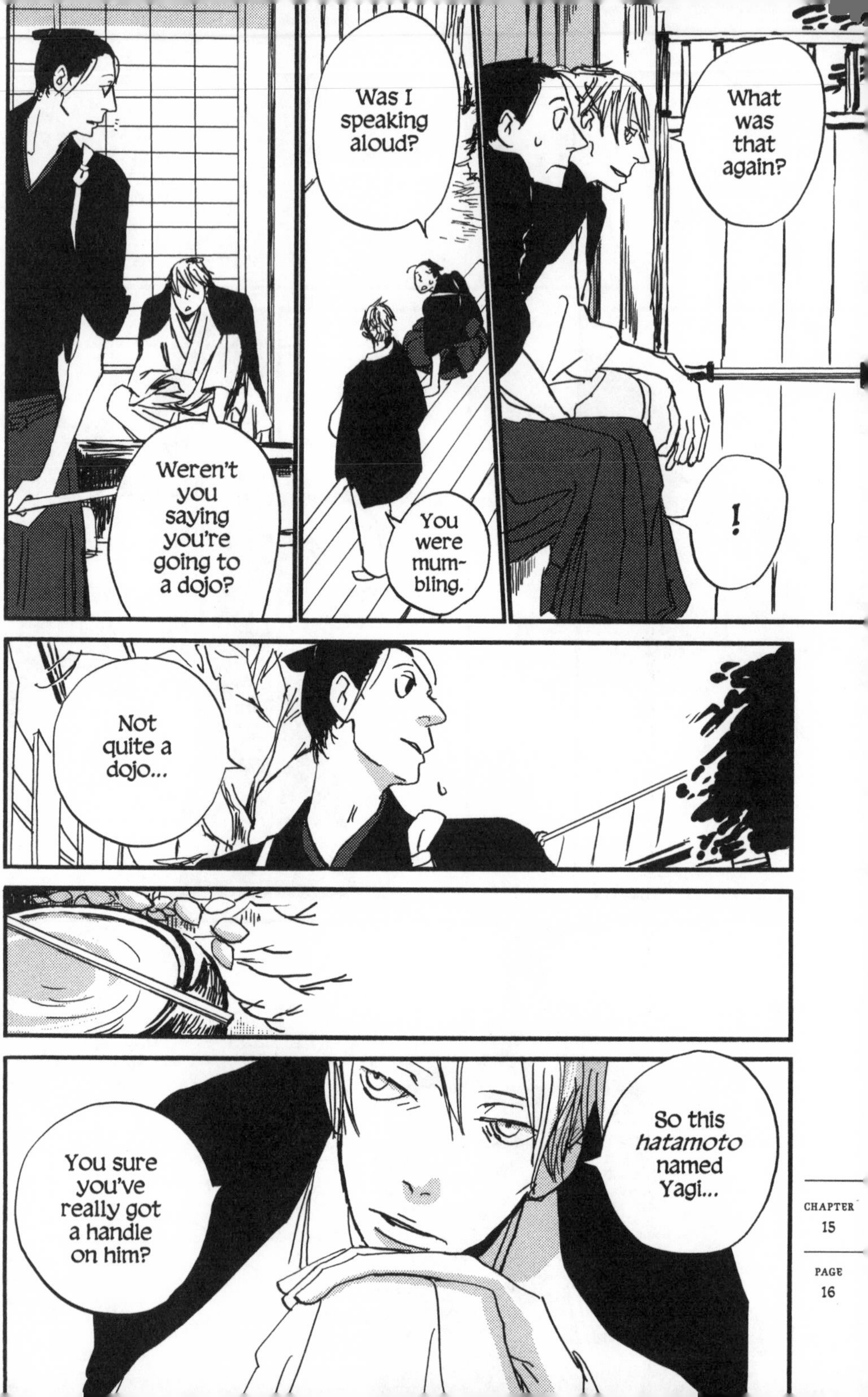
What was that again?
!
Was I speaking aloud?
You were mum-bling.
Weren't you saying you're going to a dojo?
Not quite a dojo...
So this *hatamoto* named Yagi...
You sure you've really got a handle on him?

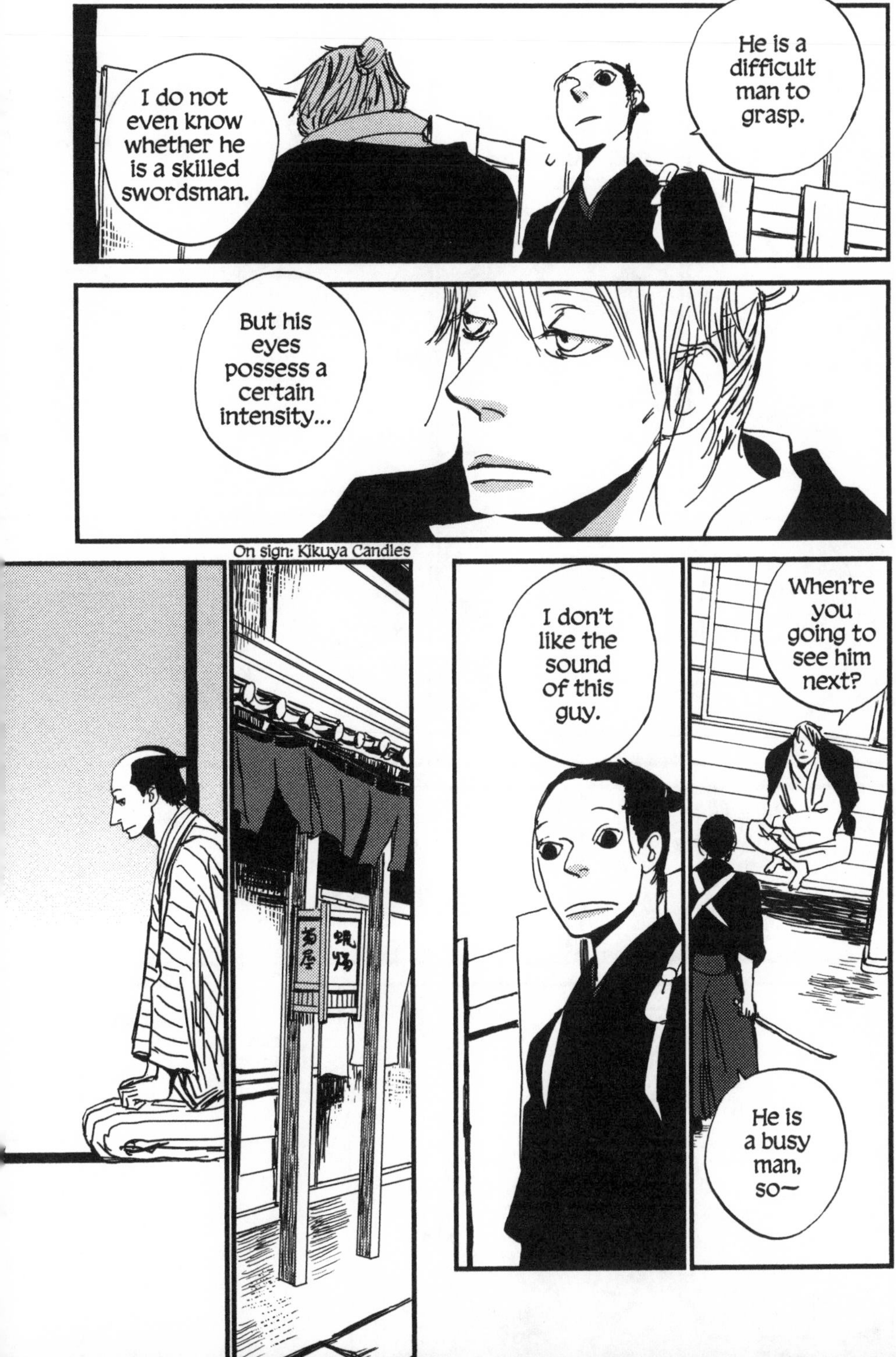
He is a difficult man to grasp.
I do not even know whether he is a skilled swordsman.
But his eyes possess a certain intensity...
When're you going to see him next?
He is a busy man, so~
I don't like the sound of this guy.
On sign: Kikuya Candles
蝋燭
菊屋

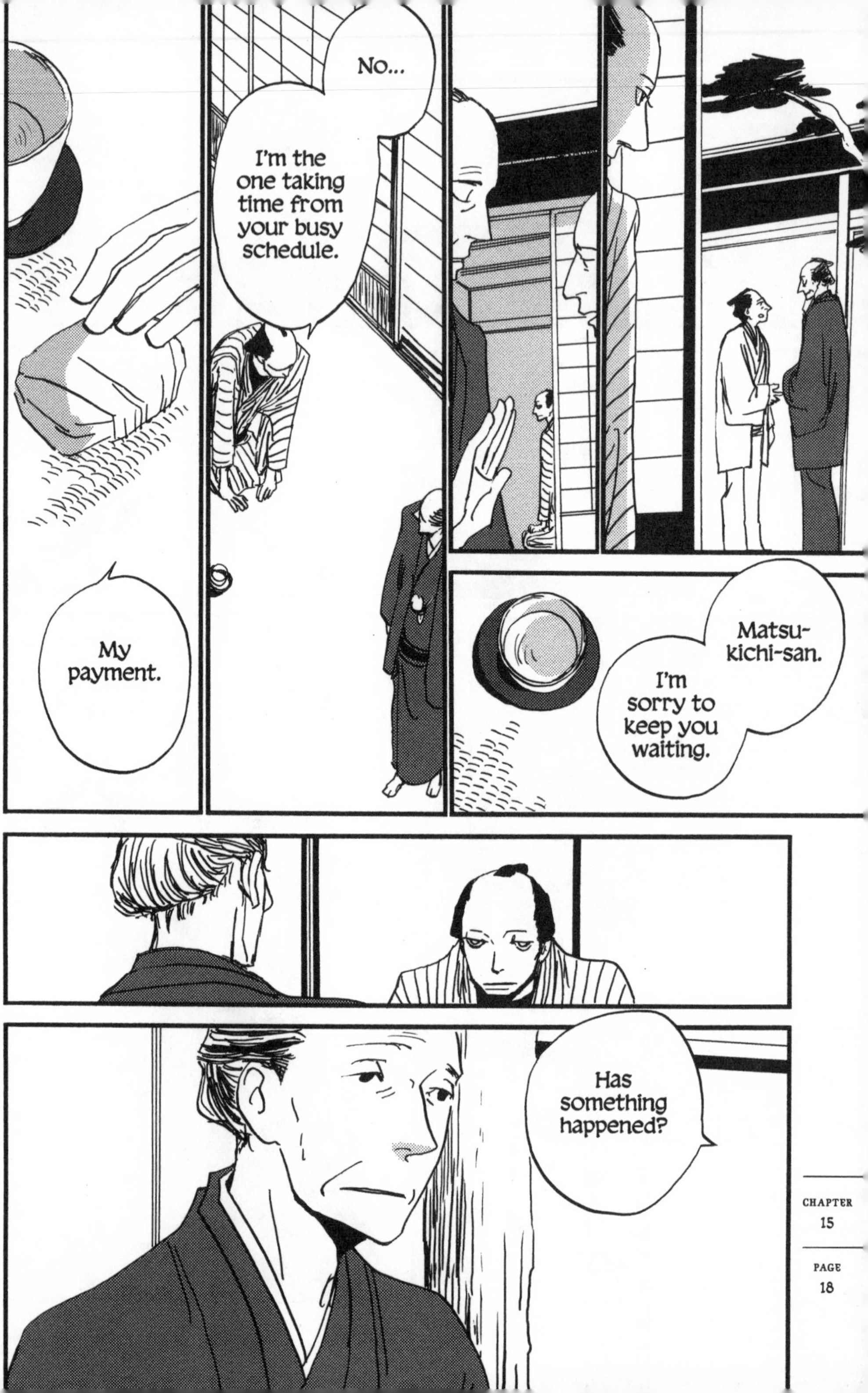
Matsu-kichi-san.
I'm sorry to keep you waiting.
No...
I'm the one taking time from your busy schedule.
My payment.
Has something happened?

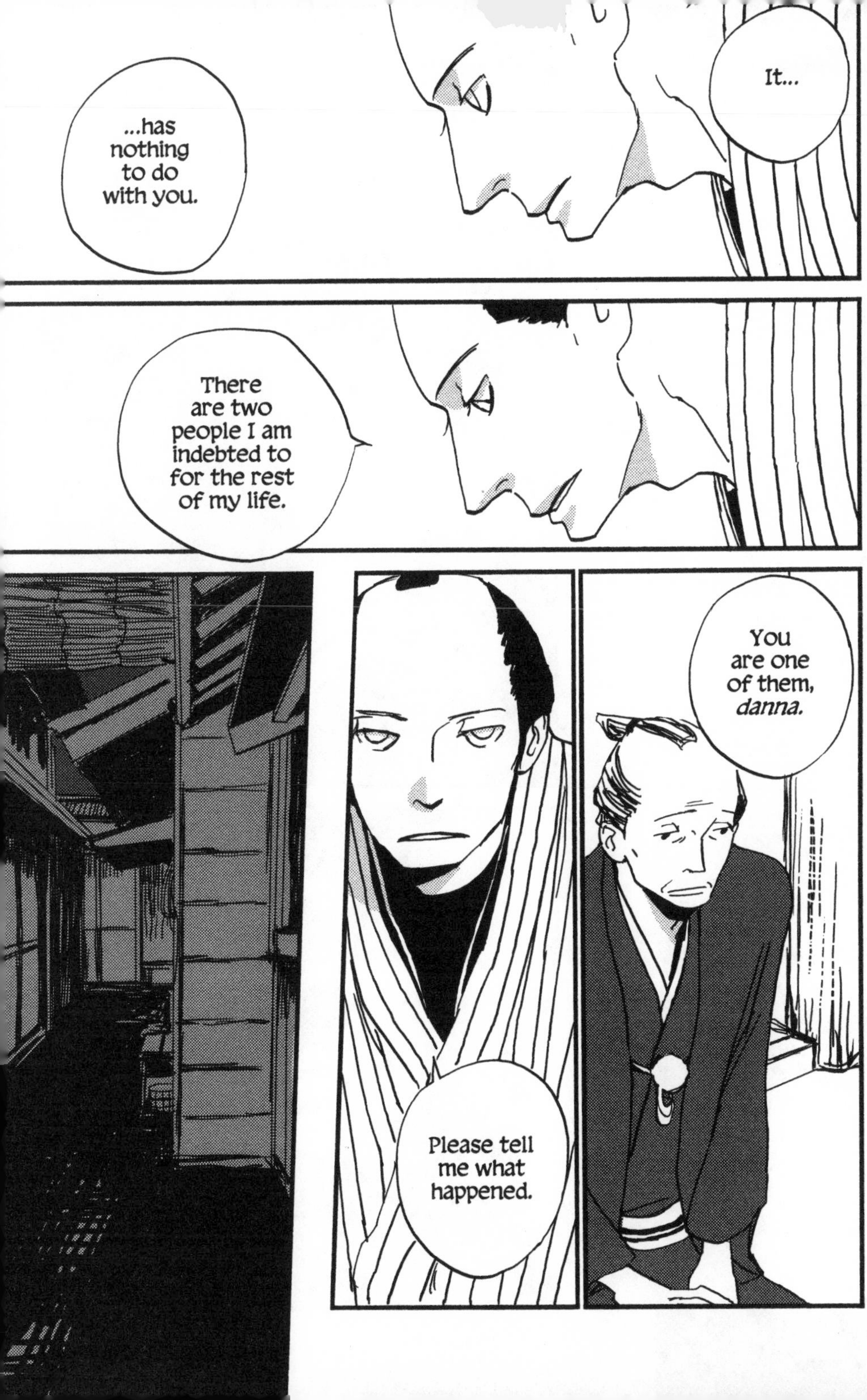
It...
...has nothing to do with you.
There are two people I am indebted to for the rest of my life.
You are one of them, *danna.*
Please tell me what happened.

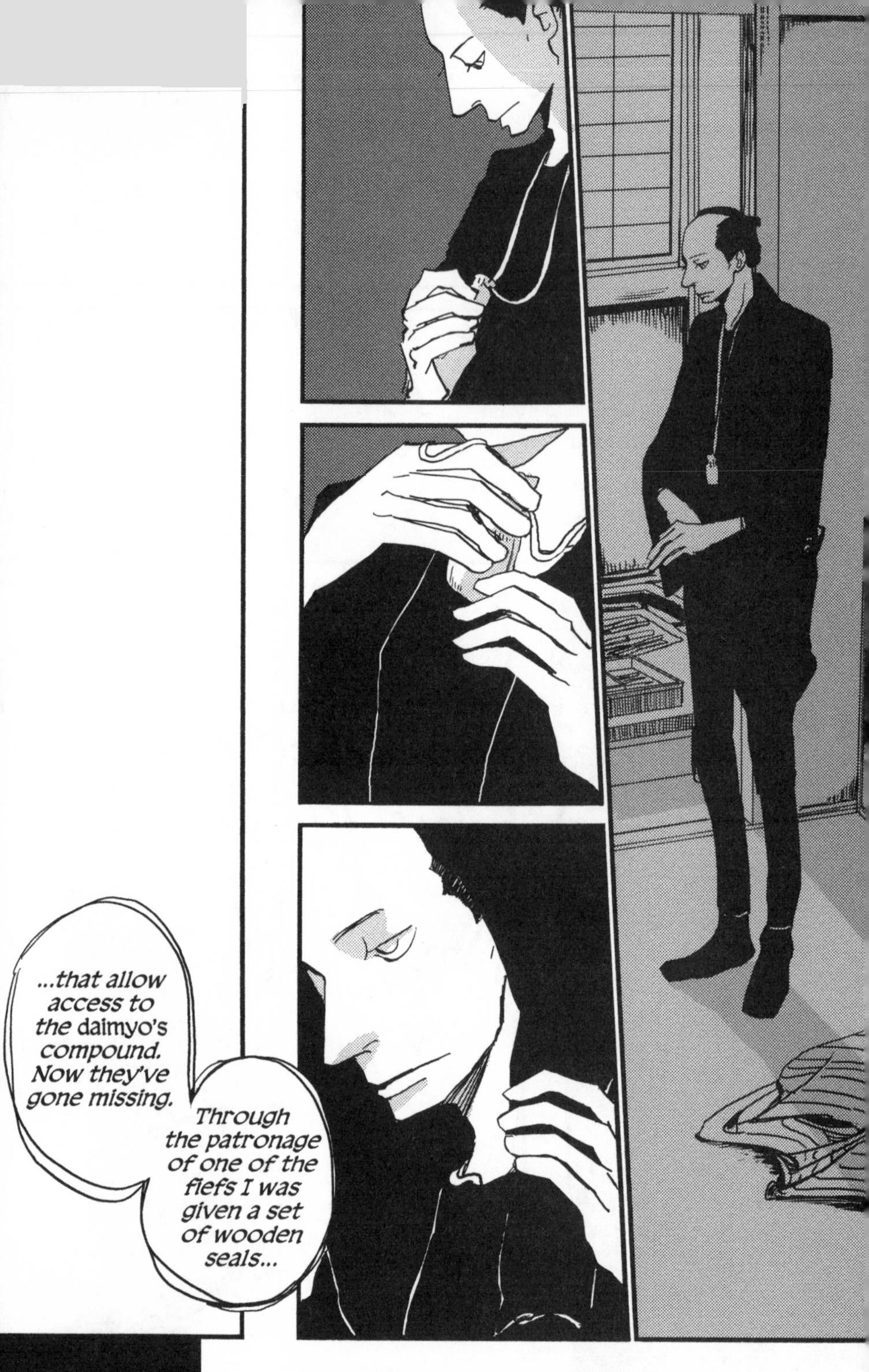
Through the patronage of one of the fiefs I was given a set of wooden seals...
...that allow access to the daimyo's compound. Now they've gone missing.

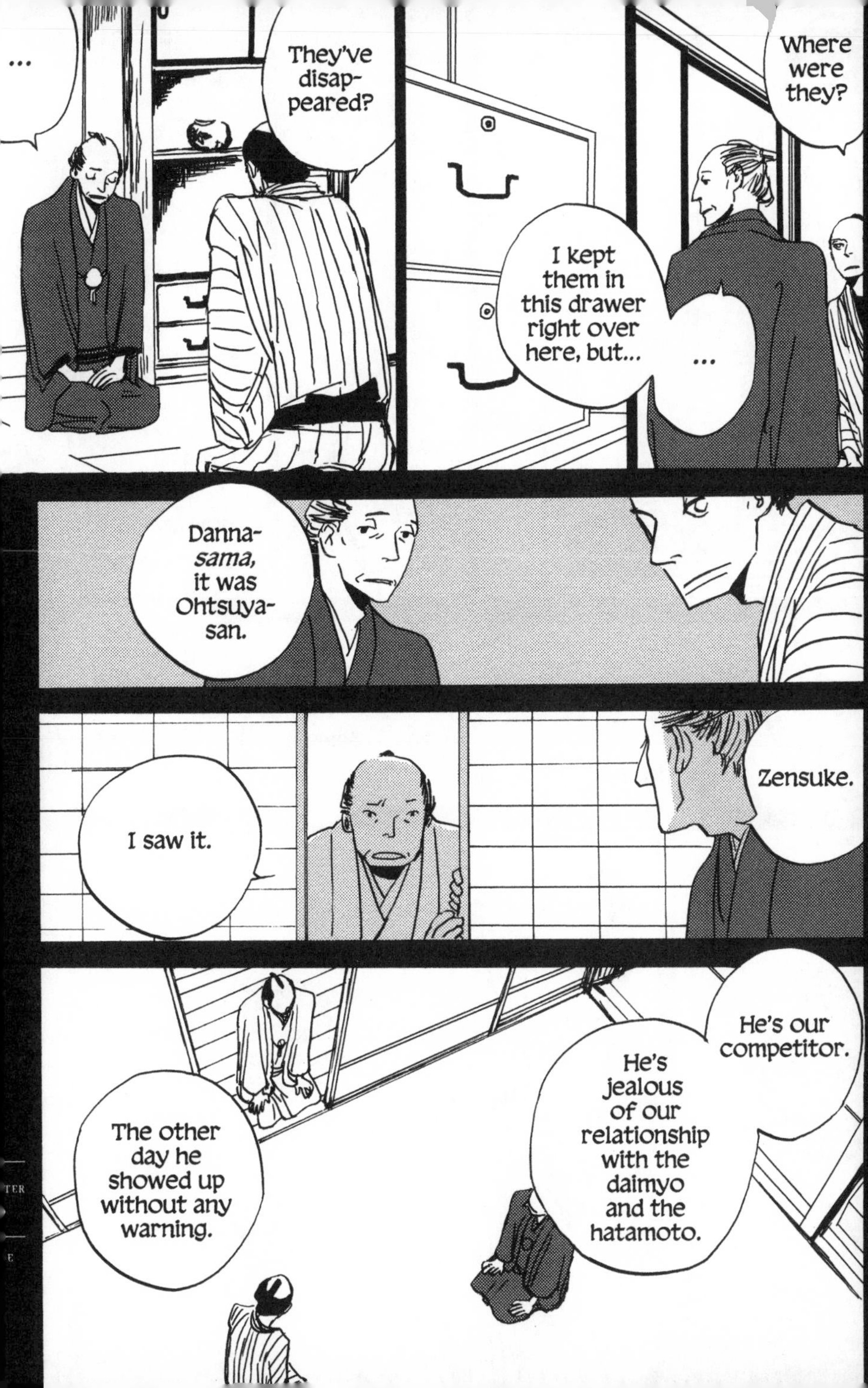
Where were they?
I kept them in this drawer right over here, but...
...
They've disap-peared?
...
Danna-*sama*, it was Ohtsuya-san.
Zensuke.
I saw it.
He's our competitor.
He's jealous of our relationship with the daimyo and the hatamoto.
The other day he showed up without any warning.

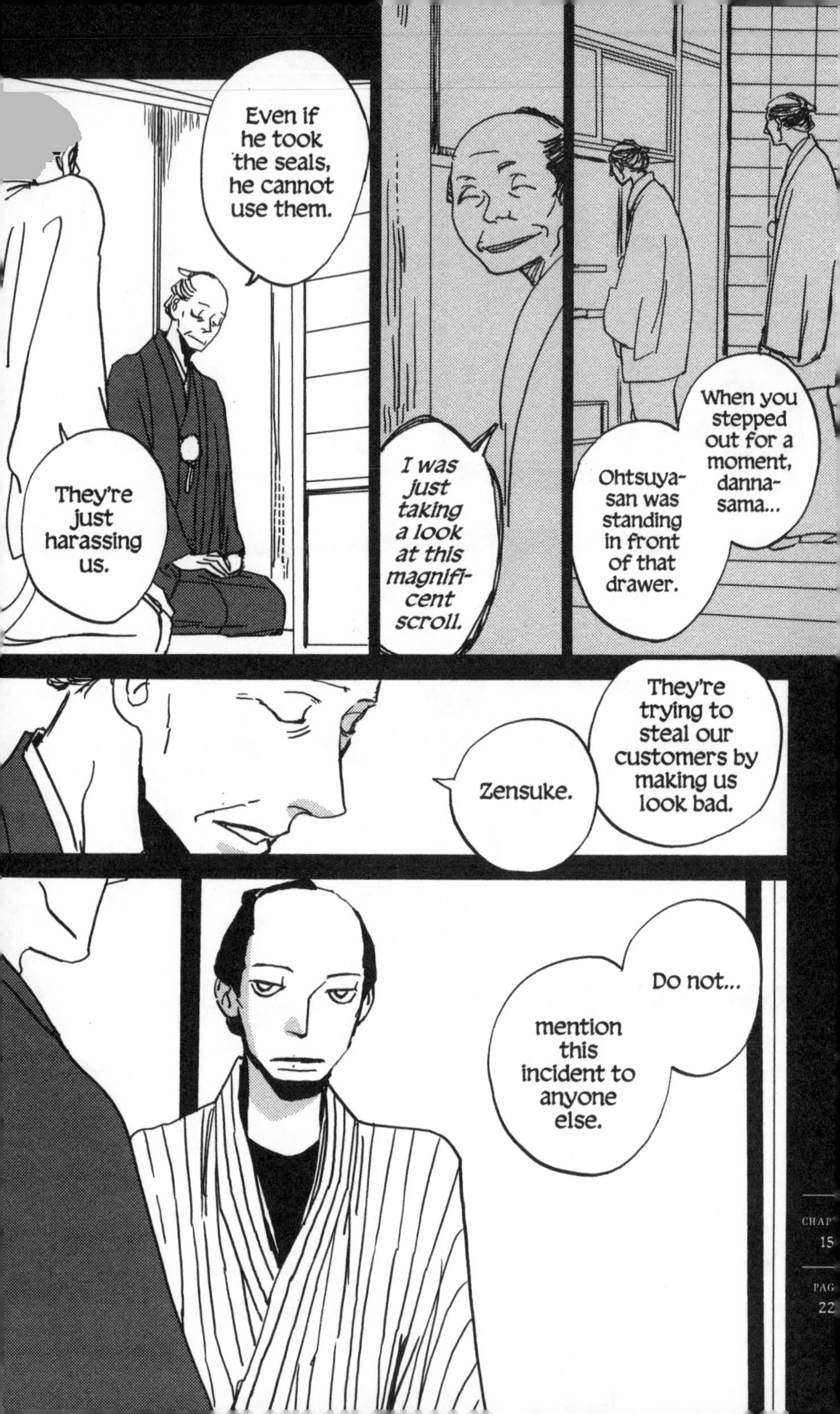
When you stepped out for a moment, danna-sama...
Ohtsuya-san was standing in front of that drawer.
I was just taking a look at this magnificent scroll.
Even if he took the seals, he cannot use them.
They're just harassing us.
They're trying to steal our customers by making us look bad.
Zensuke.
Do not...
mention this incident to anyone else.

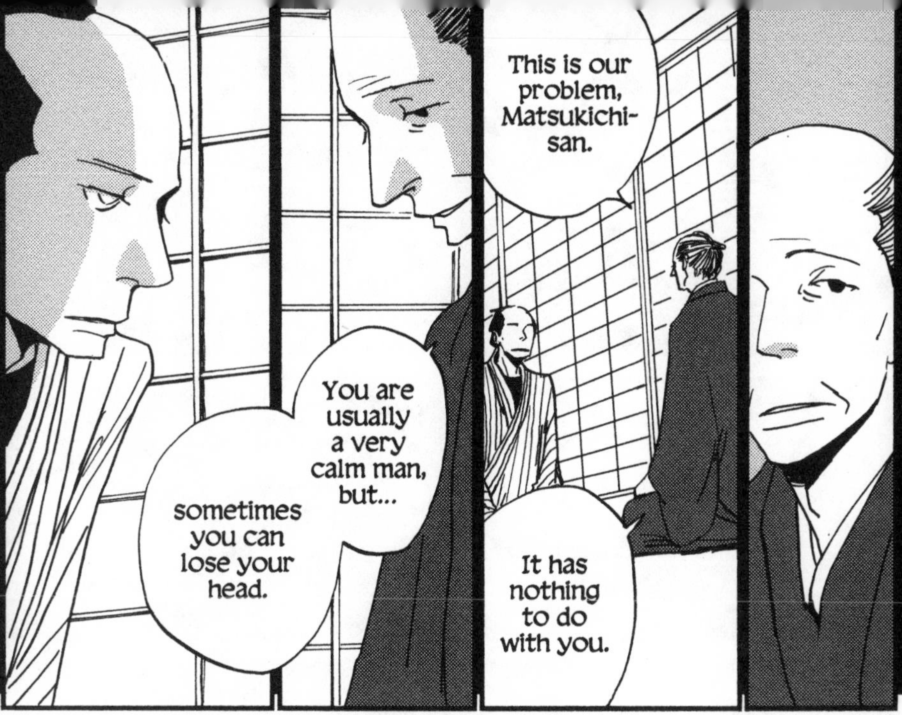
This is our problem, Matsukichi-san.
It has nothing to do with you.
You are usually a very calm man, but...
sometimes you can lose your head.

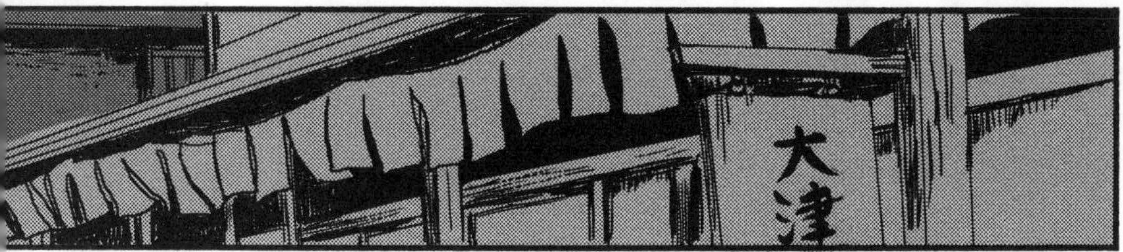
On sign: Ohtsuya

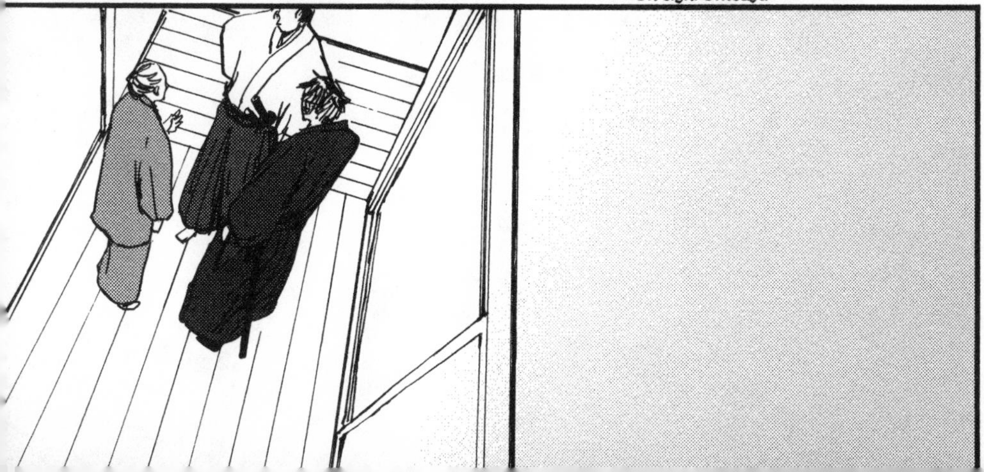

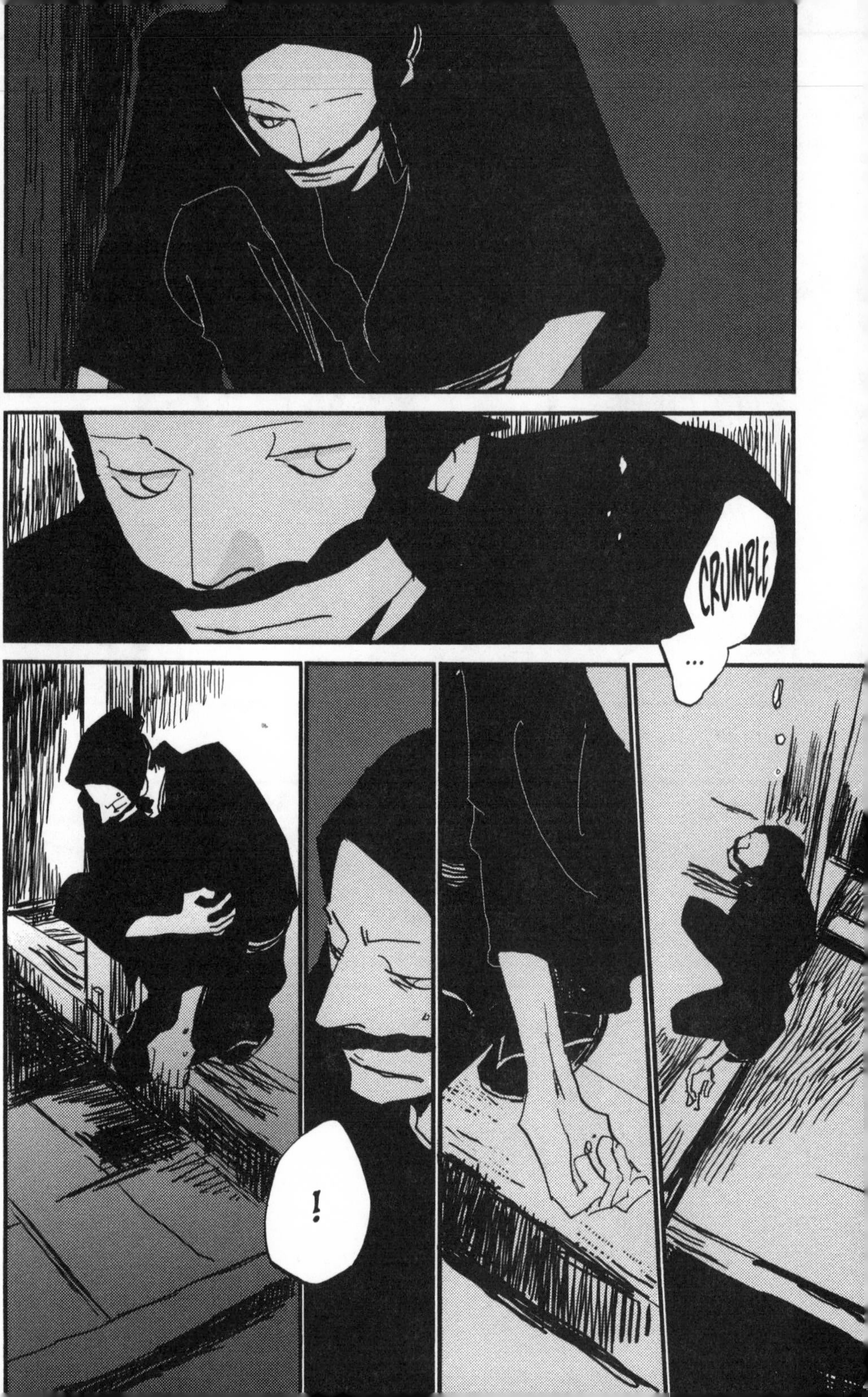
CRUMBLE
...
!

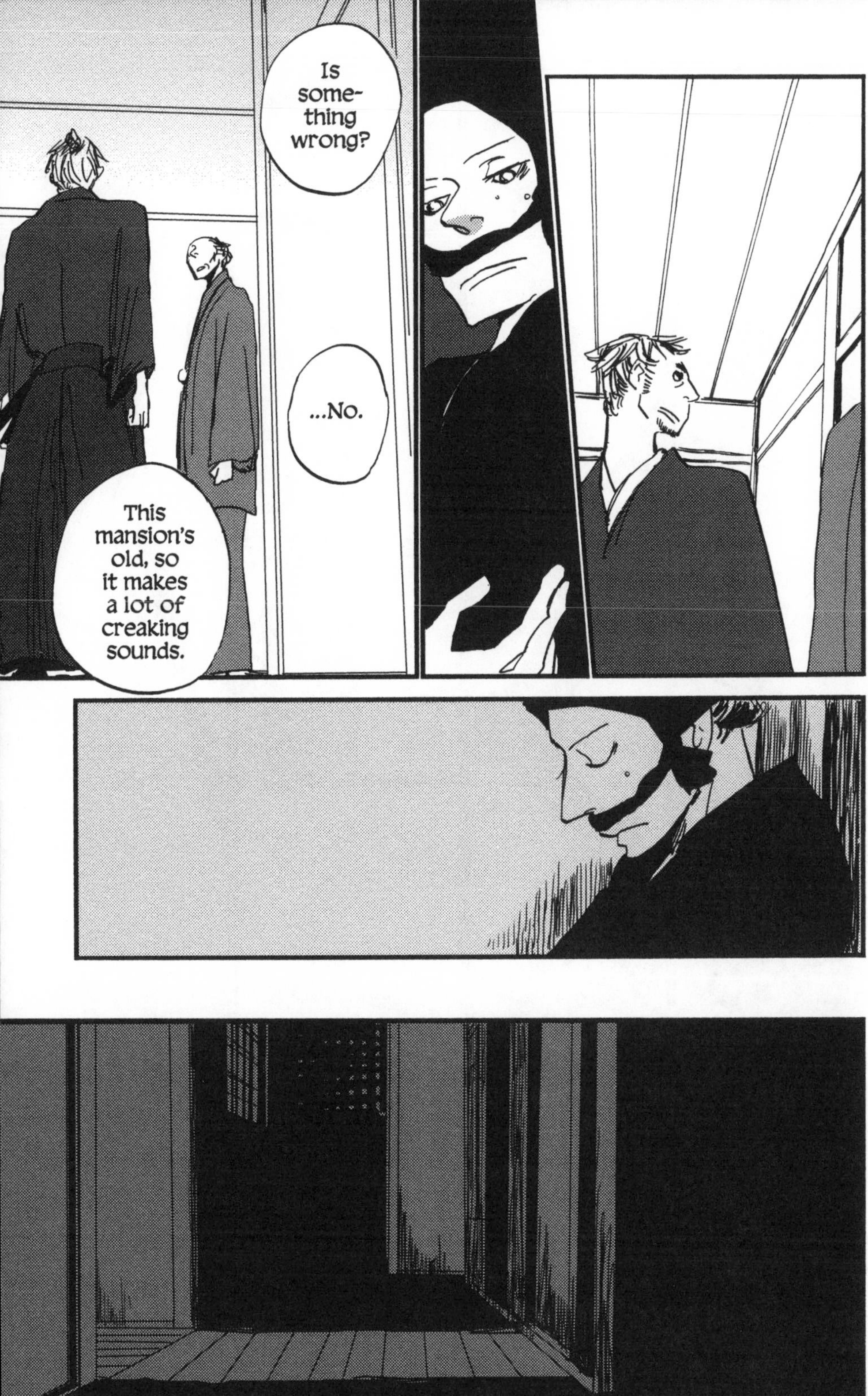
Is something wrong?
...No.
This mansion's old, so it makes a lot of creaking sounds.

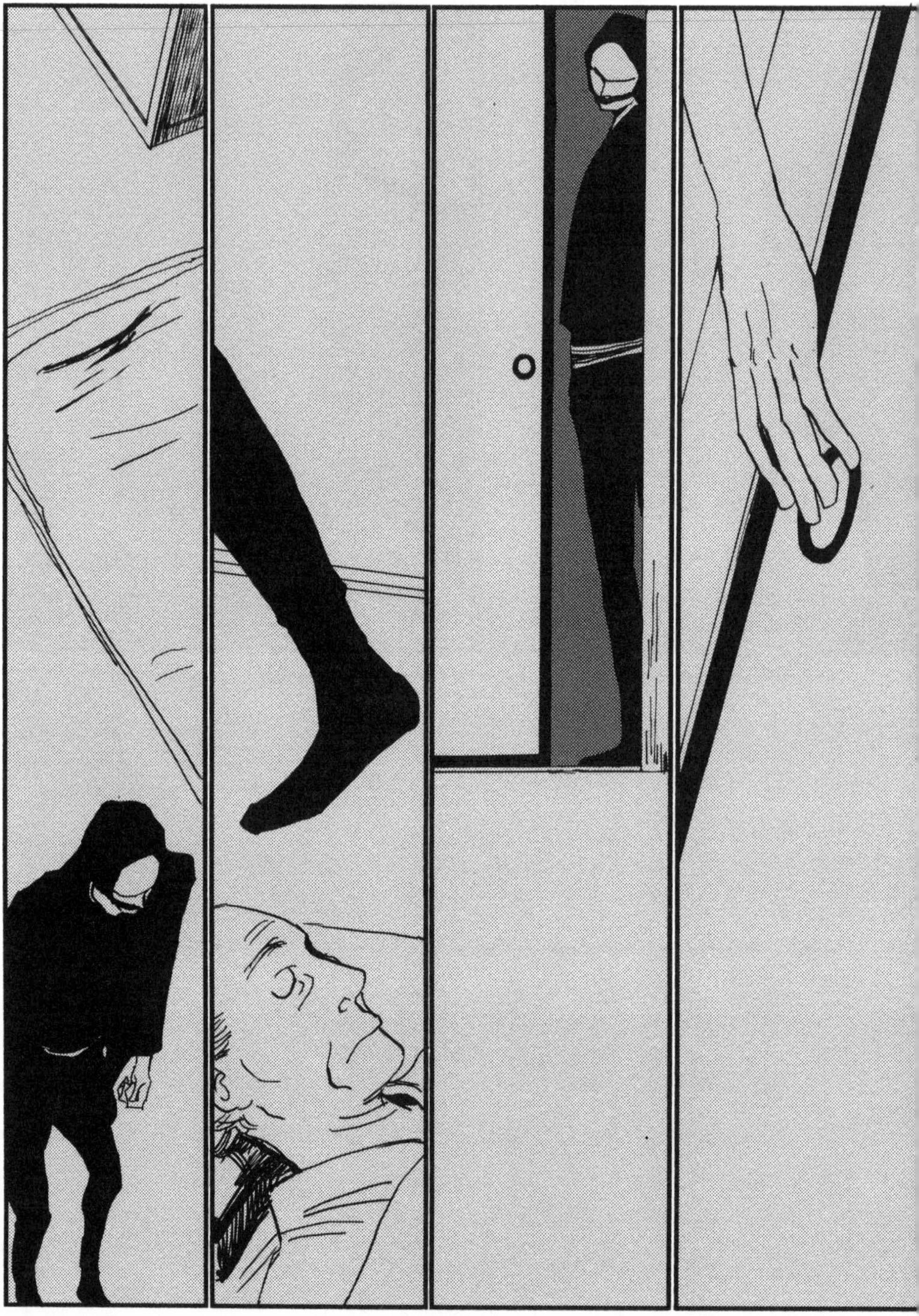

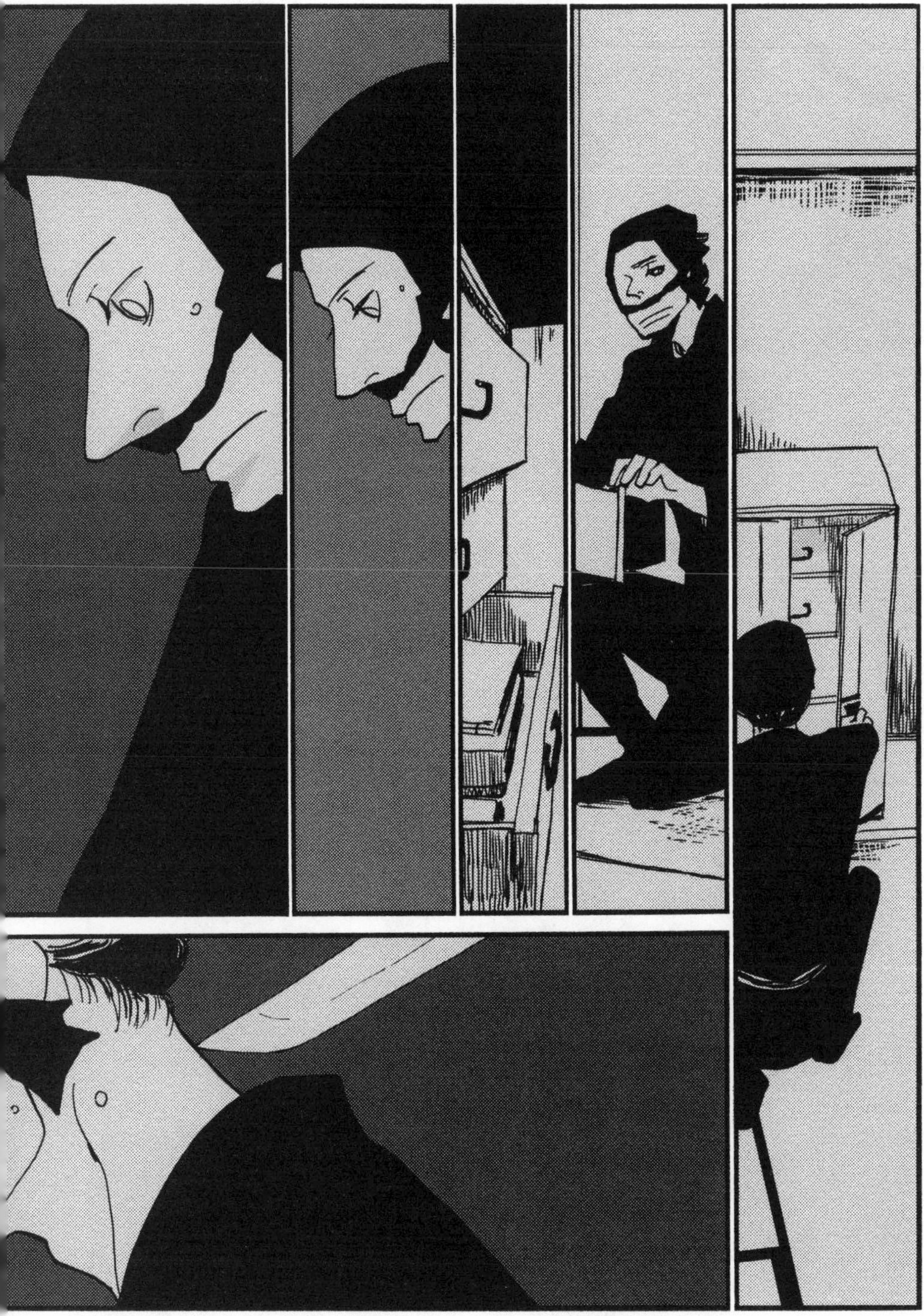

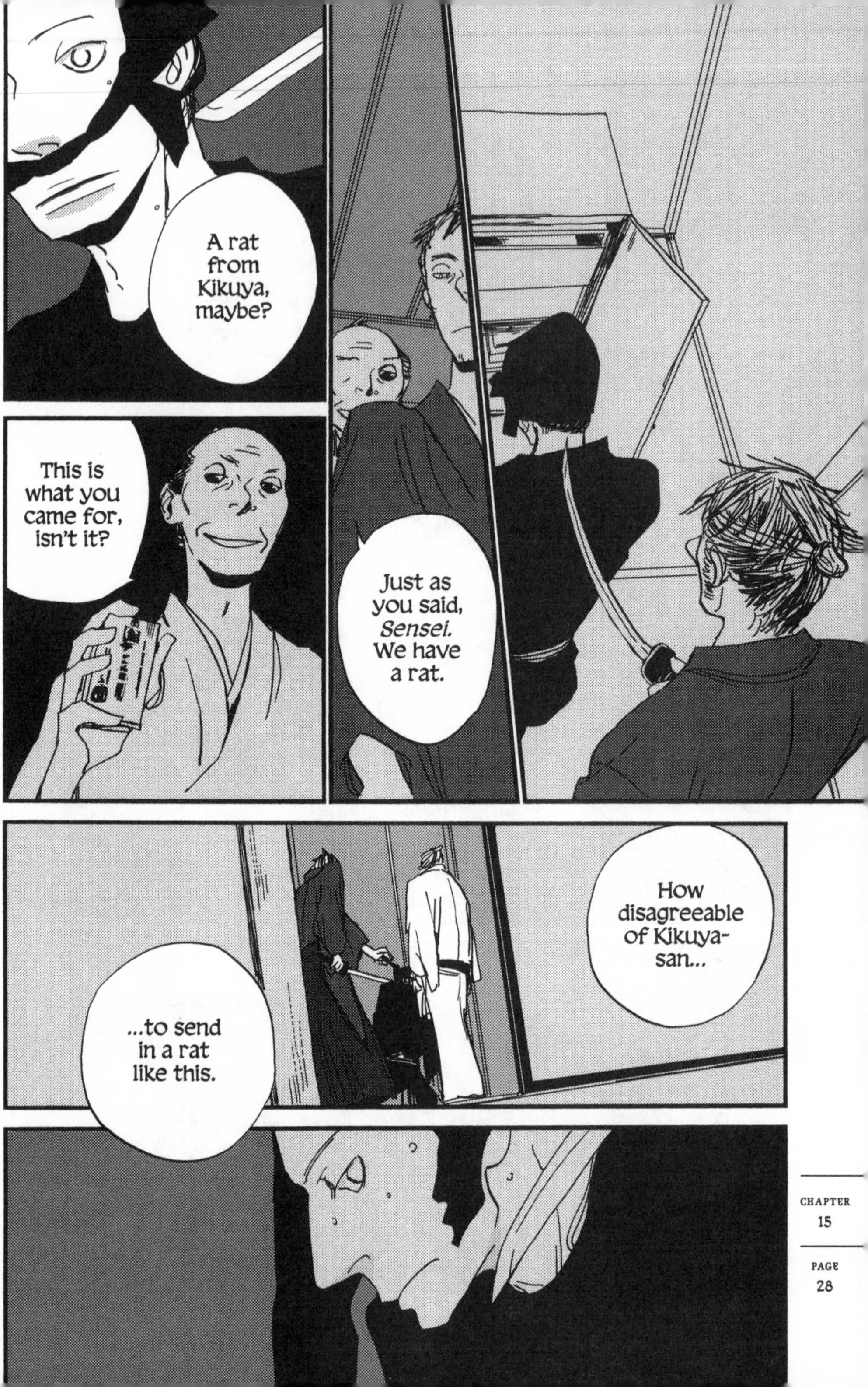
Just as you said, *Sensei.* We have a rat.
A rat from Kikuya, maybe?
This is what you came for, isn't it?
How disagreeable of Kikuya-san...
...to send in a rat like this.

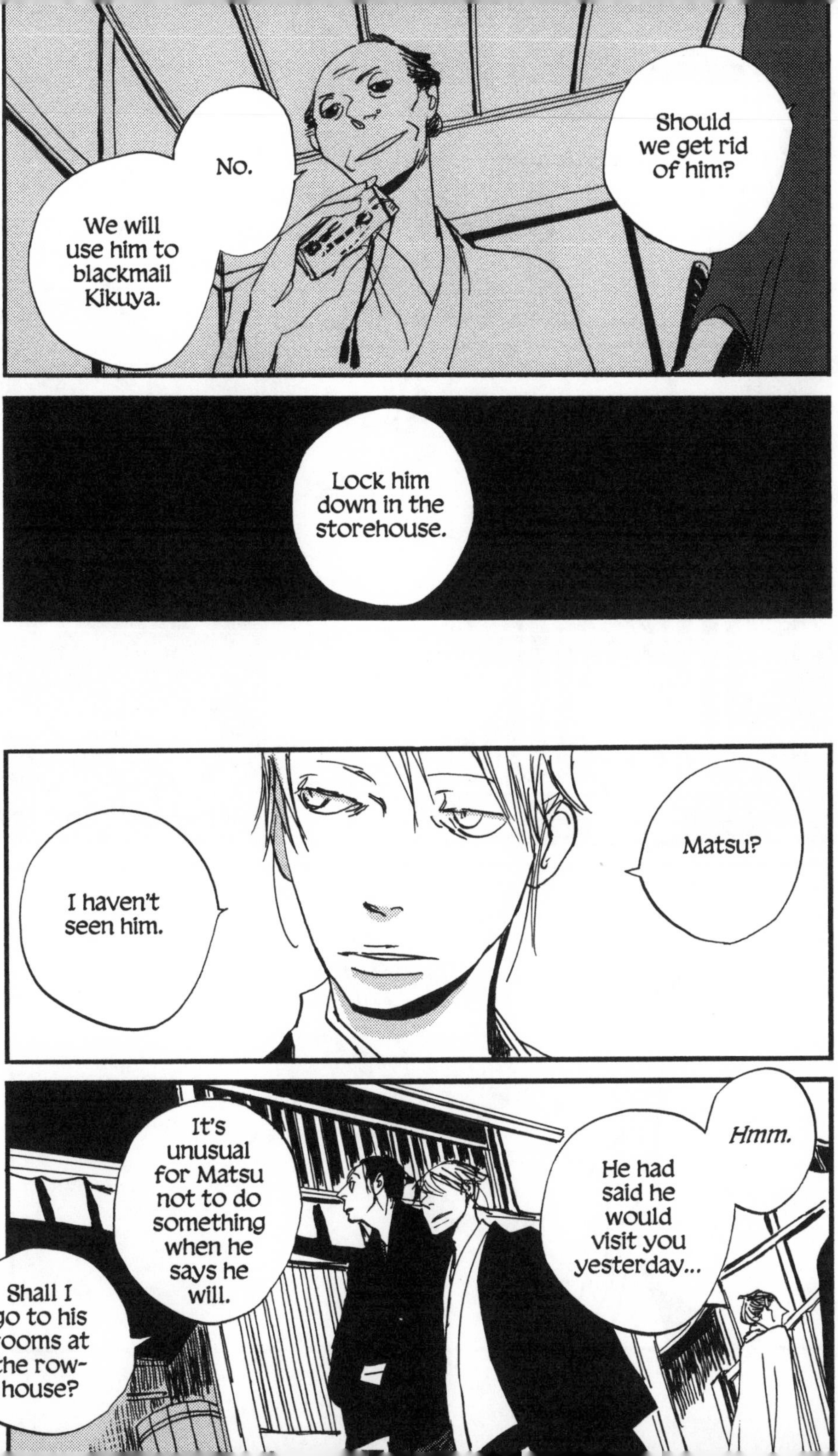
Should we get rid of him?
No.
We will use him to blackmail Kikuya.
Lock him down in the storehouse.
Matsu?
I haven't seen him.
Hmm.
He had said he would visit you yesterday...
It's unusual for Matsu not to do something when he says he will.
Shall I go to his rooms at the row-house?

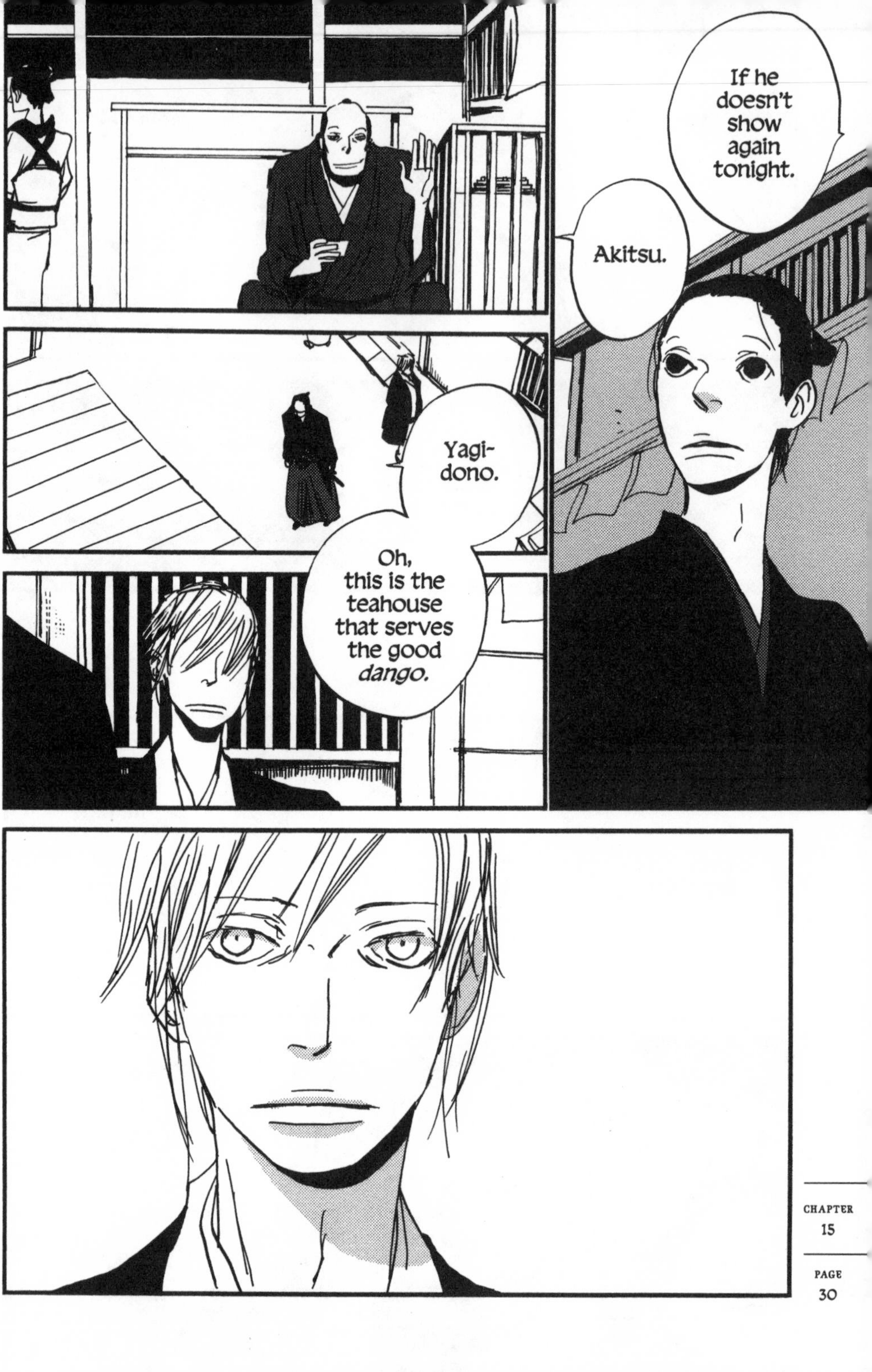

If he doesn't show again tonight.
Akitsu.
Yagi-dono.
Oh, this is the teahouse that serves the good *dango.*

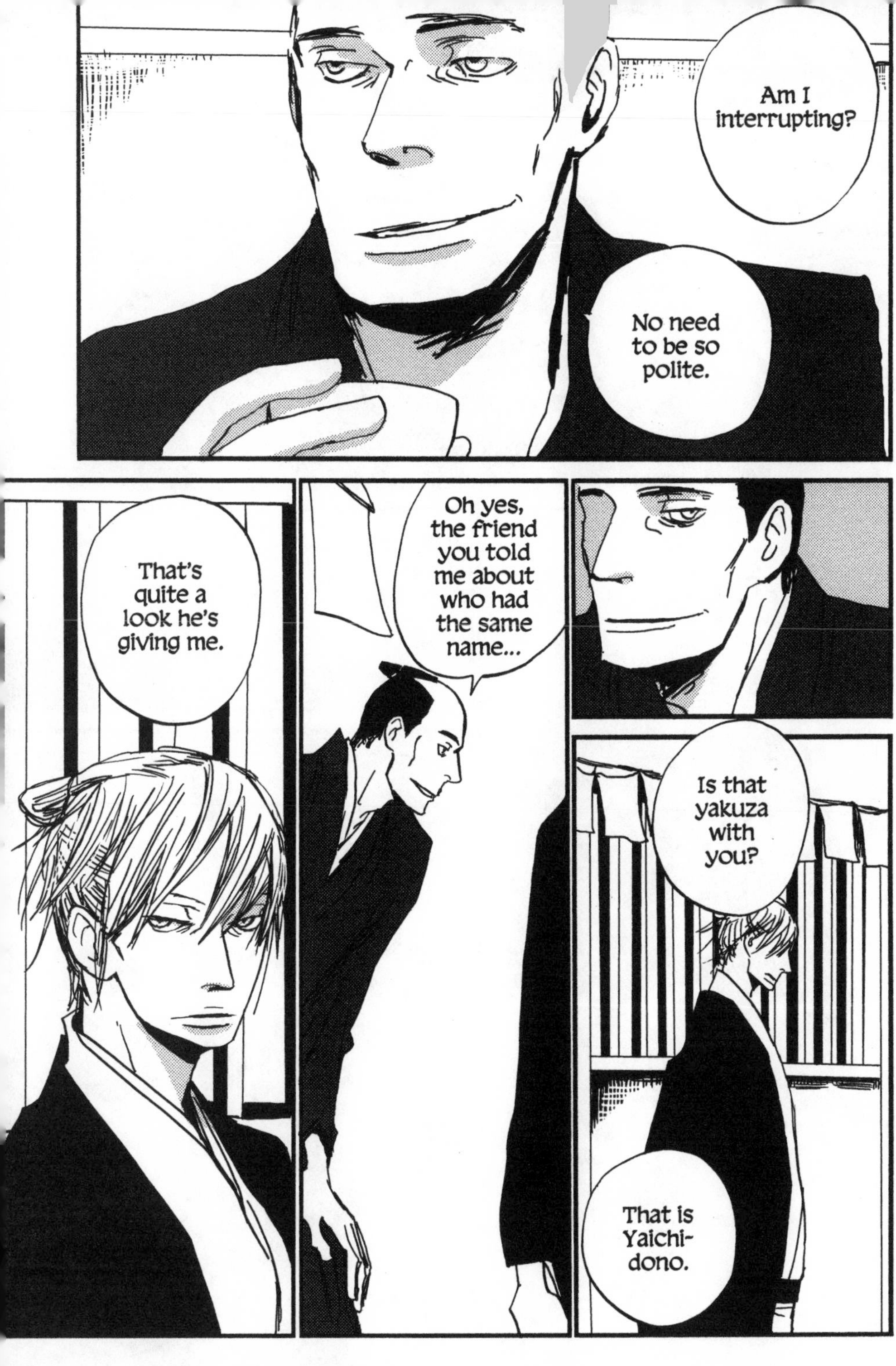
Am I interrupting?
No need to be so polite.
Is that yakuza with you?
That is Yaichi-dono.
Oh yes, the friend you told me about who had the same name...
That's quite a look he's giving me.

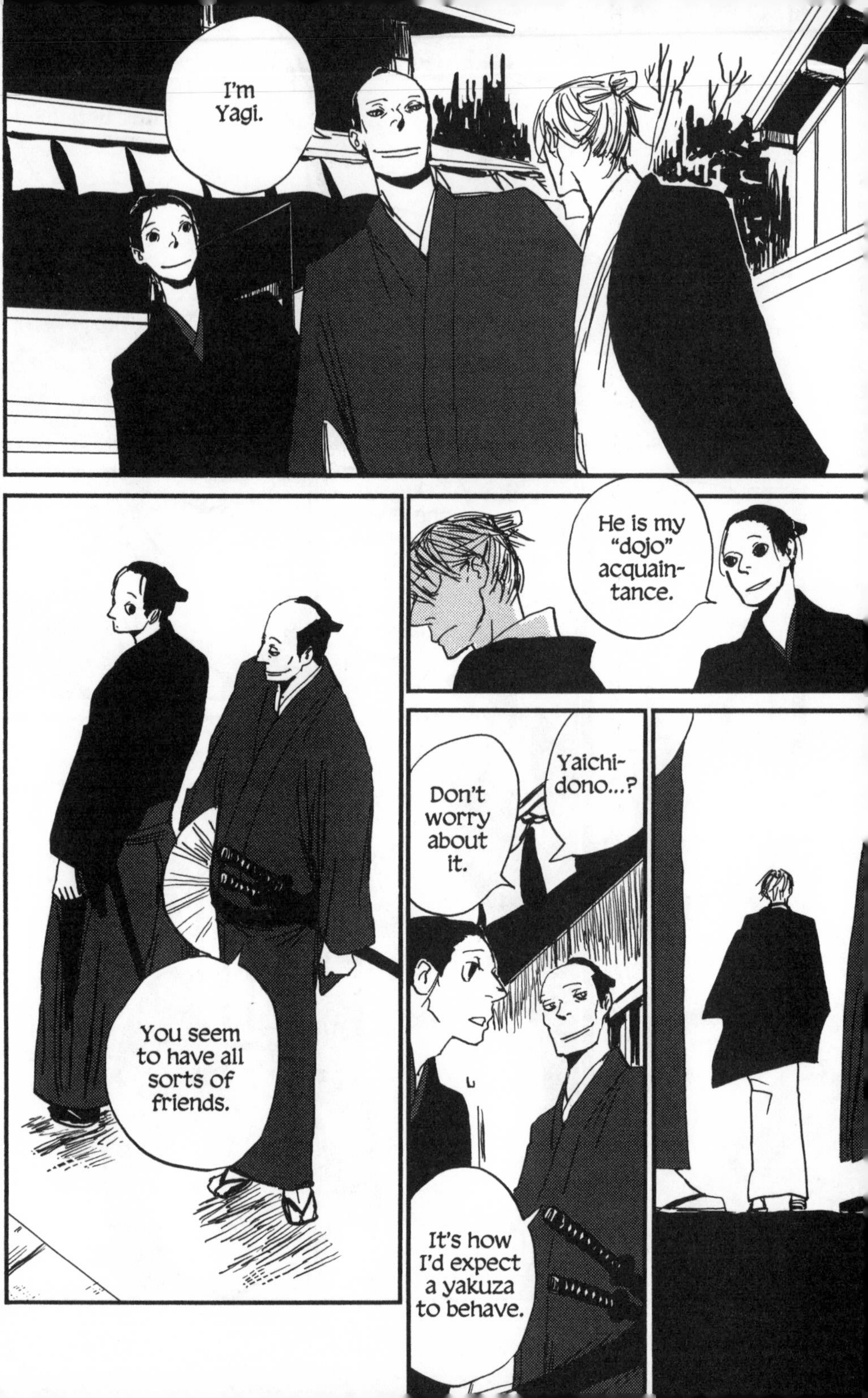
I'm Yagi.
He is my "dojo" acquaintance.
Yaichi-dono...?
Don't worry about it.
It's how I'd expect a yakuza to behave.
You seem to have all sorts of friends.

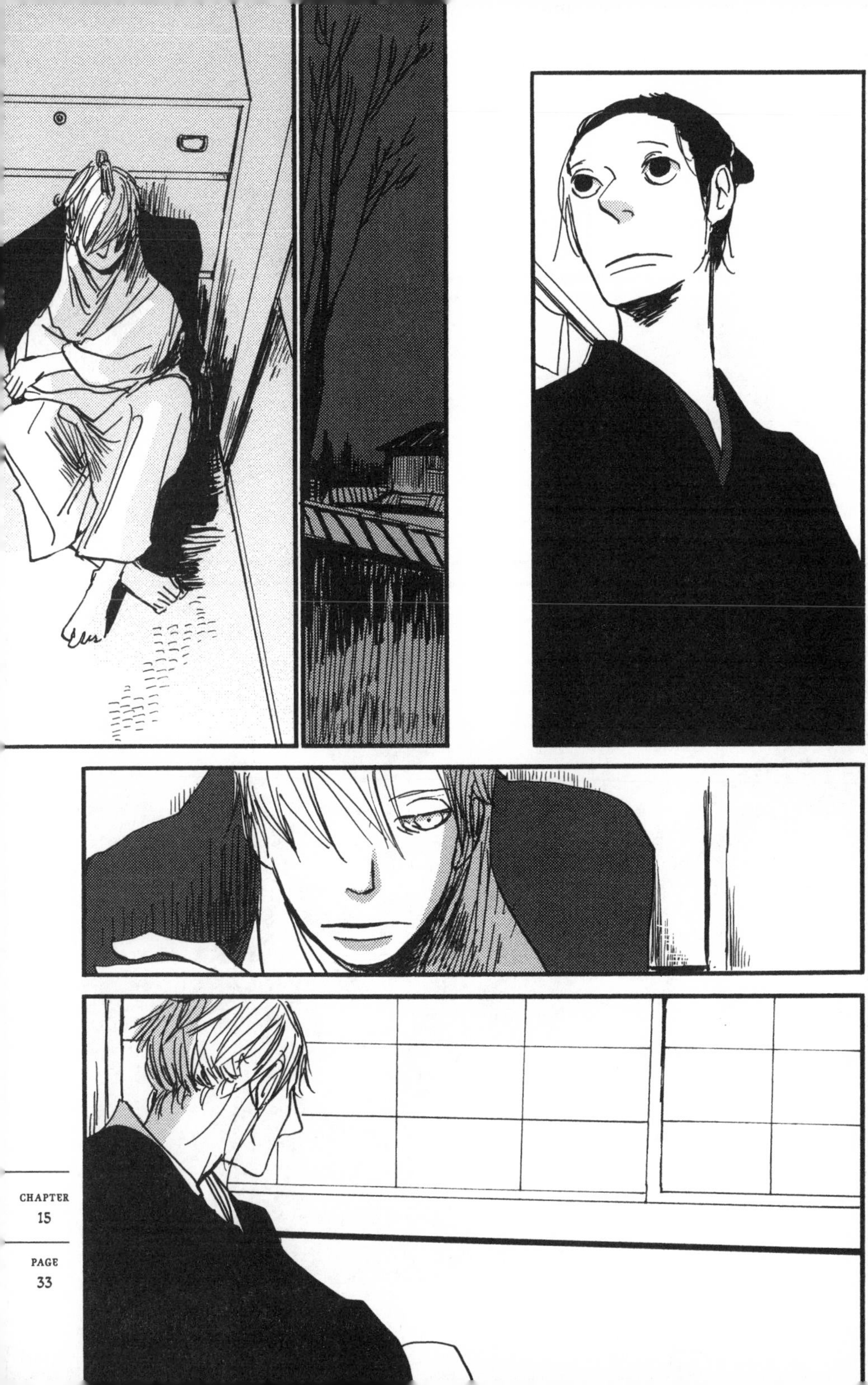

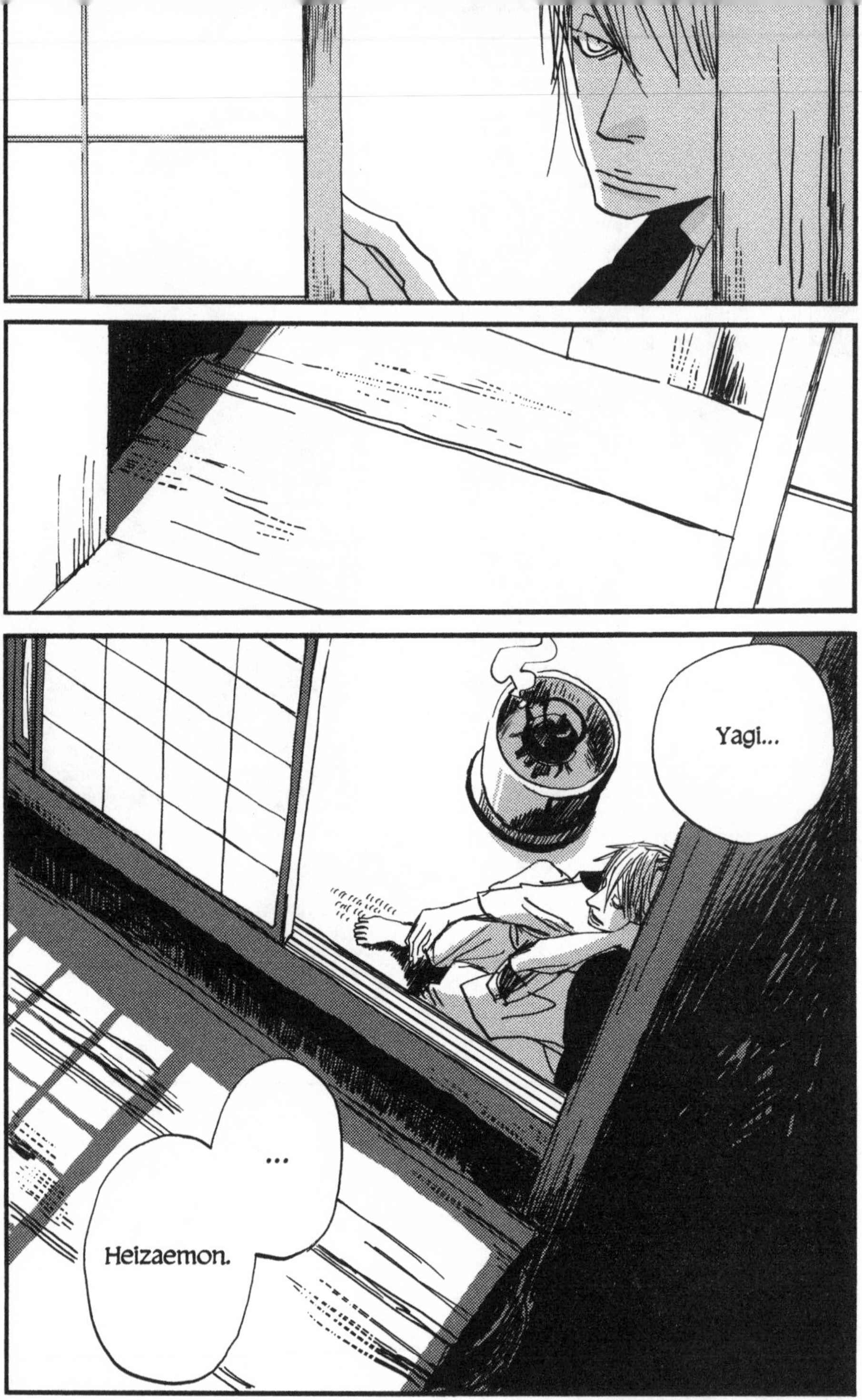
Yagi...
...
Heizaemon.

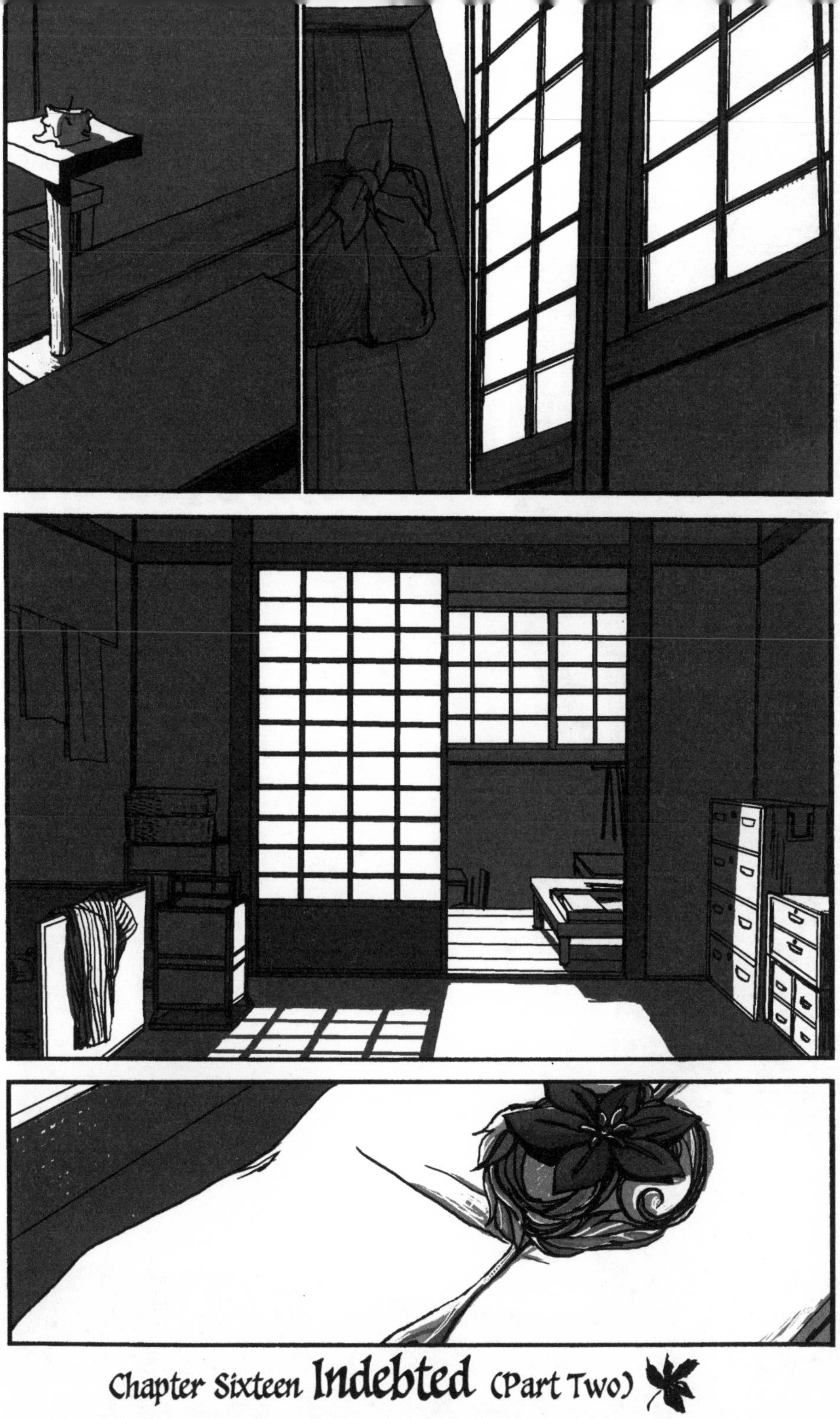

Chapter Sixteen Indebted (Part Two)

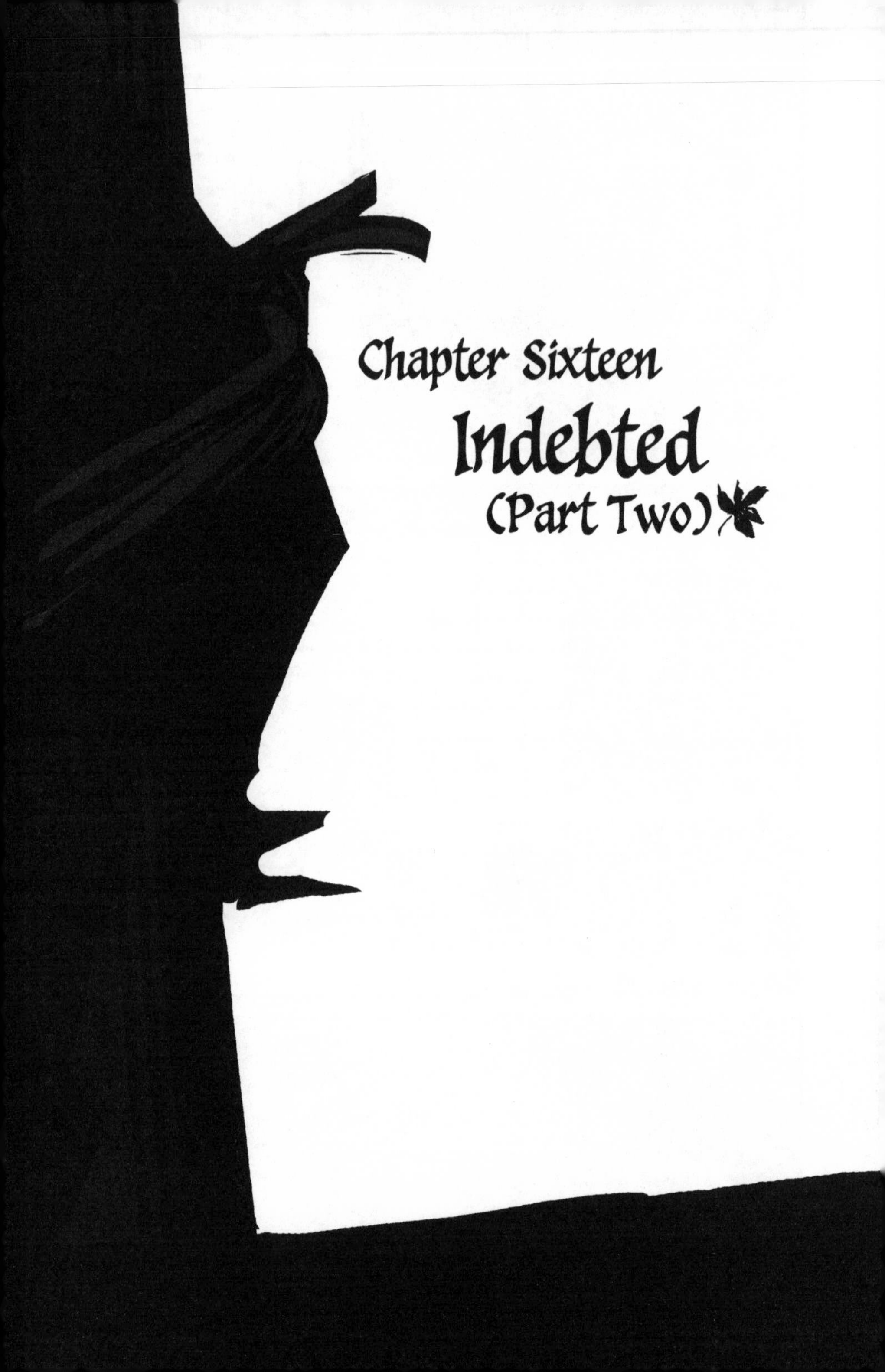

Chapter Sixteen
Indebted
(Part Two)

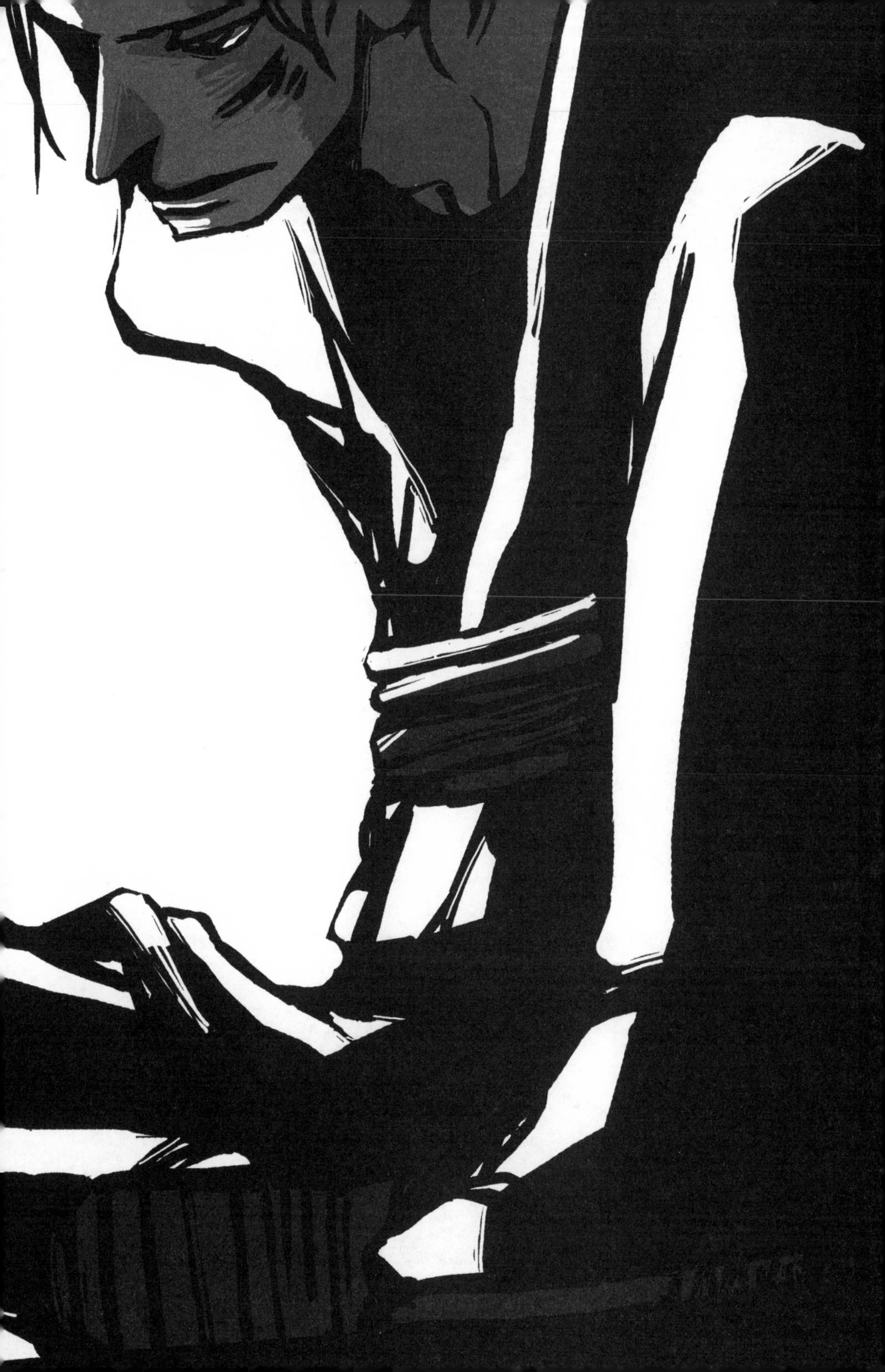

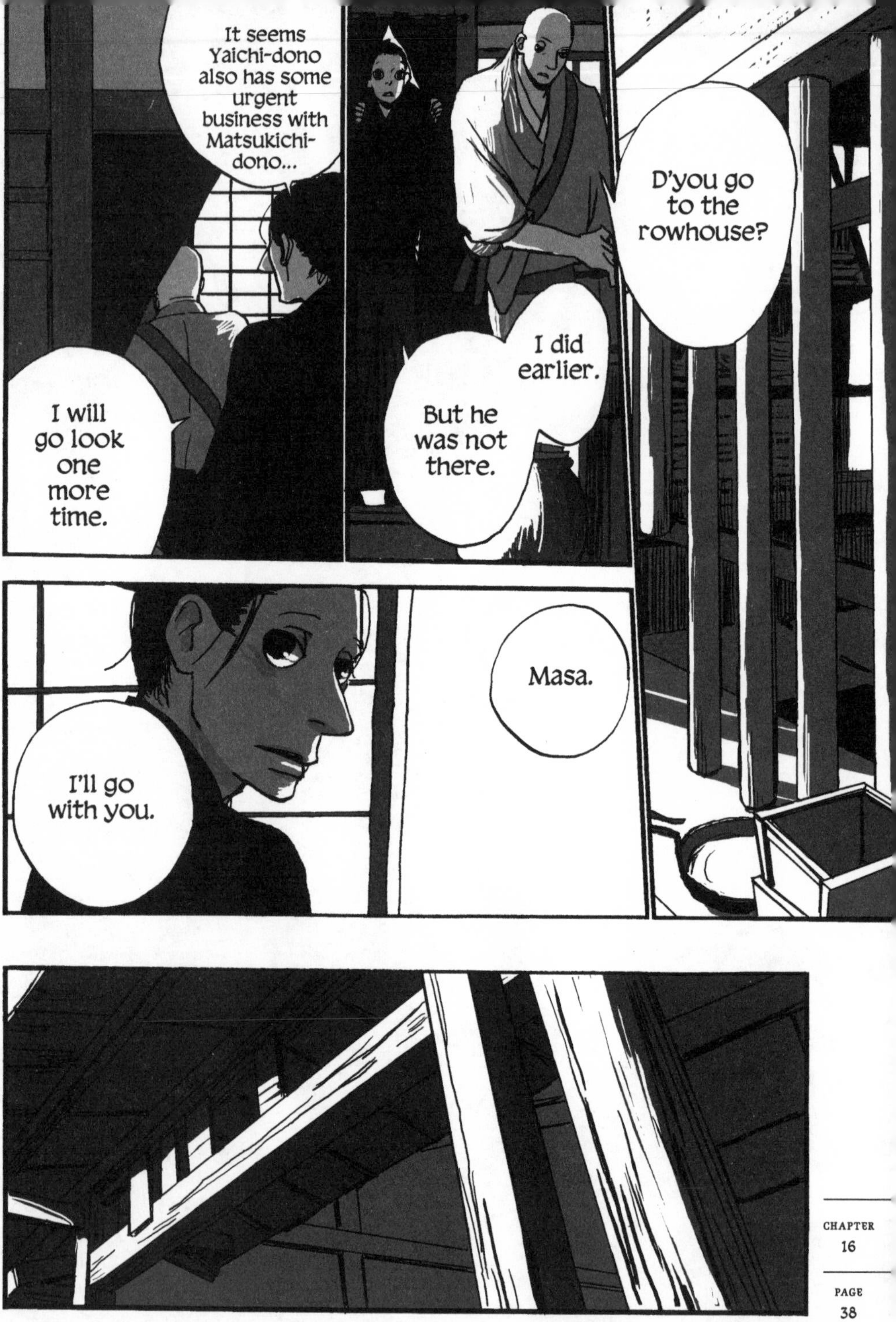
D'you go to the rowhouse?
I did earlier.
But he was not there.
It seems Yaichi-dono also has some urgent business with Matsukichi-dono...
I will go look one more time.
Masa.
I'll go with you.

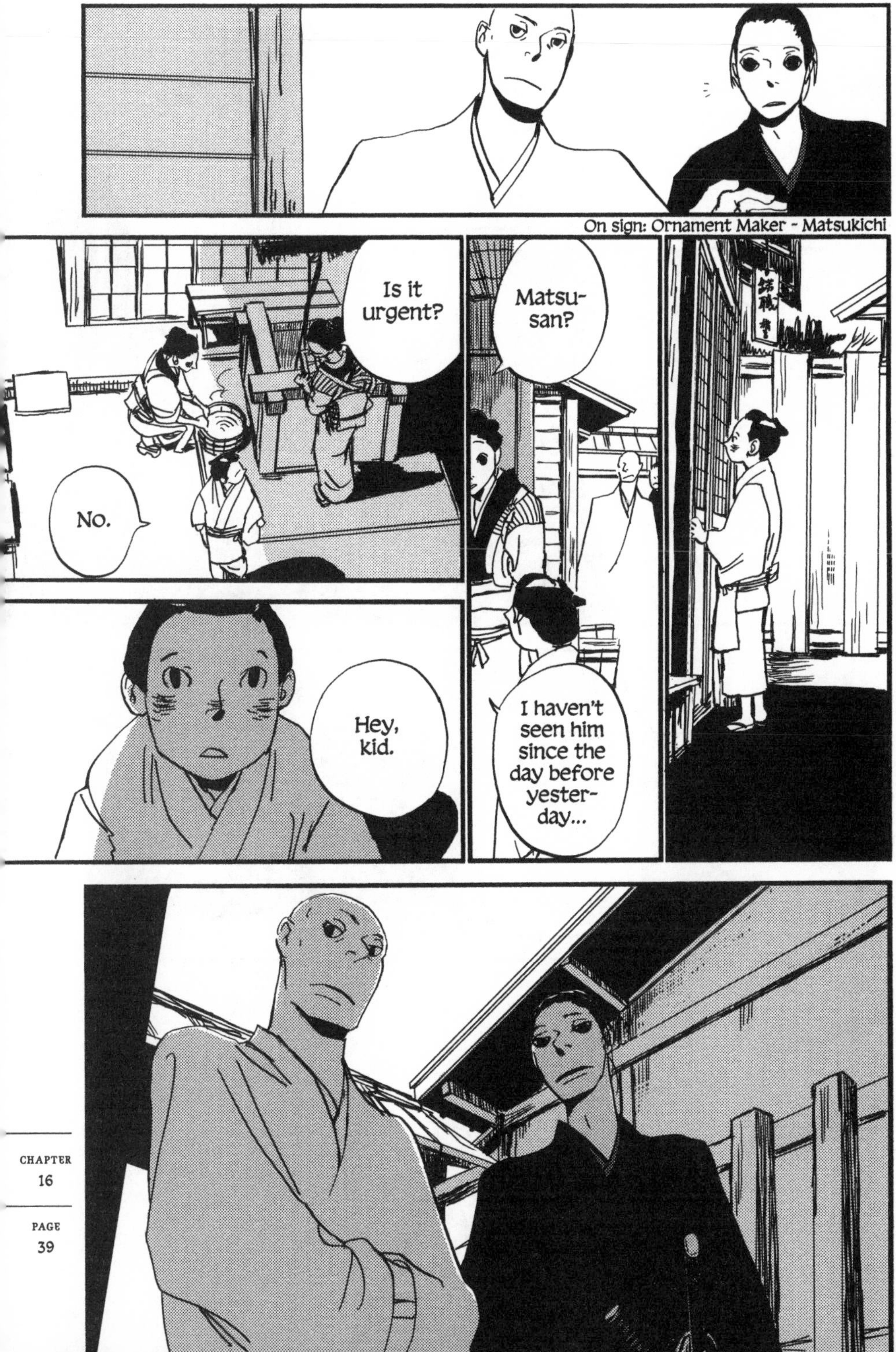
On sign: Ornament Maker - Matsukichi
Matsu-san?
I haven't seen him since the day before yester-day...
Is it urgent?
No.
Hey, kid.

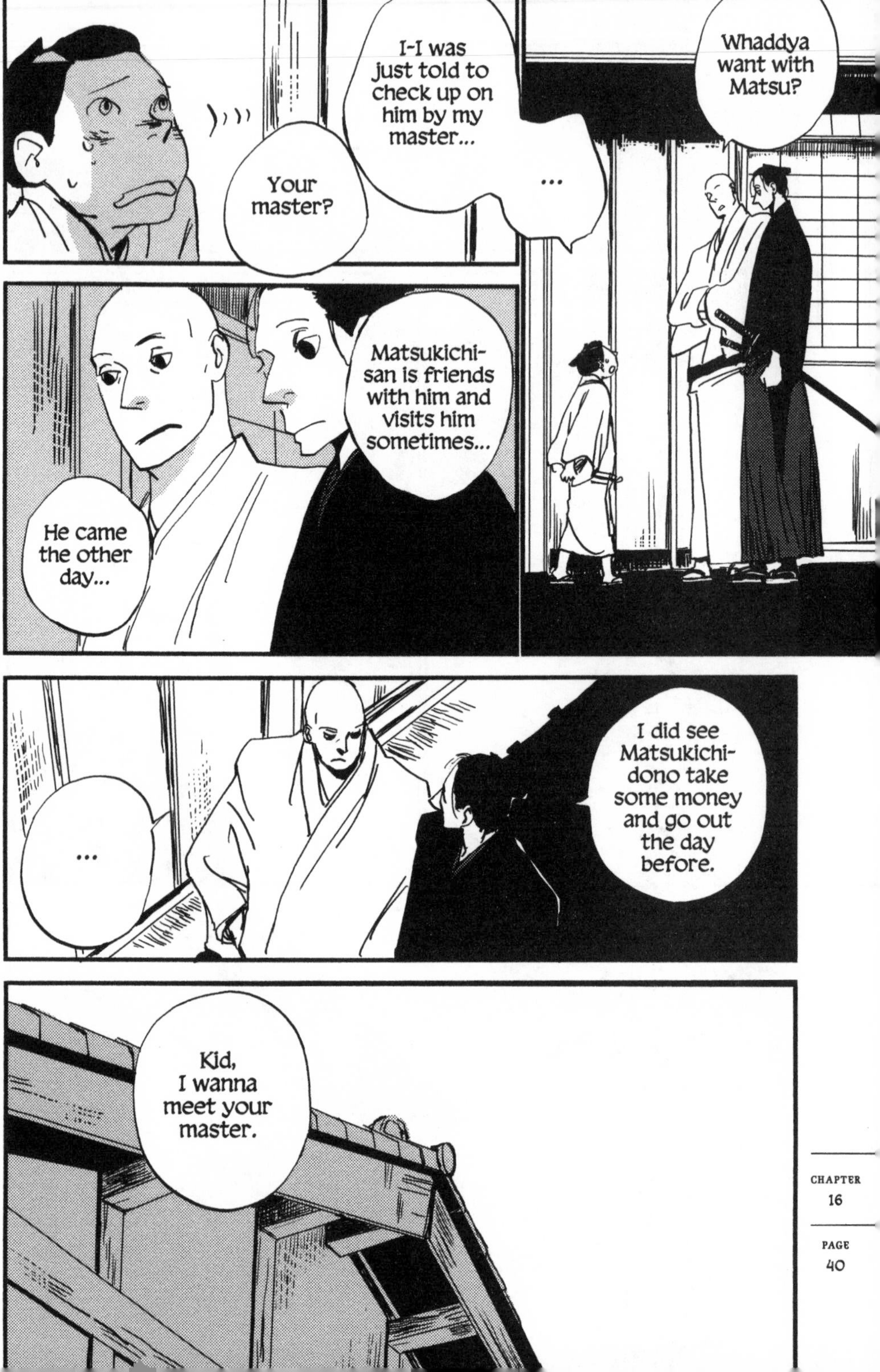
Whaddya want with Matsu?
...
I-I was just told to check up on him by my master...
Your master?
Matsukichi-san is friends with him and visits him sometimes...
He came the other day...
I did see Matsukichi-dono take some money and go out the day before.
...
Kid, I wanna meet your master.

On lantern: Kikuya Candles

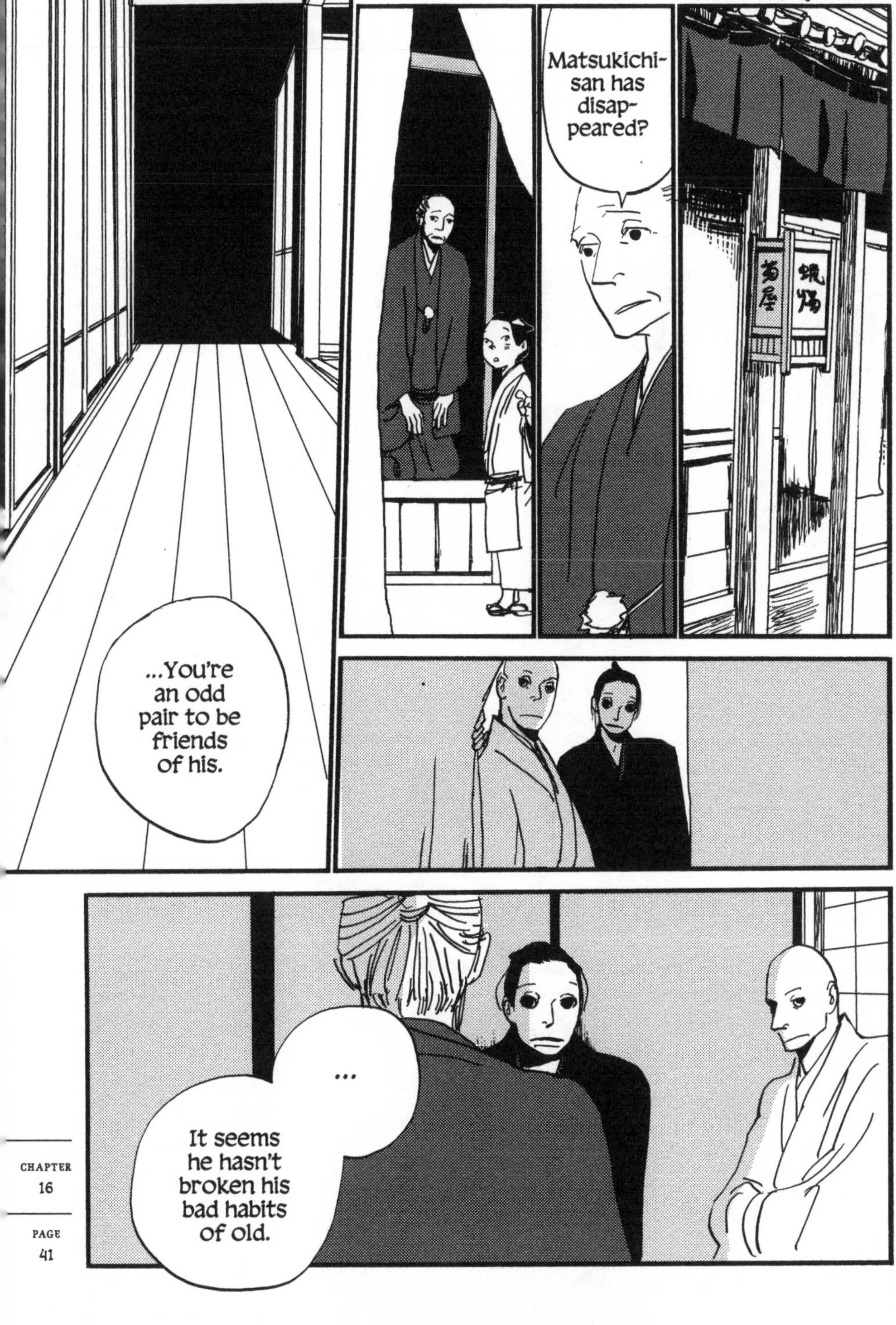

Matsukichi-san has disappeared?
...You're an odd pair to be friends of his.
...
It seems he hasn't broken his bad habits of old.

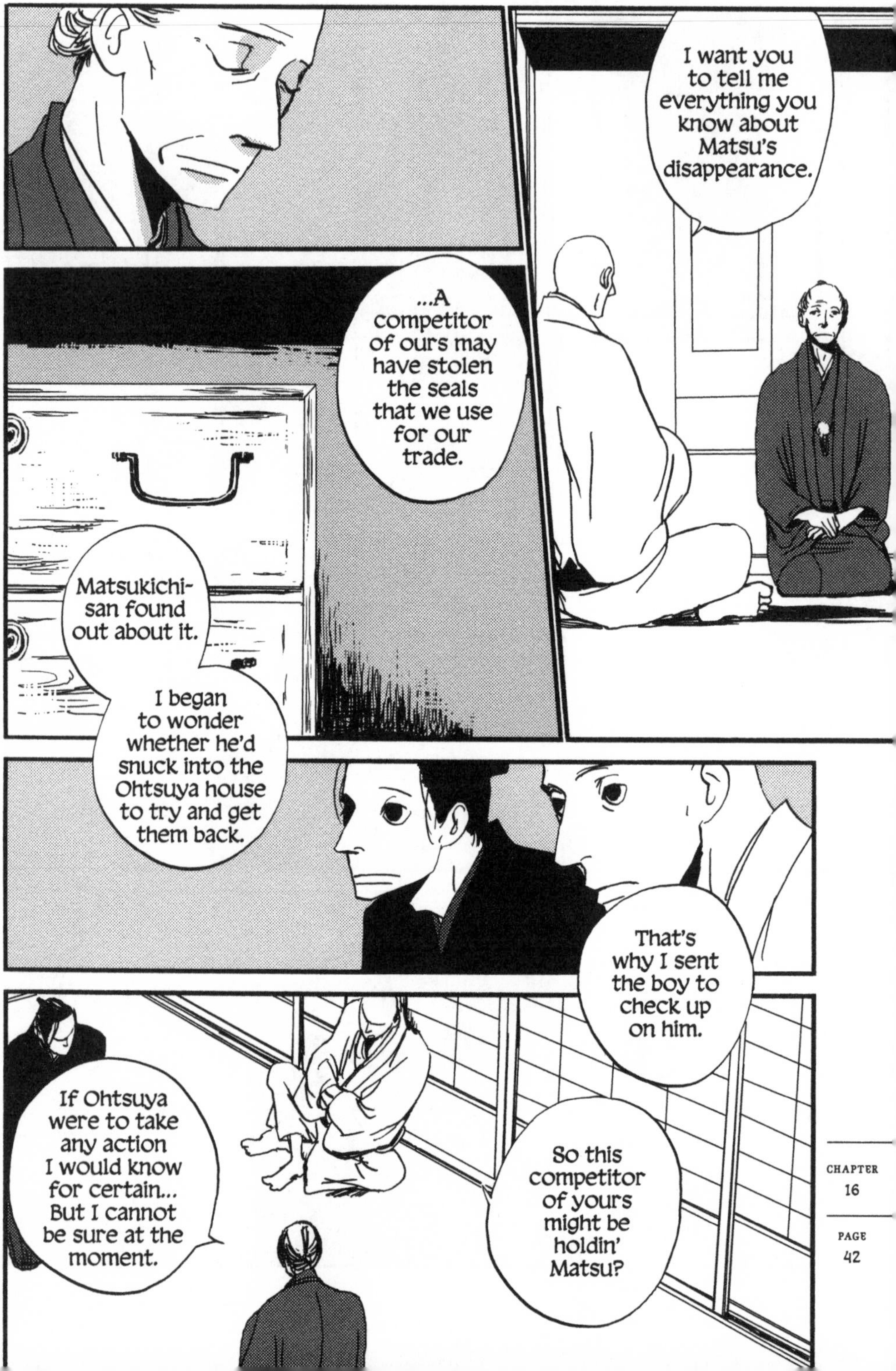
I want you to tell me everything you know about Matsu's disappearance.
...A competitor of ours may have stolen the seals that we use for our trade.
Matsukichi-san found out about it.
I began to wonder whether he'd snuck into the Ohtsuya house to try and get them back.
That's why I sent the boy to check up on him.
So this competitor of yours might be holdin' Matsu?
If Ohtsuya were to take any action I would know for certain... But I cannot be sure at the moment.

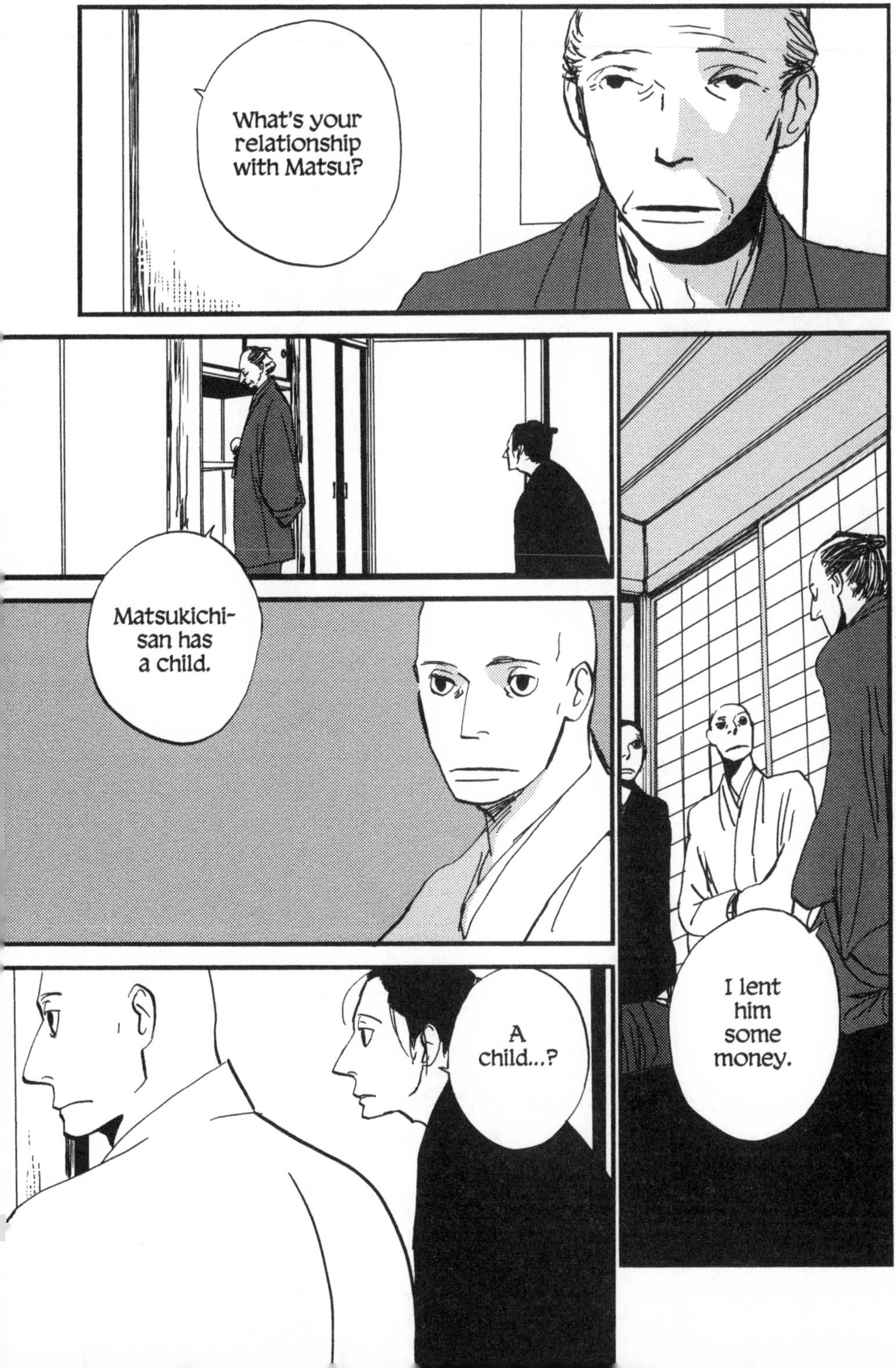
What's your relationship with Matsu?
I lent him some money.
Matsukichi-san has a child.
A child...?

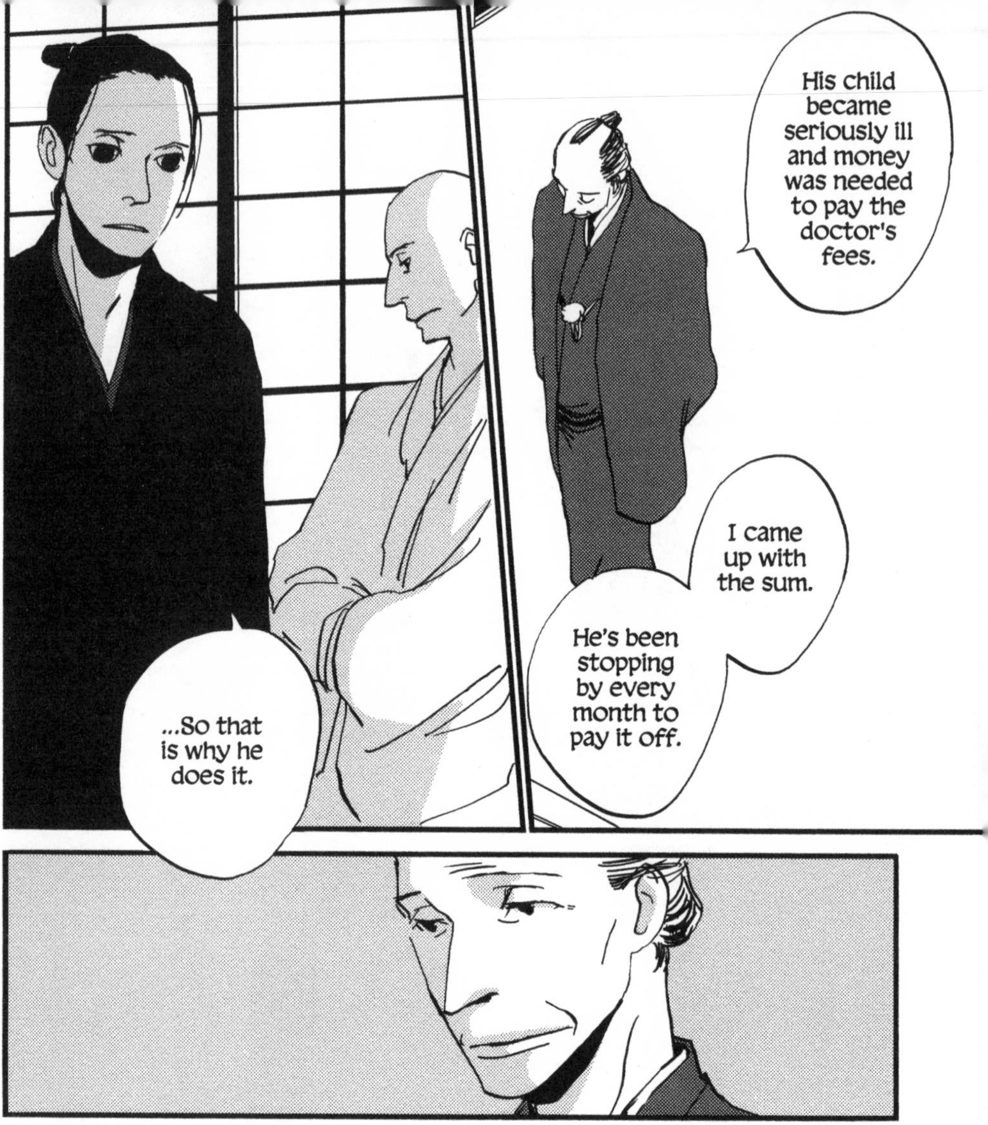
His child became seriously ill and money was needed to pay the doctor's fees.
I came up with the sum.
He's been stopping by every month to pay it off.
...So that is why he does it.

On signs: Ohtsuya Candles

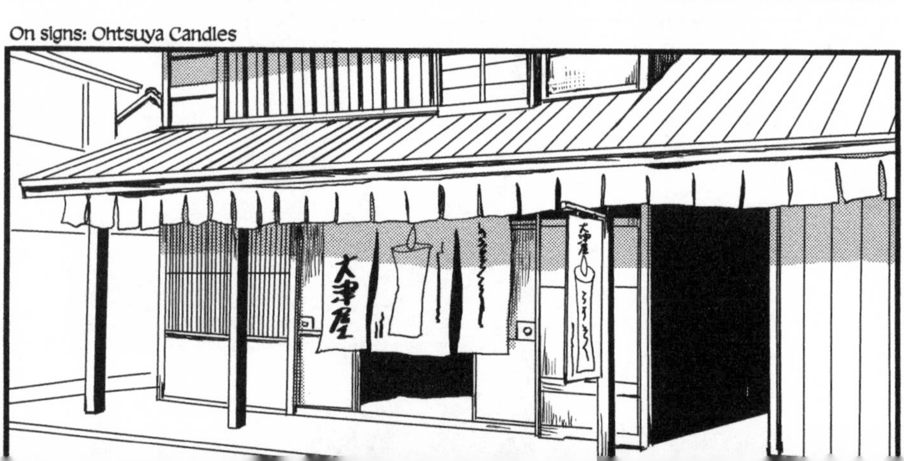

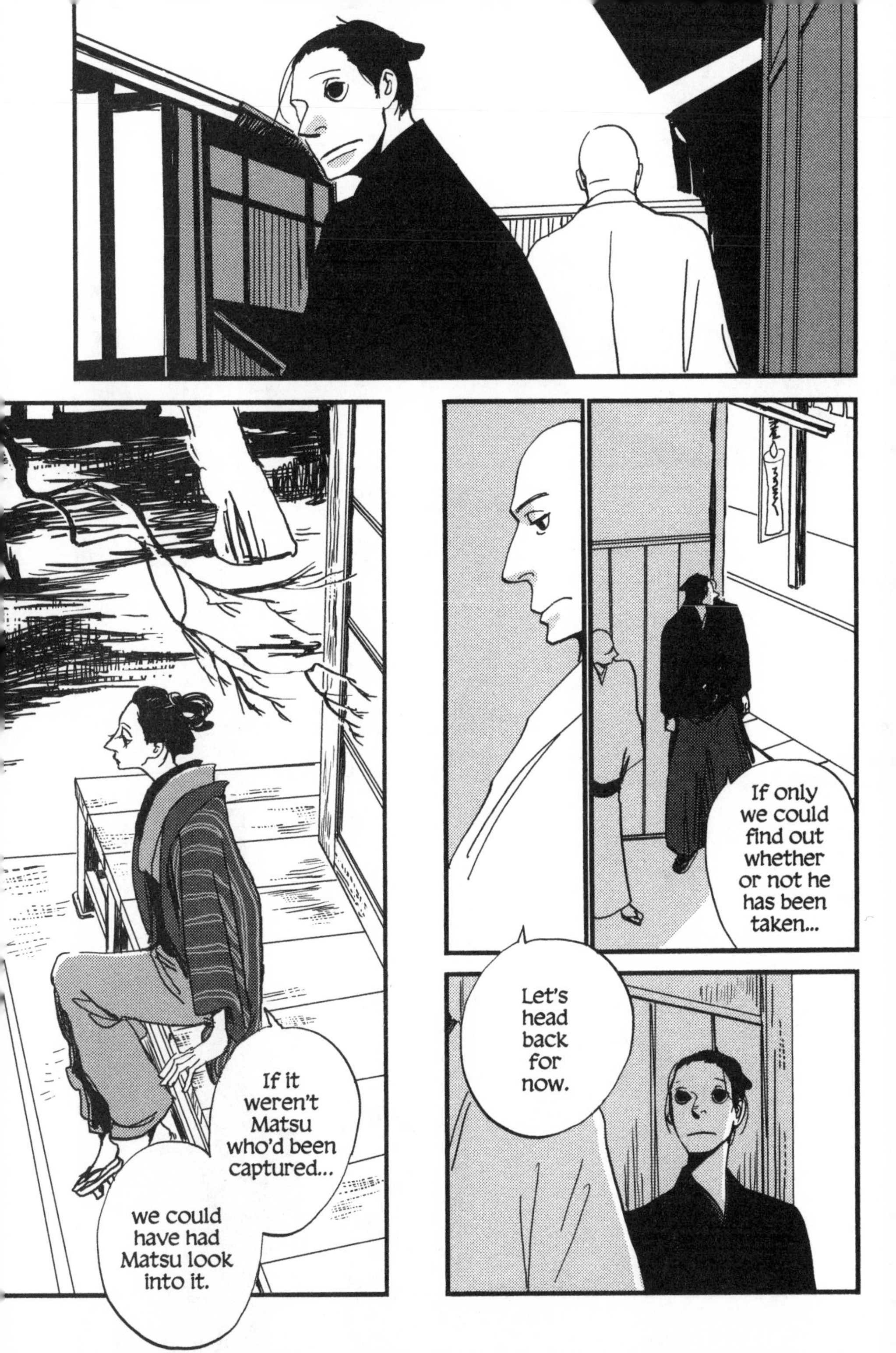
If only we could find out whether or not he has been taken...
Let's head back for now.
If it weren't Matsu who'd been captured...
we could have had Matsu look into it.

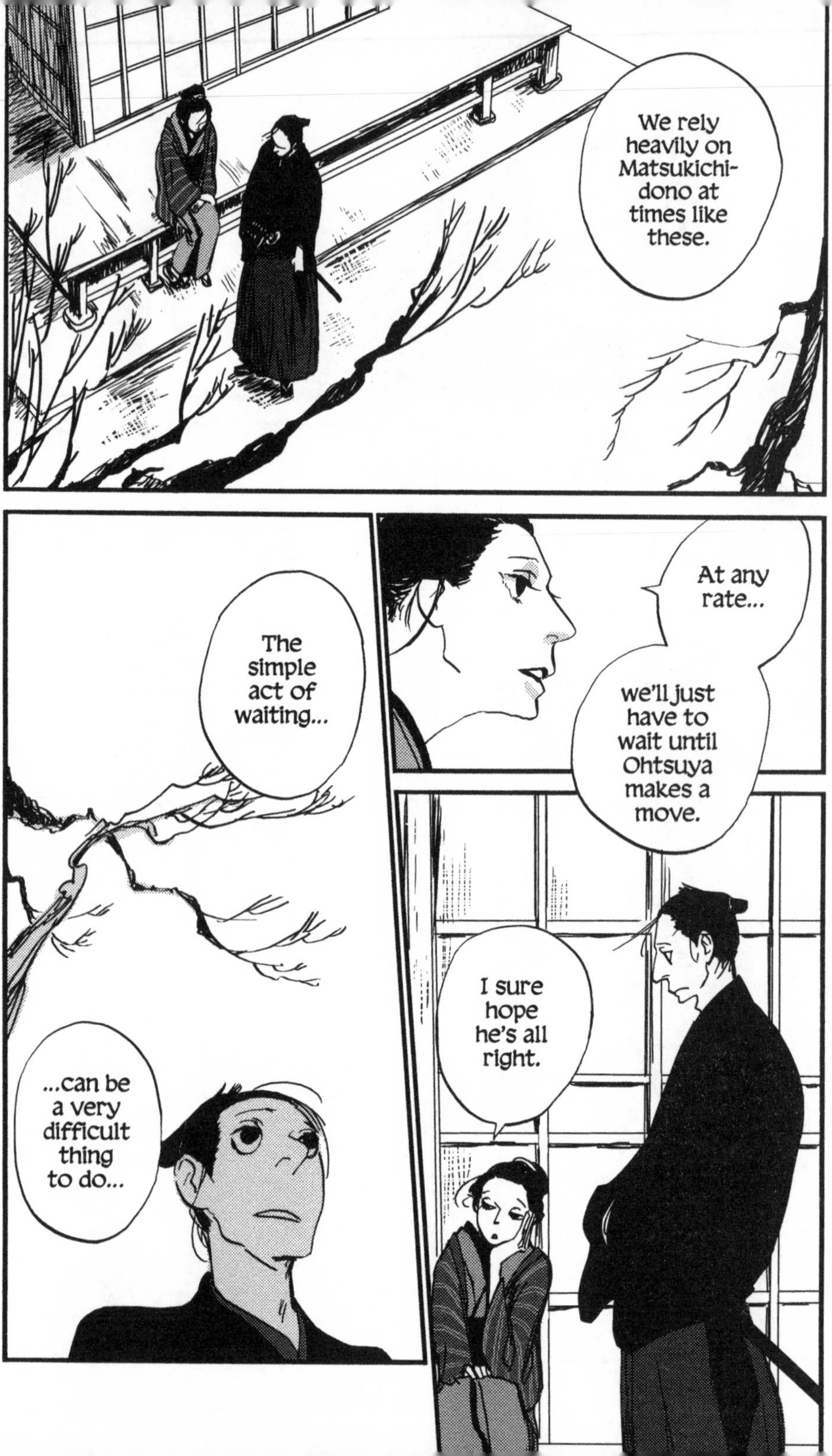
We rely heavily on Matsukichi-dono at times like these.
At any rate...
we'll just have to wait until Ohtsuya makes a move.
I sure hope he's all right.
The simple act of waiting...
...can be a very difficult thing to do...

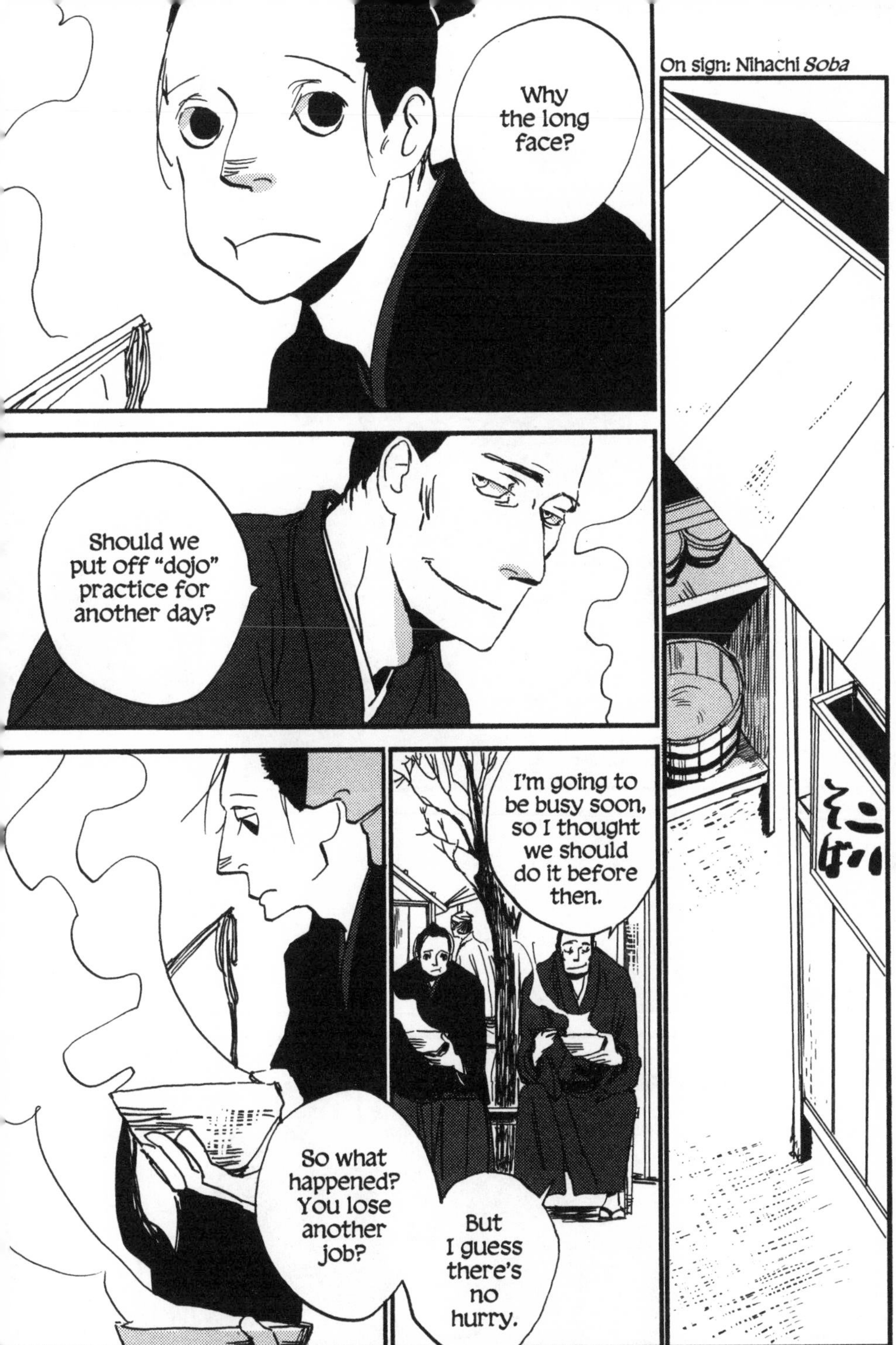
On sign: Nihachi *Soba*
Why the long face?
Should we put off "dojo" practice for another day?
I'm going to be busy soon, so I thought we should do it before then.
But I guess there's no hurry.
So what happened? You lose another job?

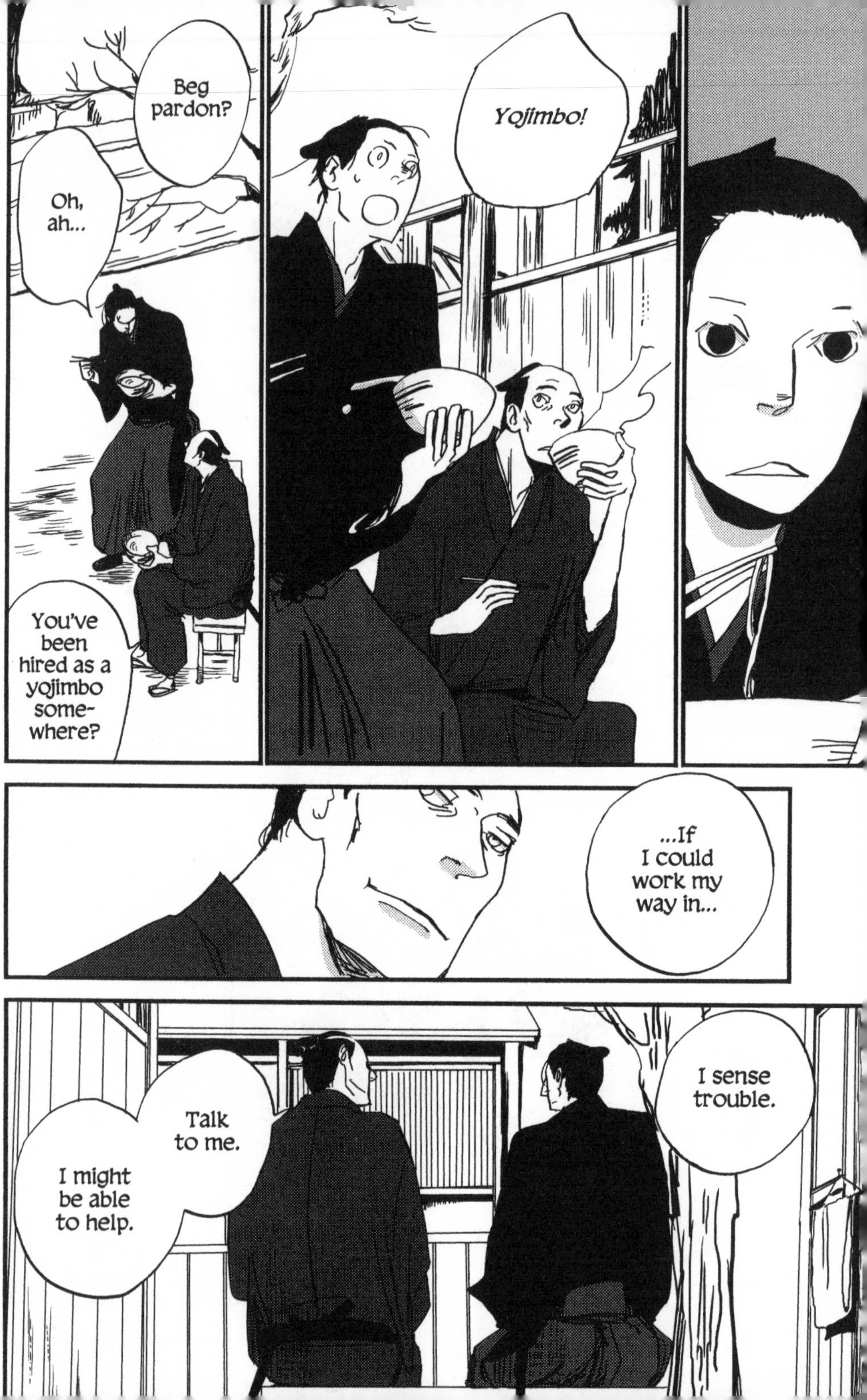
Yojimbo!
Beg pardon?
Oh, ah...
You've been hired as a yojimbo some-where?
...If I could work my way in...
I sense trouble.
Talk to me.
I might be able to help.

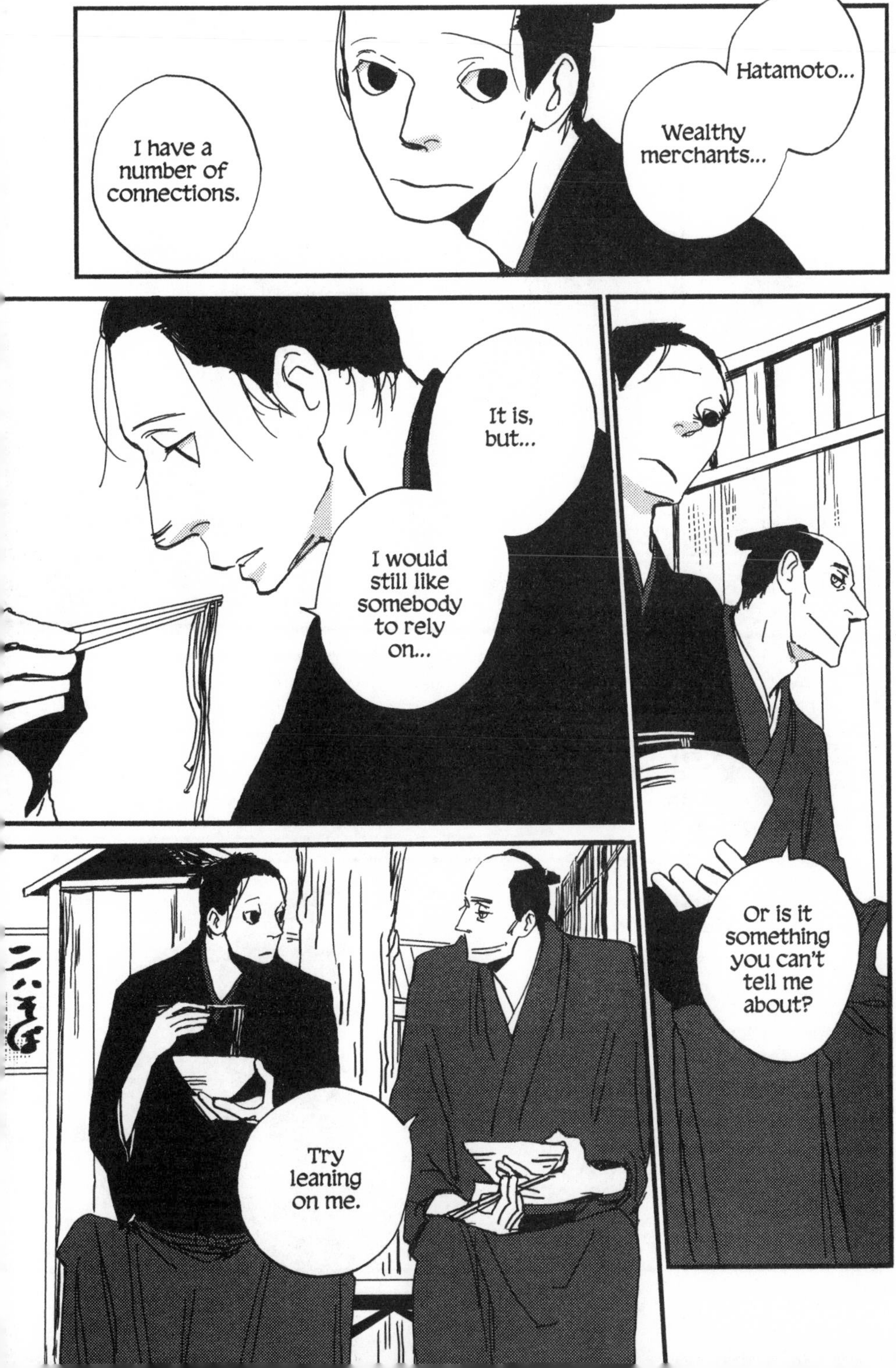
Hatamoto...
Wealthy merchants...
I have a number of connections.
Or is it something you can't tell me about?
It is, but...
I would still like somebody to rely on...
二八そば
Try leaning on me.

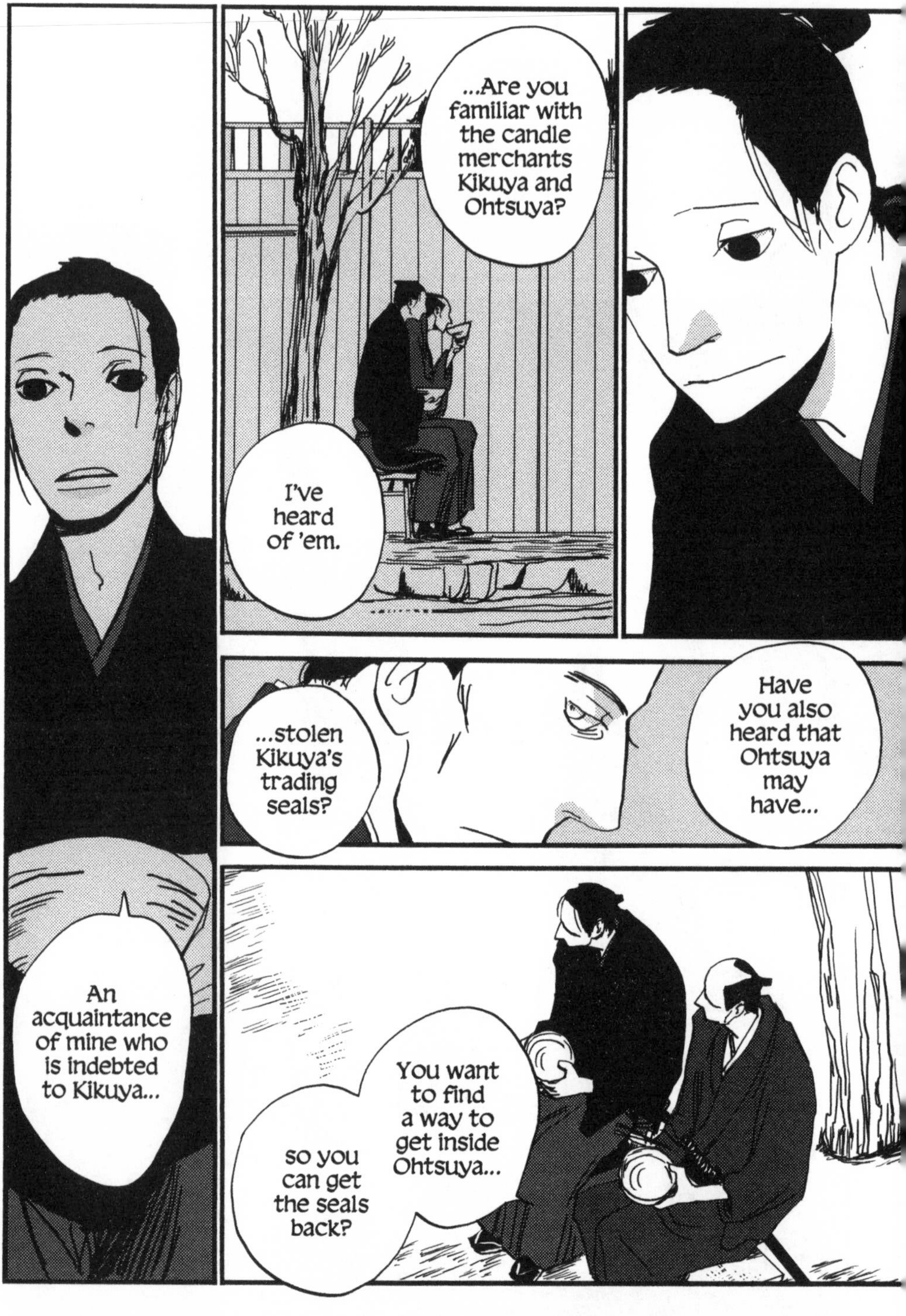
...Are you familiar with the candle merchants Kikuya and Ohtsuya?
I've heard of 'em.
Have you also heard that Ohtsuya may have...
...stolen Kikuya's trading seals?
You want to find a way to get inside Ohtsuya...
so you can get the seals back?
An acquaintance of mine who is indebted to Kikuya...

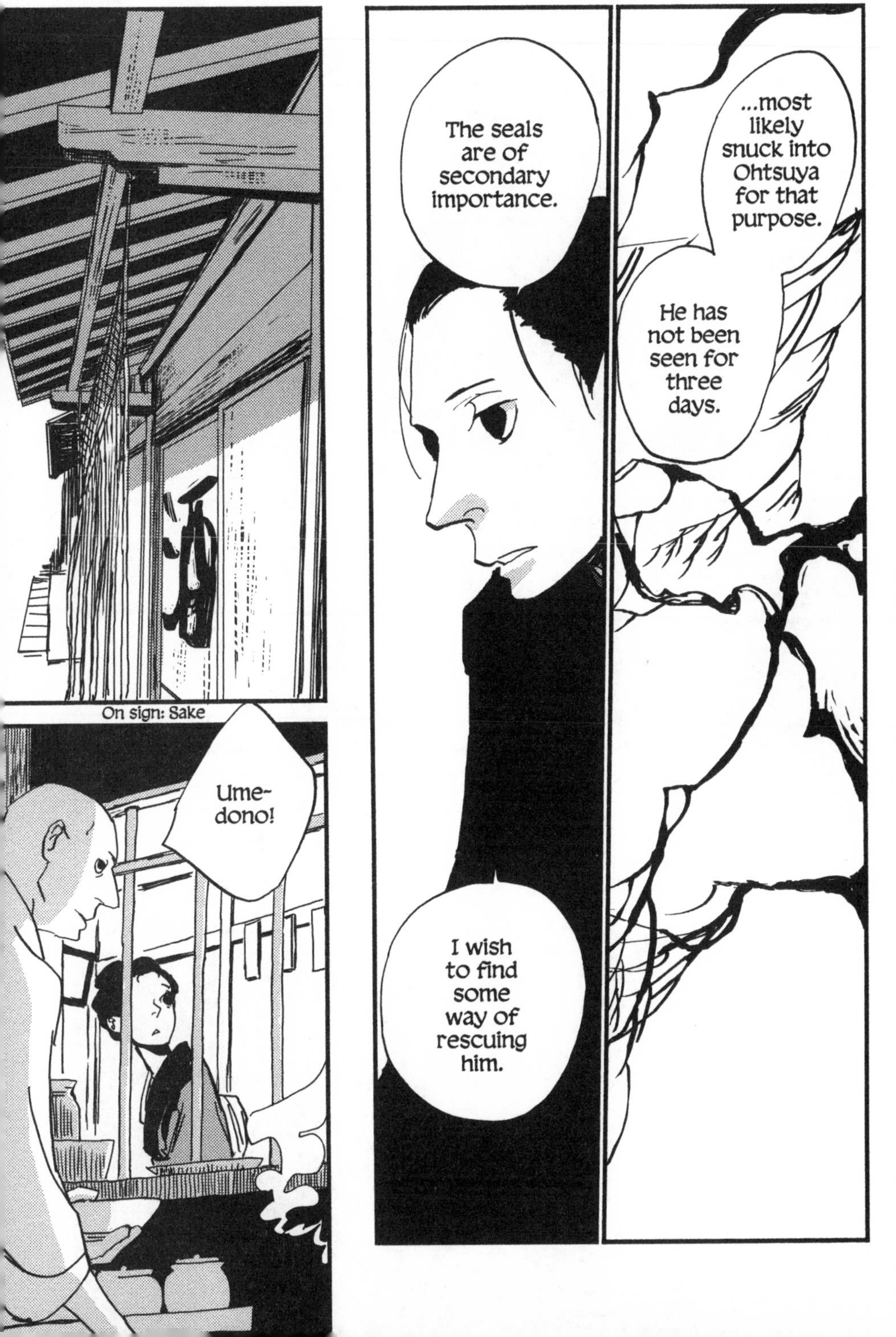
...most likely snuck into Ohtsuya for that purpose.
He has not been seen for three days.
The seals are of secondary importance.
I wish to find some way of rescuing him.
On sign: Sake
Ume-dono!

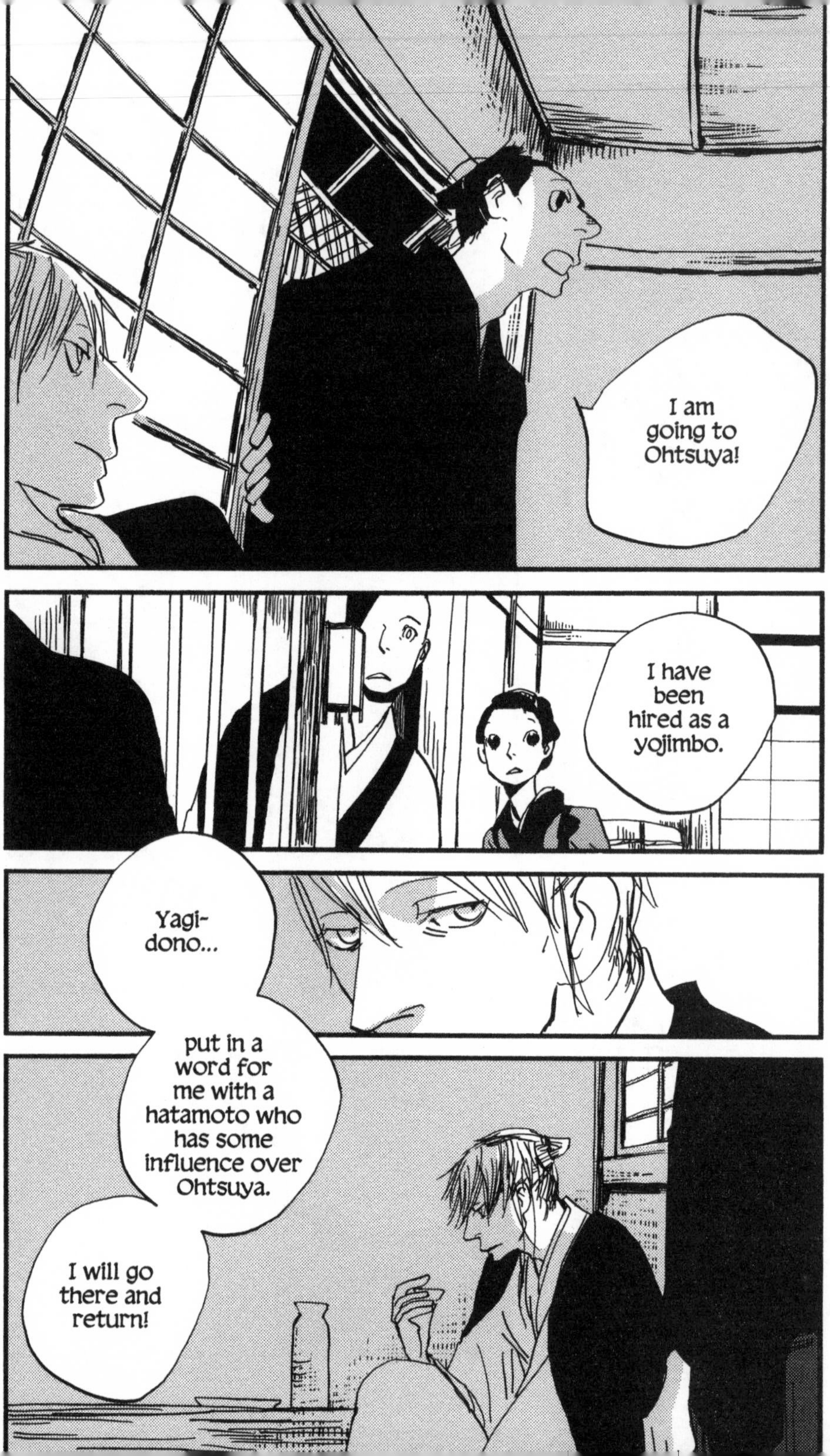
I am going to Ohtsuya!
I have been hired as a yojimbo.
Yagi-dono...
put in a word for me with a hatamoto who has some influence over Ohtsuya.
I will go there and return!

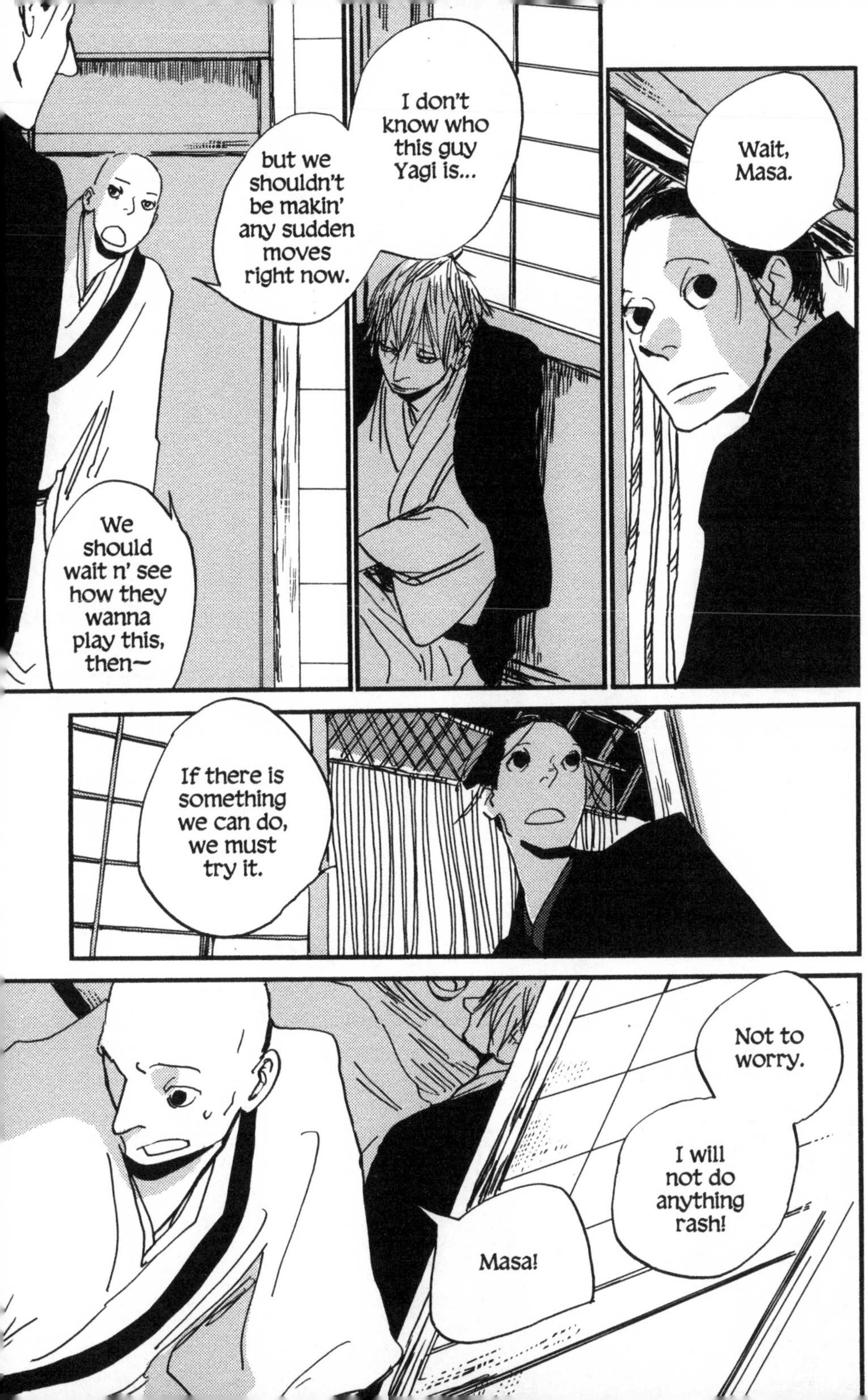
Wait, Masa.
I don't know who this guy Yagi is...
but we shouldn't be makin' any sudden moves right now.
We should wait n' see how they wanna play this, then~
If there is something we can do, we must try it.
Not to worry.
I will not do anything rash!
Masa!

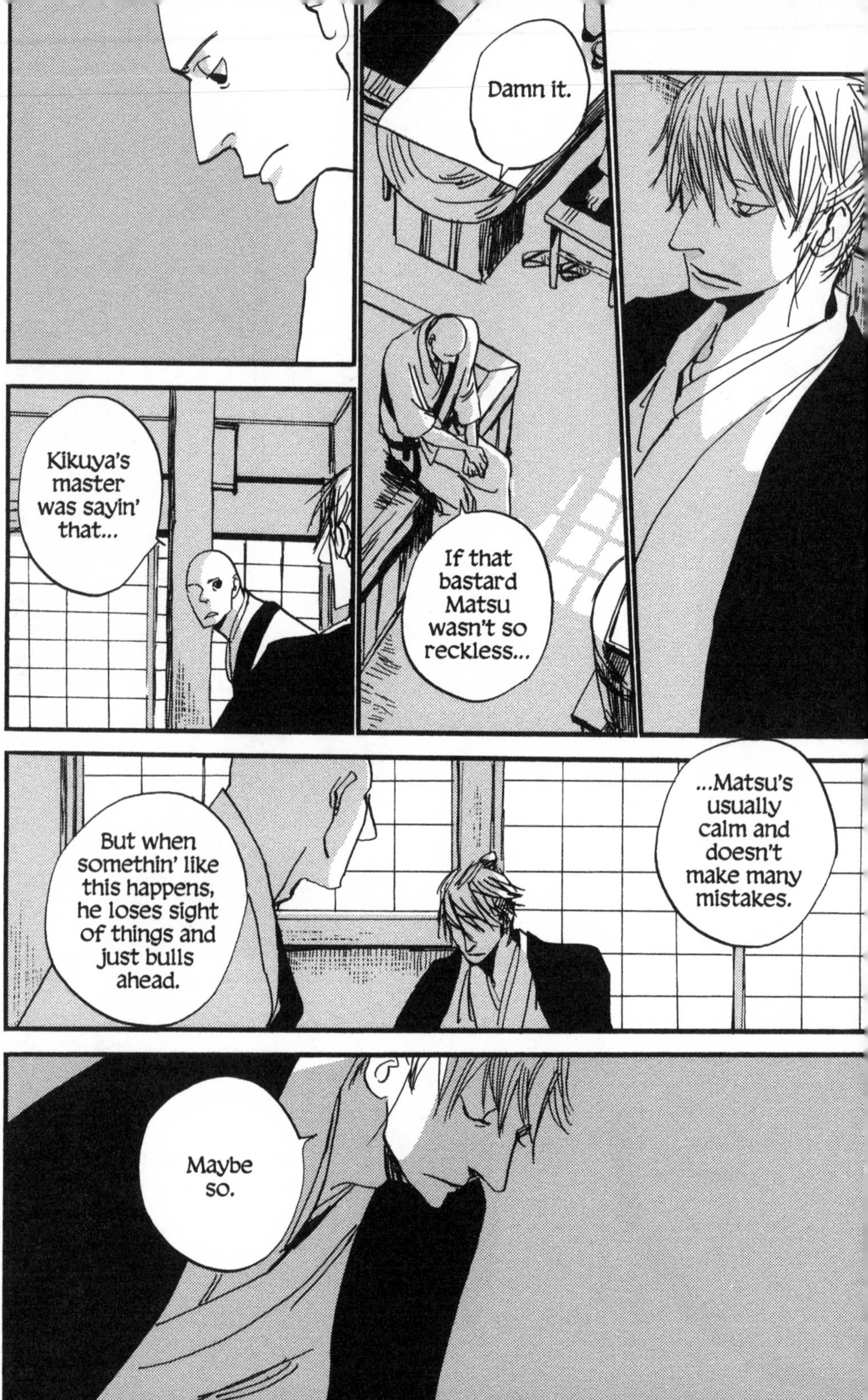
Damn it.
If that bastard Matsu wasn't so reckless...
Kikuya's master was sayin' that...
...Matsu's usually calm and doesn't make many mistakes.
But when somethin' like this happens, he loses sight of things and just bulls ahead.
Maybe so.

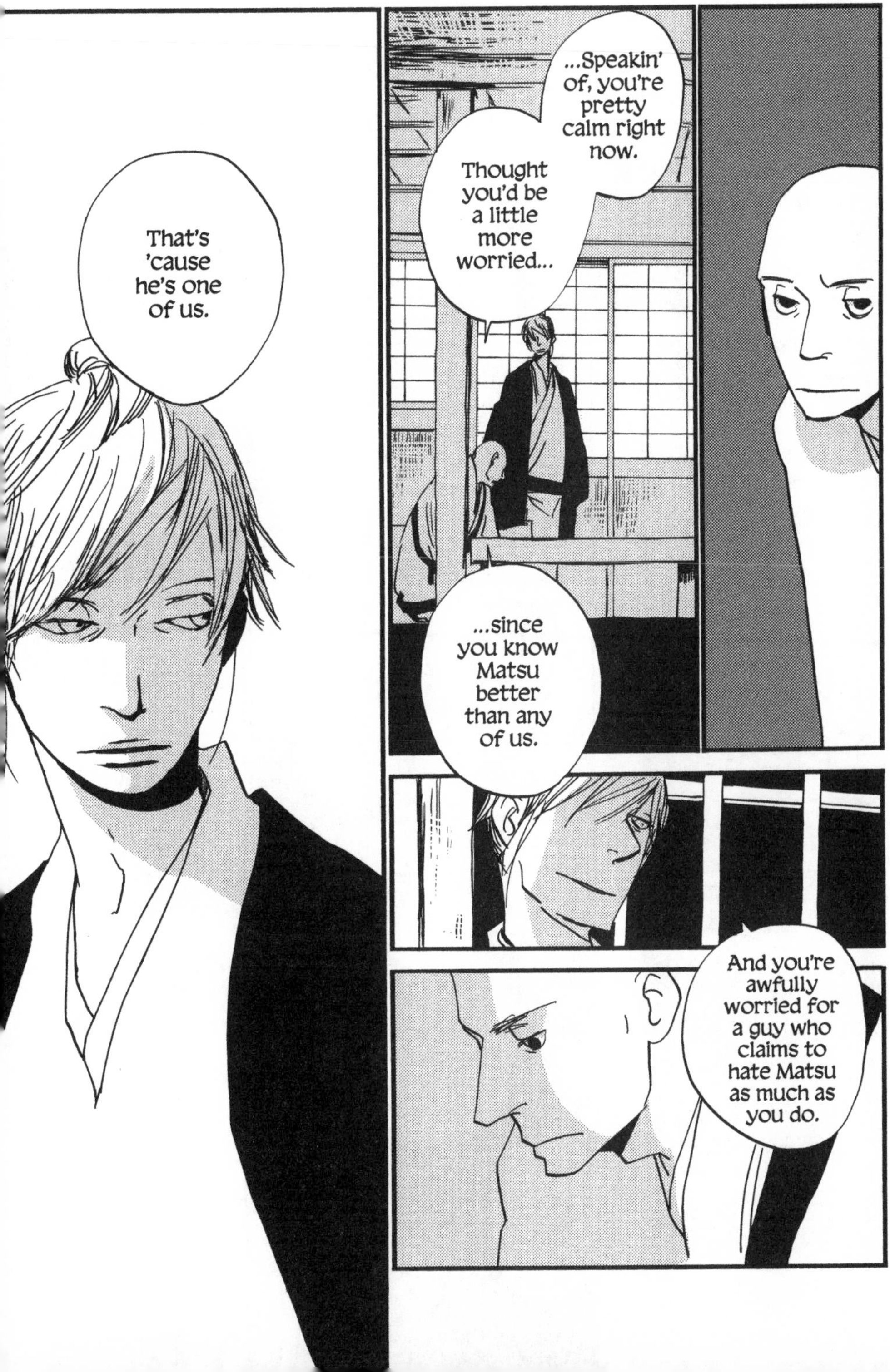
...Speakin' of, you're pretty calm right now.
Thought you'd be a little more worried...
...since you know Matsu better than any of us.
And you're awfully worried for a guy who claims to hate Matsu as much as you do.
That's 'cause he's one of us.

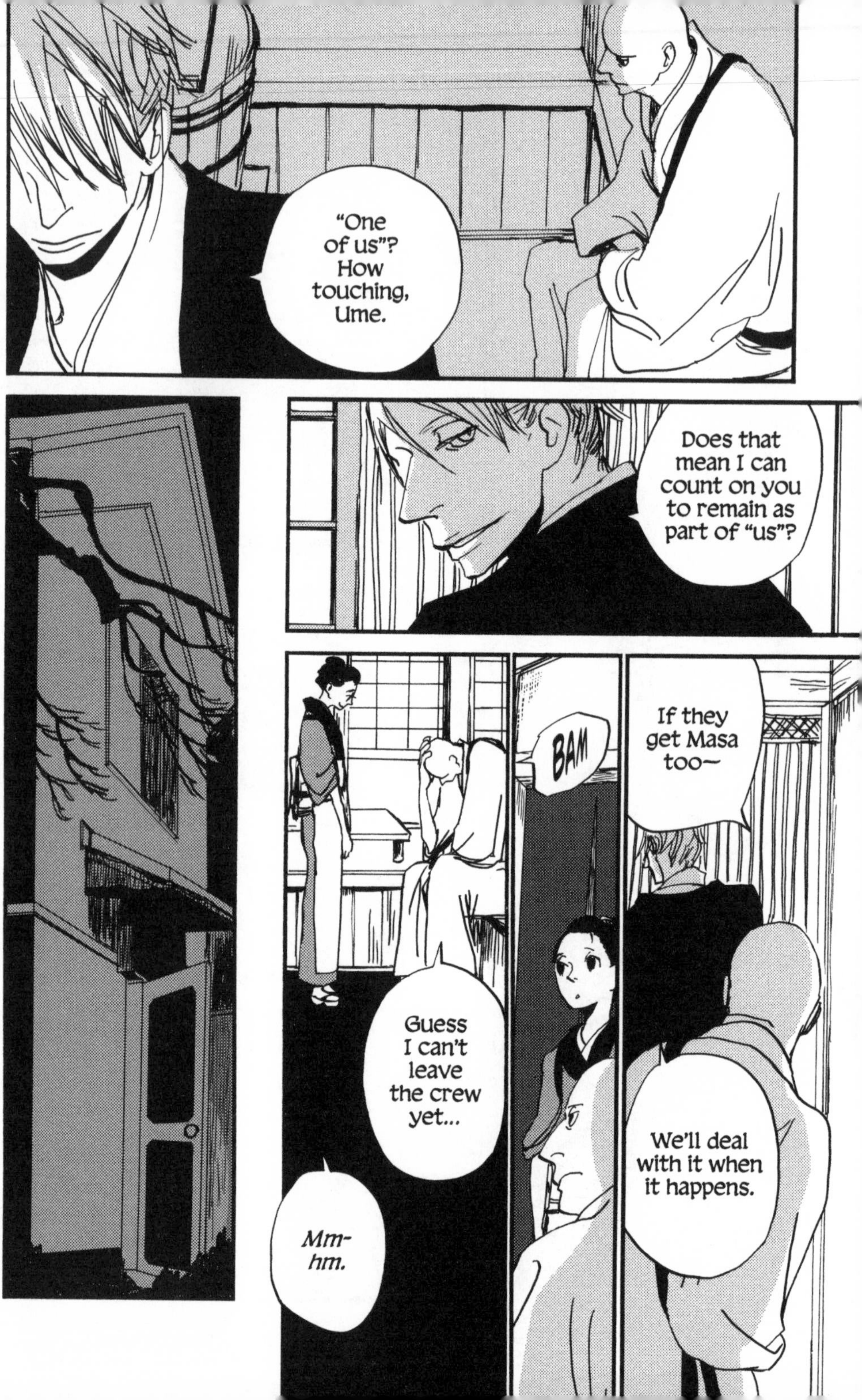
"One of us"? How touching, Ume.
Does that mean I can count on you to remain as part of "us"?
If they get Masa too~
We'll deal with it when it happens.
BAM
Guess I can't leave the crew yet...
Mm-hm.

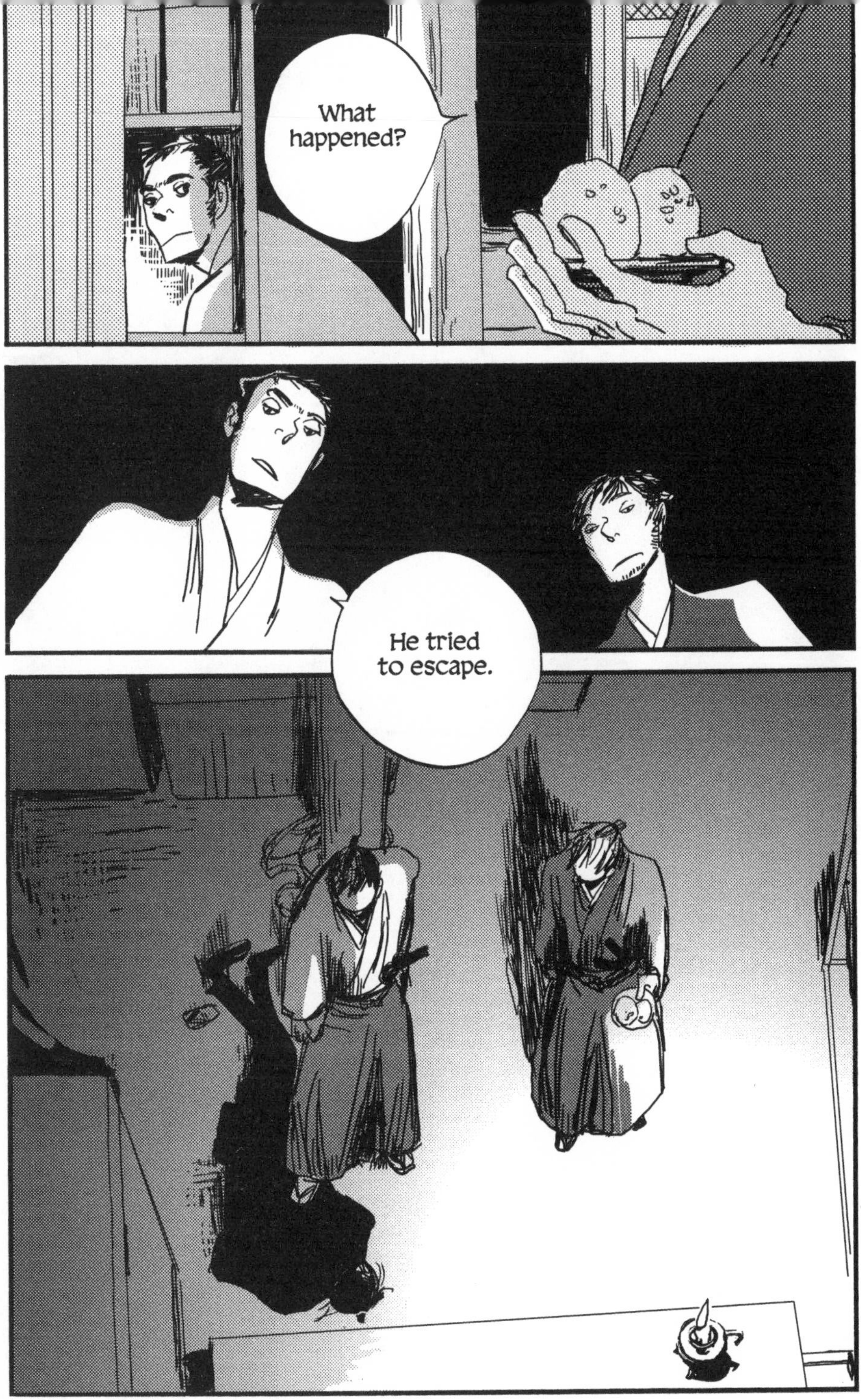
What happened?
He tried to escape.

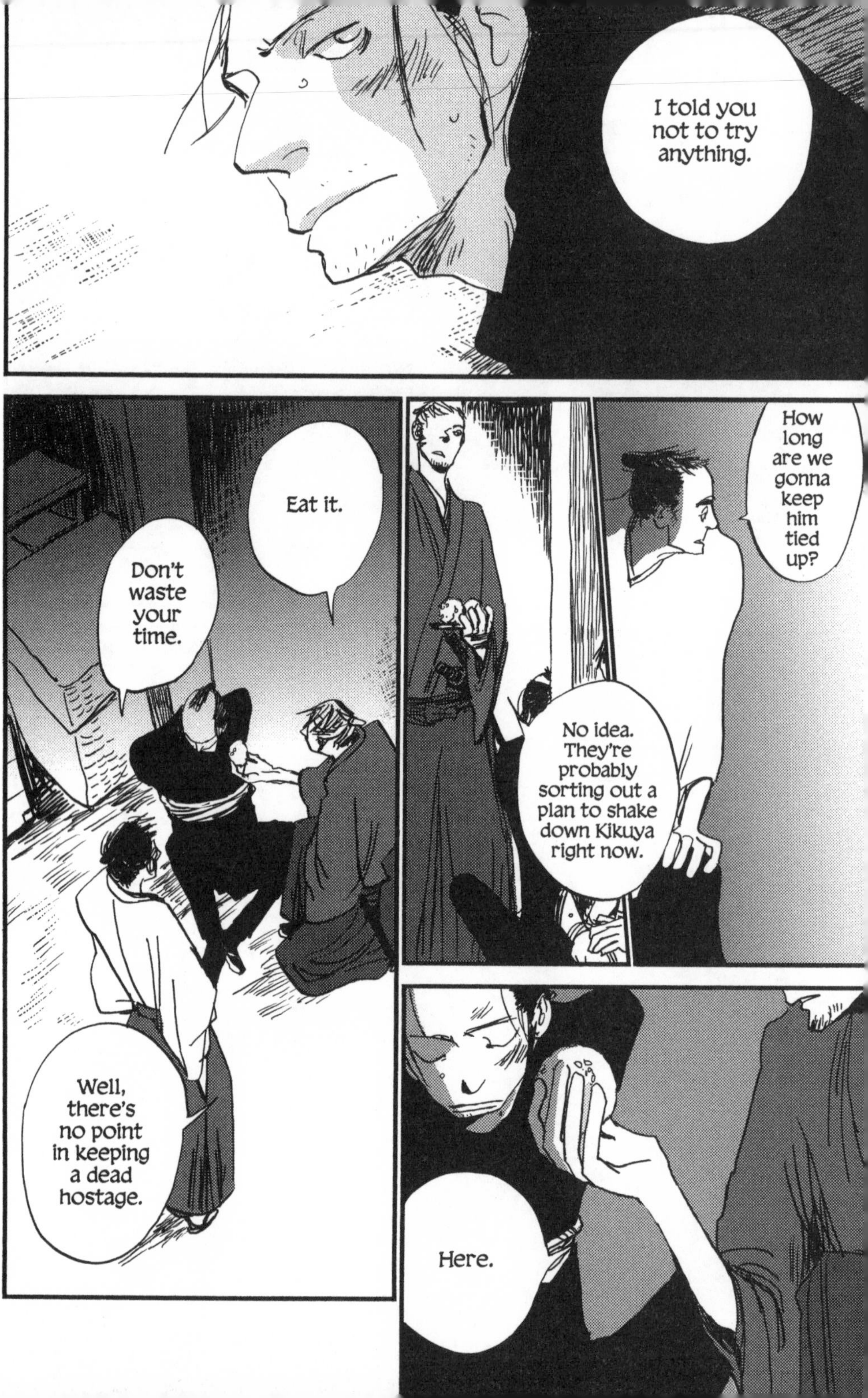
I told you not to try anything.
How long are we gonna keep him tied up?
No idea. They're probably sorting out a plan to shake down Kikuya right now.
Here.
Eat it.
Don't waste your time.
Well, there's no point in keeping a dead hostage.

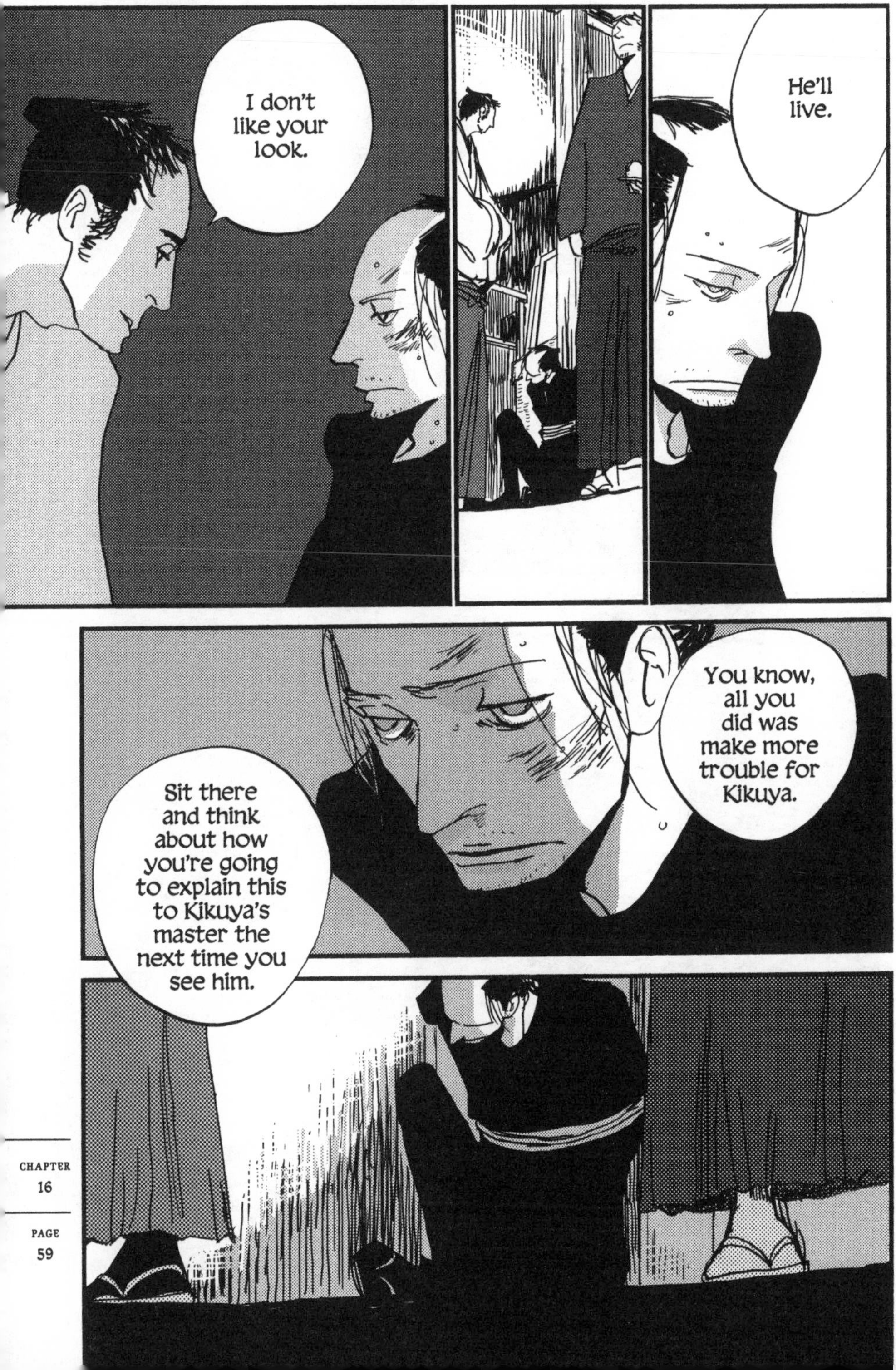
He'll live.
I don't like your look.
You know, all you did was make more trouble for Kikuya.
Sit there and think about how you're going to explain this to Kikuya's master the next time you see him.

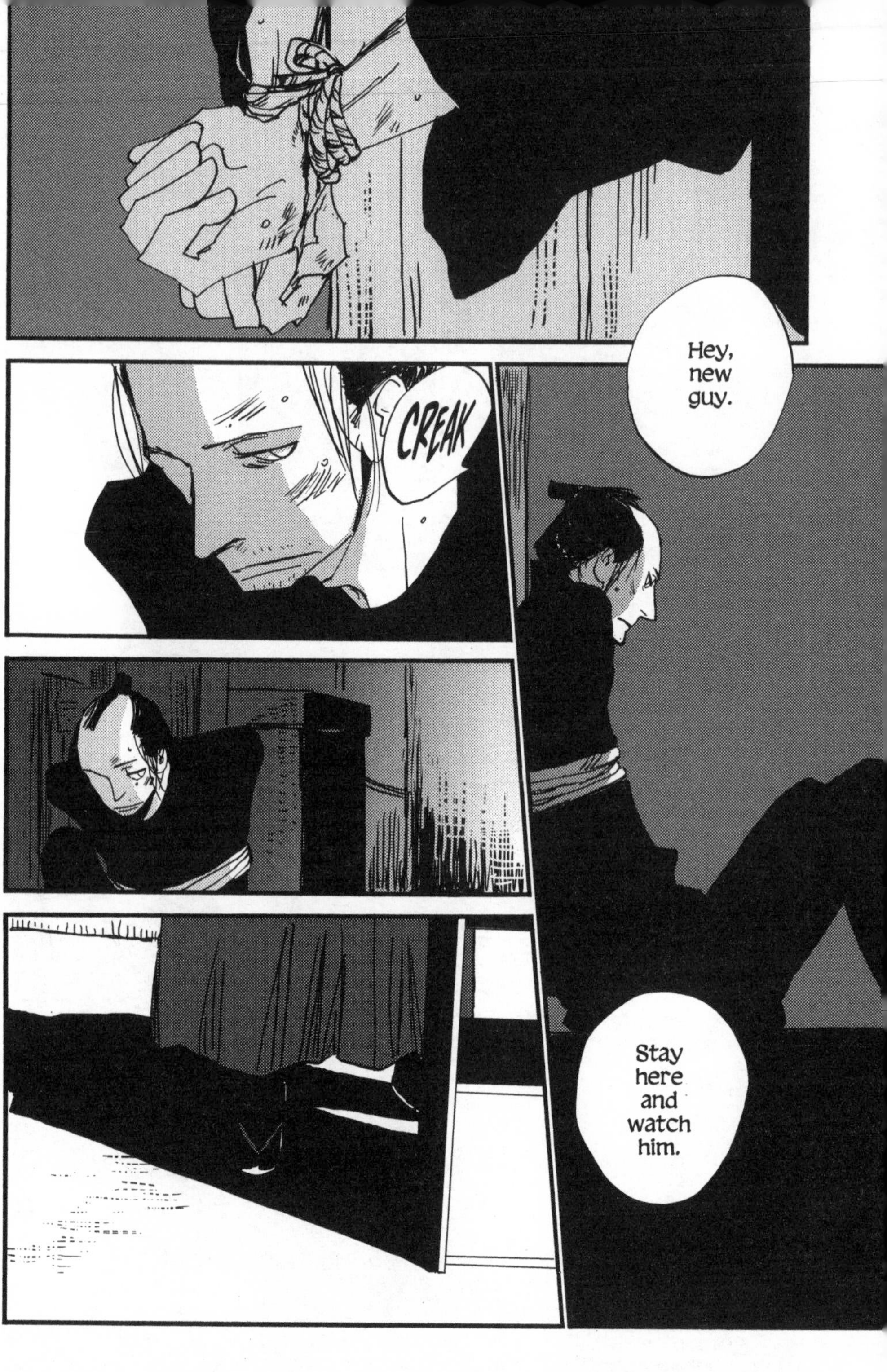
Hey, new guy.
Stay here and watch him.
CREAK

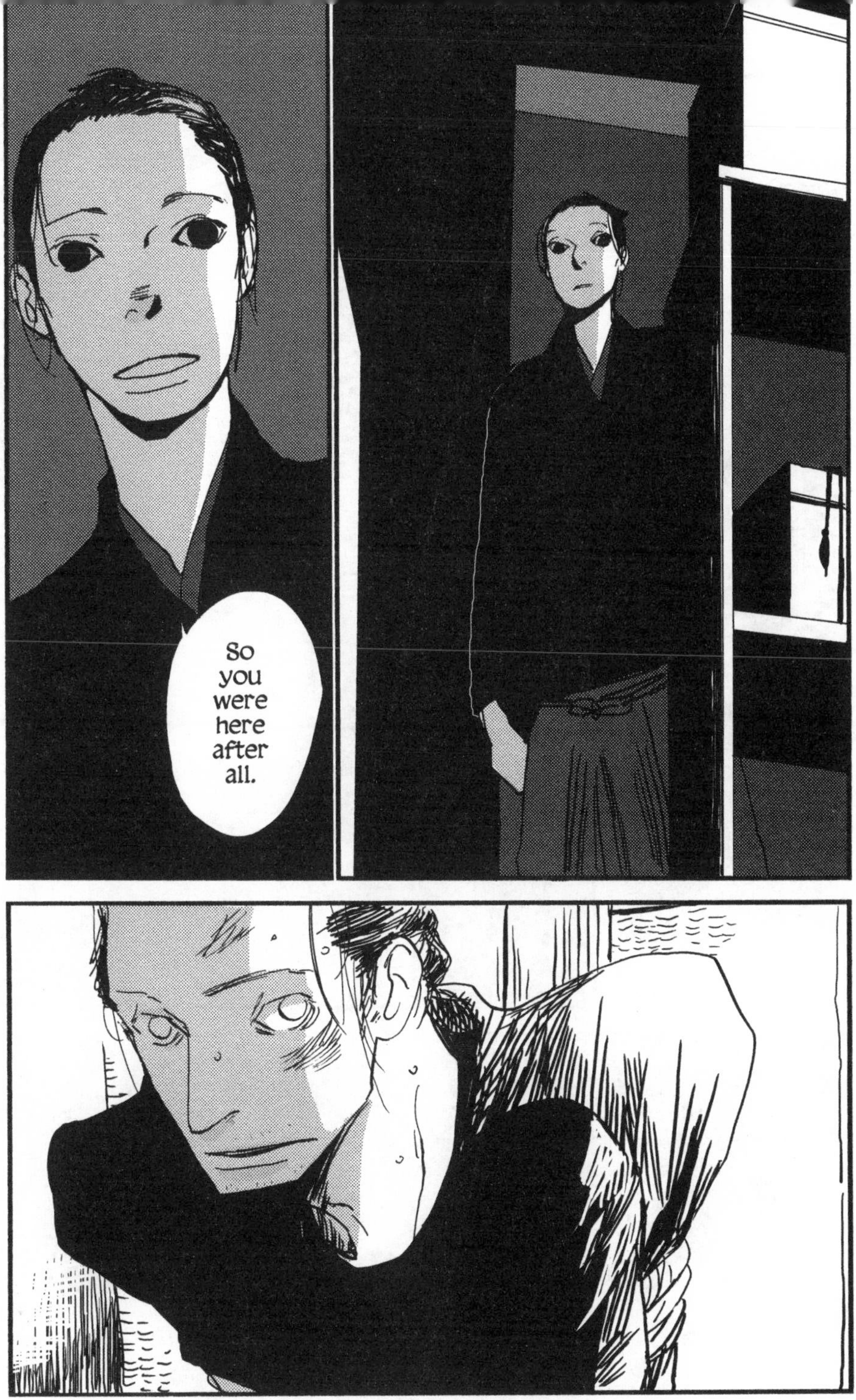
So you were here after all.

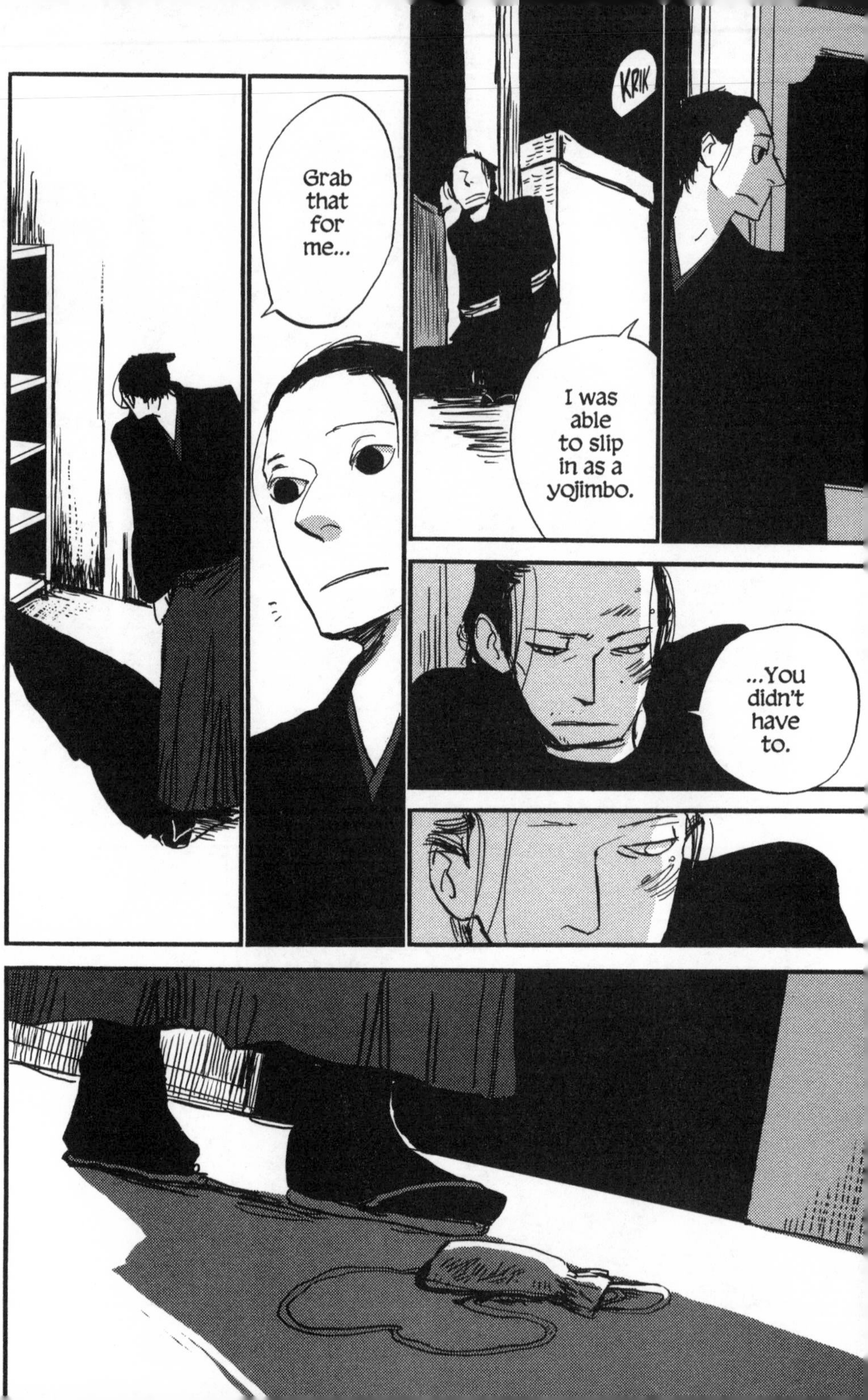
KRIK
I was able to slip in as a yojimbo.
...You didn't have to.
Grab that for me...

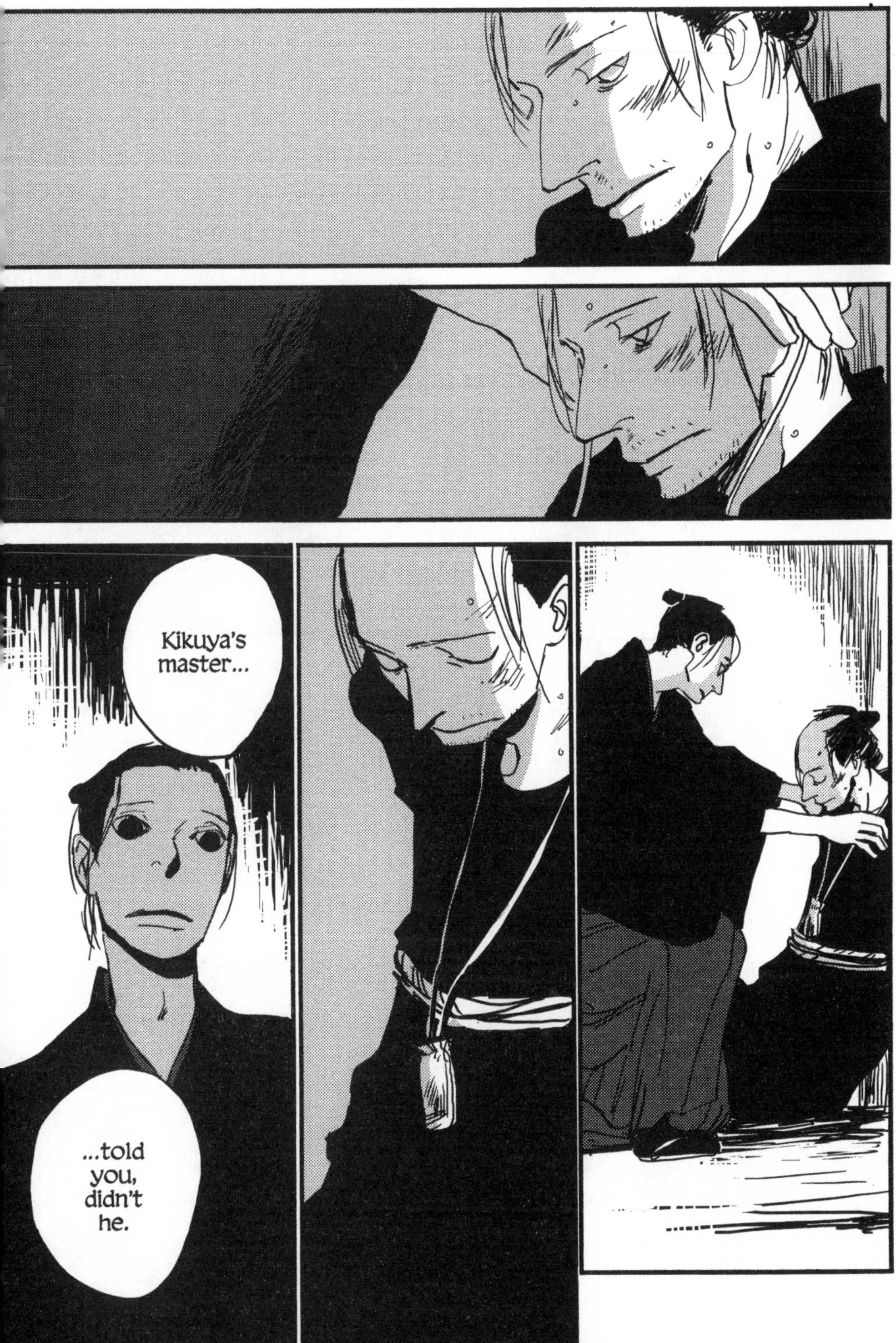
Kikuya's master...
...told you, didn't he.

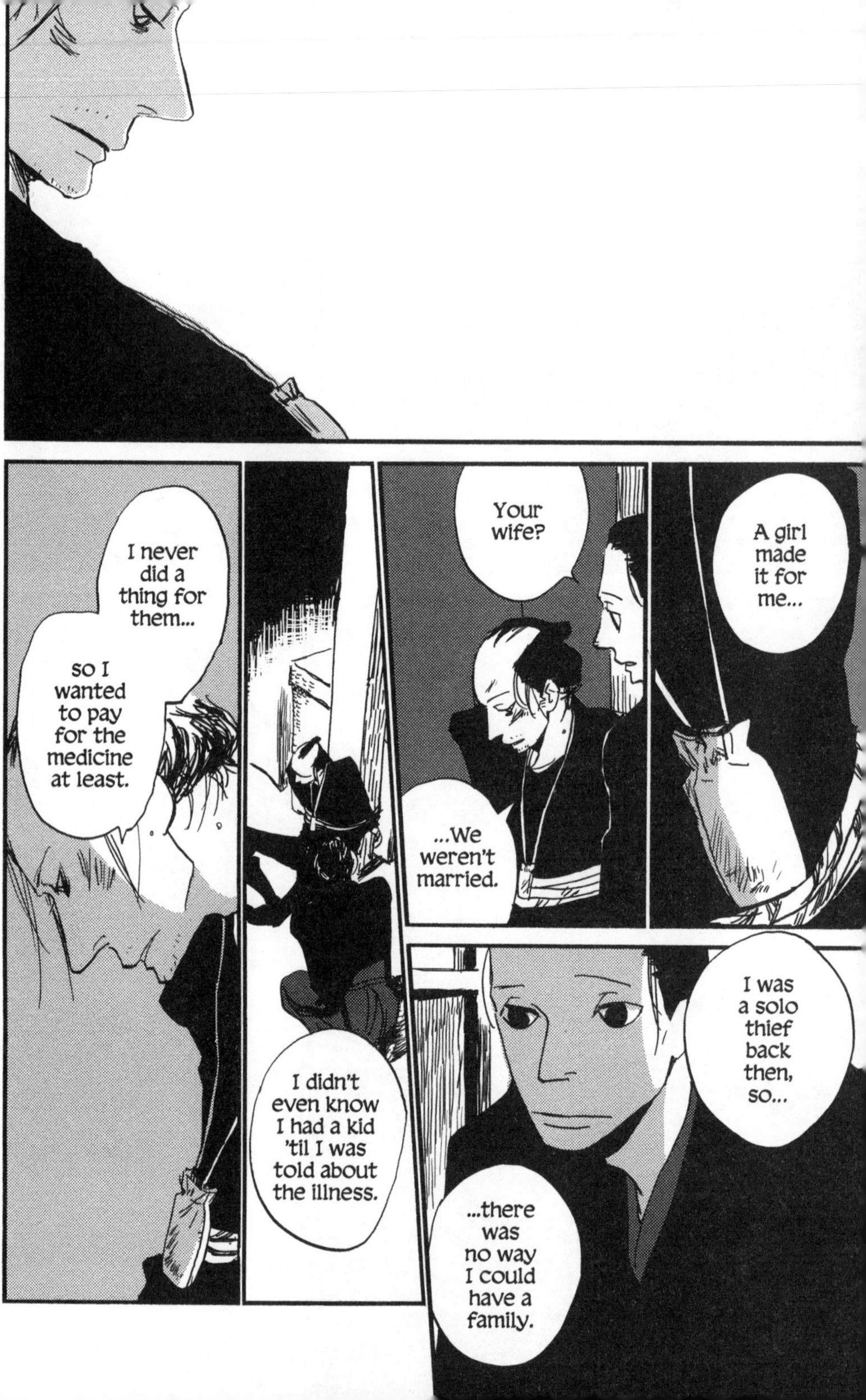
A girl made it for me...
Your wife?
...We weren't married.
I was a solo thief back then, so...
...there was no way I could have a family.
I didn't even know I had a kid 'til I was told about the illness.
I never did a thing for them...
so I wanted to pay for the medicine at least.

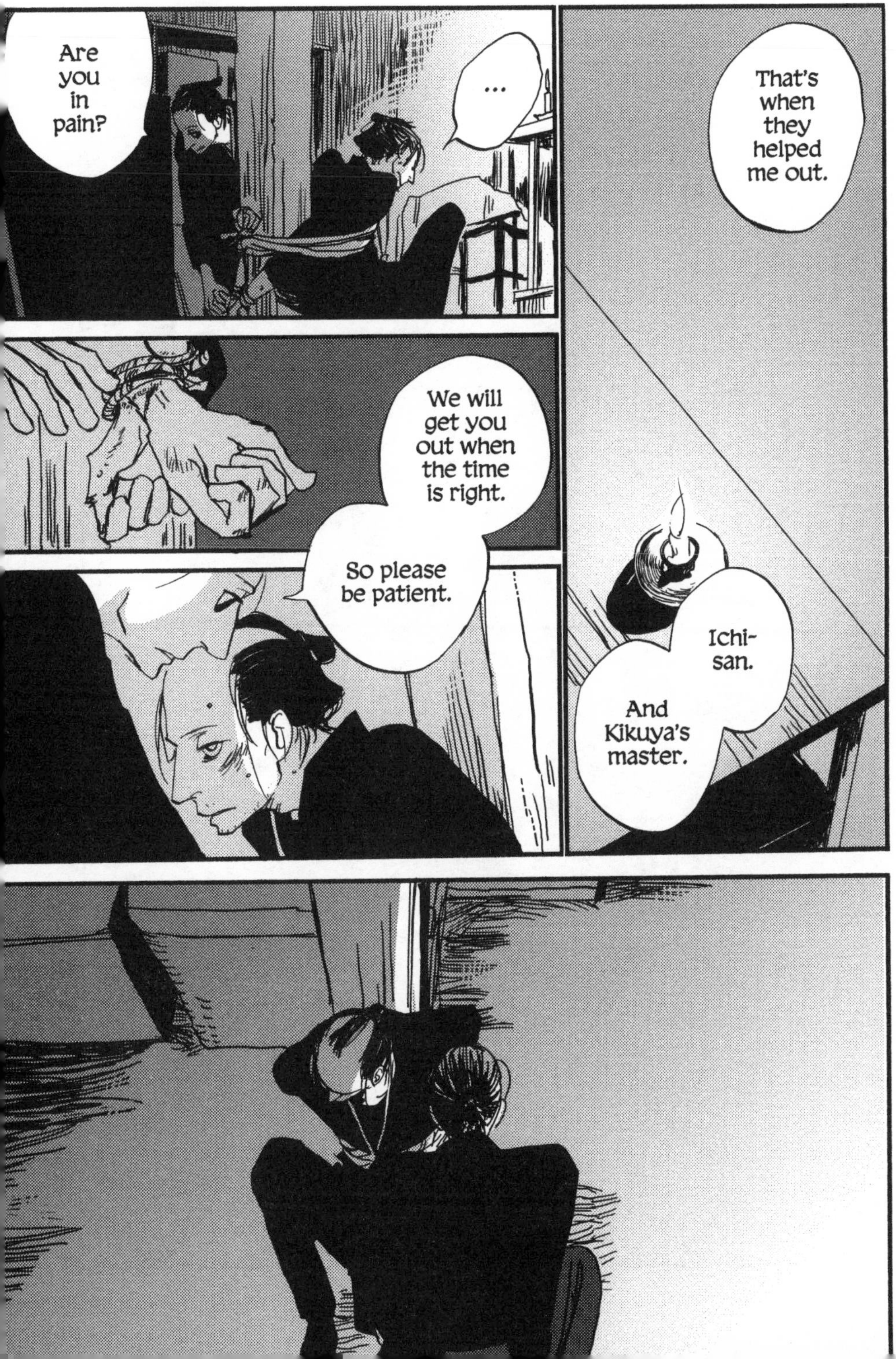
That's when they helped me out.
Ichi-san.
And Kikuya's master.
Are you in pain?
...
We will get you out when the time is right.
So please be patient.

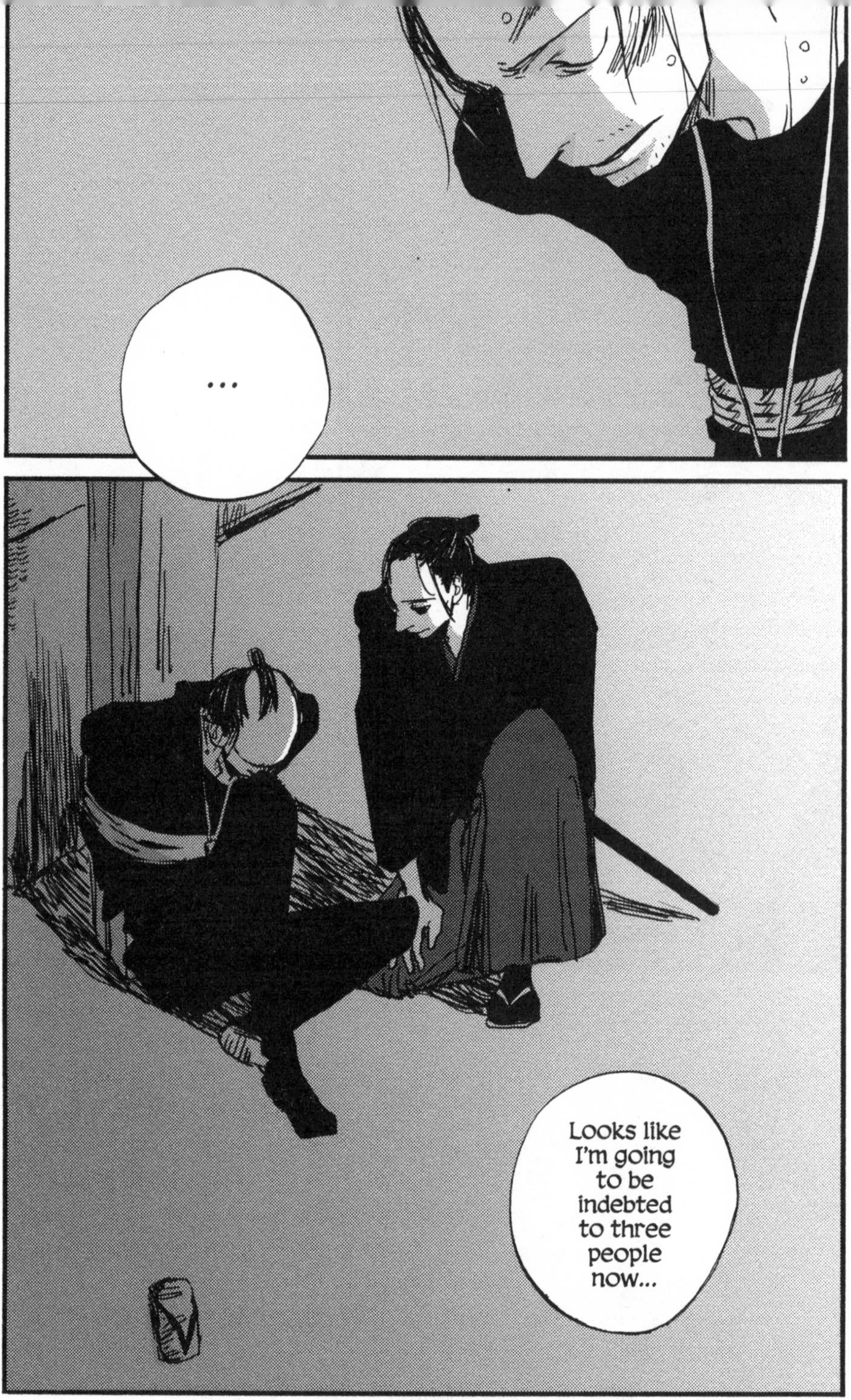
...
Looks like I'm going to be indebted to three people now...

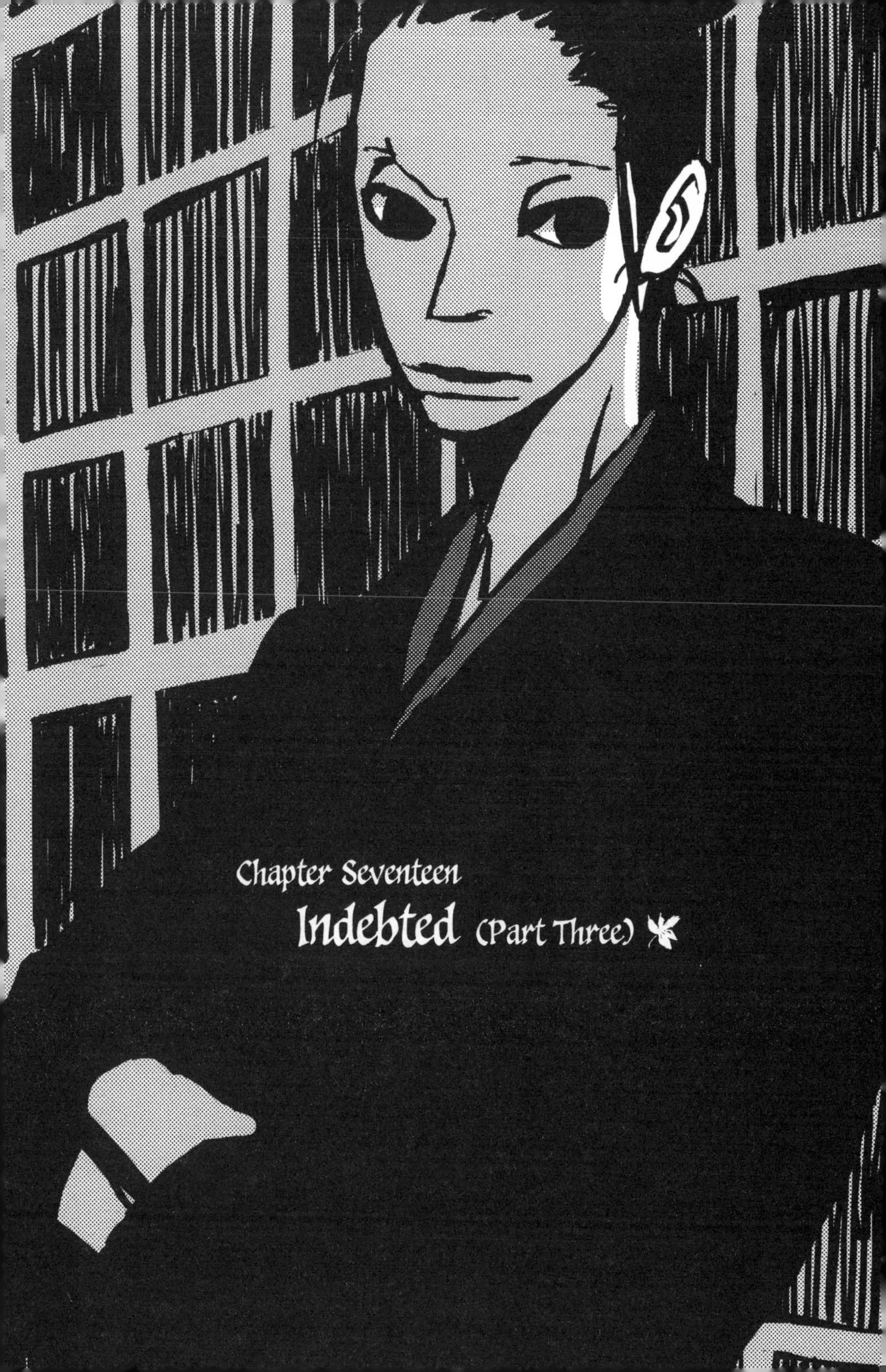
Chapter Seventeen
Indebted (Part Three)

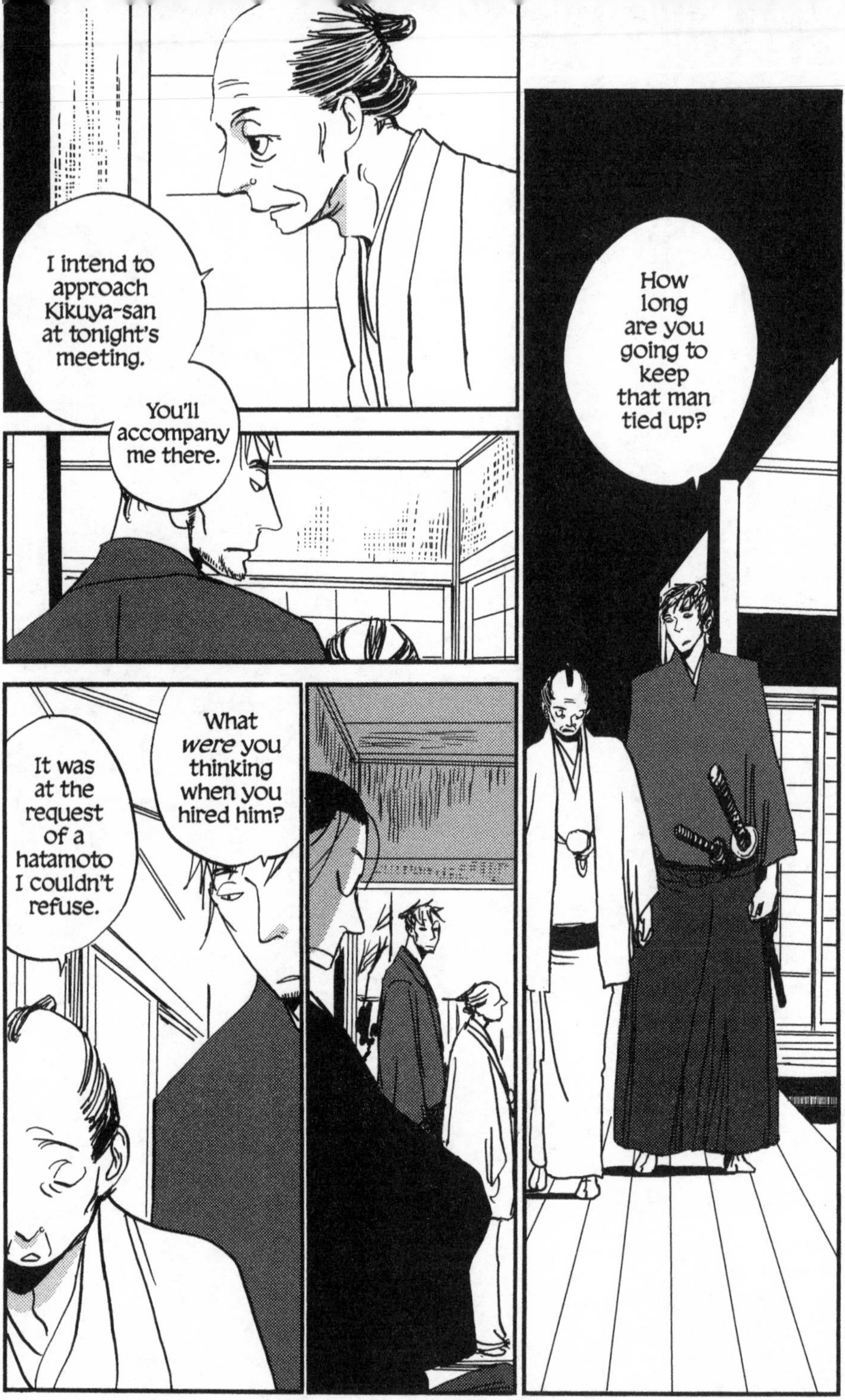
How long are you going to keep that man tied up?
I intend to approach Kikuya-san at tonight's meeting.
You'll accompany me there.
What *were* you thinking when you hired him?
It was at the request of a hatamoto I couldn't refuse.

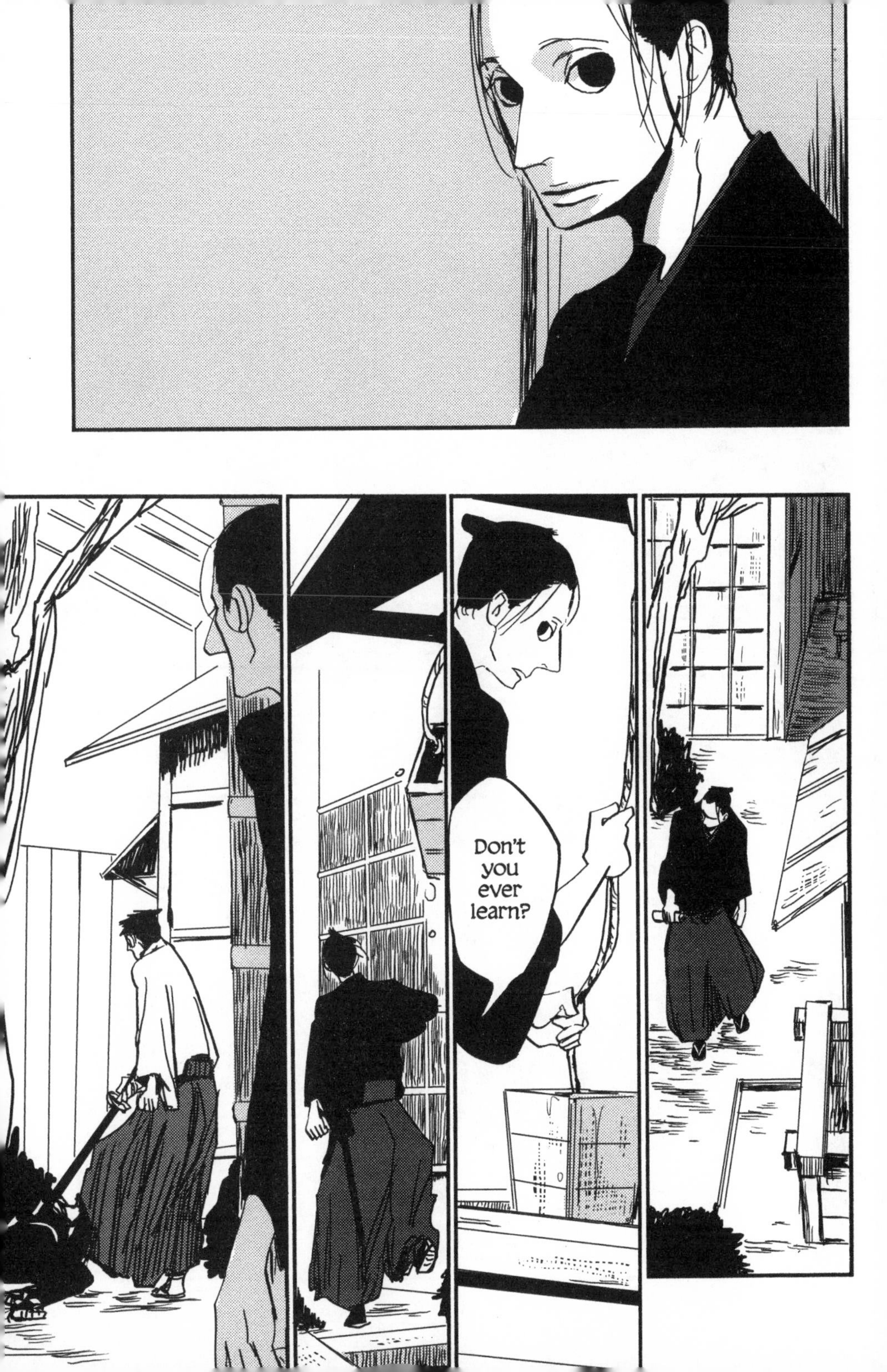
Don't you ever learn?

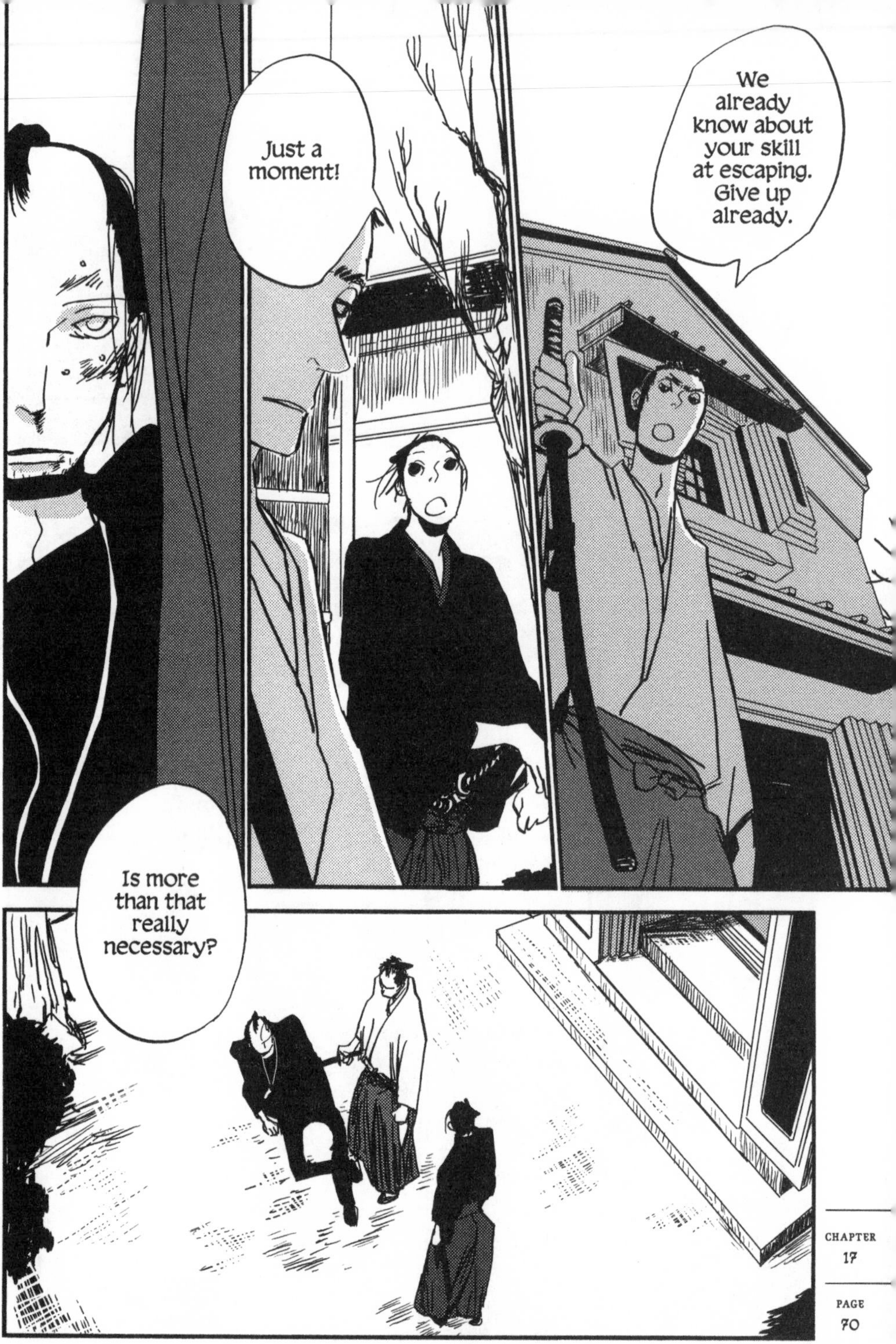
We already know about your skill at escaping. Give up already.
Just a moment!
Is more than that really necessary?

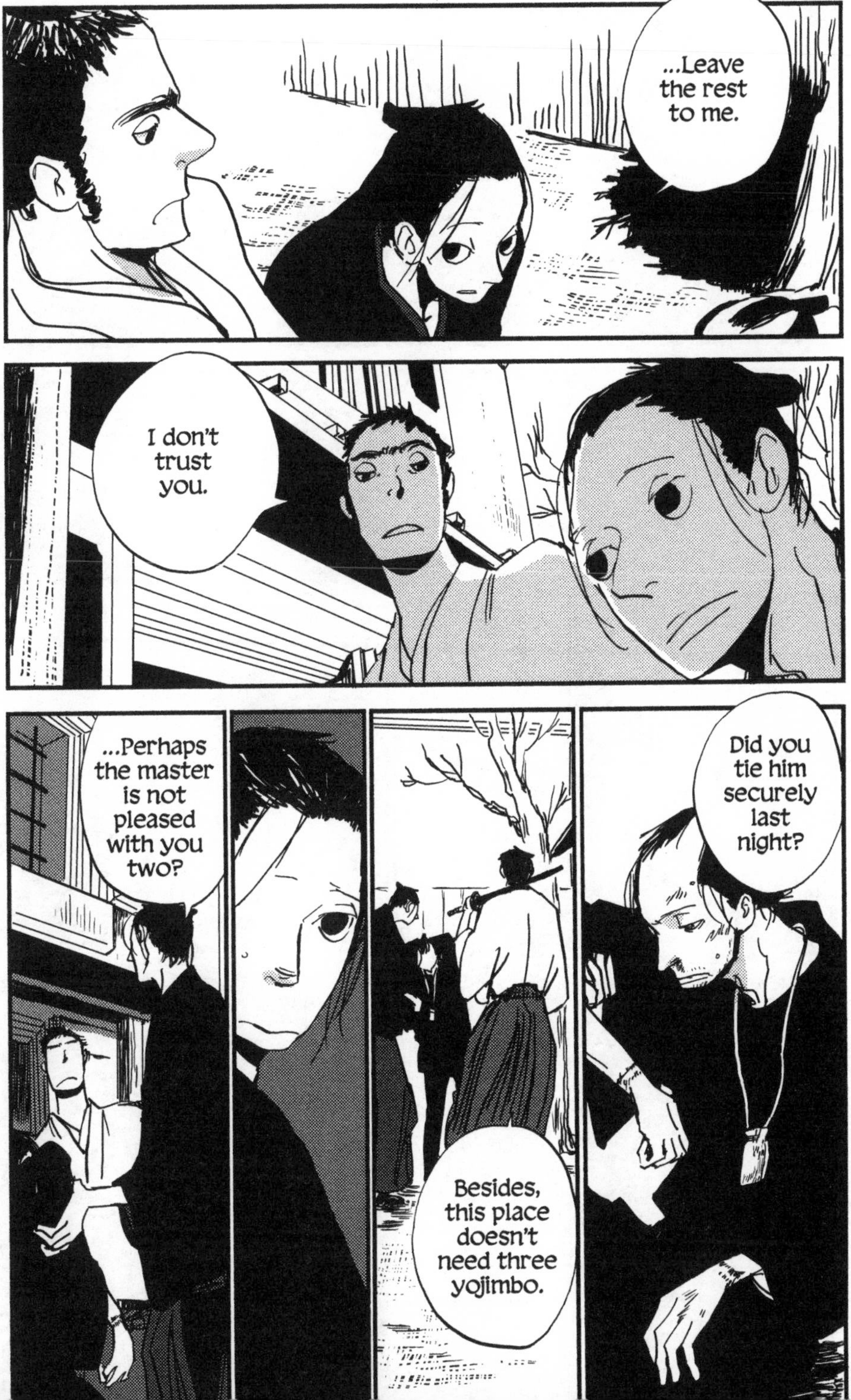
...Leave the rest to me.
I don't trust you.
Did you tie him securely last night?
Besides, this place doesn't need three yojimbo.
...Perhaps the master is not pleased with you two?

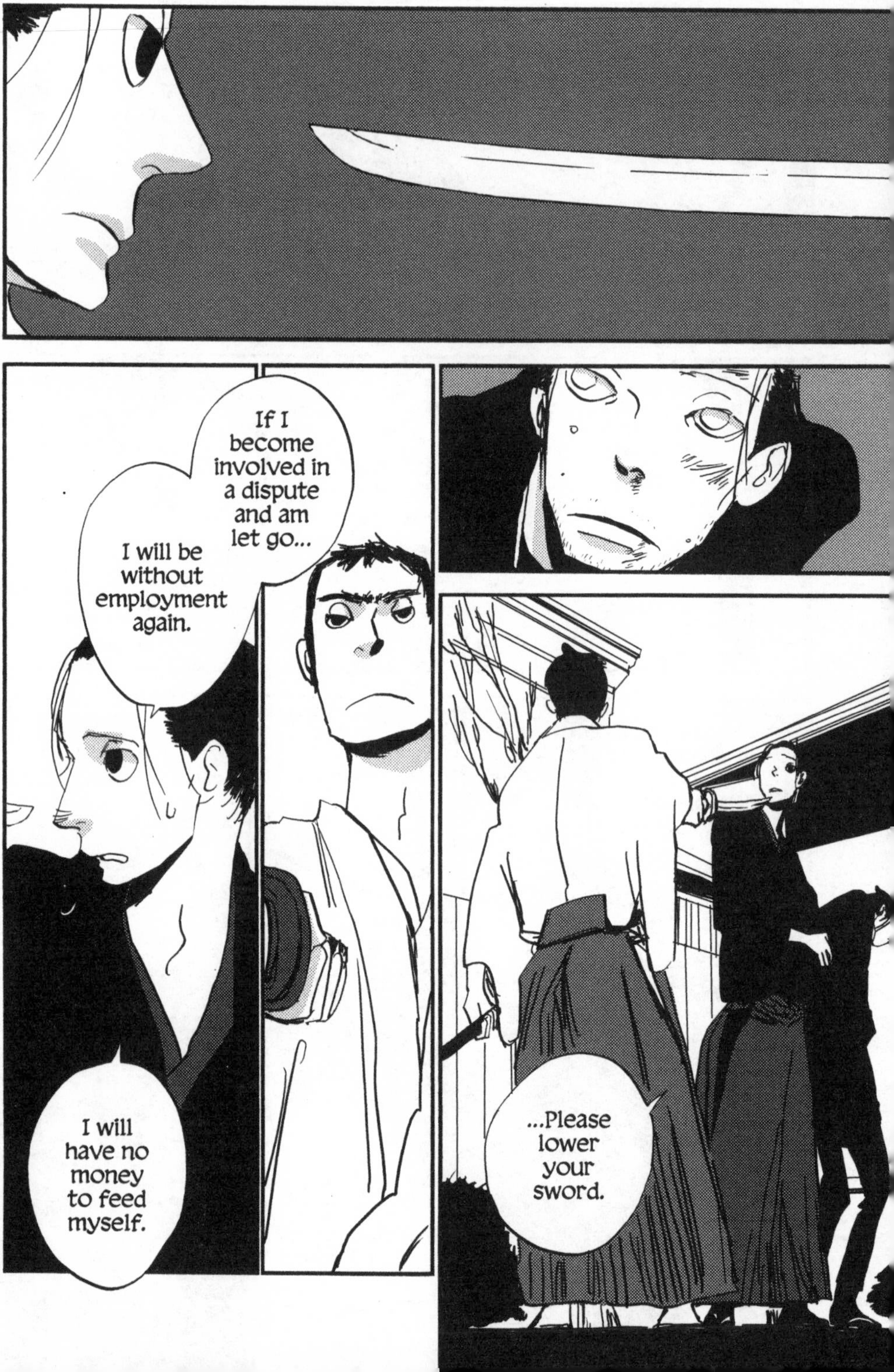
...Please lower your sword.
If I become involved in a dispute and am let go...
I will be without employment again.
I will have no money to feed myself.

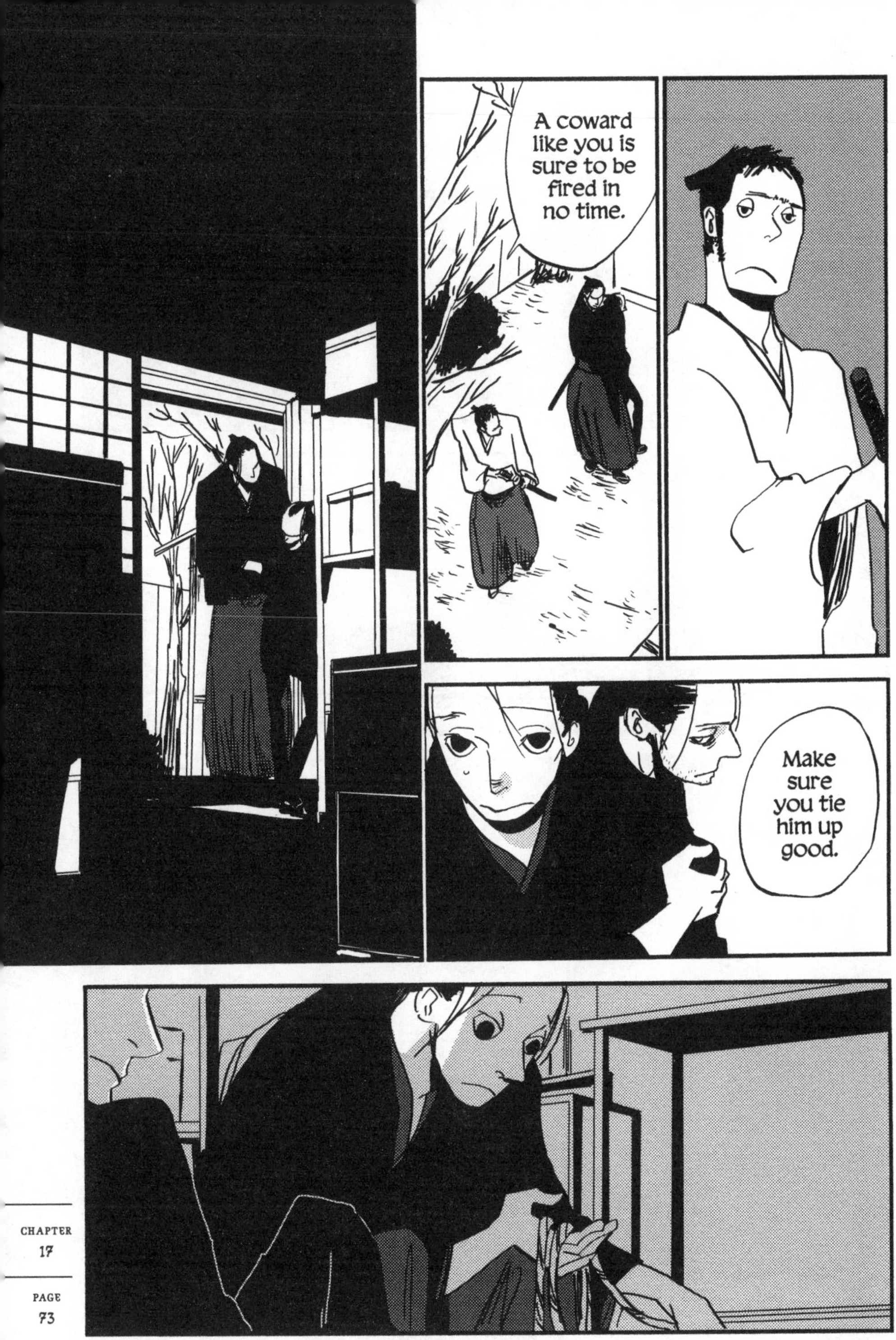
A coward like you is sure to be fired in no time.
Make sure you tie him up good.

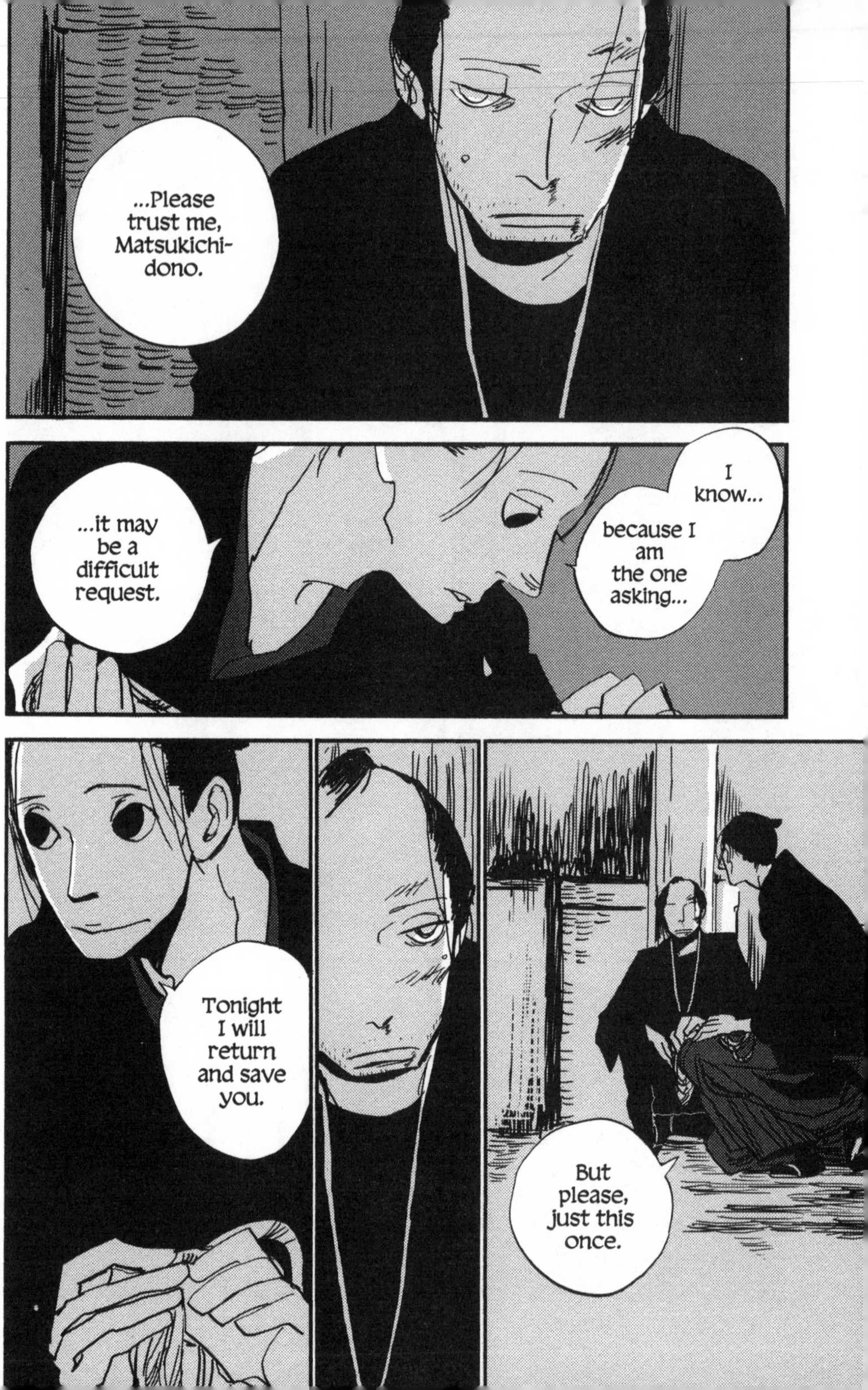
...Please trust me, Matsukichi-dono.
I know... because I am the one asking...
...it may be a difficult request.
But please, just this once.
Tonight I will return and save you.

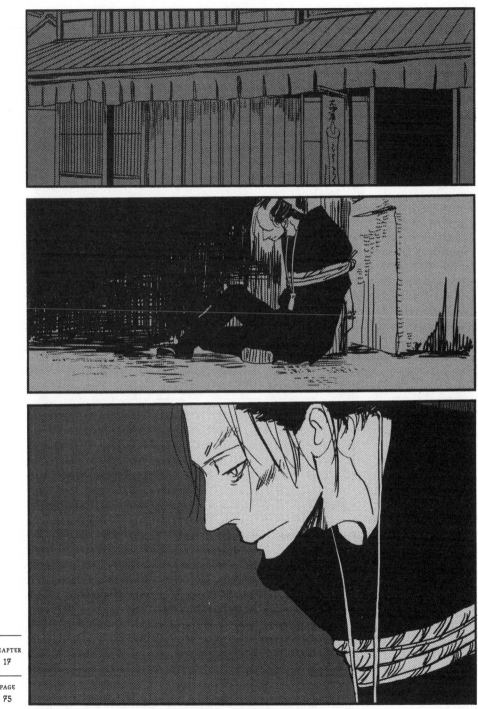

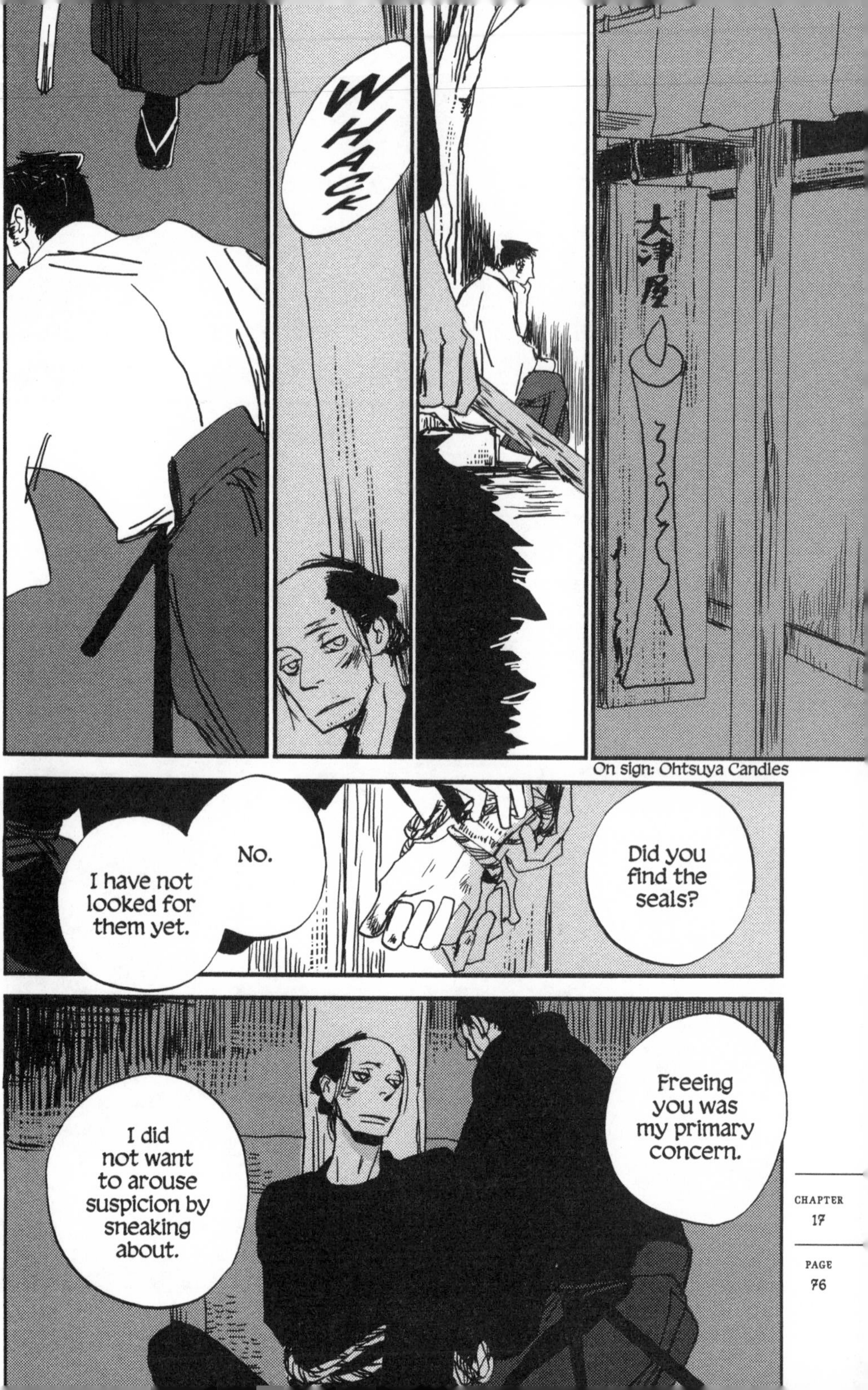
WHACK
On sign: Ohtsuya Candles
Did you find the seals?
No.
I have not looked for them yet.
Freeing you was my primary concern.
I did not want to arouse suspicion by sneaking about.

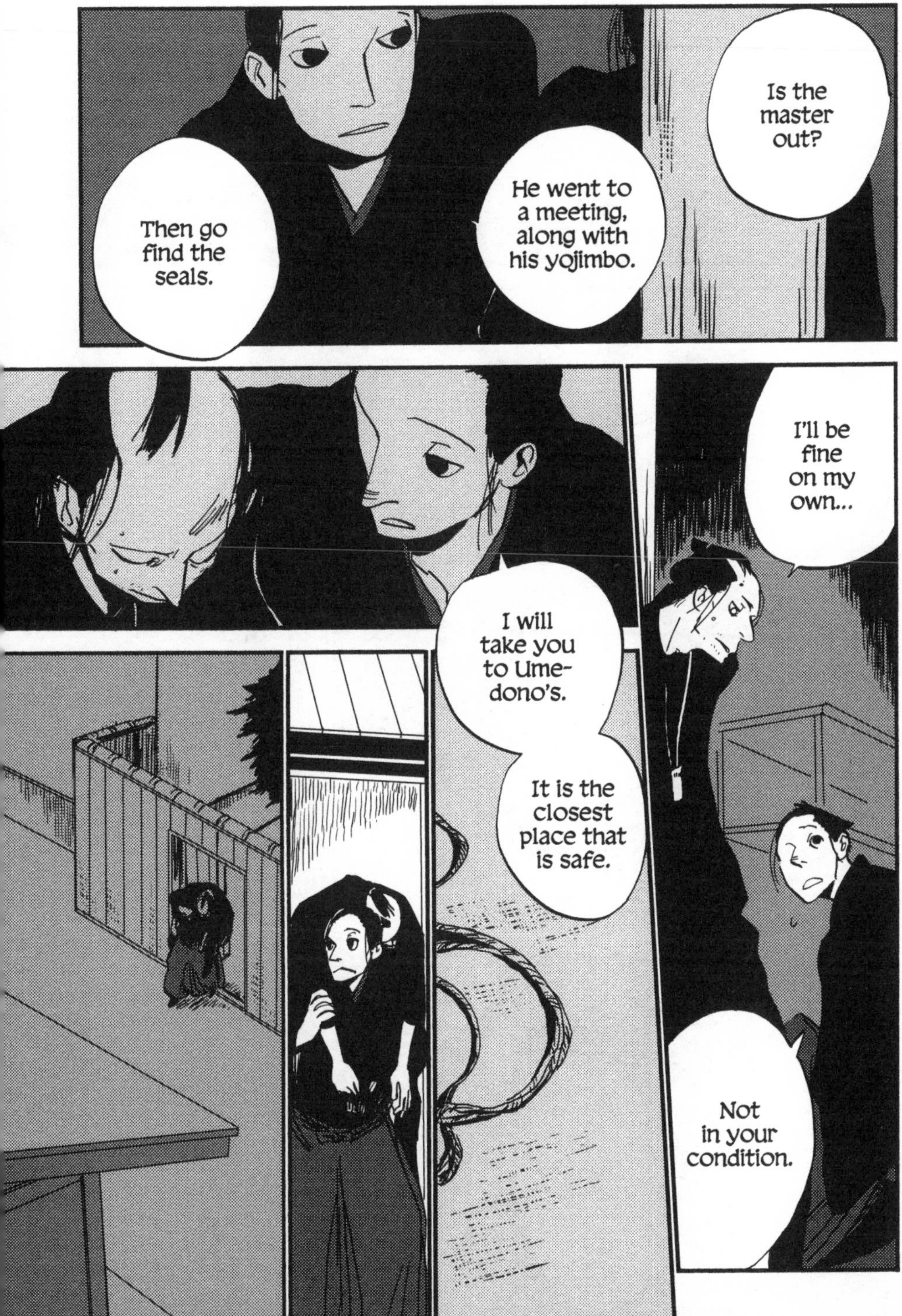
Is the master out?
He went to a meeting, along with his yojimbo.
Then go find the seals.
I'll be fine on my own...
Not in your condition.
I will take you to Ume-dono's.
It is the closest place that is safe.

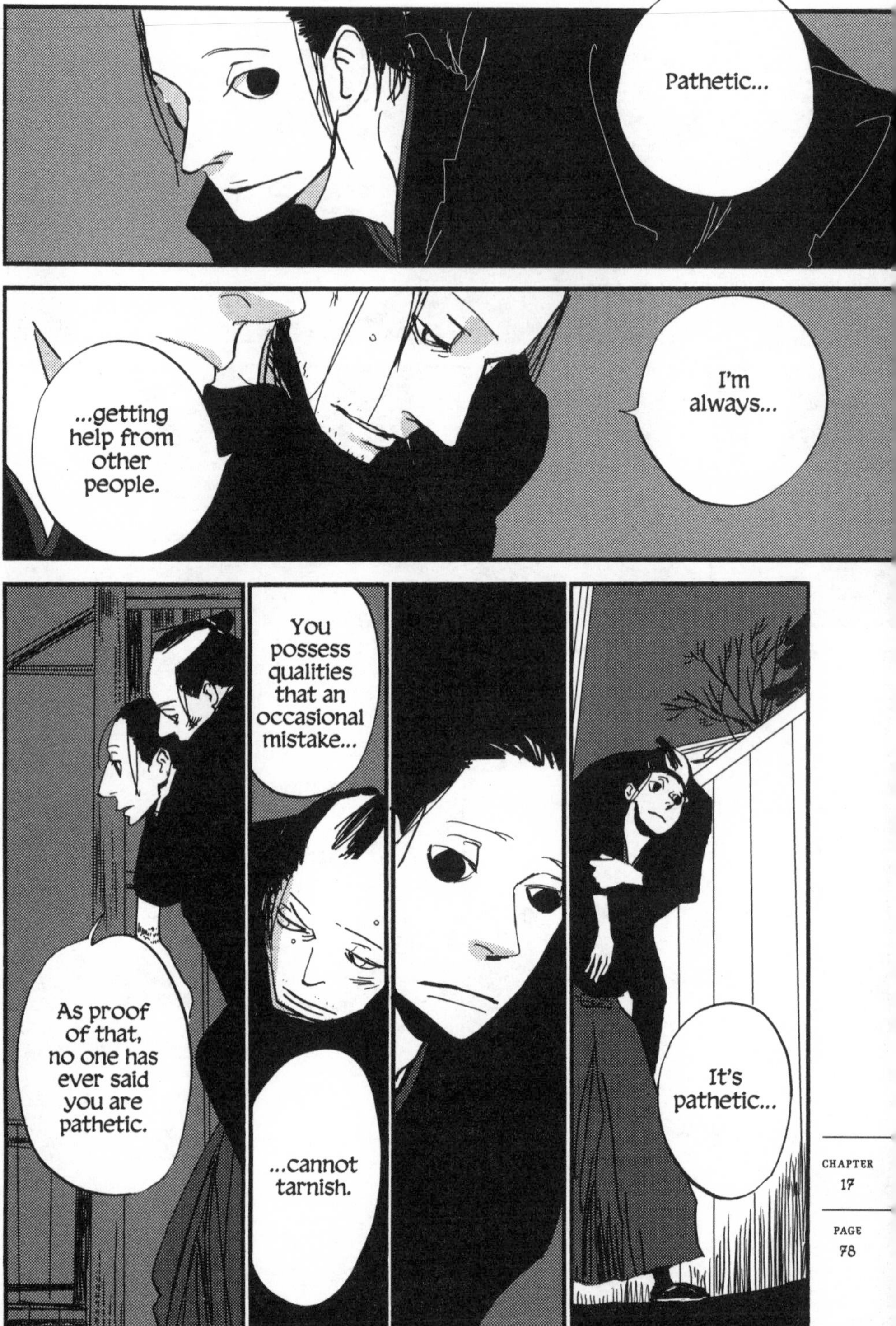
Pathetic...
I'm always...
...getting help from other people.
It's pathetic...
You possess qualities that an occasional mistake...
...cannot tarnish.
As proof of that, no one has ever said you are pathetic.

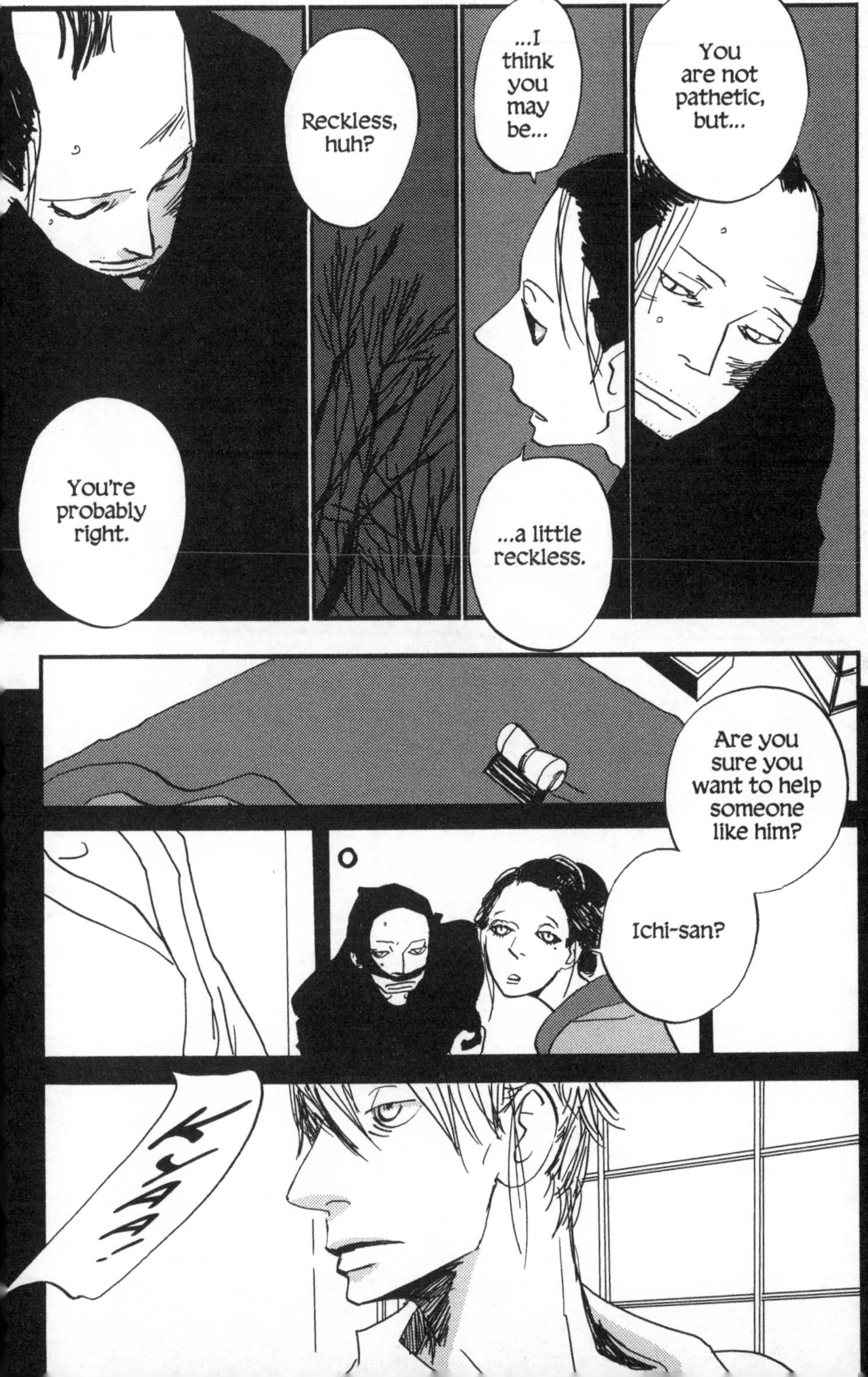
You are not pathetic, but...
...I think you may be...
...a little reckless.
Reckless, huh?
You're probably right.
Are you sure you want to help someone like him?
Ichi-san?
KYAA!

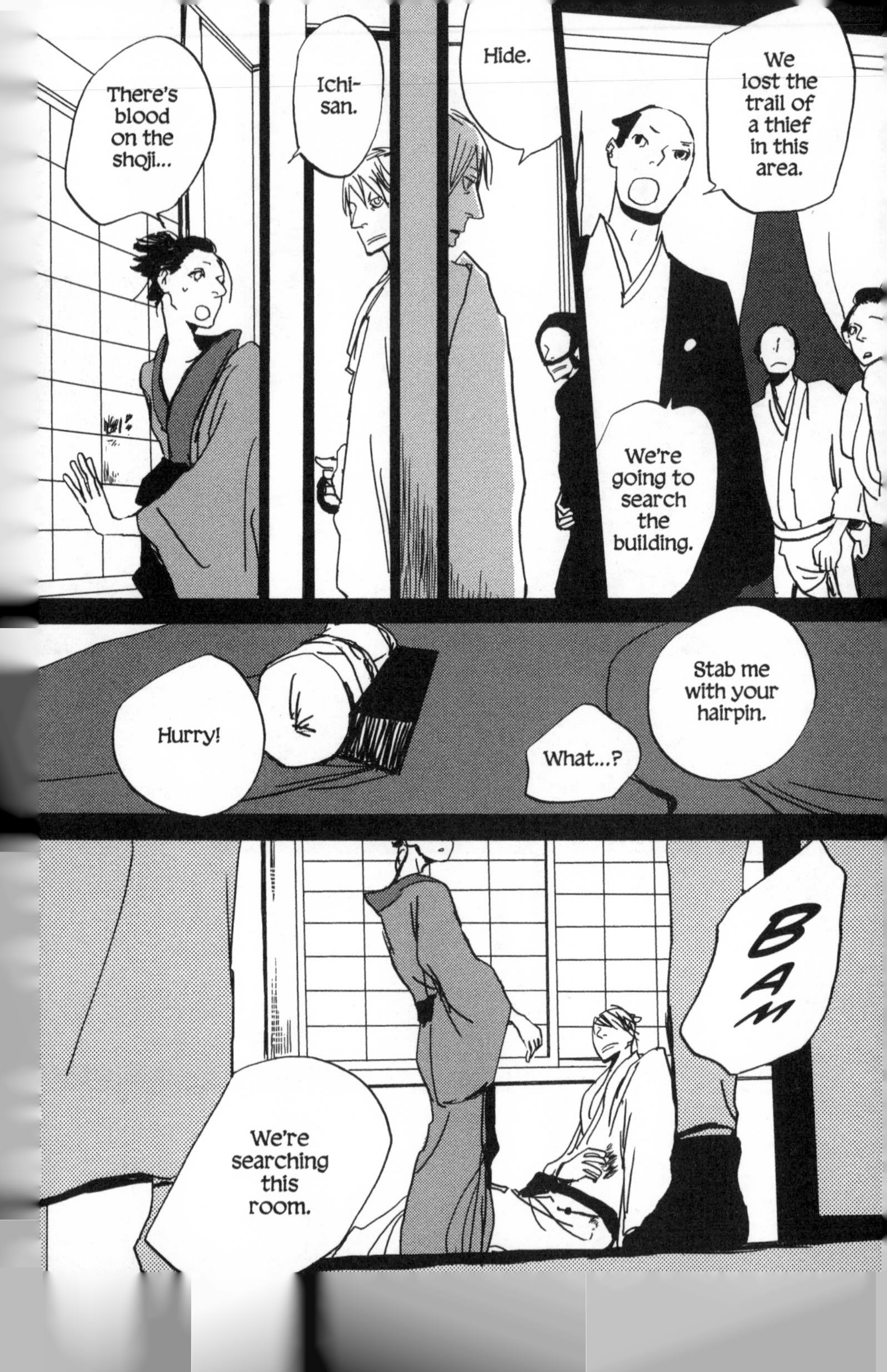

We lost the trail of a thief in this area.
We're going to search the building.
Hide.
Ichi-san.
There's blood on the shoji...
Stab me with your hairpin.
What...?
Hurry!
BAM
We're searching this room.

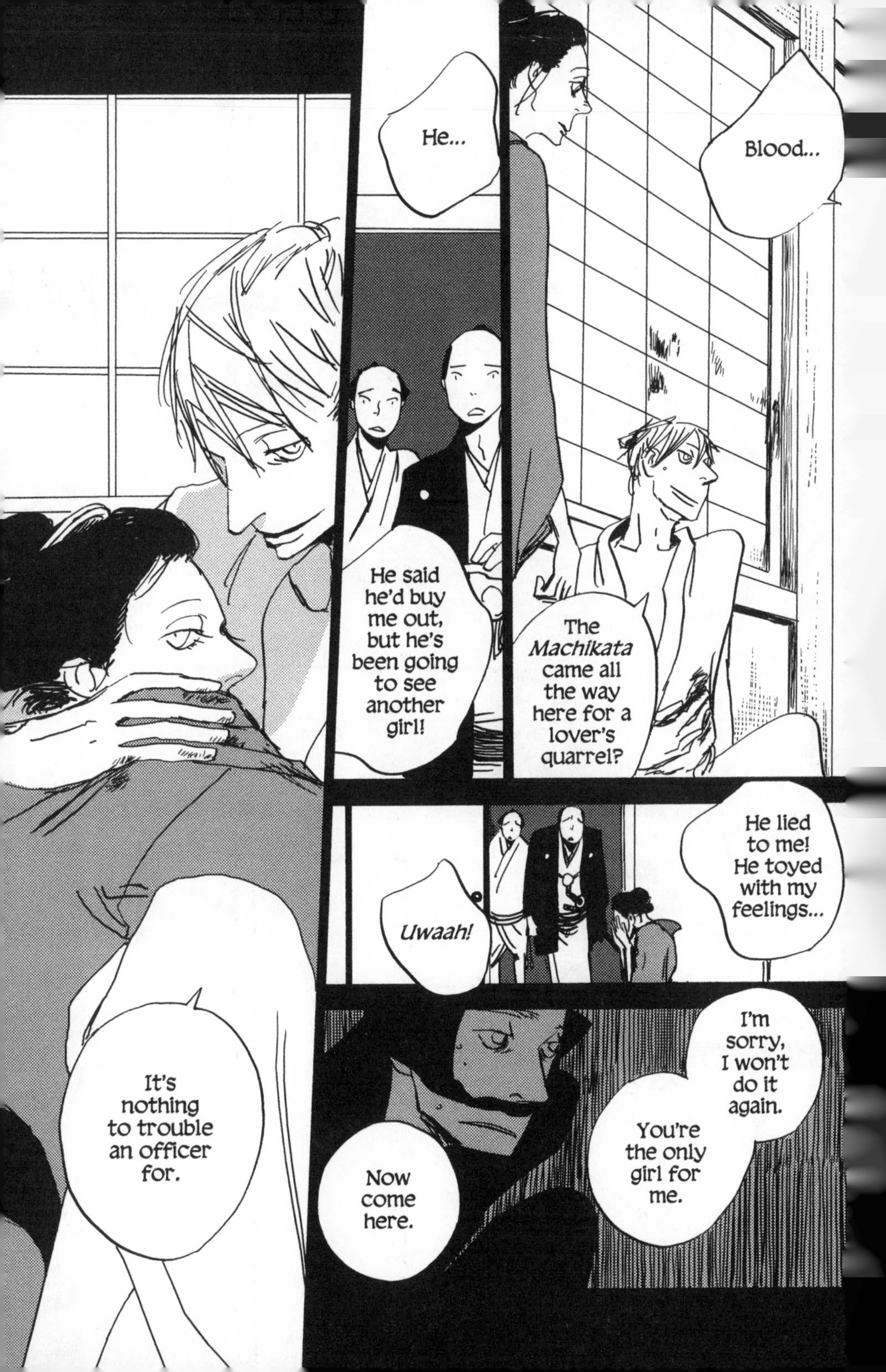
Blood...
The *Machikata* came all the way here for a lover's quarrel?
He...
He said he'd buy me out, but he's been going to see another girl!
He lied to me! He toyed with my feelings...
Uwaah!
I'm sorry, I won't do it again.
You're the only girl for me.
Now come here.
It's nothing to trouble an officer for.

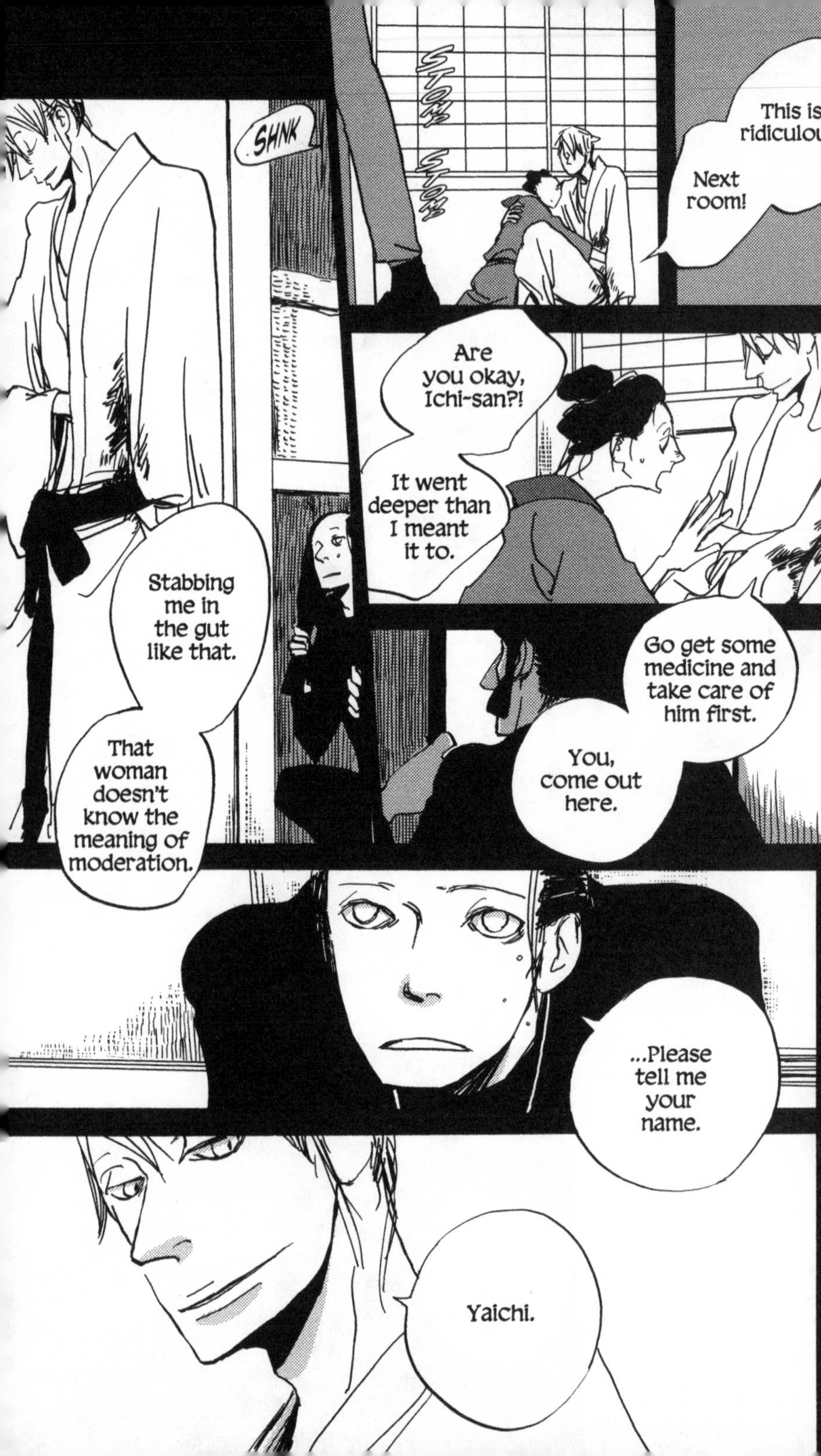
STOMP STOMP
This is ridiculous.
Next room!
SHNK
Are you okay, Ichi-san?!
It went deeper than I meant it to.
Go get some medicine and take care of him first.
You, come out here.
Stabbing me in the gut like that.
That woman doesn't know the meaning of moderation.
...Please tell me your name.
Yaichi.

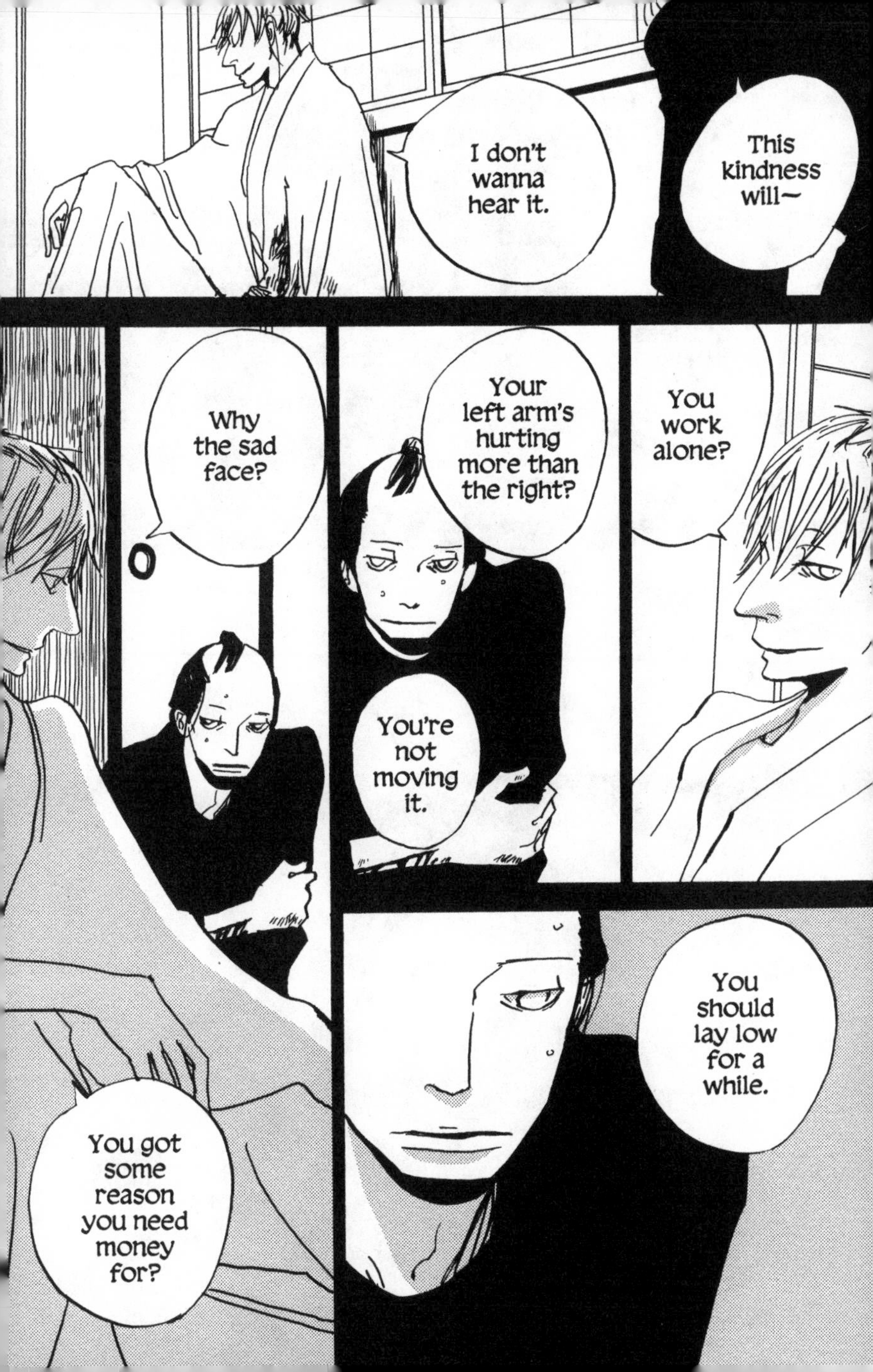
This kindness will~
I don't wanna hear it.
You work alone?
Your left arm's hurting more than the right?
You're not moving it.
You should lay low for a while.
Why the sad face?
You got some reason you need money for?

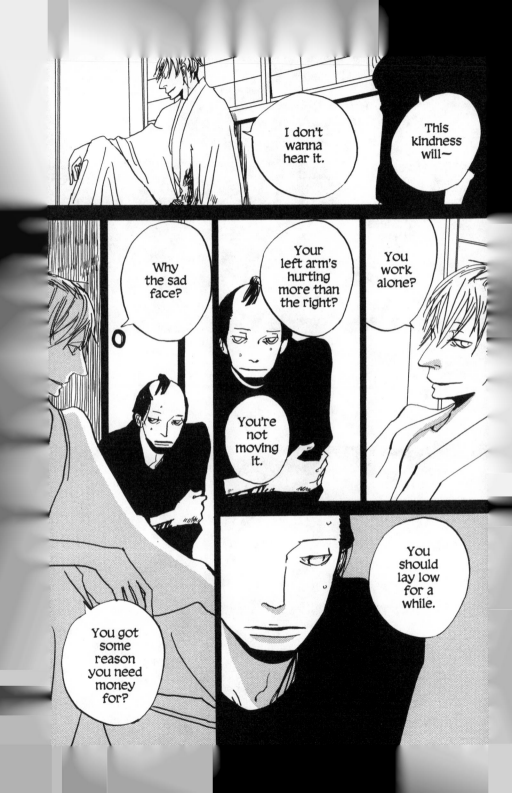

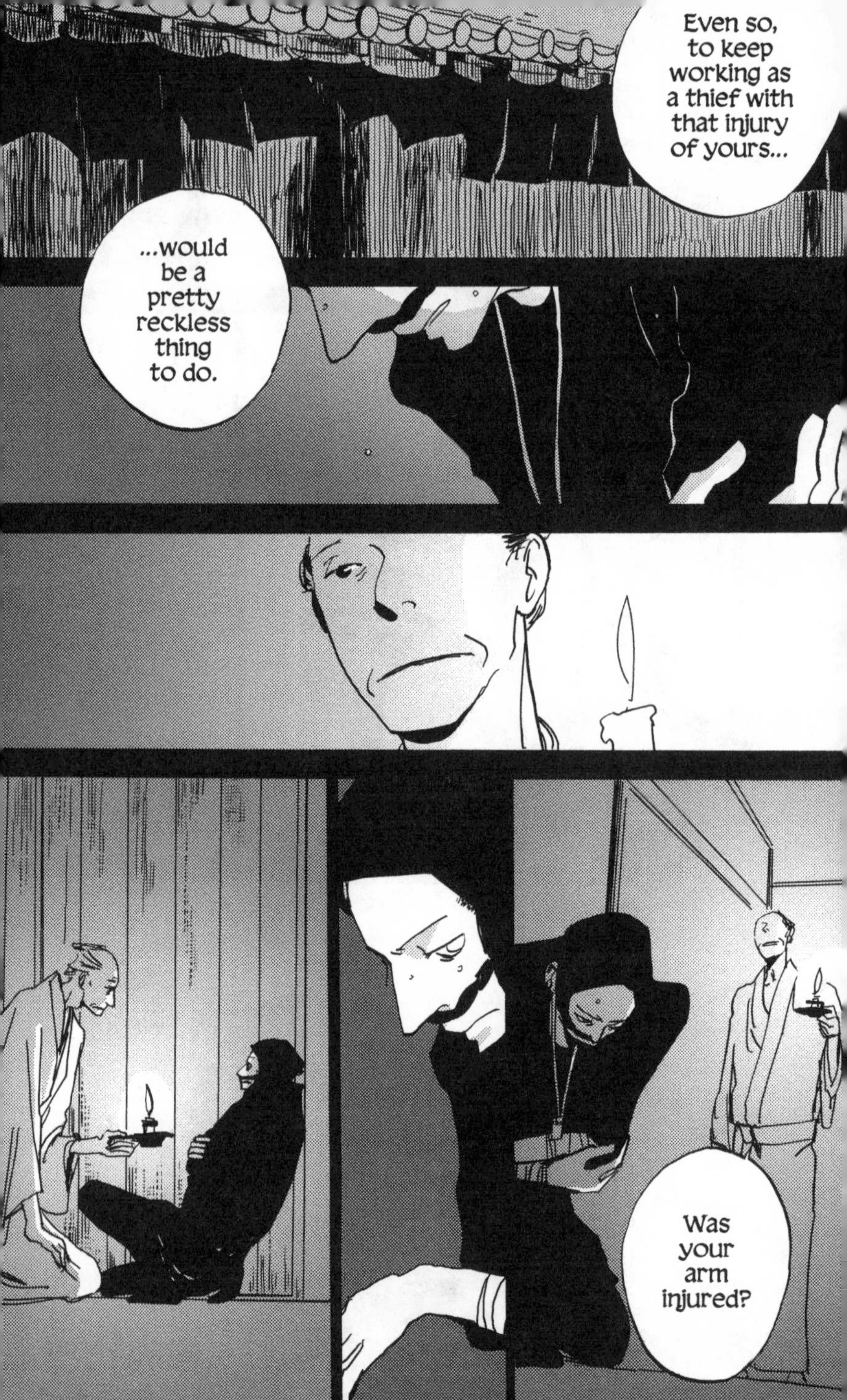
Even so, to keep working as a thief with that injury of yours...
...would be a pretty reckless thing to do.
Was your arm injured?

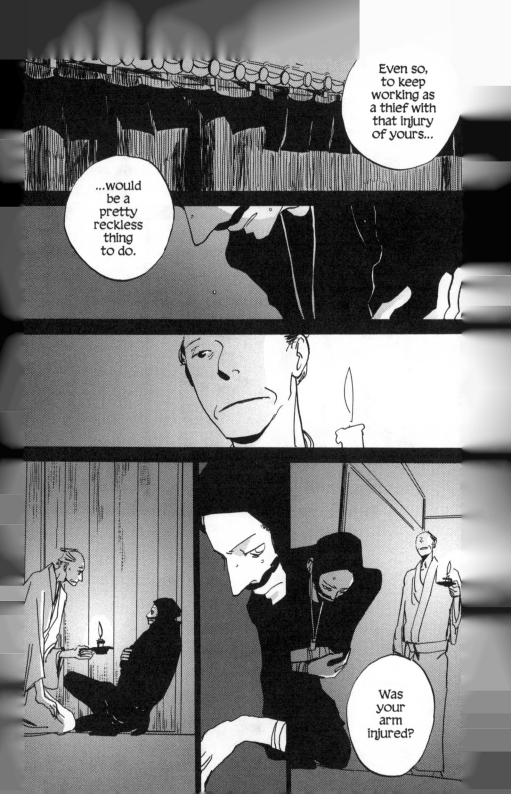

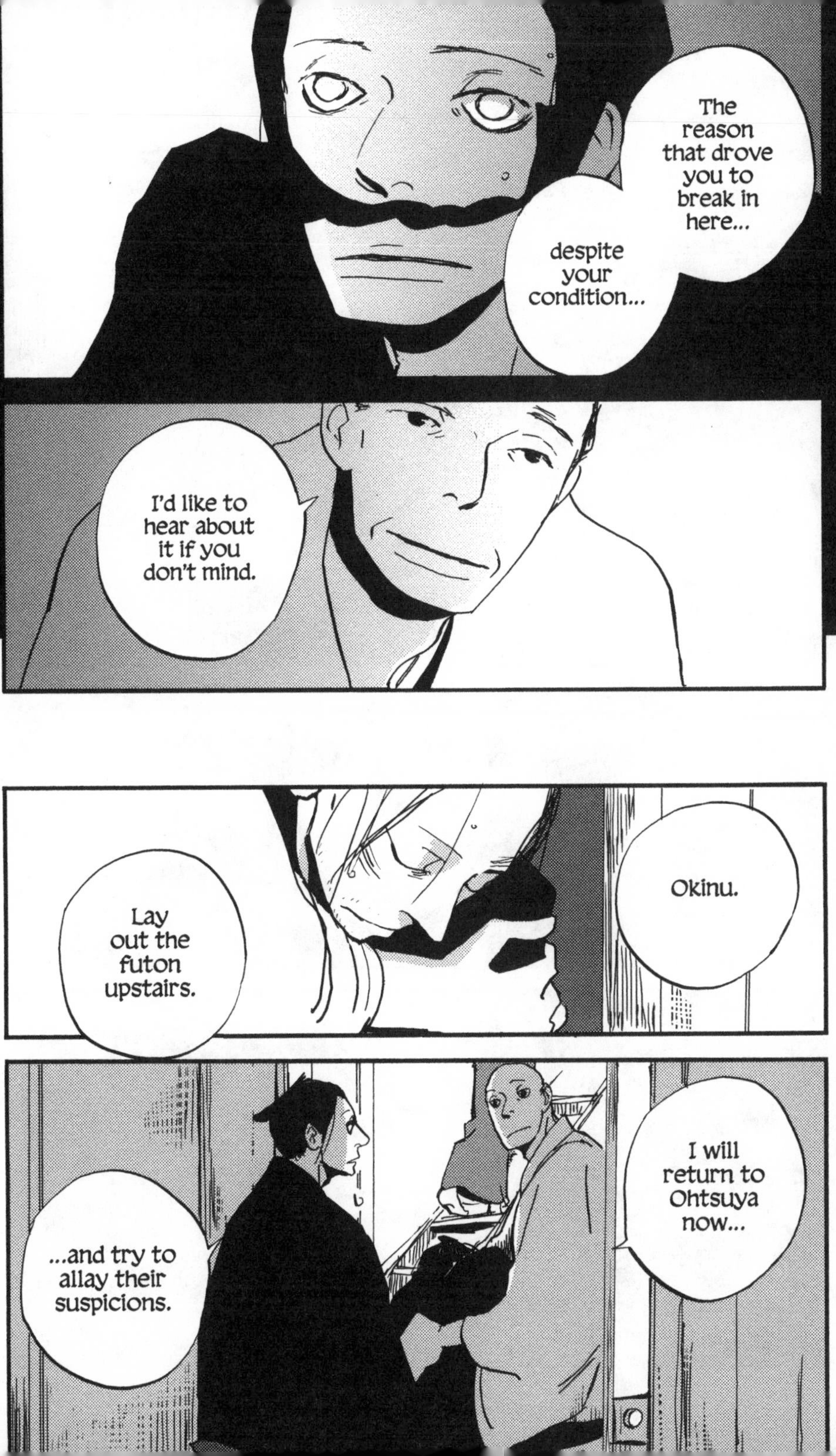
The reason that drove you to break in here...
despite your condition...
I'd like to hear about it if you don't mind.
Okinu.
Lay out the futon upstairs.
I will return to Ohtsuya now...
...and try to allay their suspicions.

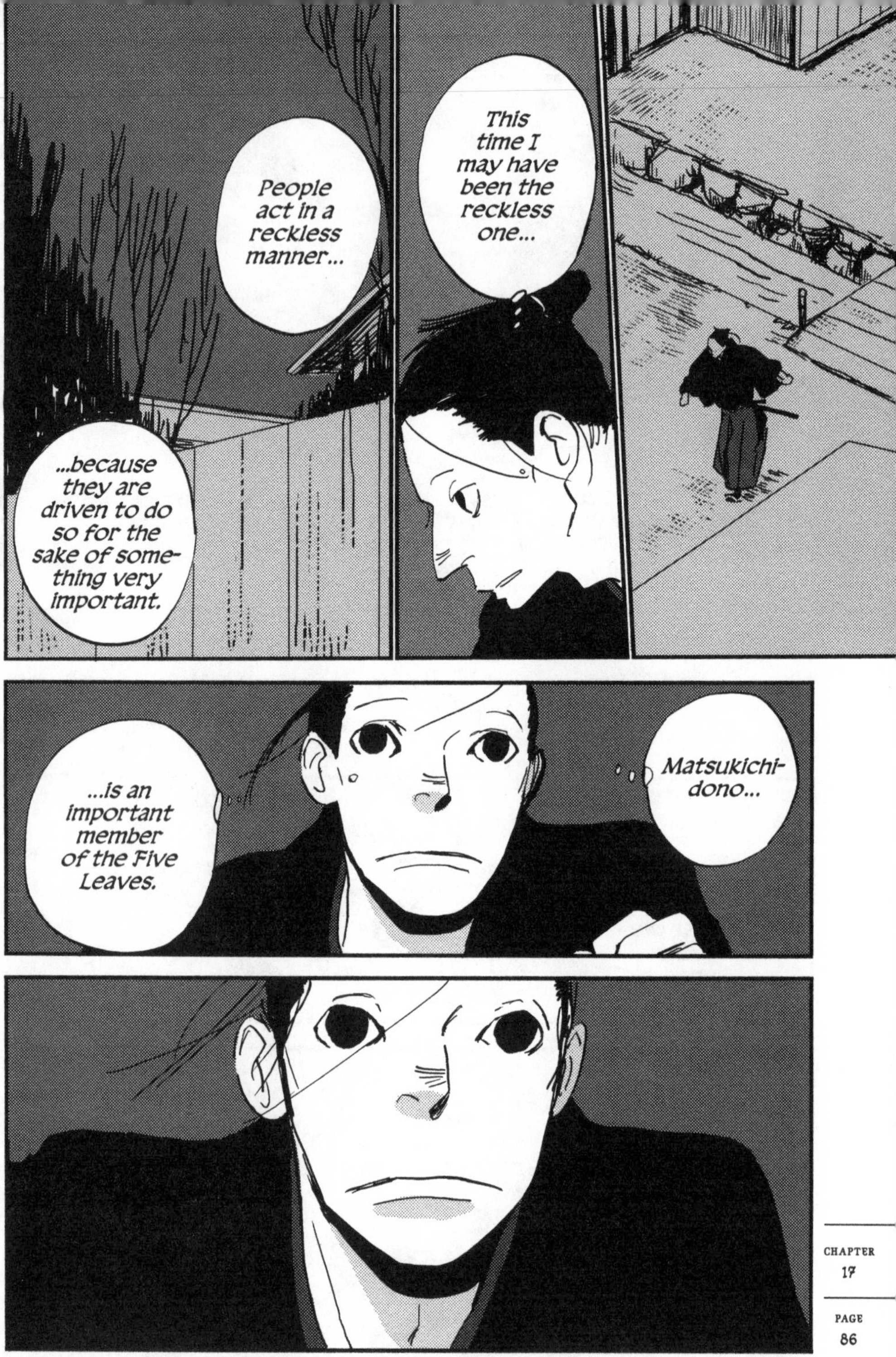
This time I may have been the reckless one...
People act in a reckless manner...
...because they are driven to do so for the sake of some-thing very important.
Matsukichi-dono...
...is an important member of the Five Leaves.

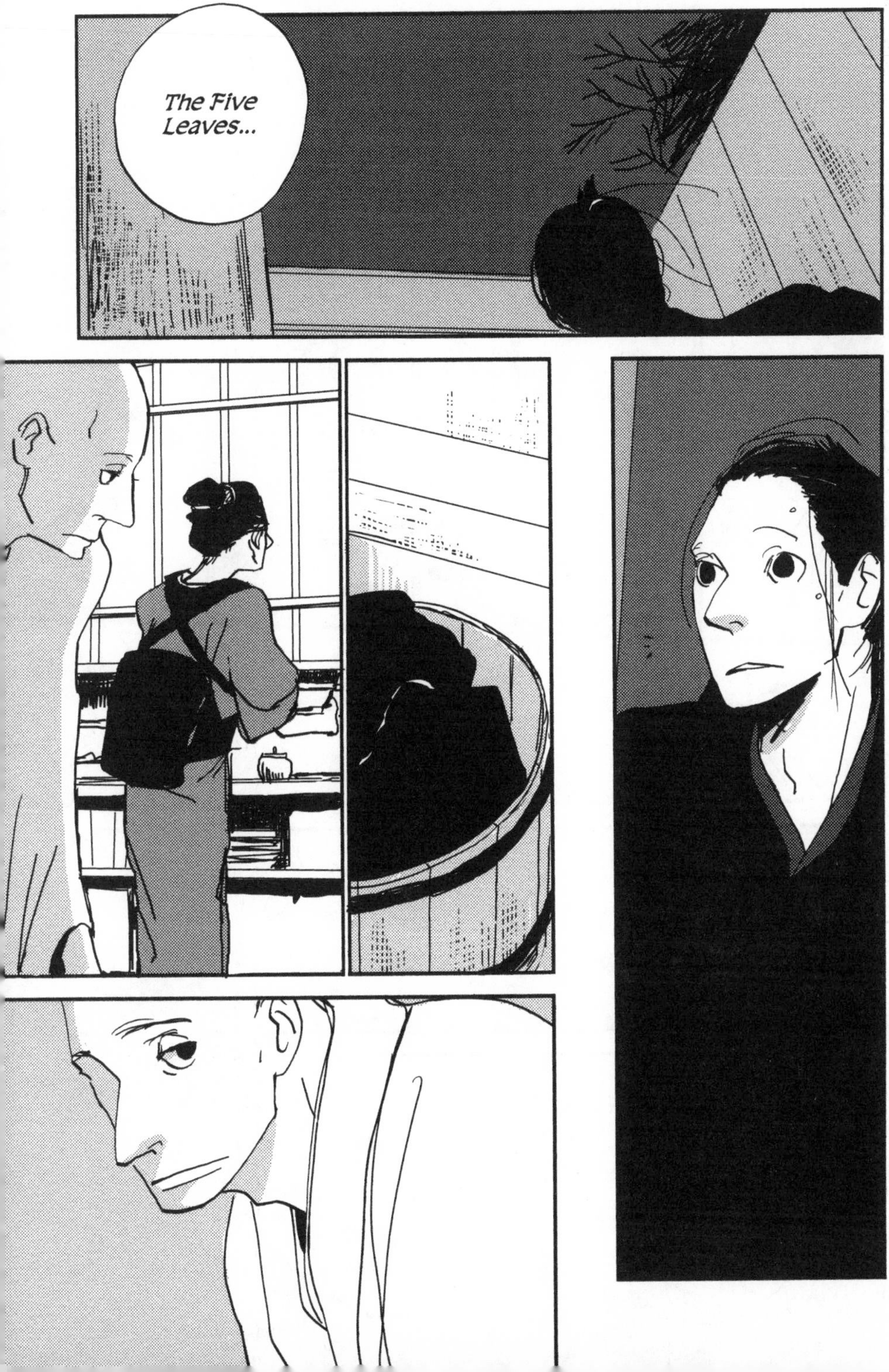
The Five Leaves...

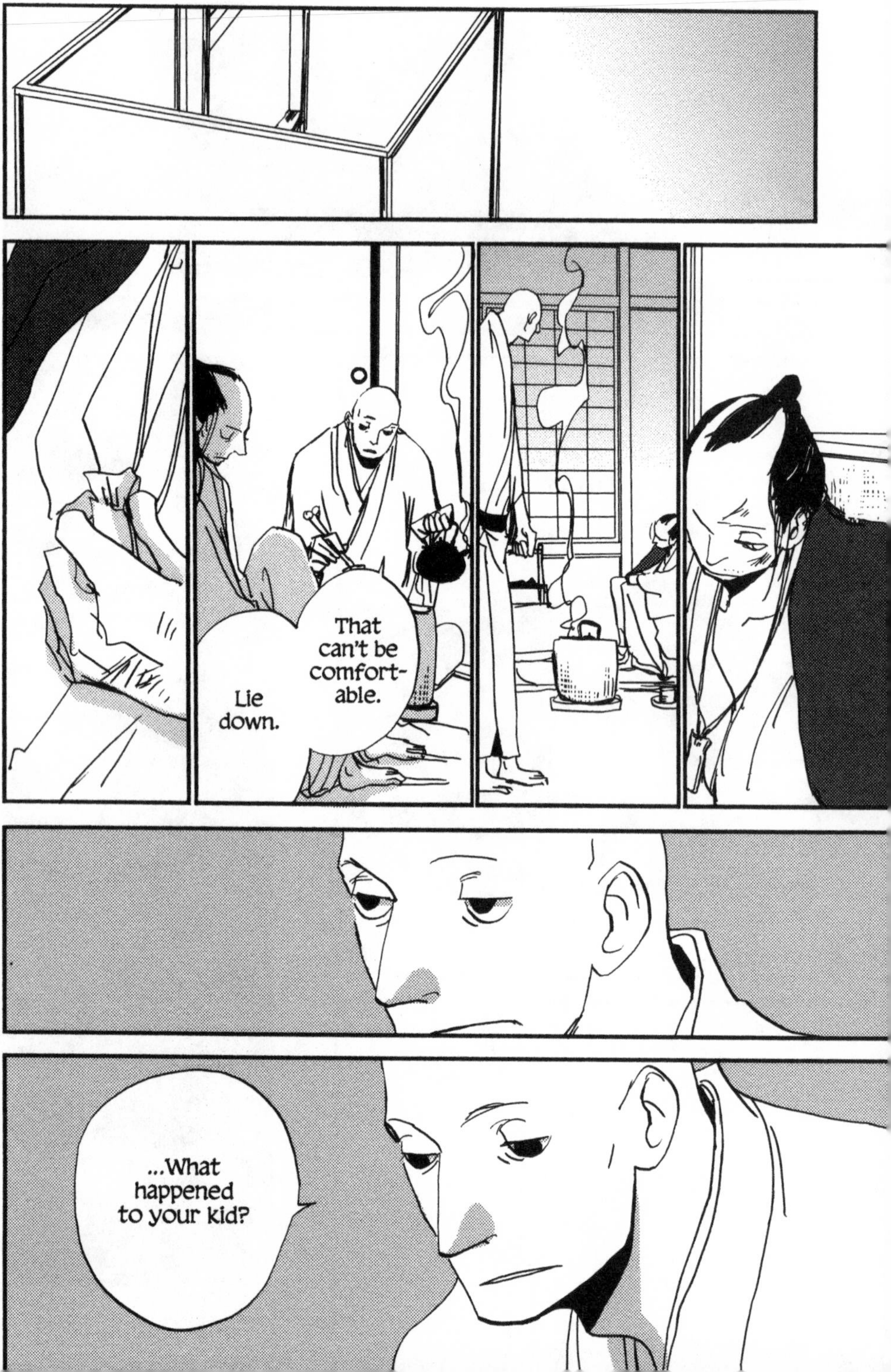
That can't be comfort-able.
Lie down.
...What happened to your kid?

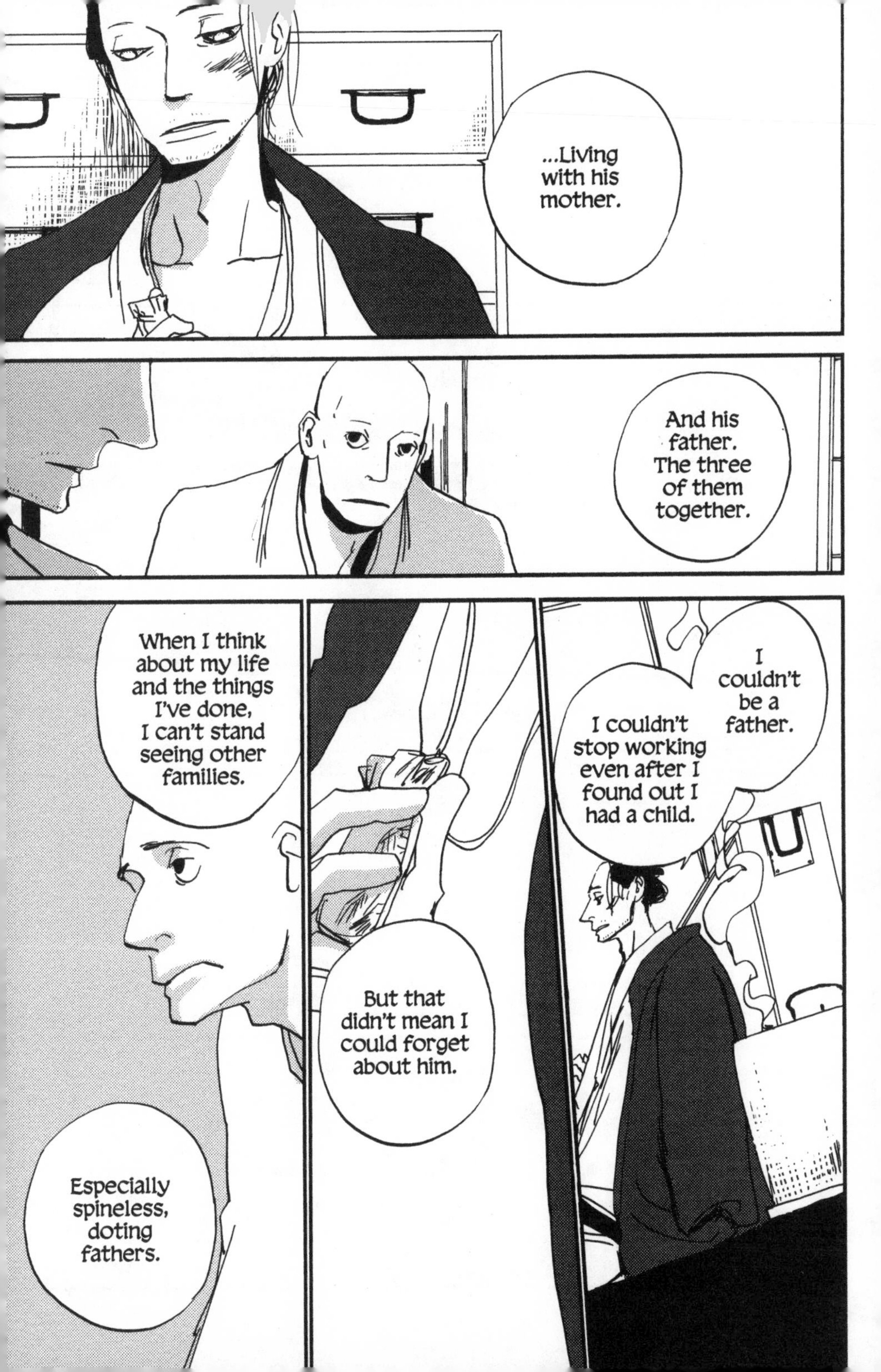
...Living with his mother.
And his father. The three of them together.
I couldn't be a father.
I couldn't stop working even after I found out I had a child.
But that didn't mean I could forget about him.
When I think about my life and the things I've done, I can't stand seeing other families.
Especially spineless, doting fathers.

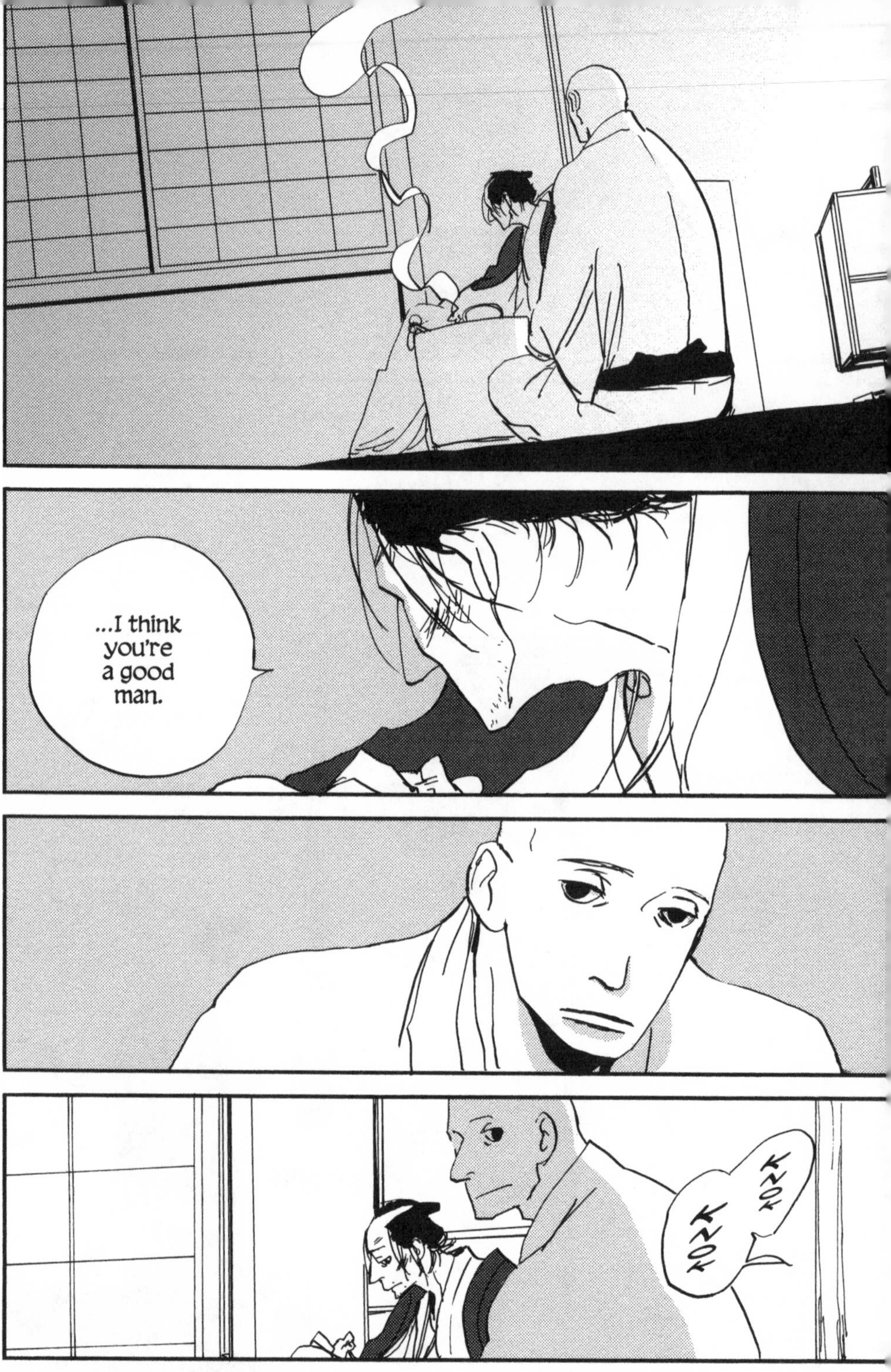
...I think you're a good man.
KNOK KNOK

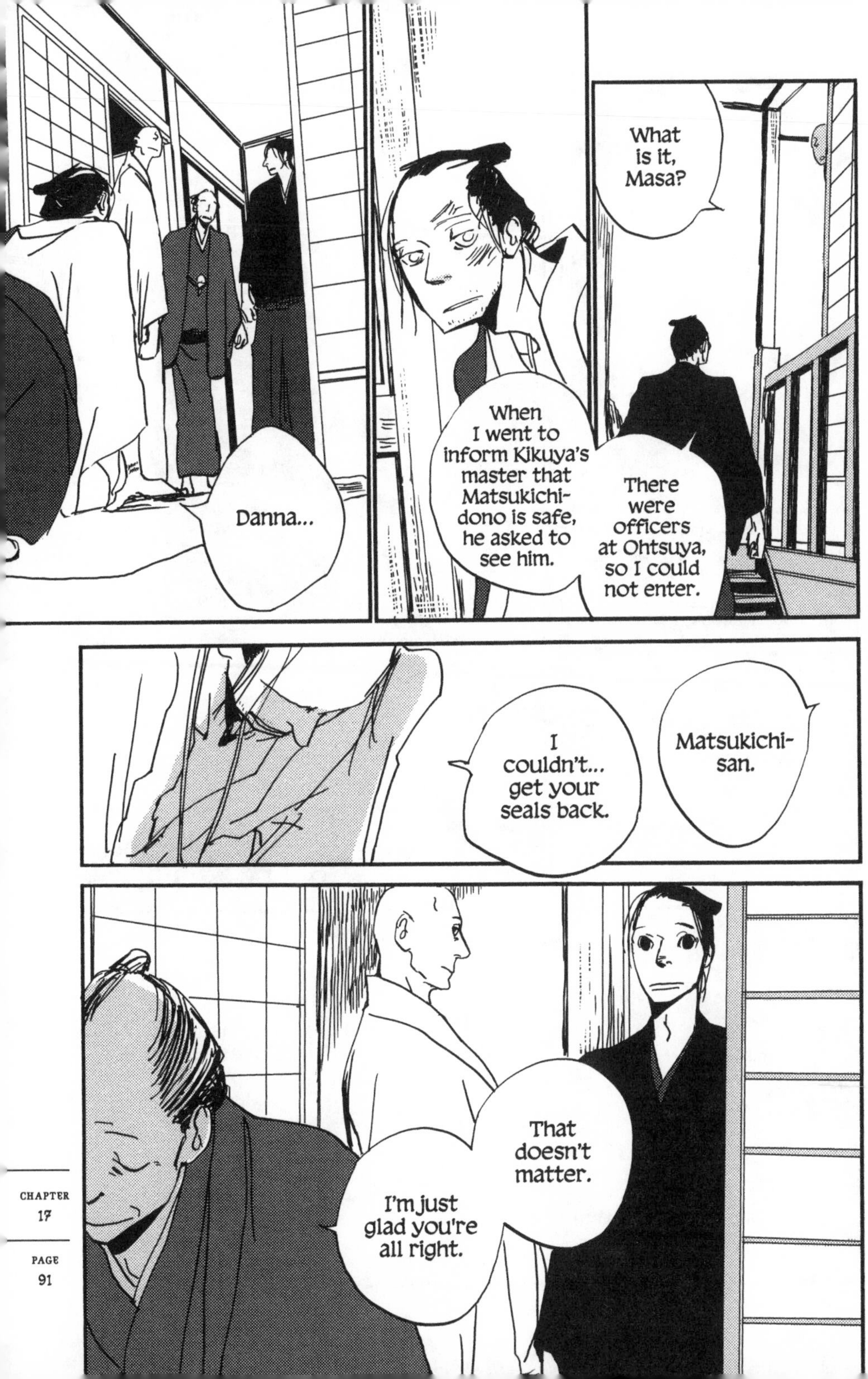
What is it, Masa?
There were officers at Ohtsuya, so I could not enter.
When I went to inform Kikuya's master that Matsukichi-dono is safe, he asked to see him.
Danna...
Matsukichi-san.
I couldn't... get your seals back.
That doesn't matter.
I'm just glad you're all right.

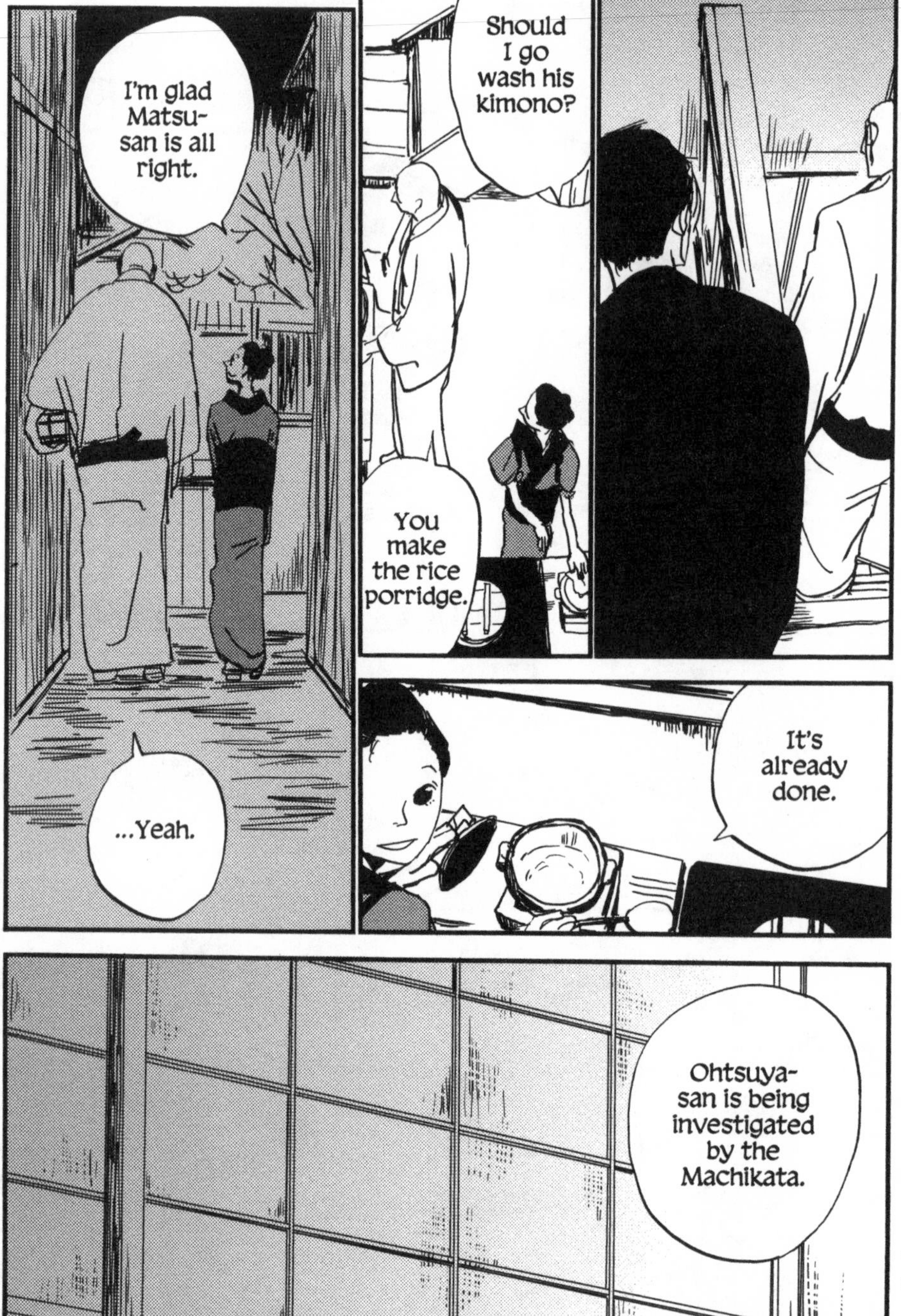
Should I go wash his kimono?
You make the rice porridge.
It's already done.
I'm glad Matsu-san is all right.
...Yeah.
Ohtsuya-san is being investigated by the Machikata.

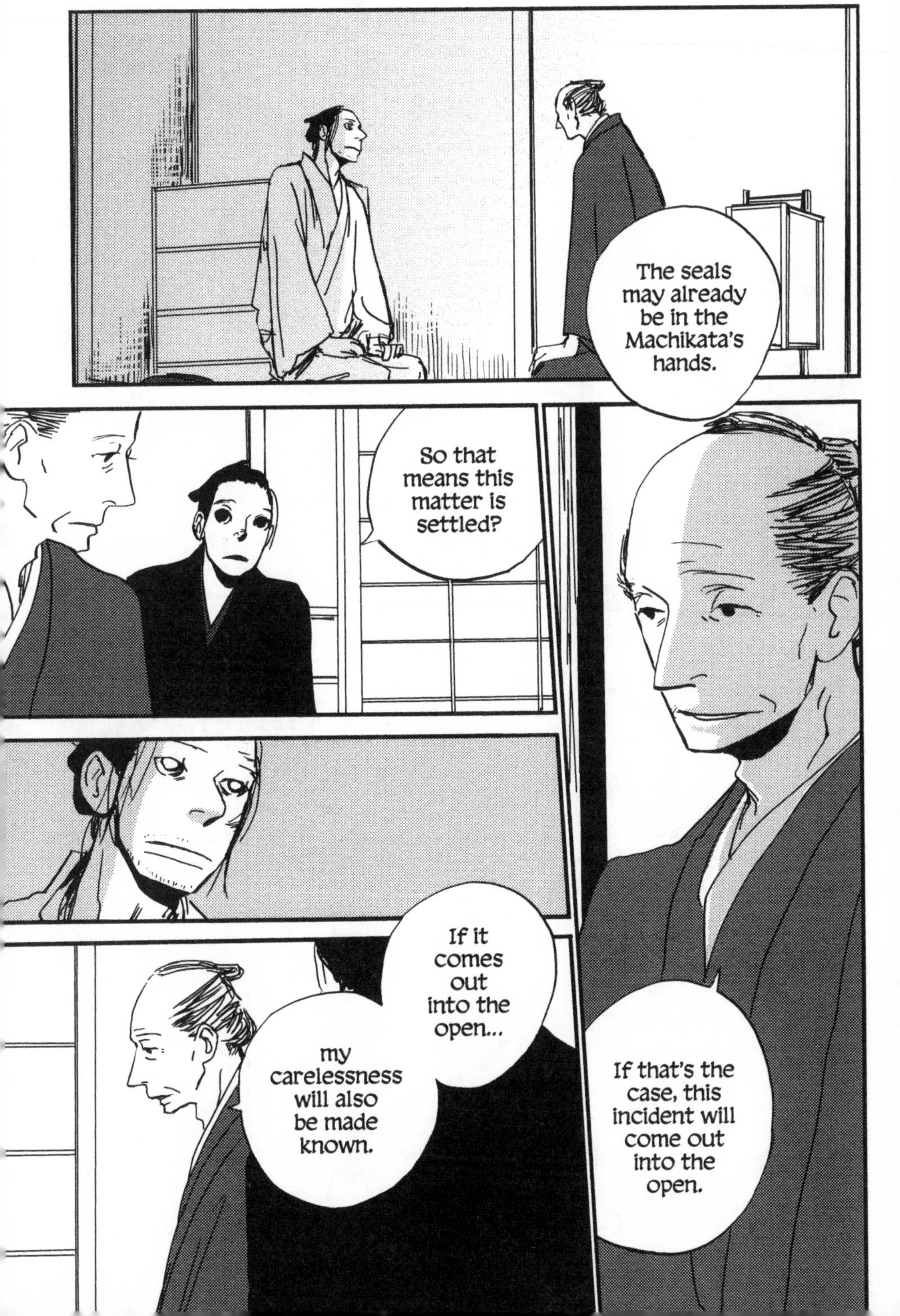
The seals may already be in the Machikata's hands.
If that's the case, this incident will come out into the open.
So that means this matter is settled?
If it comes out into the open...
my carelessness will also be made known.

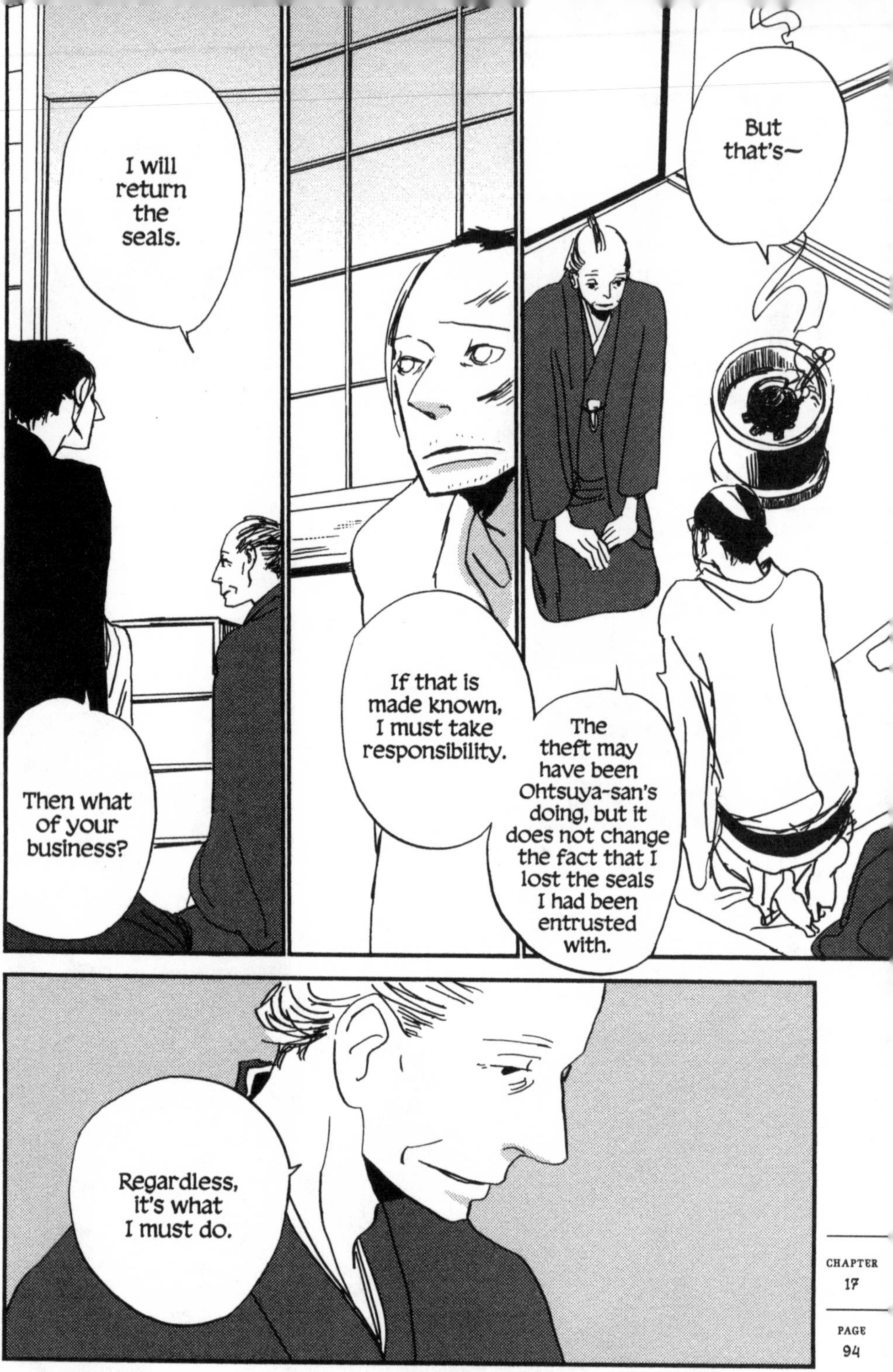
But that's~
The theft may have been Ohtsuya-san's doing, but it does not change the fact that I lost the seals I had been entrusted with.
If that is made known, I must take responsibility.
I will return the seals.
Then what of your business?
Regardless, it's what I must do.

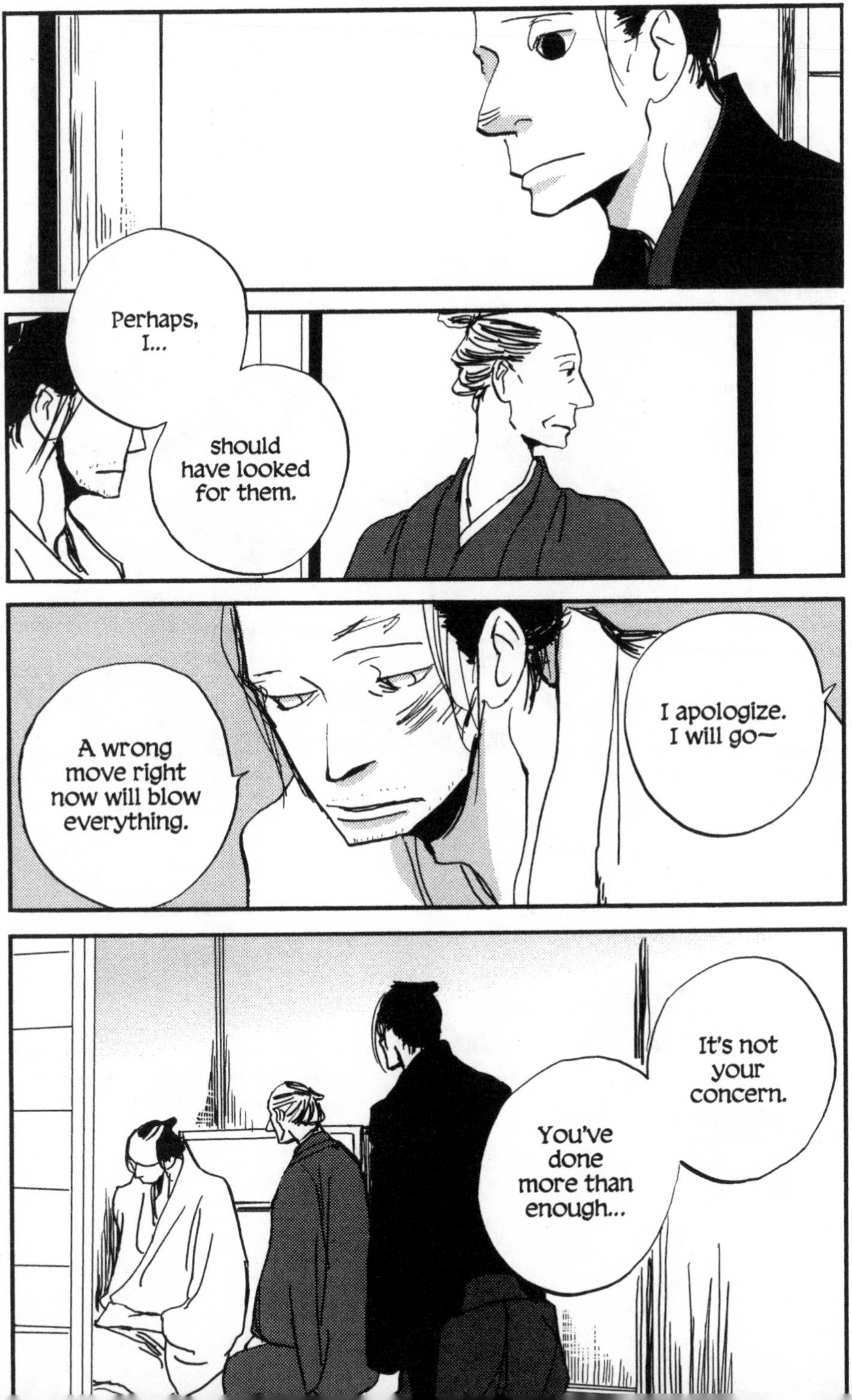
Perhaps, I...
should have looked for them.
I apologize. I will go~
A wrong move right now will blow everything.
It's not your concern.
You've done more than enough...

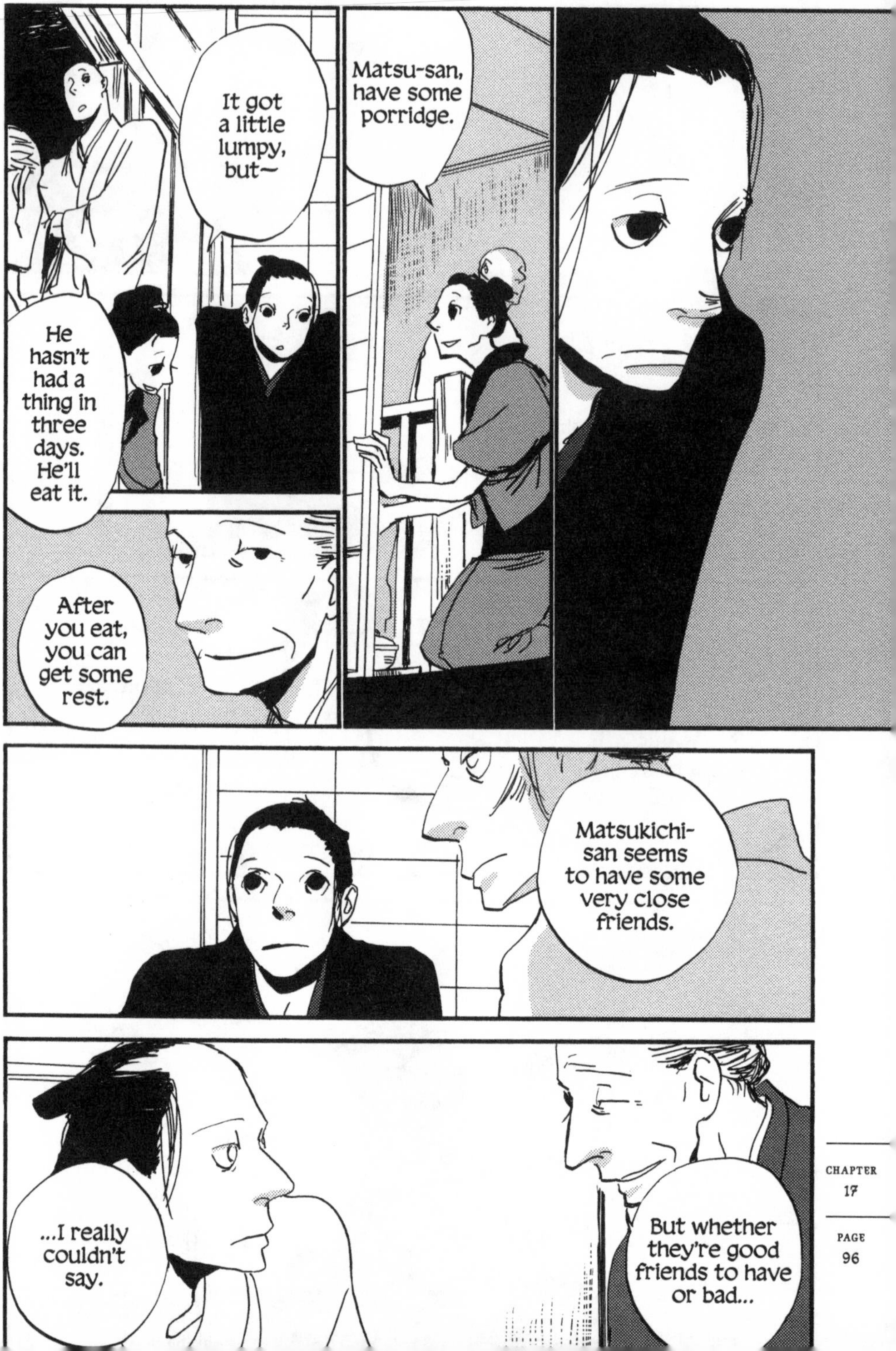
Matsu-san, have some porridge.
It got a little lumpy, but~
He hasn't had a thing in three days. He'll eat it.
After you eat, you can get some rest.
Matsukichi-san seems to have some very close friends.
But whether they're good friends to have or bad...
...I really couldn't say.

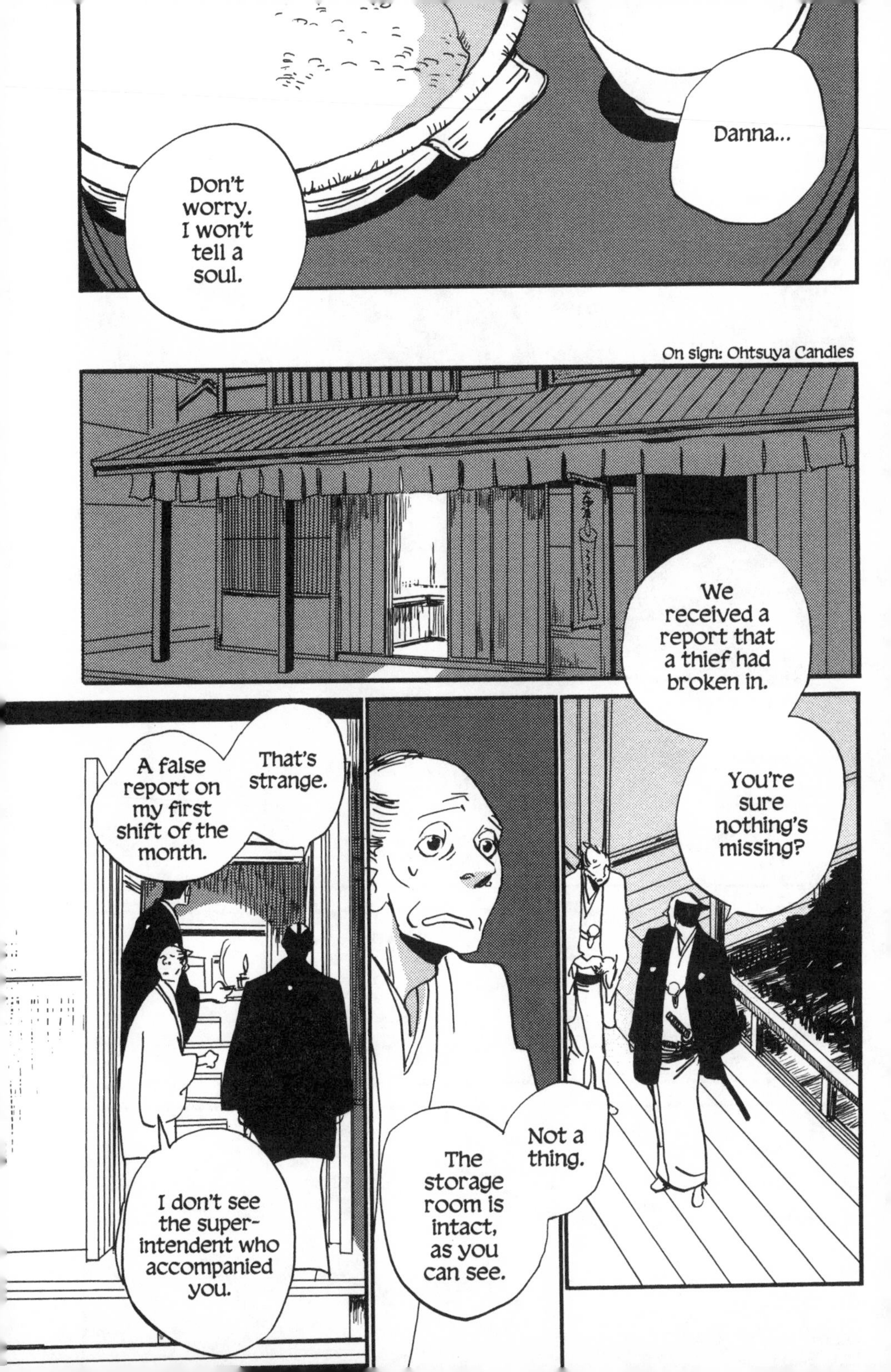
Danna...
Don't worry. I won't tell a soul.
On sign: Ohtsuya Candles
We received a report that a thief had broken in.
You're sure nothing's missing?
Not a thing.
The storage room is intact, as you can see.
That's strange.
A false report on my first shift of the month.
I don't see the super-intendent who accompanied you.

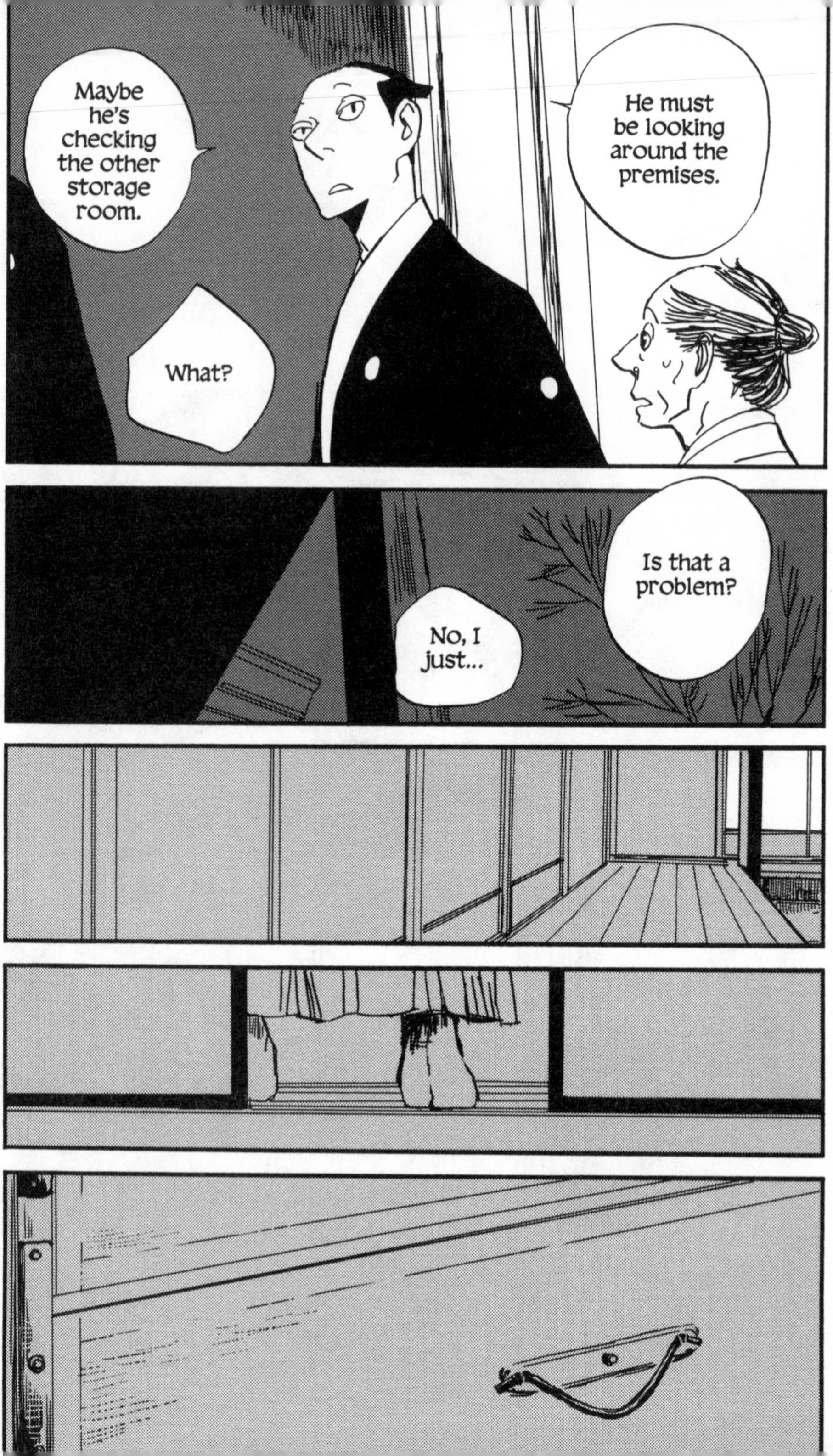
He must be looking around the premises.
Maybe he's checking the other storage room.
What?
Is that a problem?
No, I just...

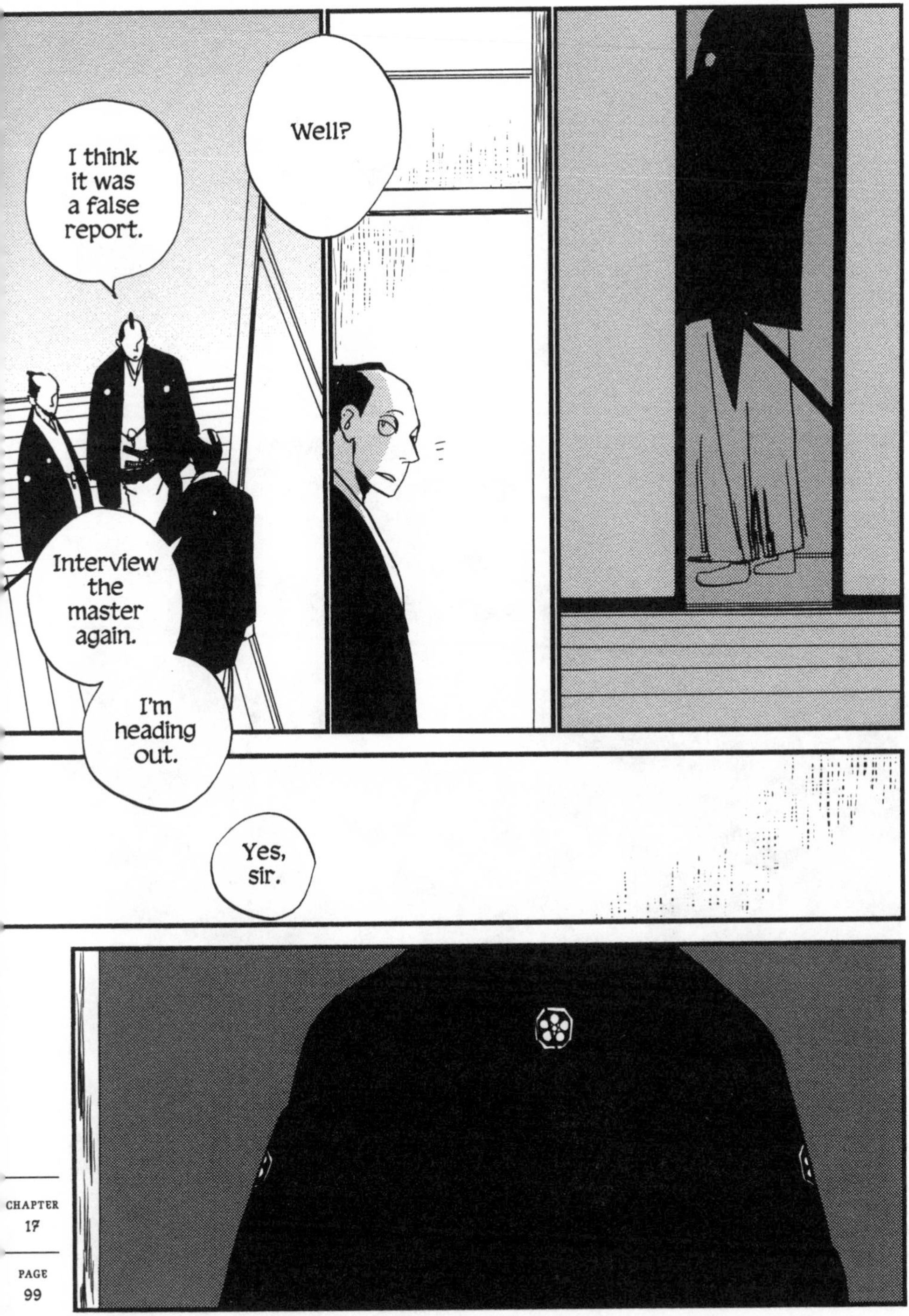
Well?
I think it was a false report.
Interview the master again.
I'm heading out.
Yes, sir.

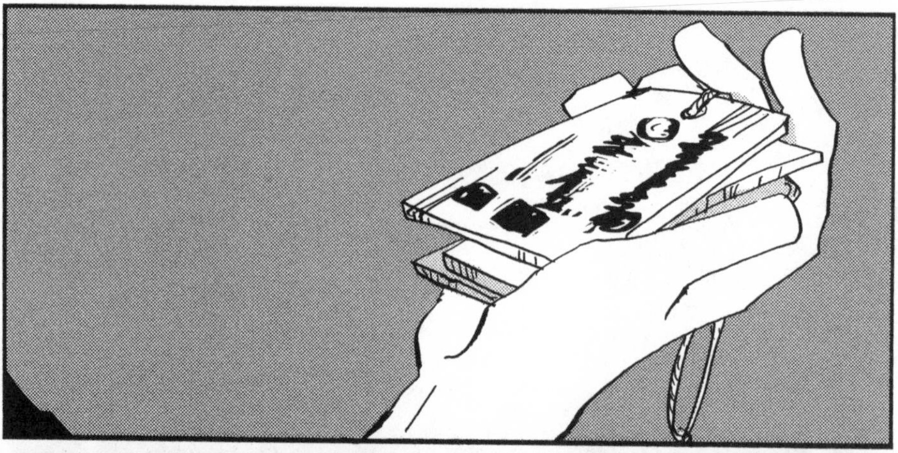

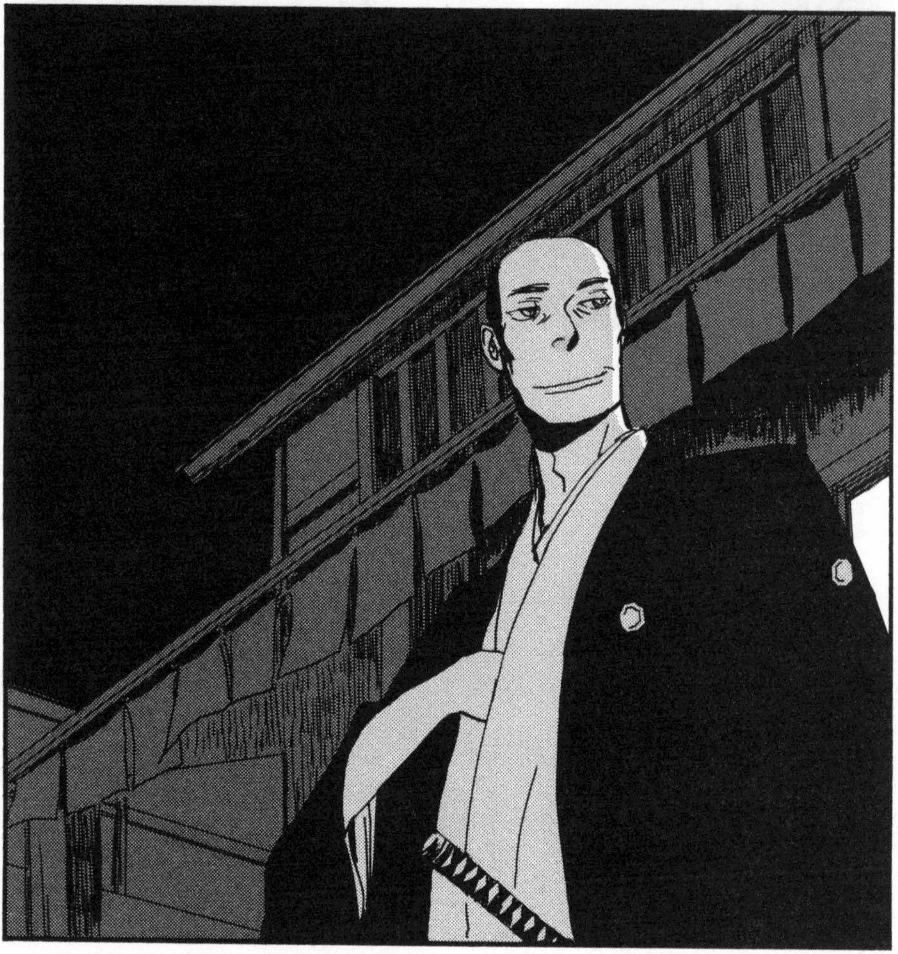

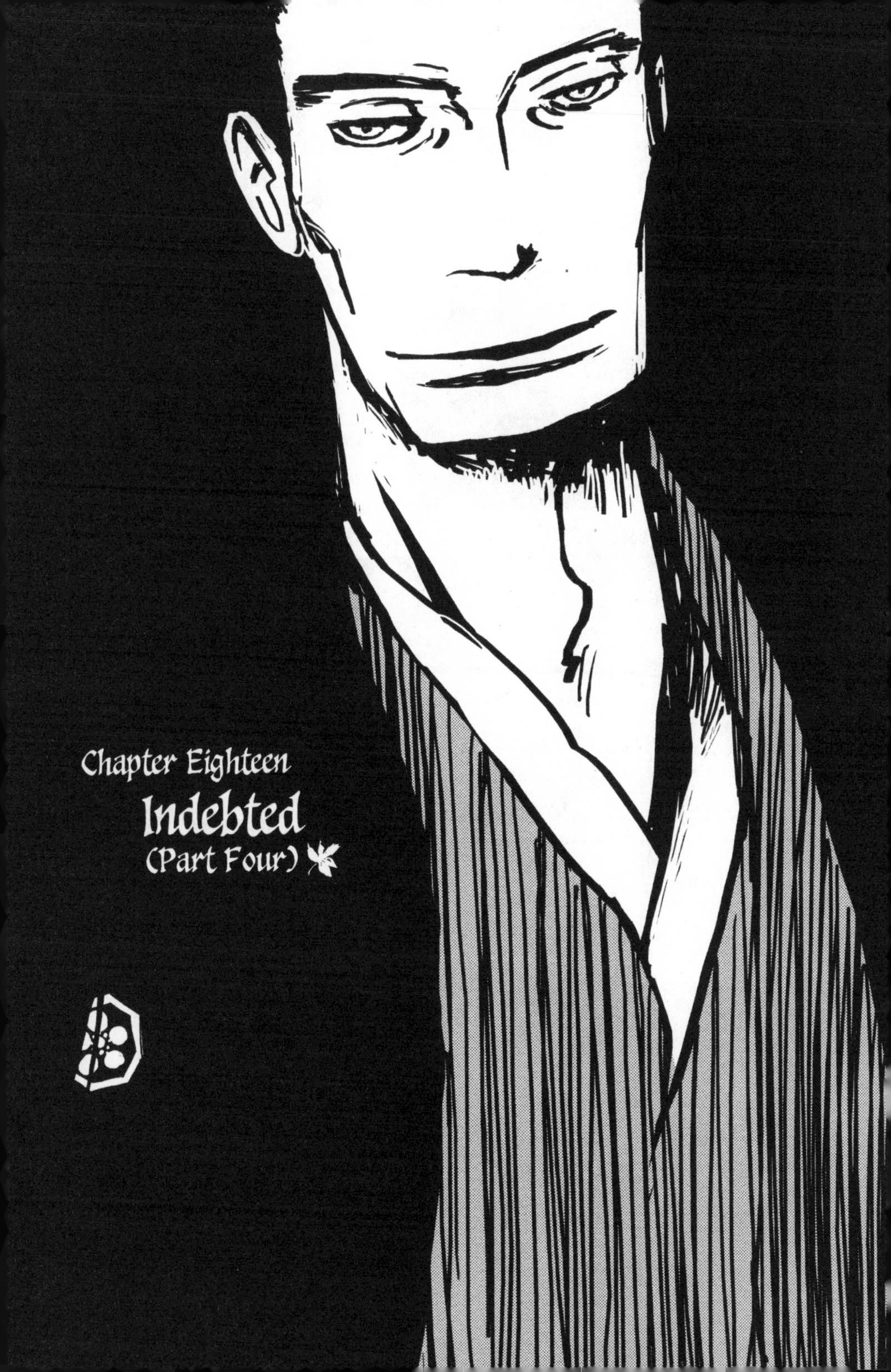
Chapter Eighteen
Indebted
(Part Four)

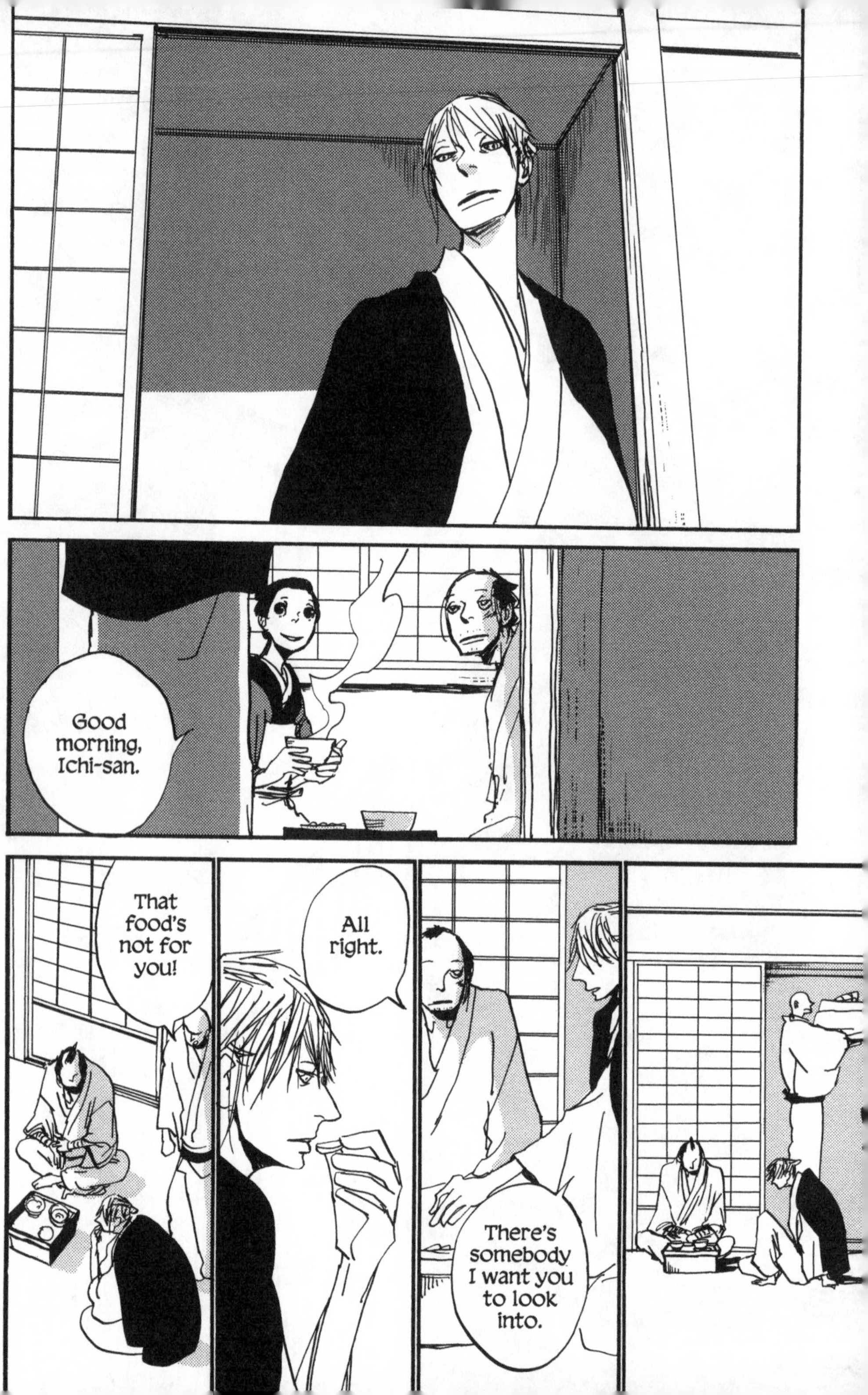
Good morning, Ichi-san.
There's somebody I want you to look into.
All right.
That food's not for you!

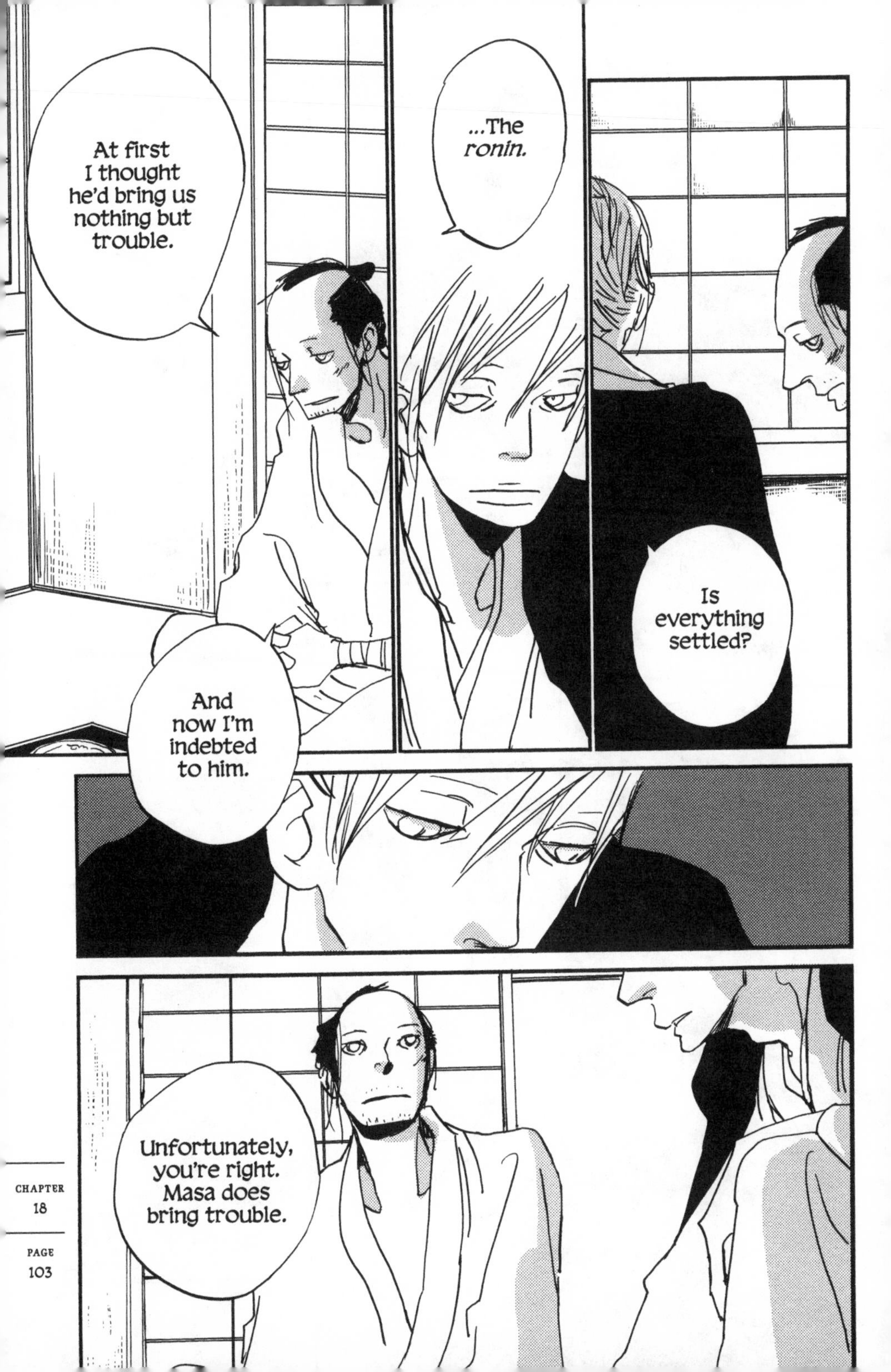
Is everything settled?
...The *ronin.*
At first I thought he'd bring us nothing but trouble.
And now I'm indebted to him.
Unfortunately, you're right. Masa does bring trouble.

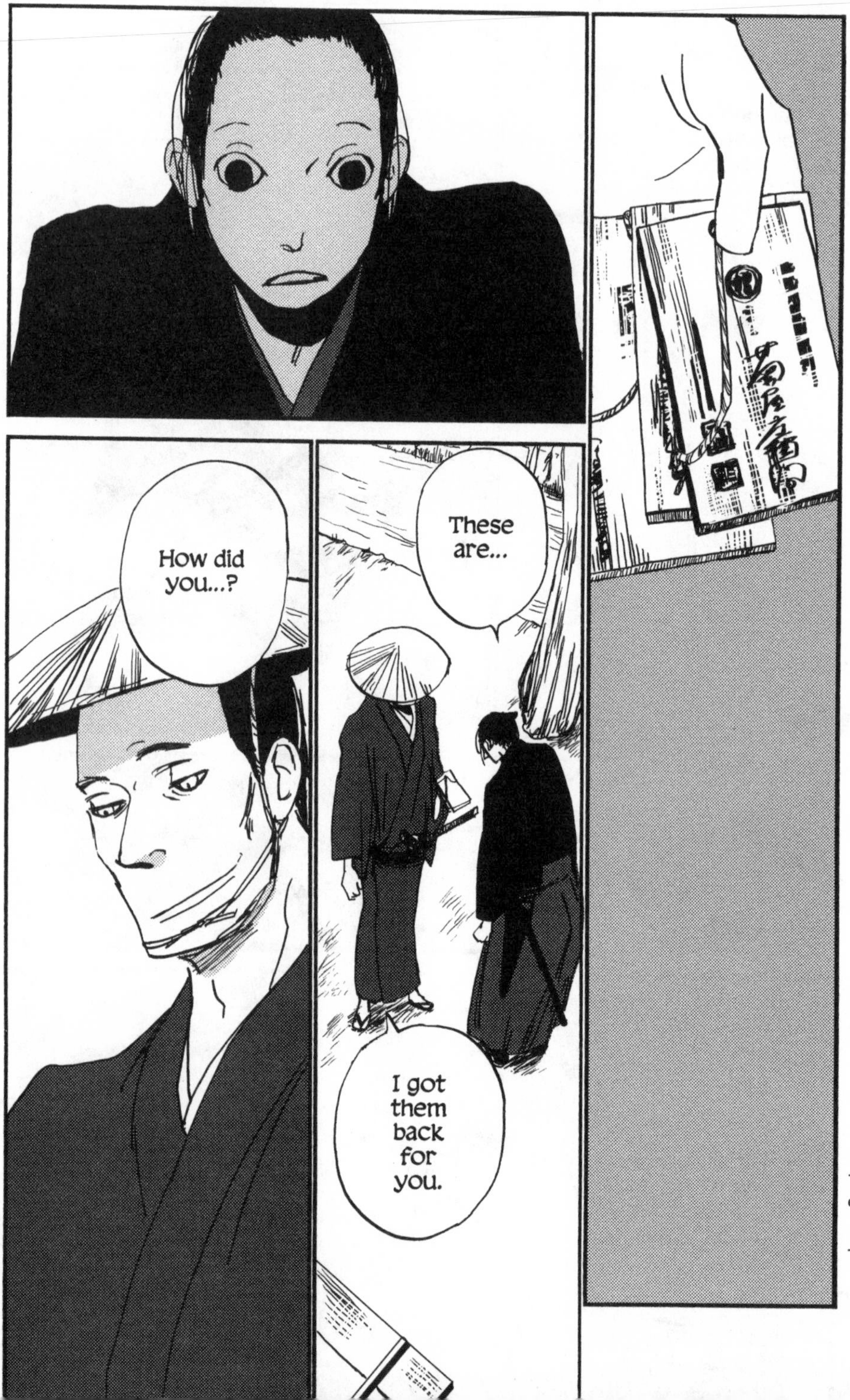
These are...
I got them back for you.
How did you...?

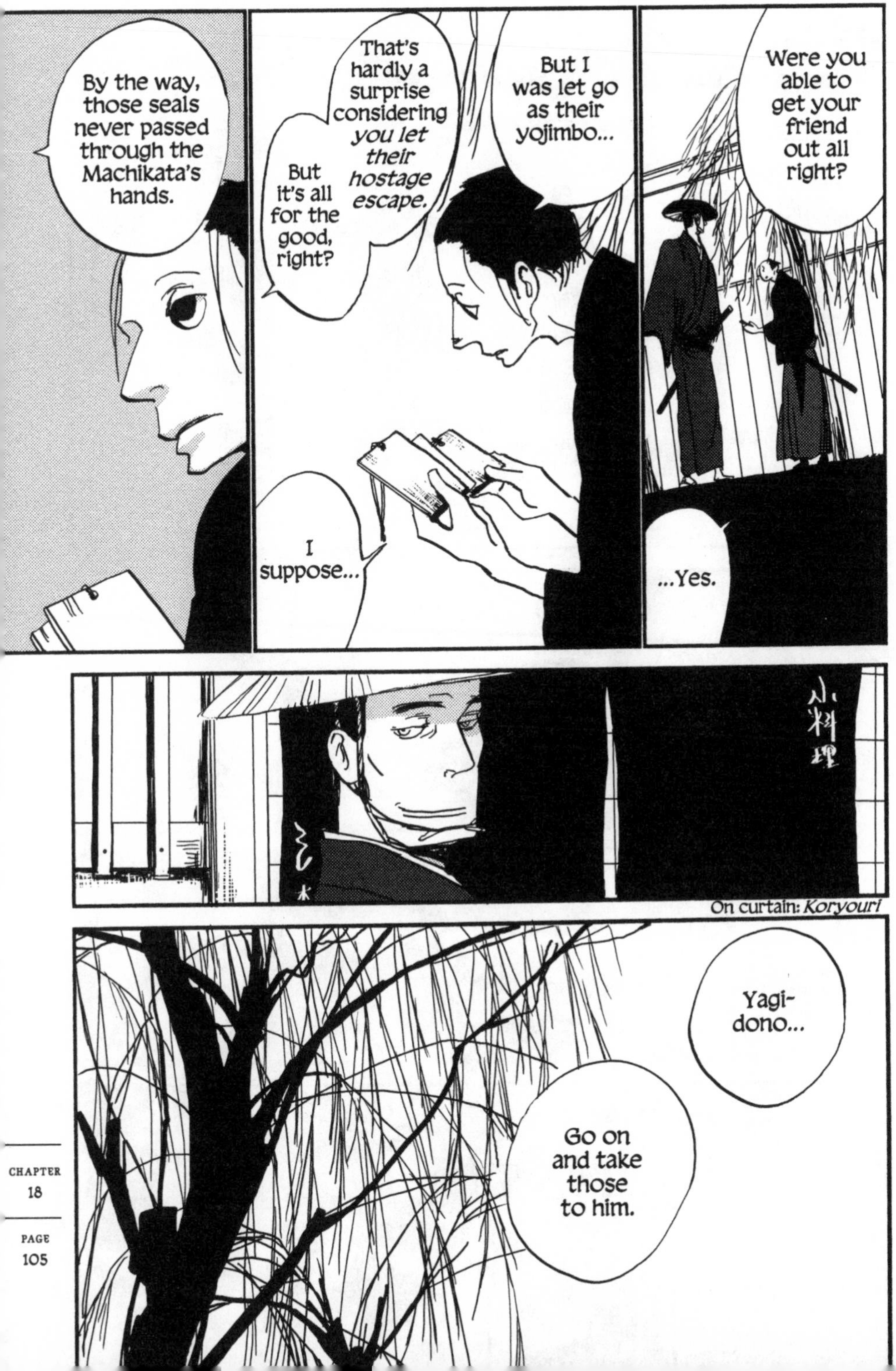
Were you able to get your friend out all right?
...Yes.
But I was let go as their yojimbo...
That's hardly a surprise considering *you let their hostage escape.*
But it's all for the good, right?
I suppose...
By the way, those seals never passed through the Machikata's hands.
On curtain: *Koryouri*
Yagi-dono...
Go on and take those to him.

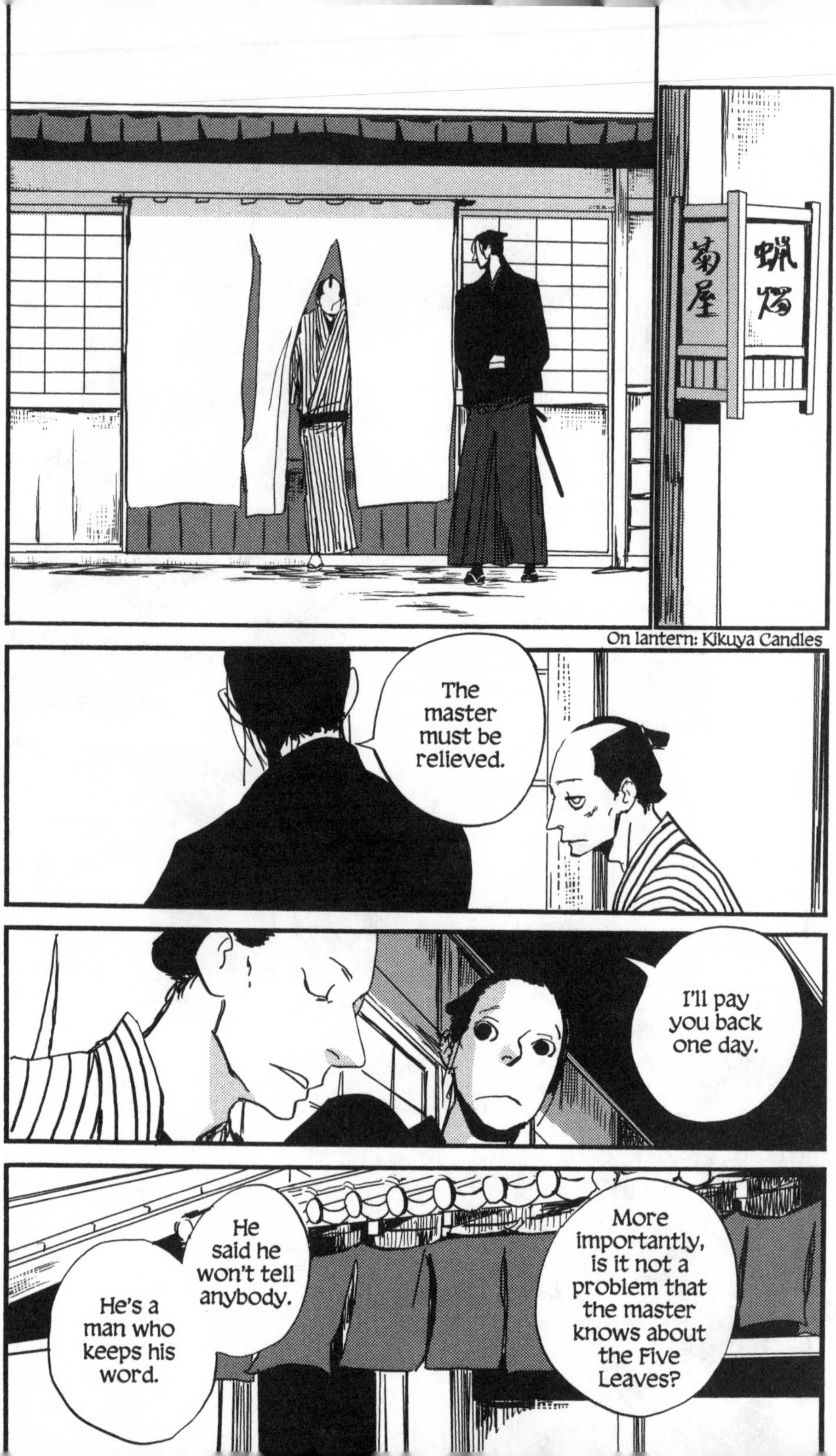
蝋燭
菊屋
On lantern: Kikuya Candles
The master must be relieved.
I'll pay you back one day.
More importantly, is it not a problem that the master knows about the Five Leaves?
He said he won't tell anybody.
He's a man who keeps his word.

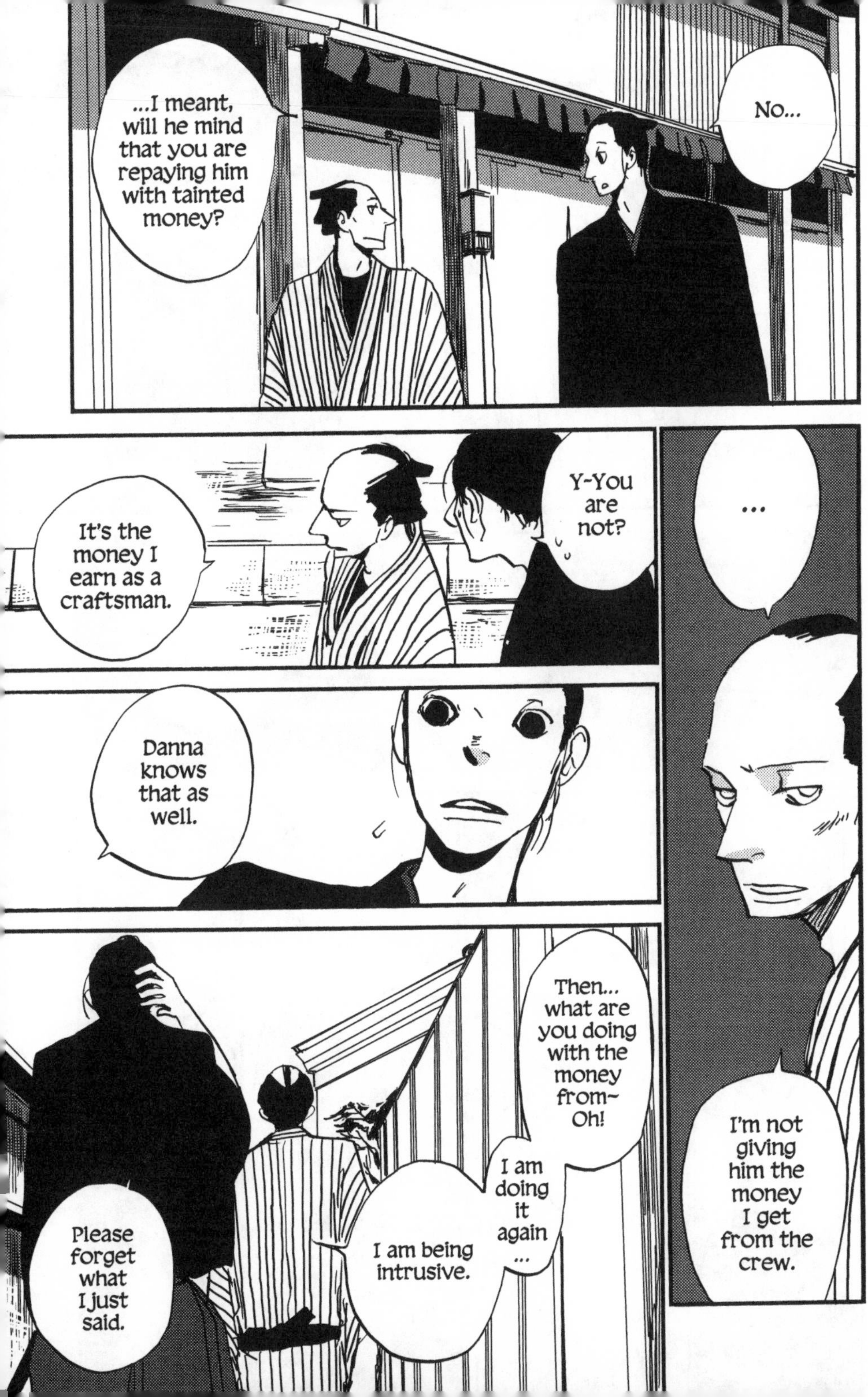
No...
...I meant, will he mind that you are repaying him with tainted money?
...
I'm not giving him the money I get from the crew.
Y-You are not?
It's the money I earn as a craftsman.
Danna knows that as well.
Then... what are you doing with the money from~ Oh!
I am doing it again ...
I am being intrusive.
Please forget what I just said.

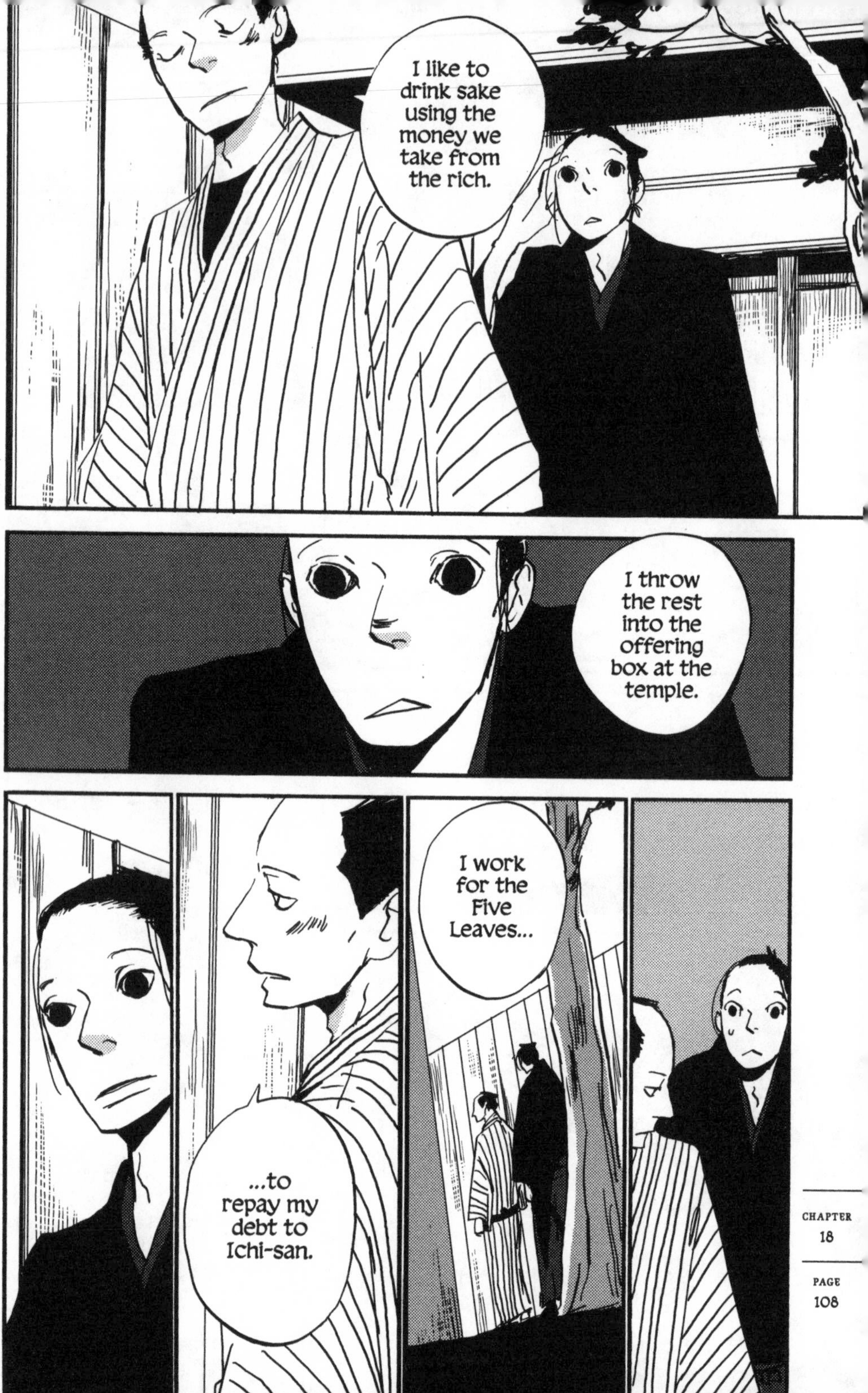
I like to drink sake using the money we take from the rich.
I throw the rest into the offering box at the temple.
I work for the Five Leaves...
...to repay my debt to Ichi-san.

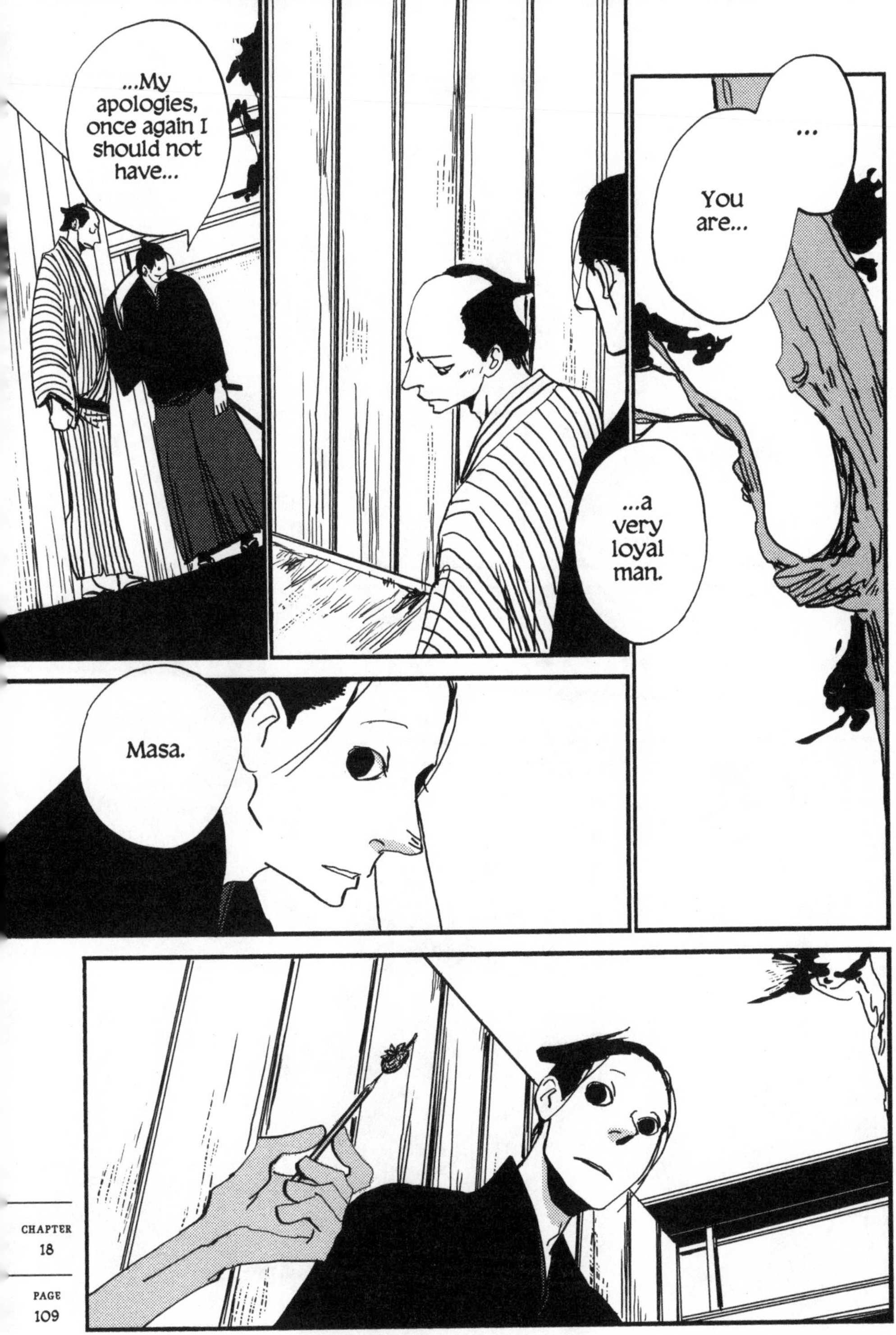
...
You are...
...a very loyal man.
...My apologies, once again I should not have...
Masa.

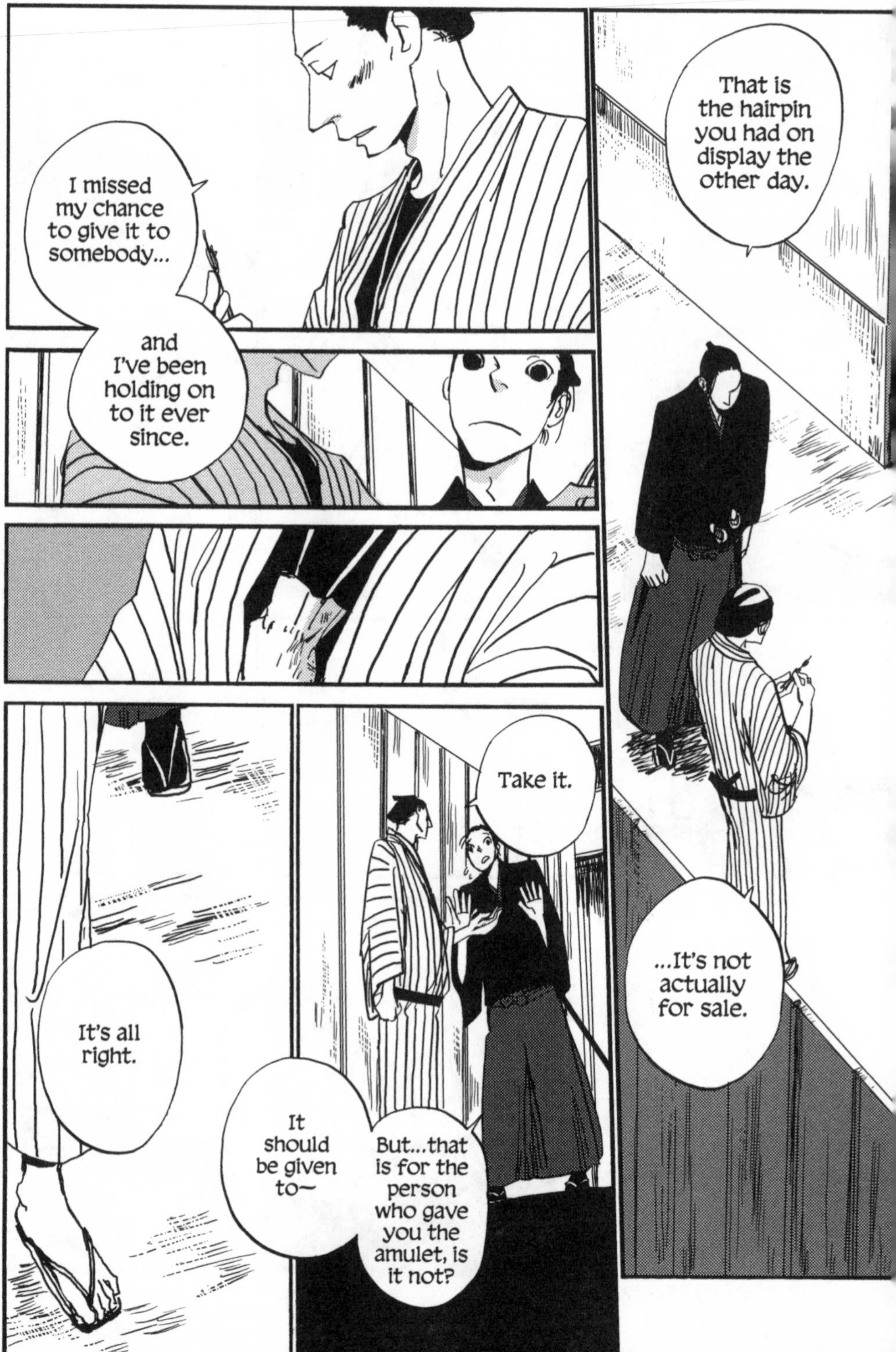
That is the hairpin you had on display the other day.
...It's not actually for sale.
I missed my chance to give it to somebody...
and I've been holding on to it ever since.
Take it.
But...that is for the person who gave you the amulet, is it not?
It should be given to~
It's all right.

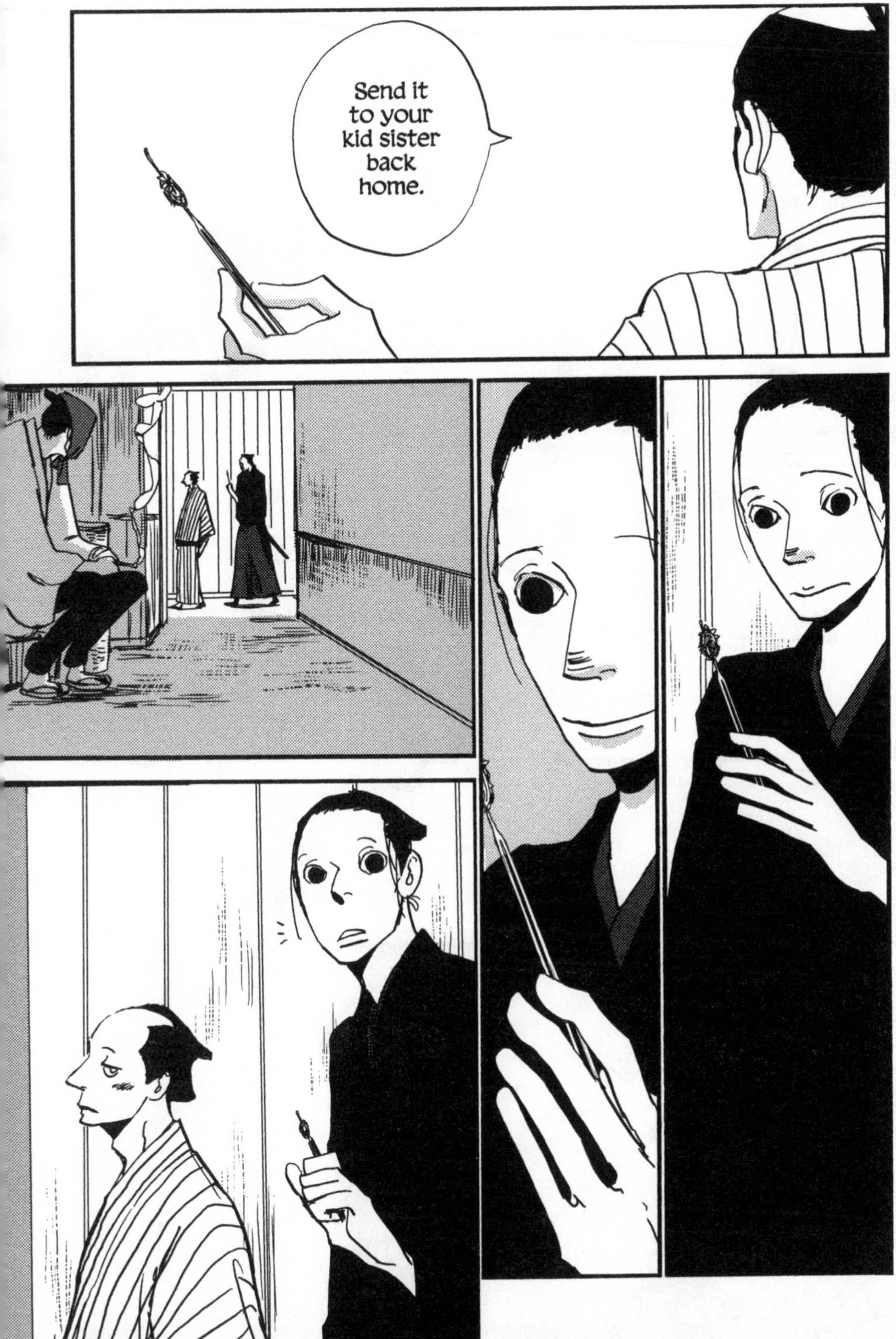
Send it to your kid sister back home.

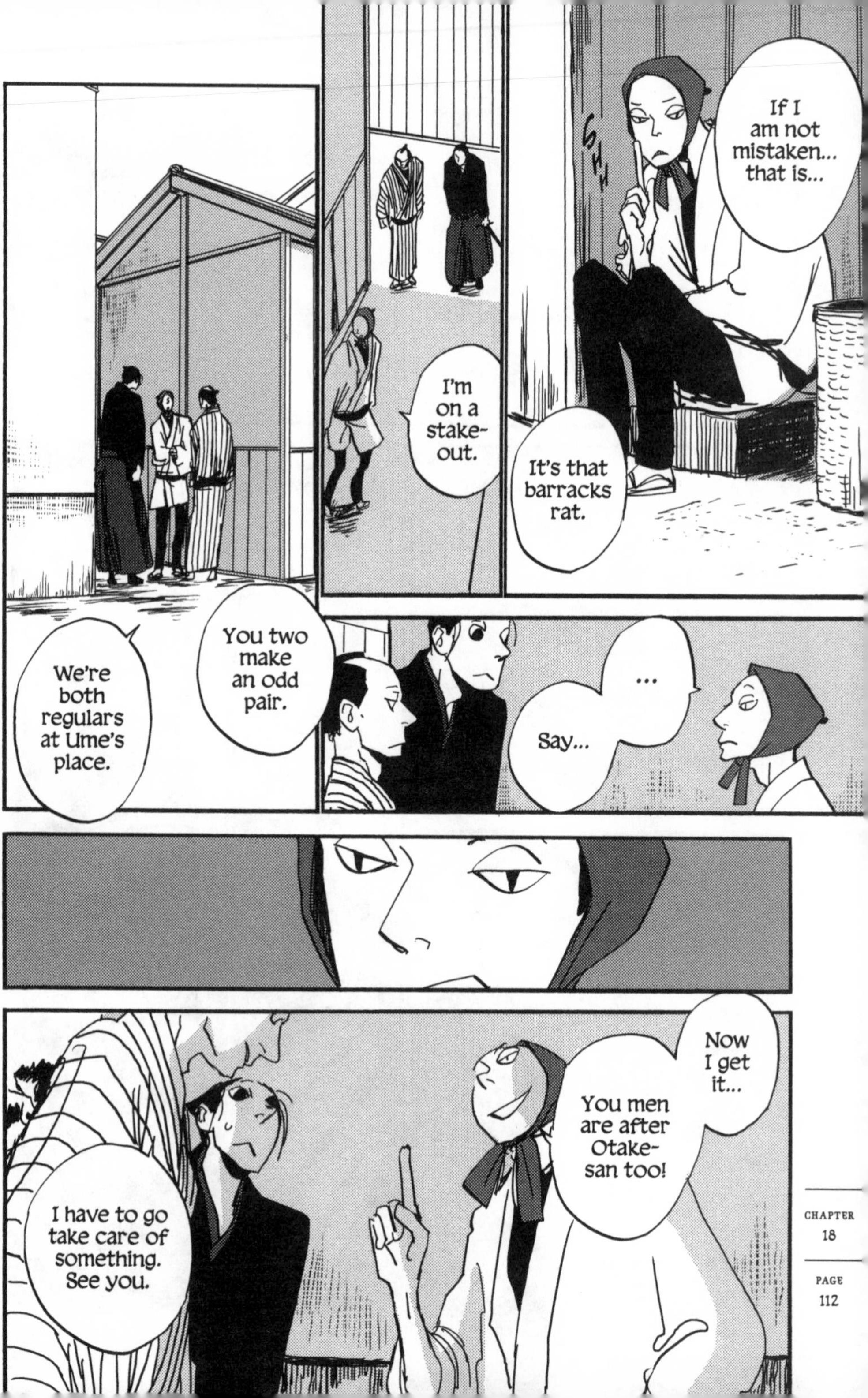
If I am not mistaken... that is...
SHH
It's that barracks rat.
I'm on a stake-out.
...
Say...
You two make an odd pair.
We're both regulars at Ume's place.
Now I get it...
You men are after Otake-san too!
I have to go take care of something. See you.

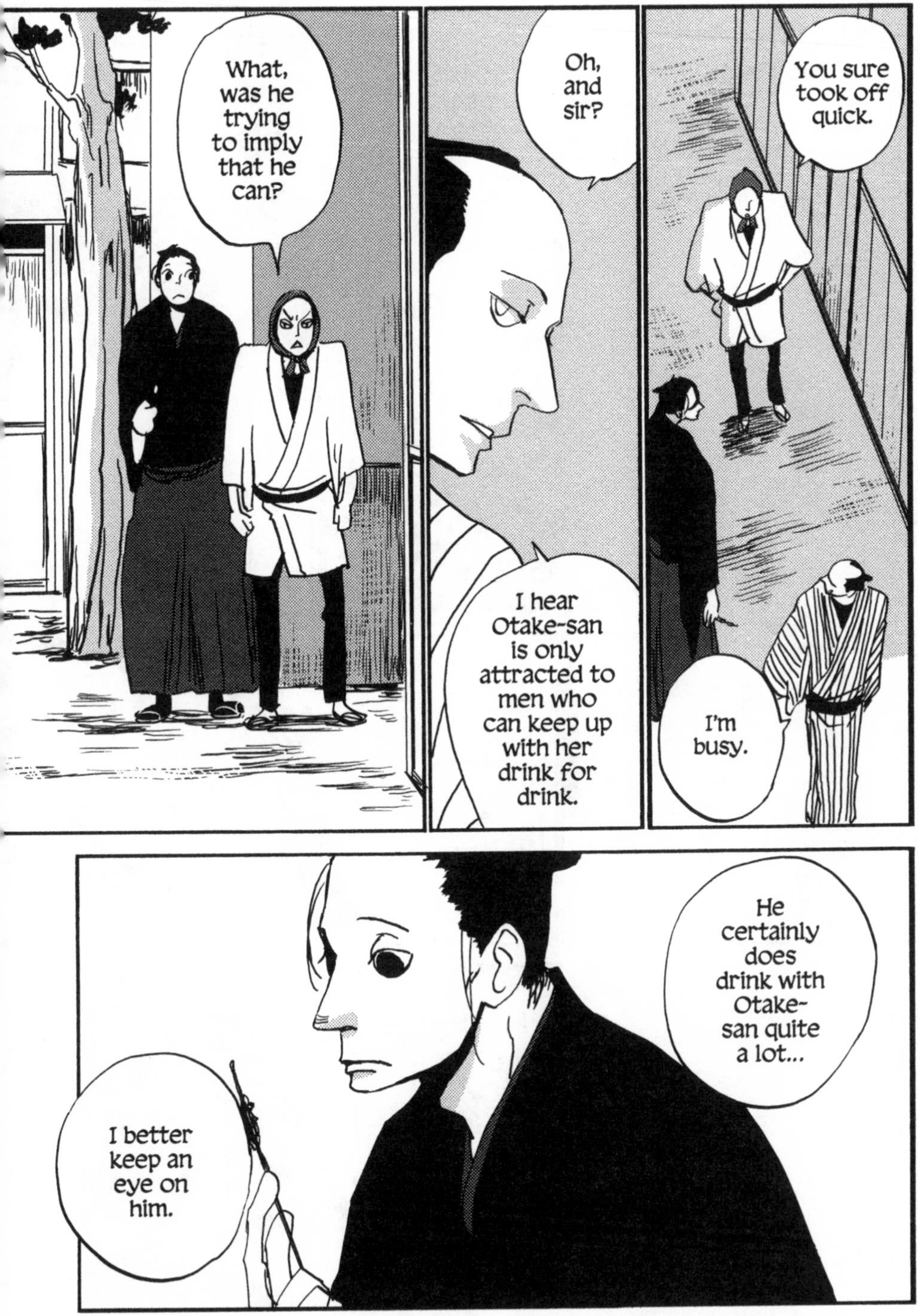
You sure took off quick.
I'm busy.
Oh, and sir?
I hear Otake-san is only attracted to men who can keep up with her drink for drink.
What, was he trying to imply that he can?
He certainly does drink with Otake-san quite a lot...
I better keep an eye on him.

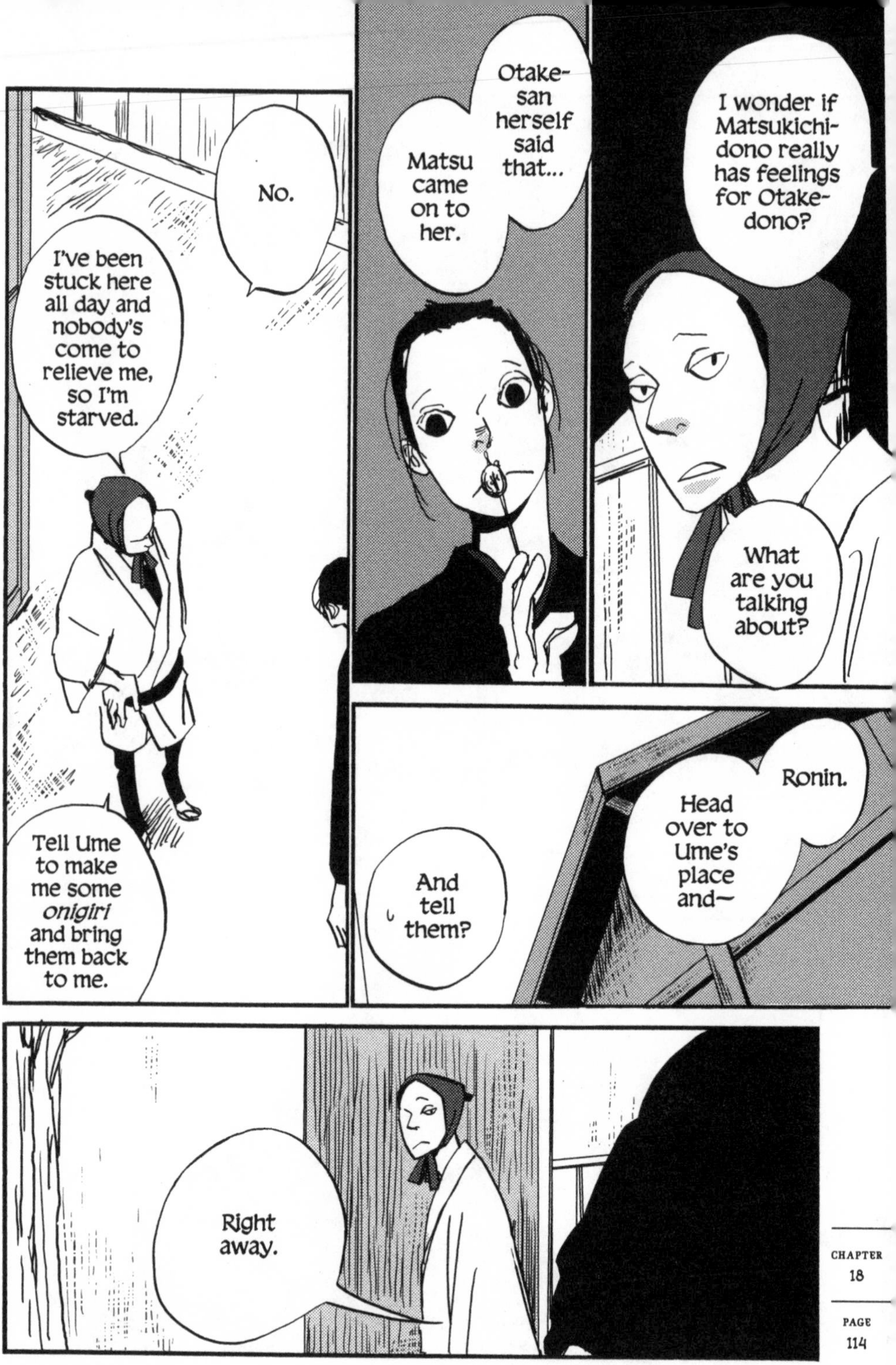
I wonder if Matsukichi-dono really has feelings for Otake-dono?
What are you talking about?
Otake-san herself said that...
Matsu came on to her.
Ronin.
Head over to Ume's place and~
And tell them?
No.
I've been stuck here all day and nobody's come to relieve me, so I'm starved.
Tell Ume to make me some *onigiri* and bring them back to me.
Right away.

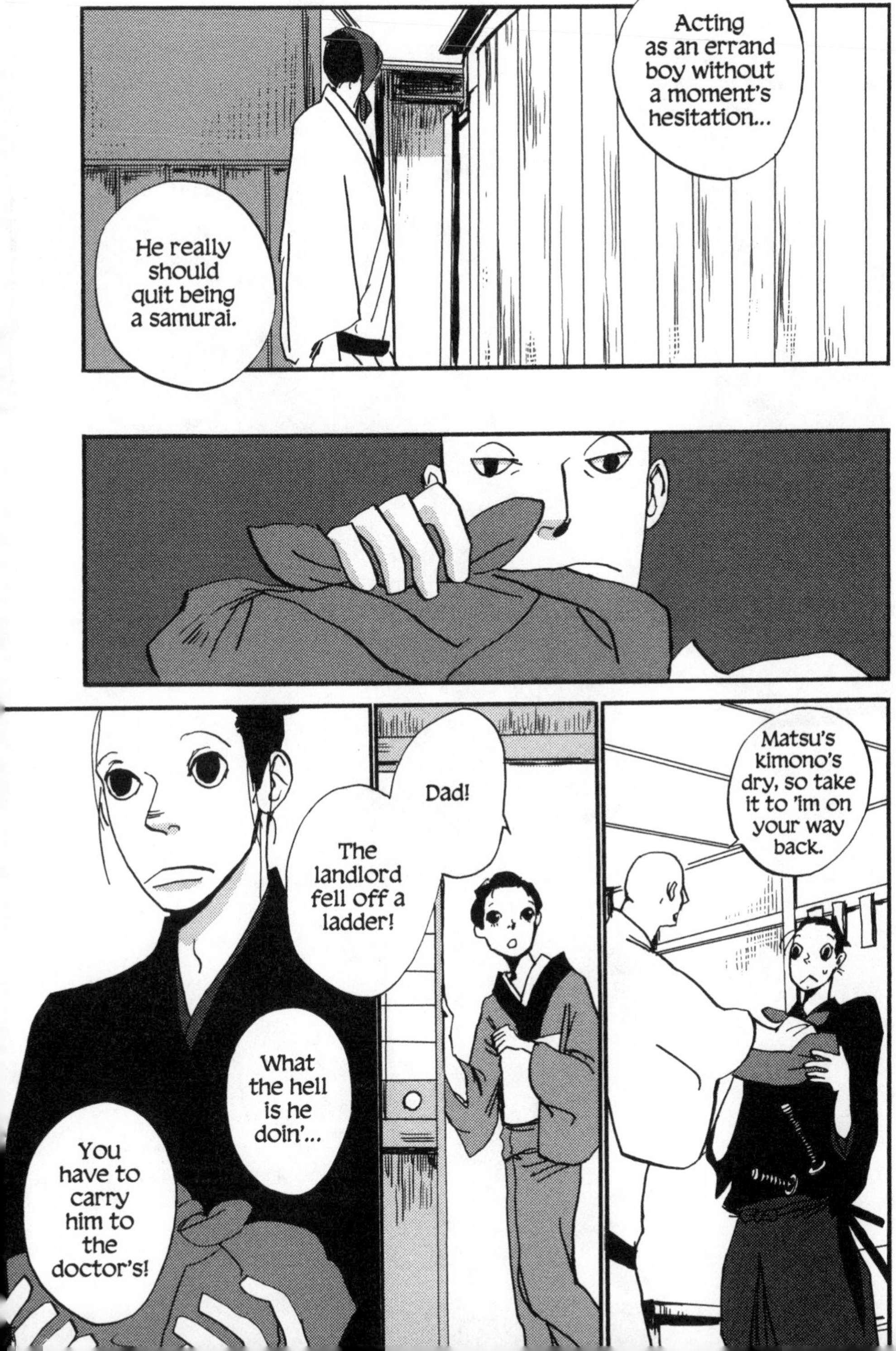
Acting as an errand boy without a moment's hesitation...
He really should quit being a samurai.
Matsu's kimono's dry, so take it to 'im on your way back.
Dad!
The landlord fell off a ladder!
What the hell is he doin'...
You have to carry him to the doctor's!

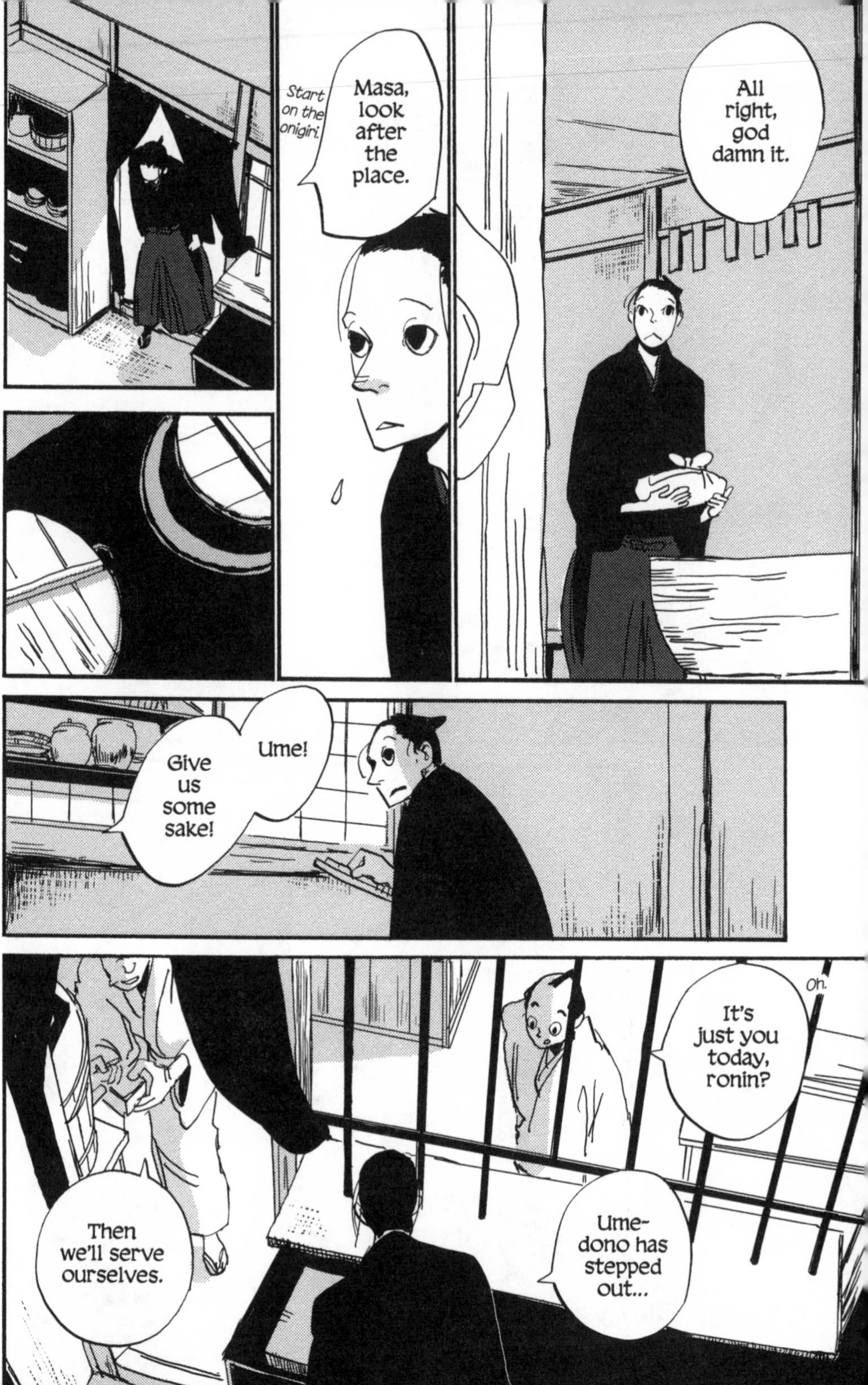
All right, god damn it.
Masa, look after the place.
Start on the onigiri.
Ume!
Give us some sake!
Oh.
It's just you today, ronin?
Ume-dono has stepped out...
Then we'll serve ourselves.

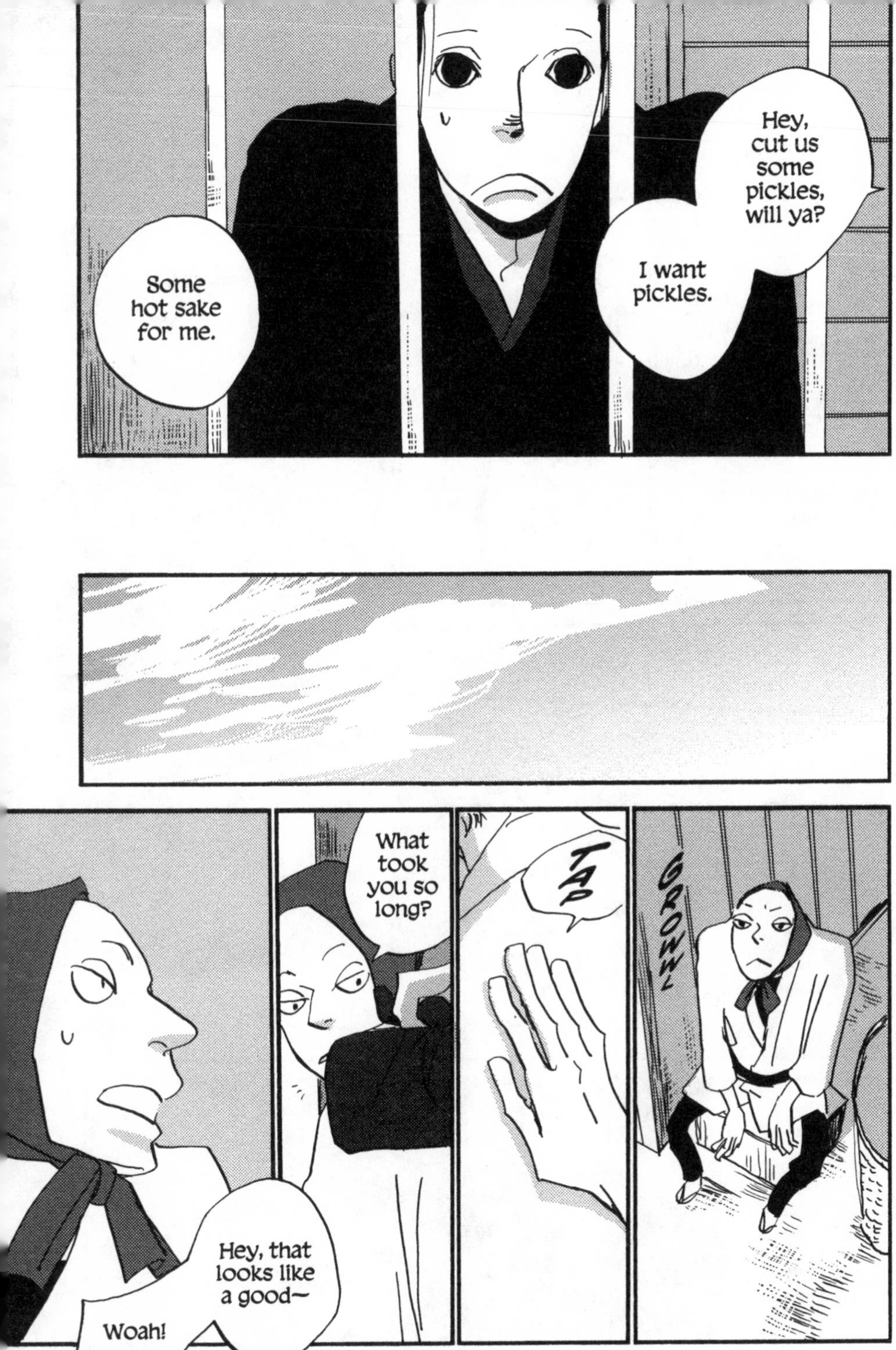
Hey, cut us some pickles, will ya?
I want pickles.
Some hot sake for me.
GROWL
TAP
What took you so long?
Hey, that looks like a good~
Woah!

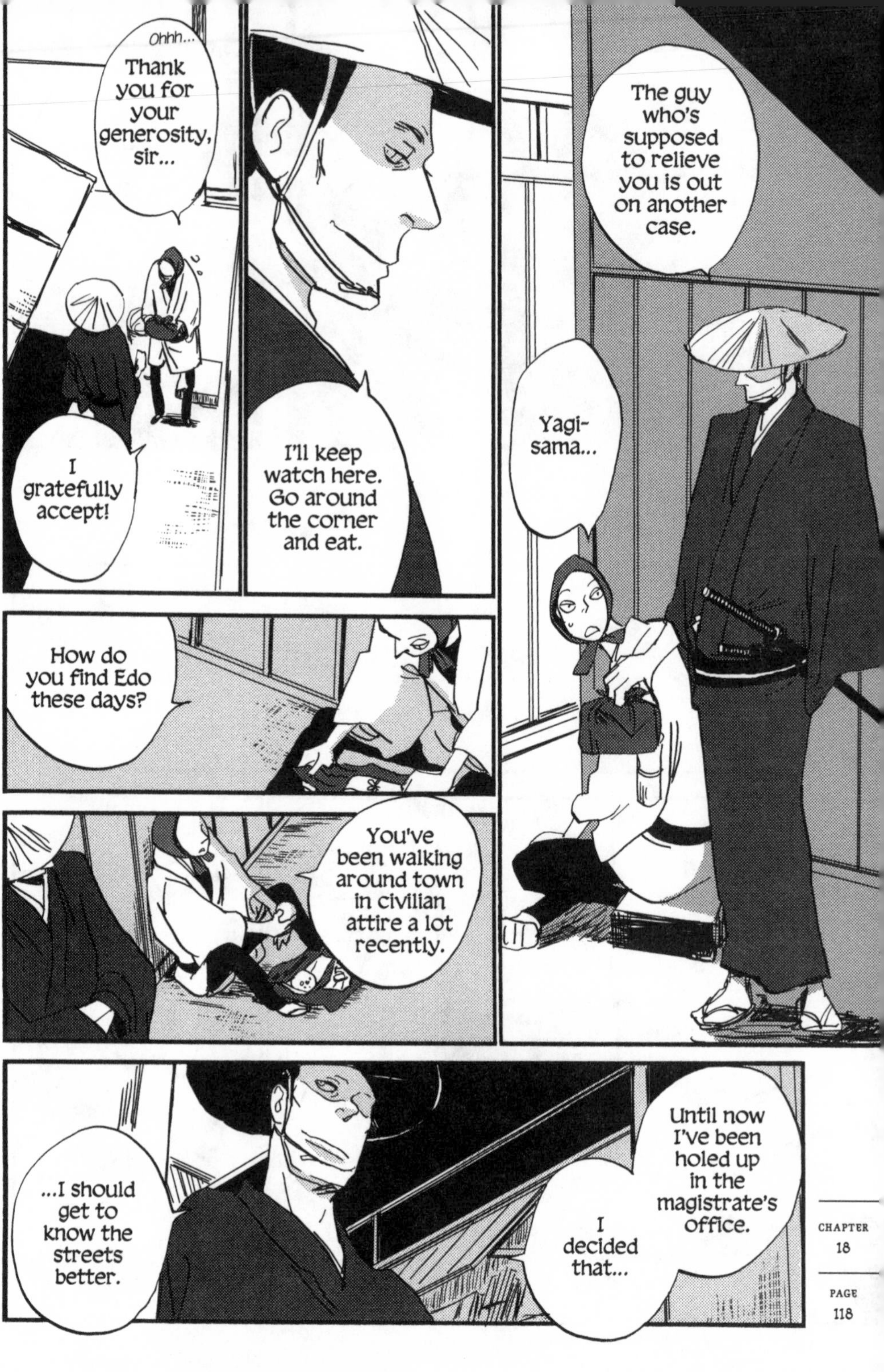
The guy who's supposed to relieve you is out on another case.
Yagi-sama...
I'll keep watch here. Go around the corner and eat.
Ohhh...
Thank you for your generosity, sir...
I gratefully accept!
How do you find Edo these days?
You've been walking around town in civilian attire a lot recently.
Until now I've been holed up in the magistrate's office.
I decided that...
...I should get to know the streets better.

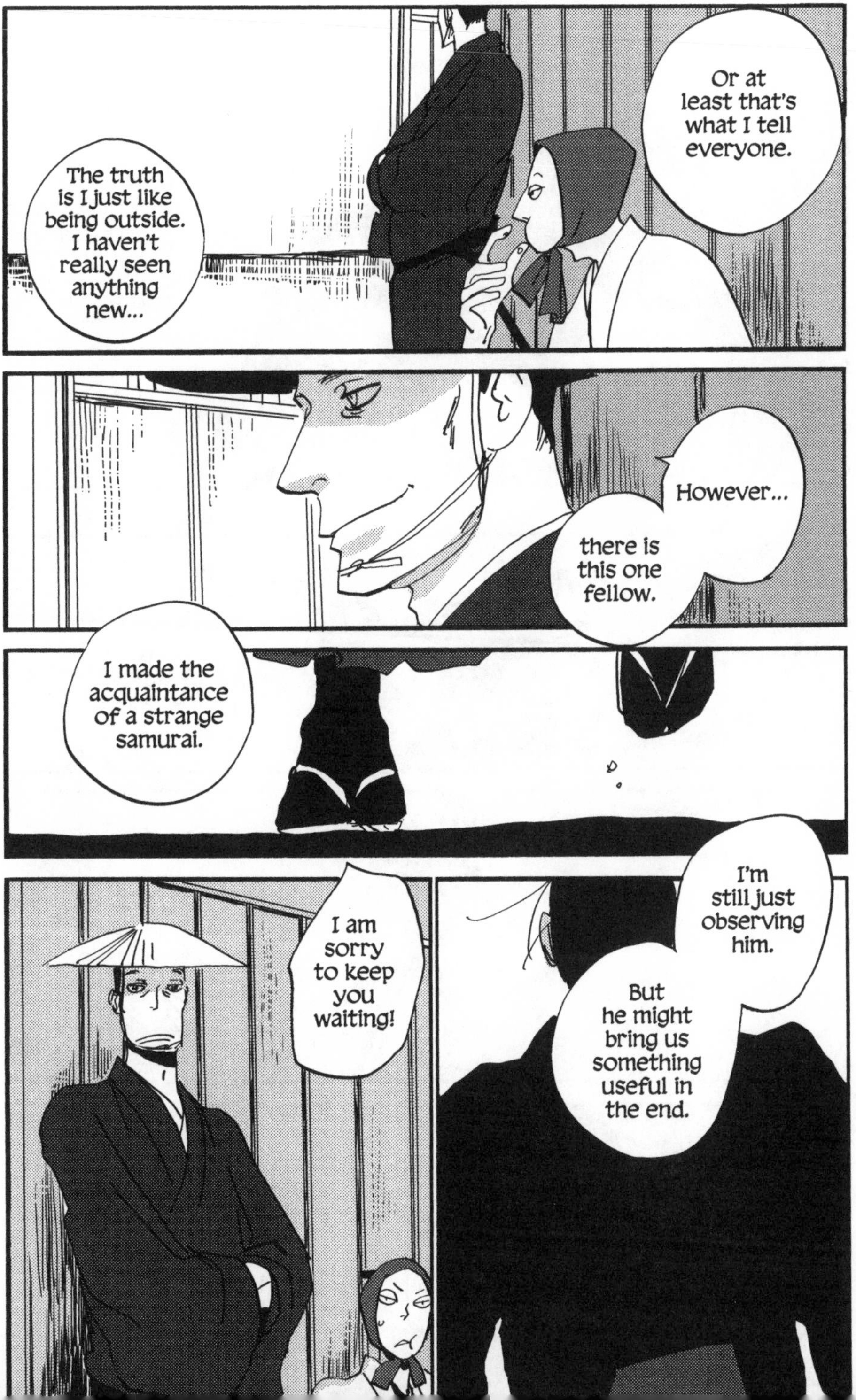

Or at least that's what I tell everyone.
The truth is I just like being outside. I haven't really seen anything new...
However...
there is this one fellow.
I made the acquaintance of a strange samurai.
I'm still just observing him.
But he might bring us something useful in the end.
I am sorry to keep you waiting!

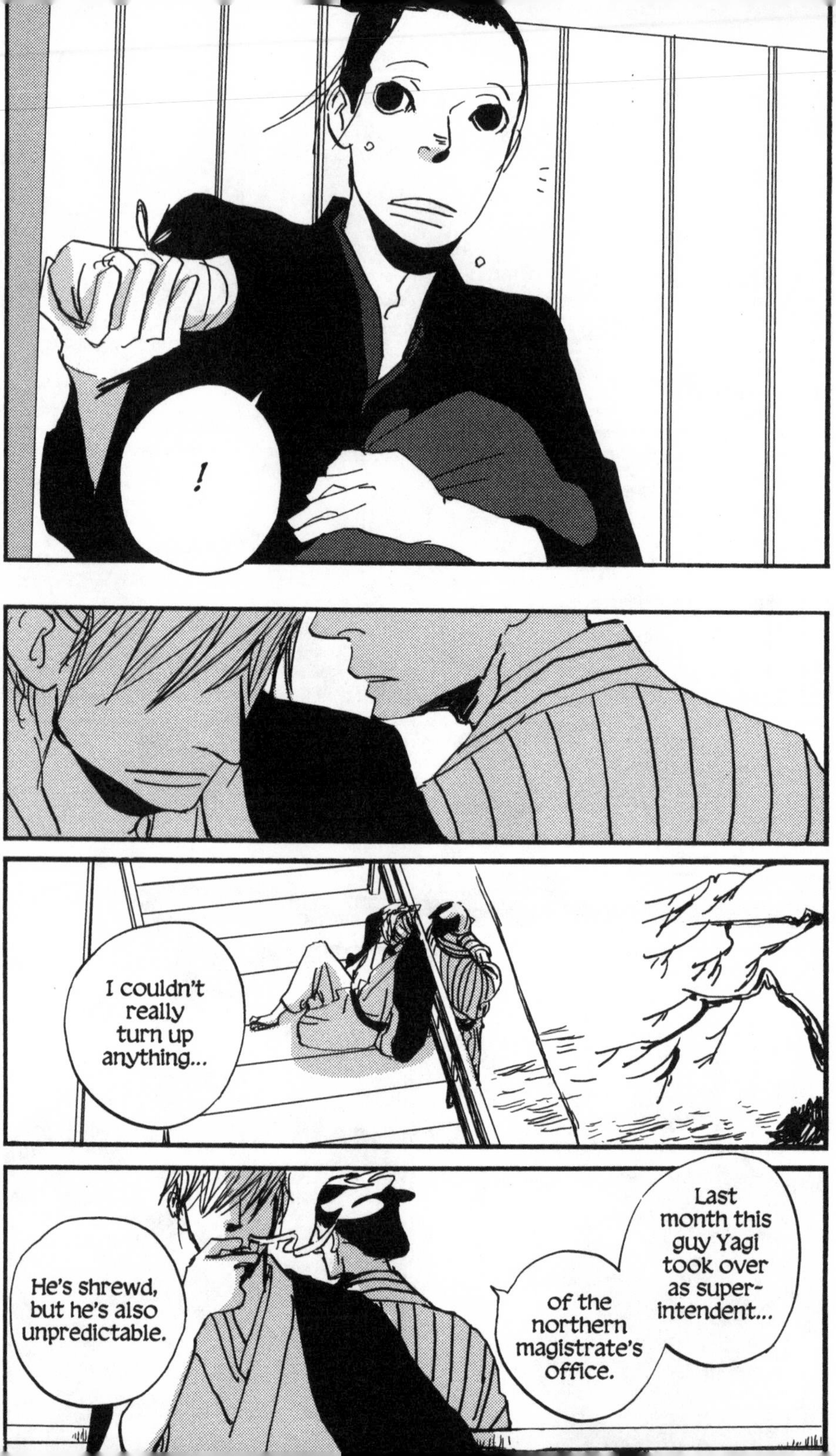
!
I couldn't really turn up anything...
Last month this guy Yagi took over as super-intendent...
of the northern magistrate's office.
He's shrewd, but he's also unpredictable.

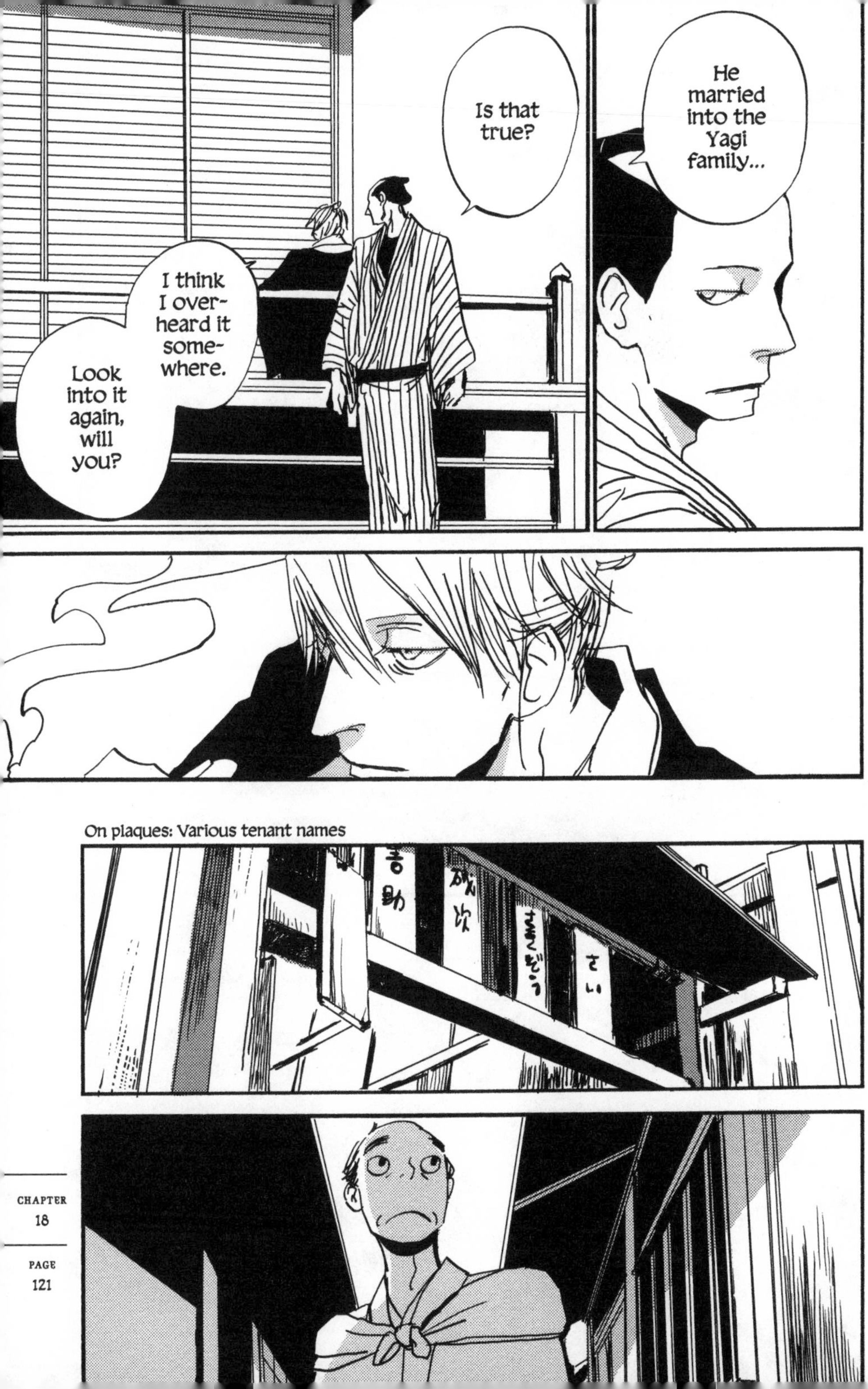
He married into the Yagi family...
Is that true?
I think I overheard it somewhere.
Look into it again, will you?
On plaques: Various tenant names

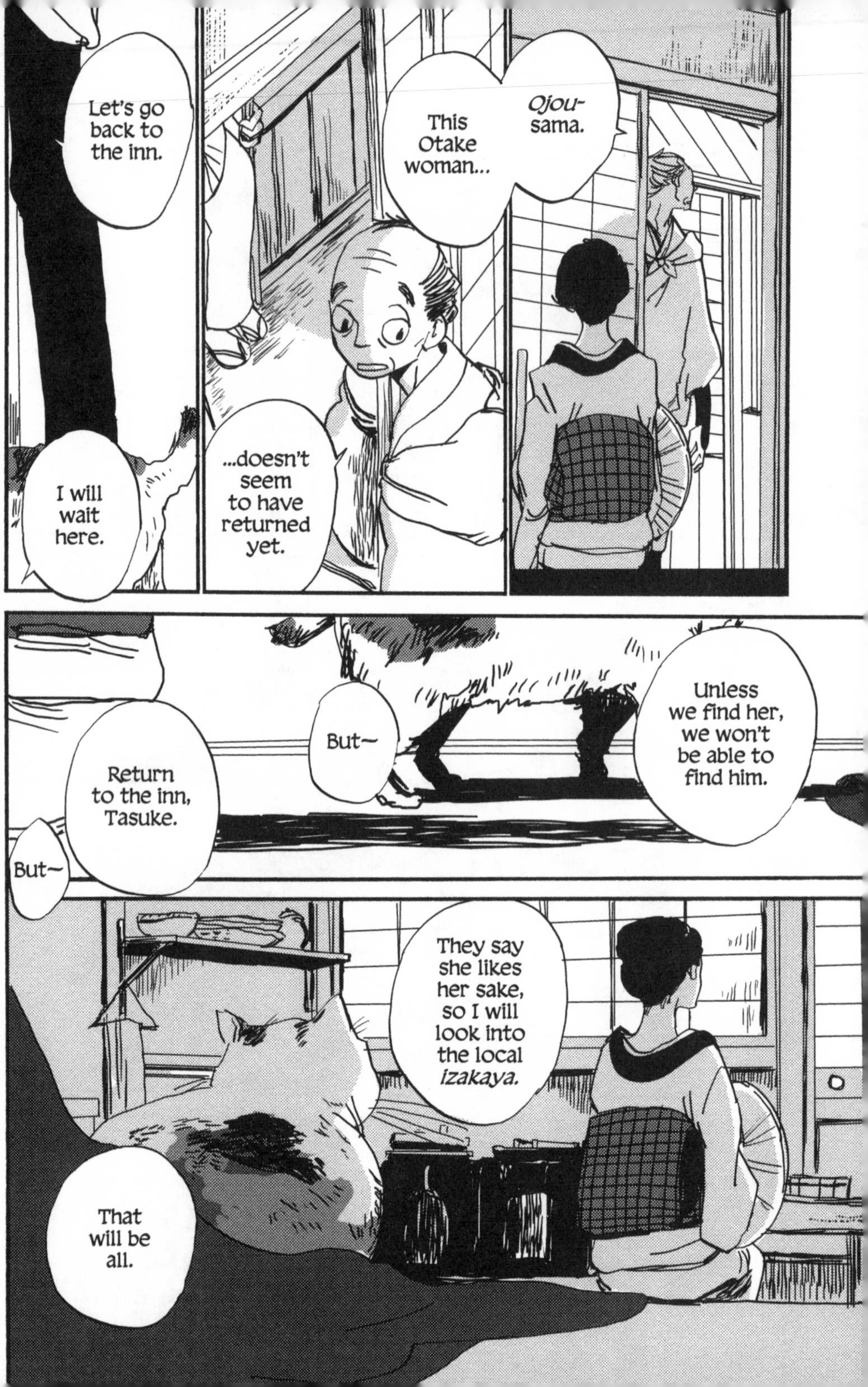
Ojou-sama.
This Otake woman...
...doesn't seem to have returned yet.
Let's go back to the inn.
I will wait here.
Unless we find her, we won't be able to find him.
But~
Return to the inn, Tasuke.
But~
They say she likes her sake, so I will look into the local izakaya.
That will be all.

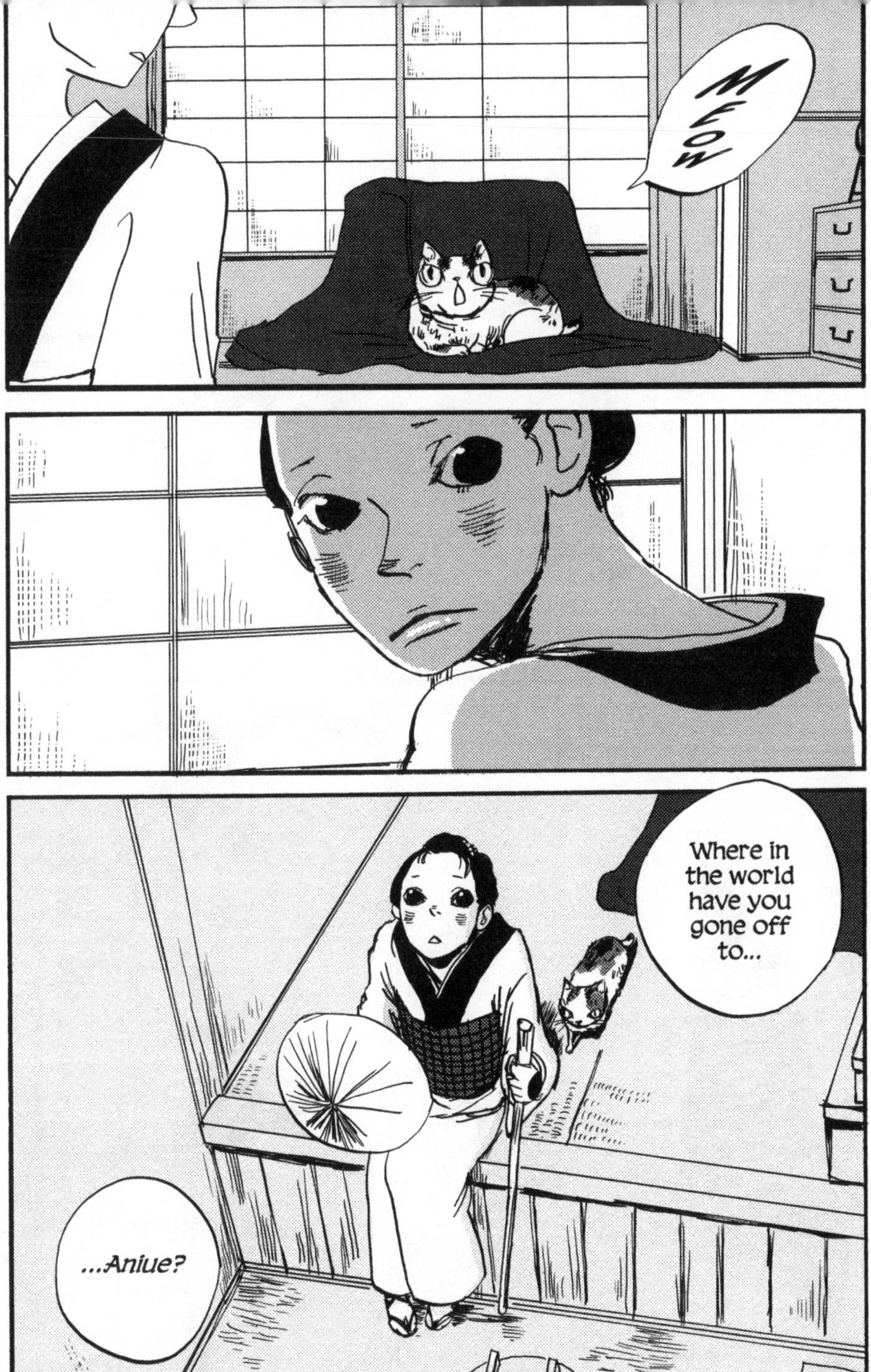
MEOW
Where in the world have you gone off to...
...Aniue?

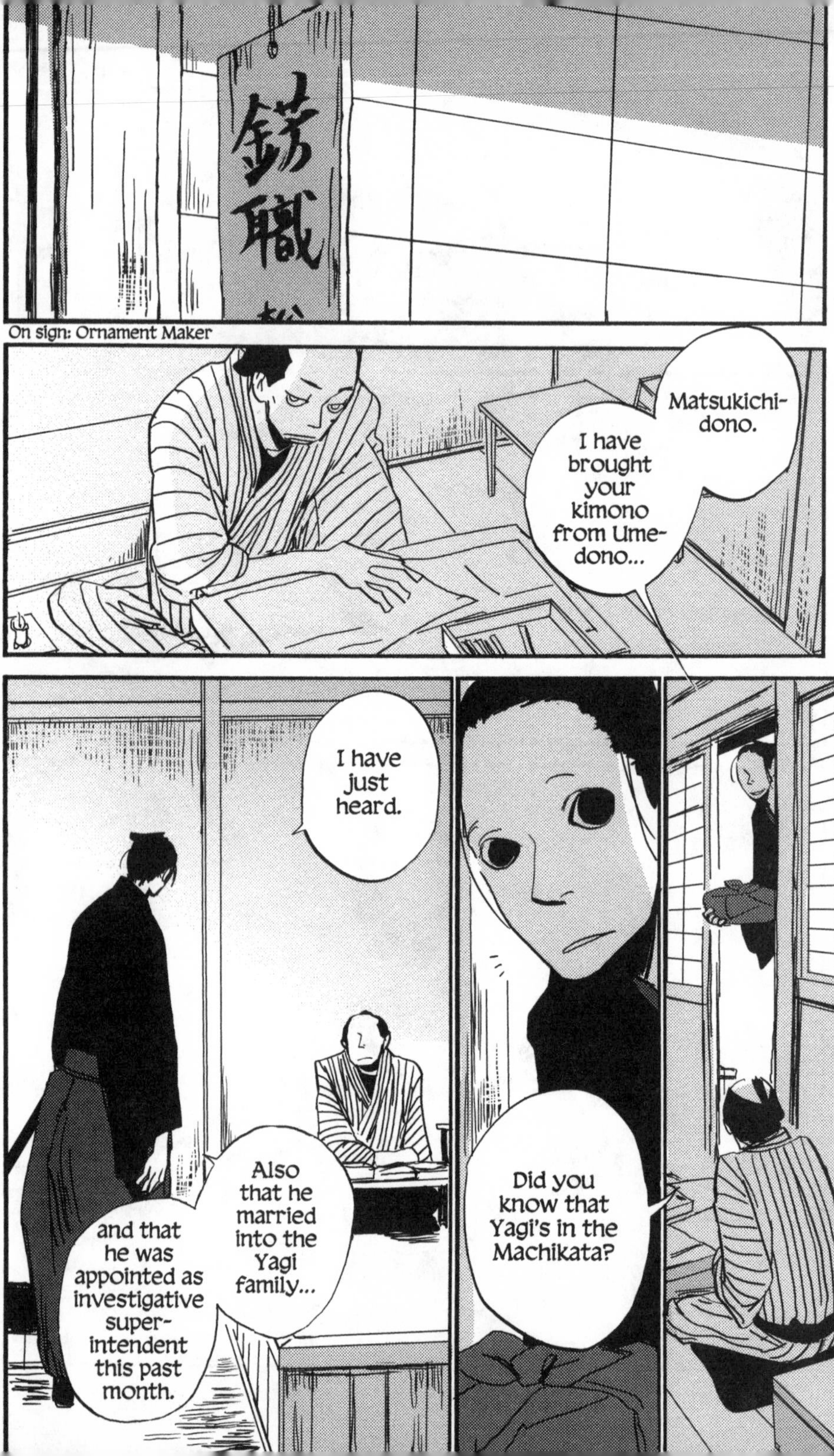
錺職
On sign: Ornament Maker
Matsukichi-dono.
I have brought your kimono from Ume-dono...
Did you know that Yagi's in the Machikata?
I have just heard.
Also that he married into the Yagi family...
and that he was appointed as investigative super-intendent this past month.

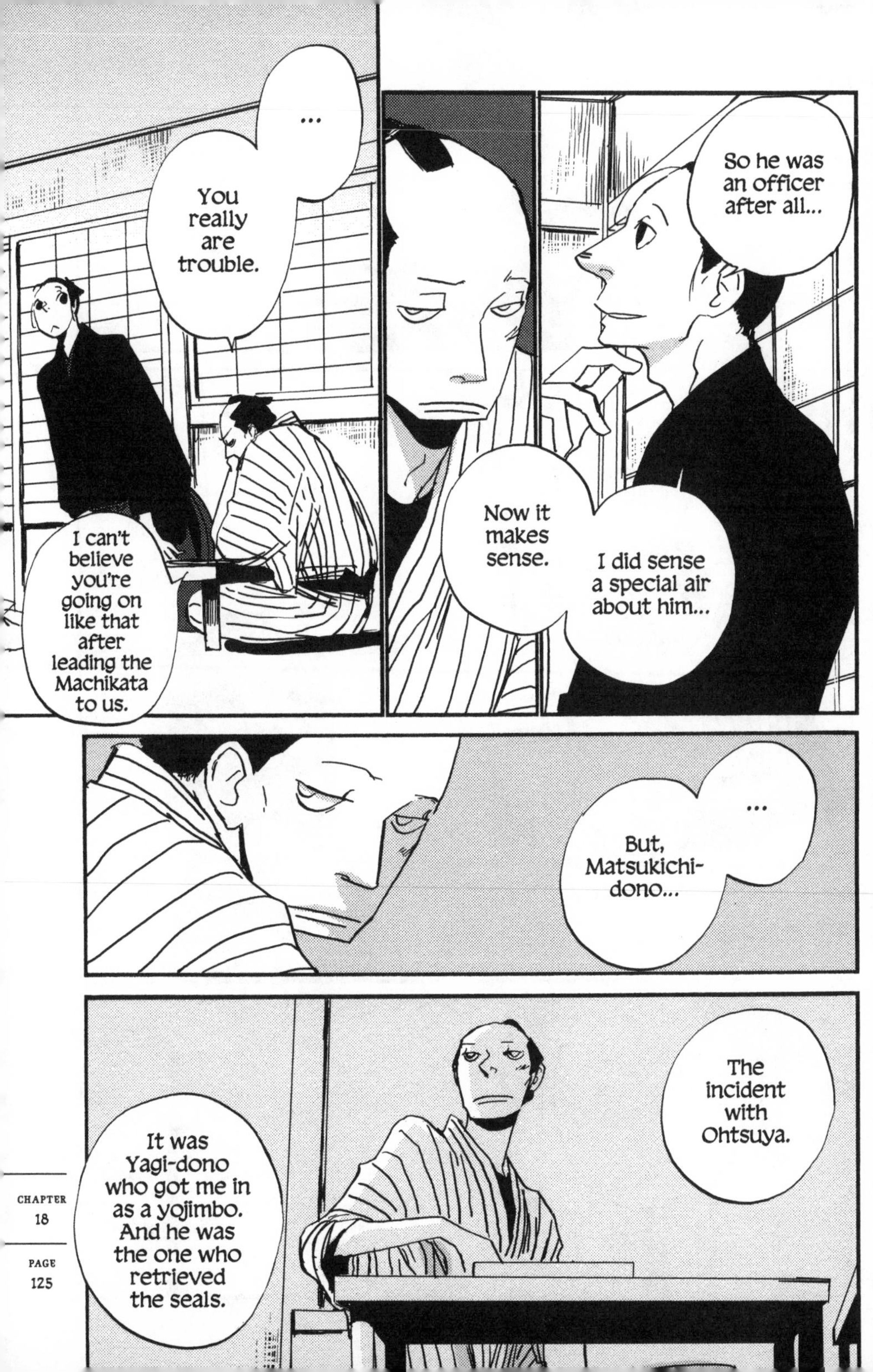
So he was an officer after all...
I did sense a special air about him...
Now it makes sense.
...
You really are trouble.
I can't believe you're going on like that after leading the Machikata to us.
...
But, Matsukichi-dono...
The incident with Ohtsuya.
It was Yagi-dono who got me in as a yojimbo. And he was the one who retrieved the seals.

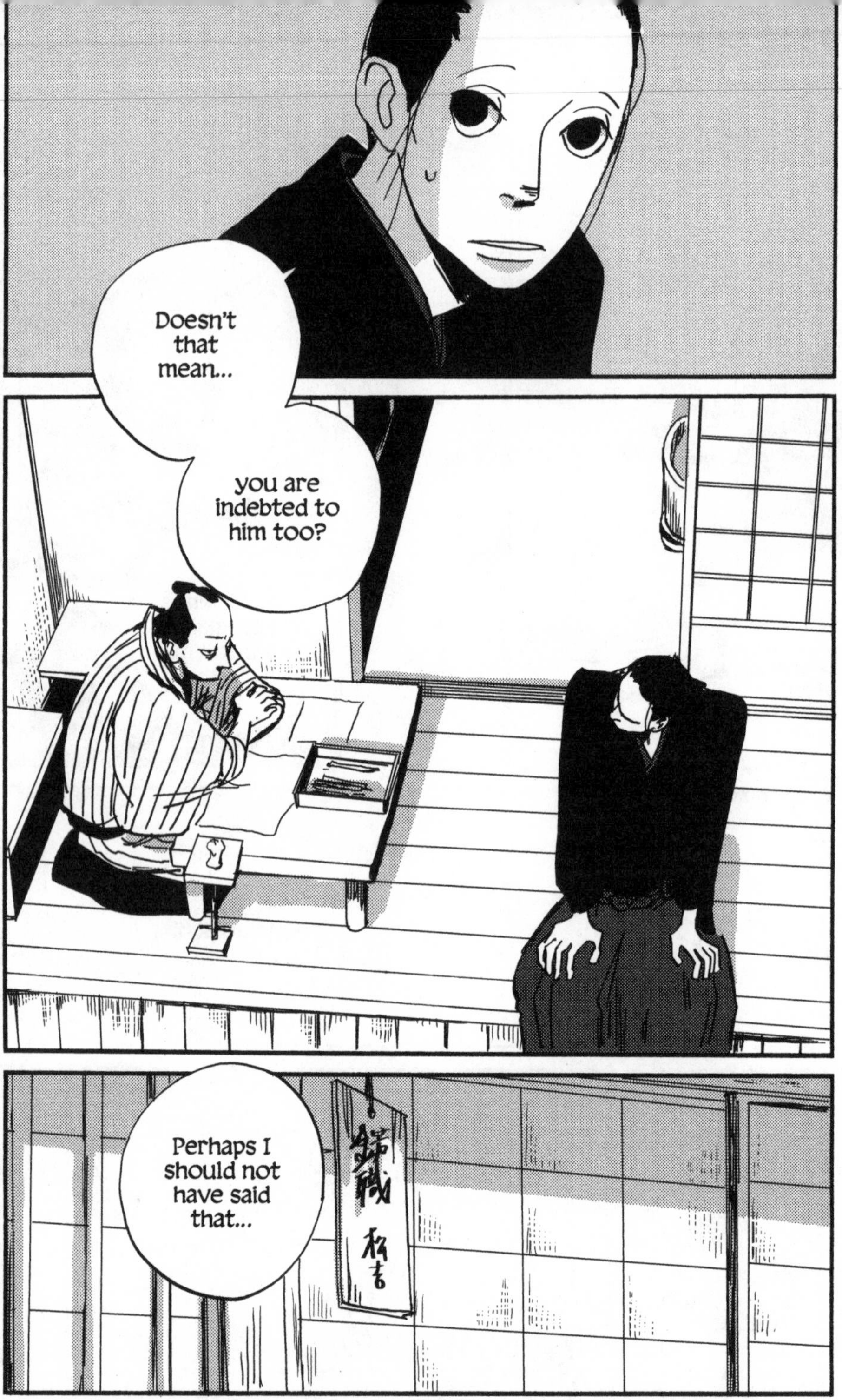
Doesn't that mean...
you are indebted to him too?
Perhaps I should not have said that...

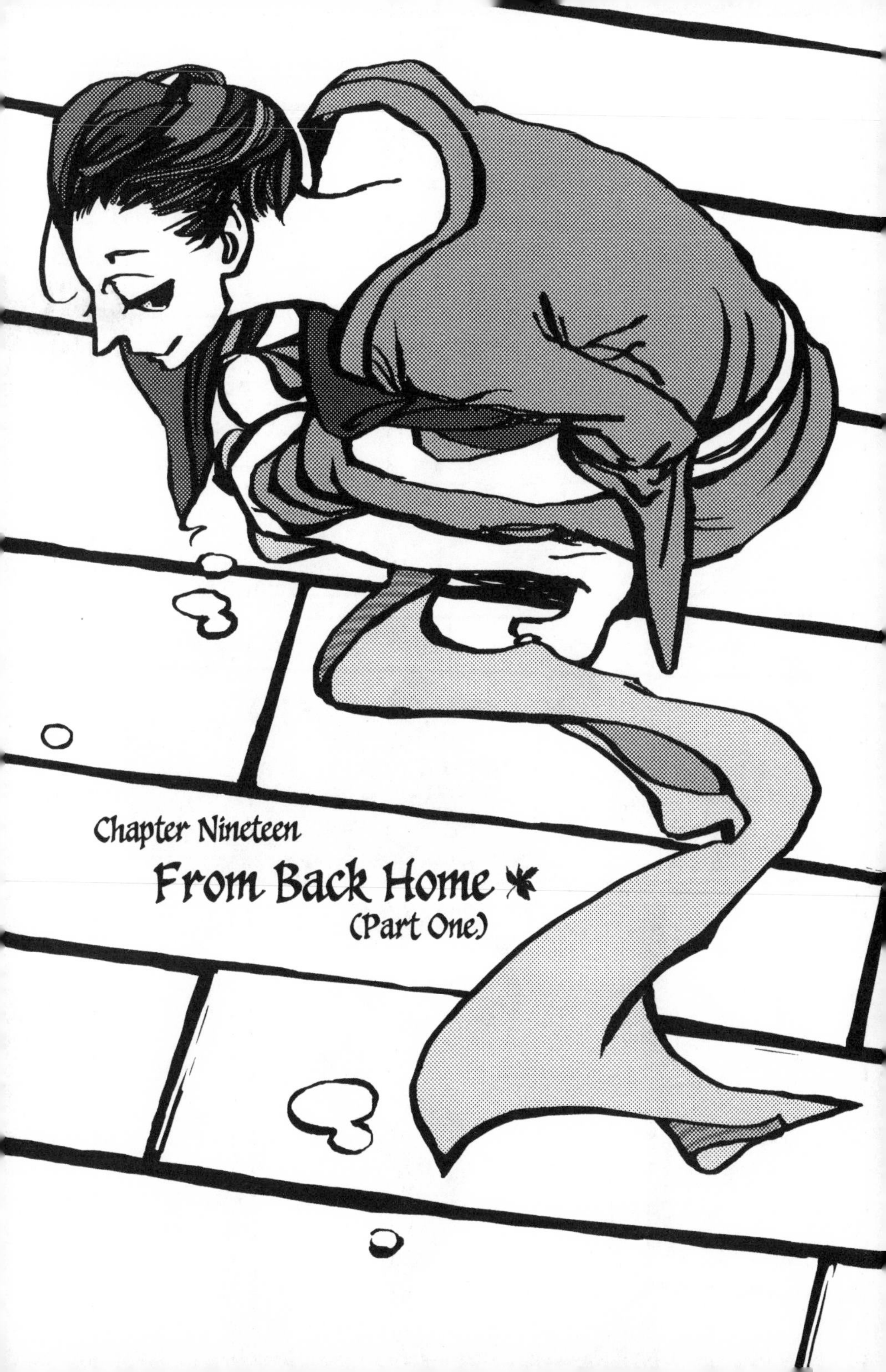

Chapter Nineteen

From Back Home

(Part One)

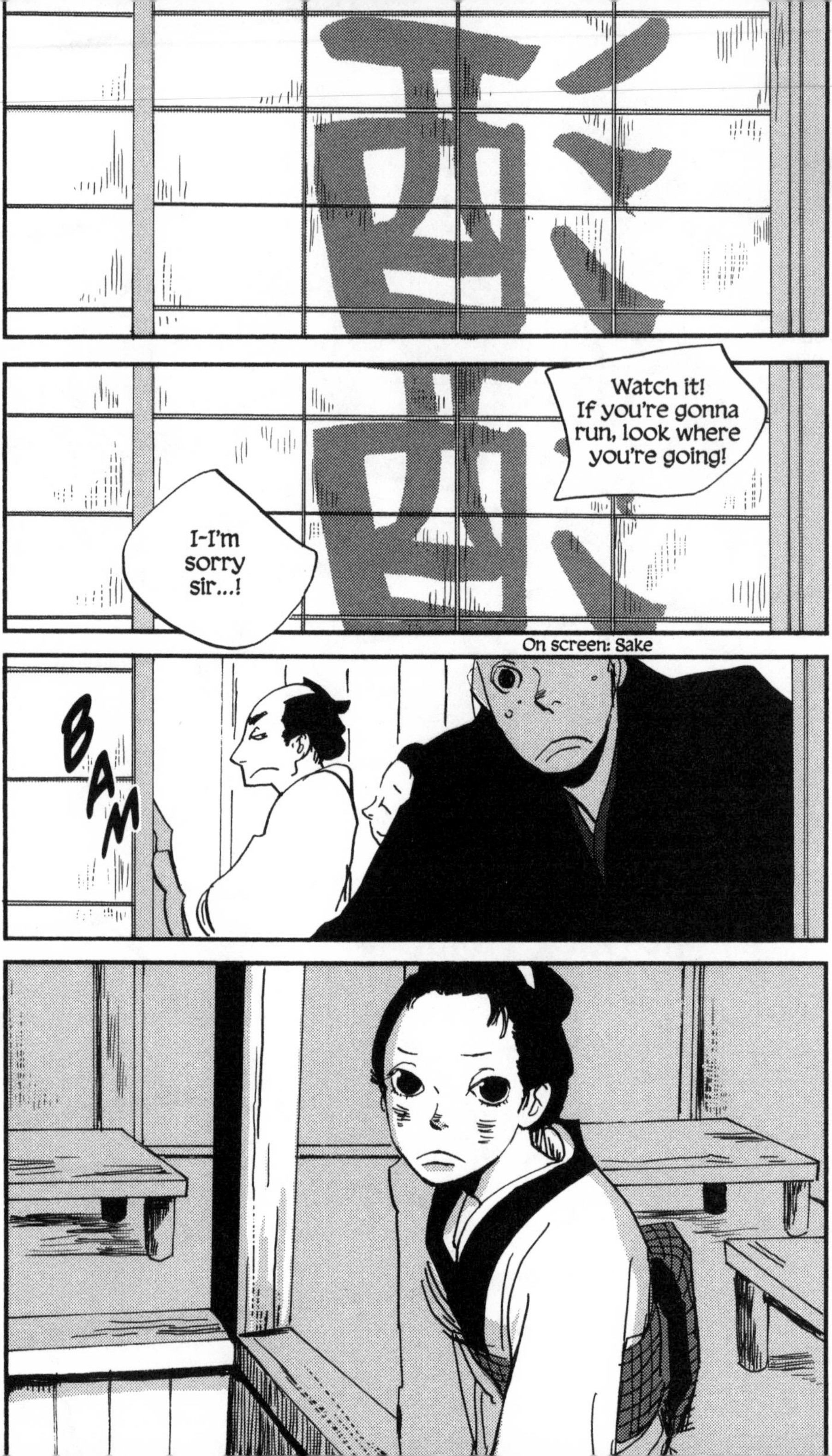
Watch it! If you're gonna run, look where you're going!
I-I'm sorry sir...!
On screen: Sake
BAM

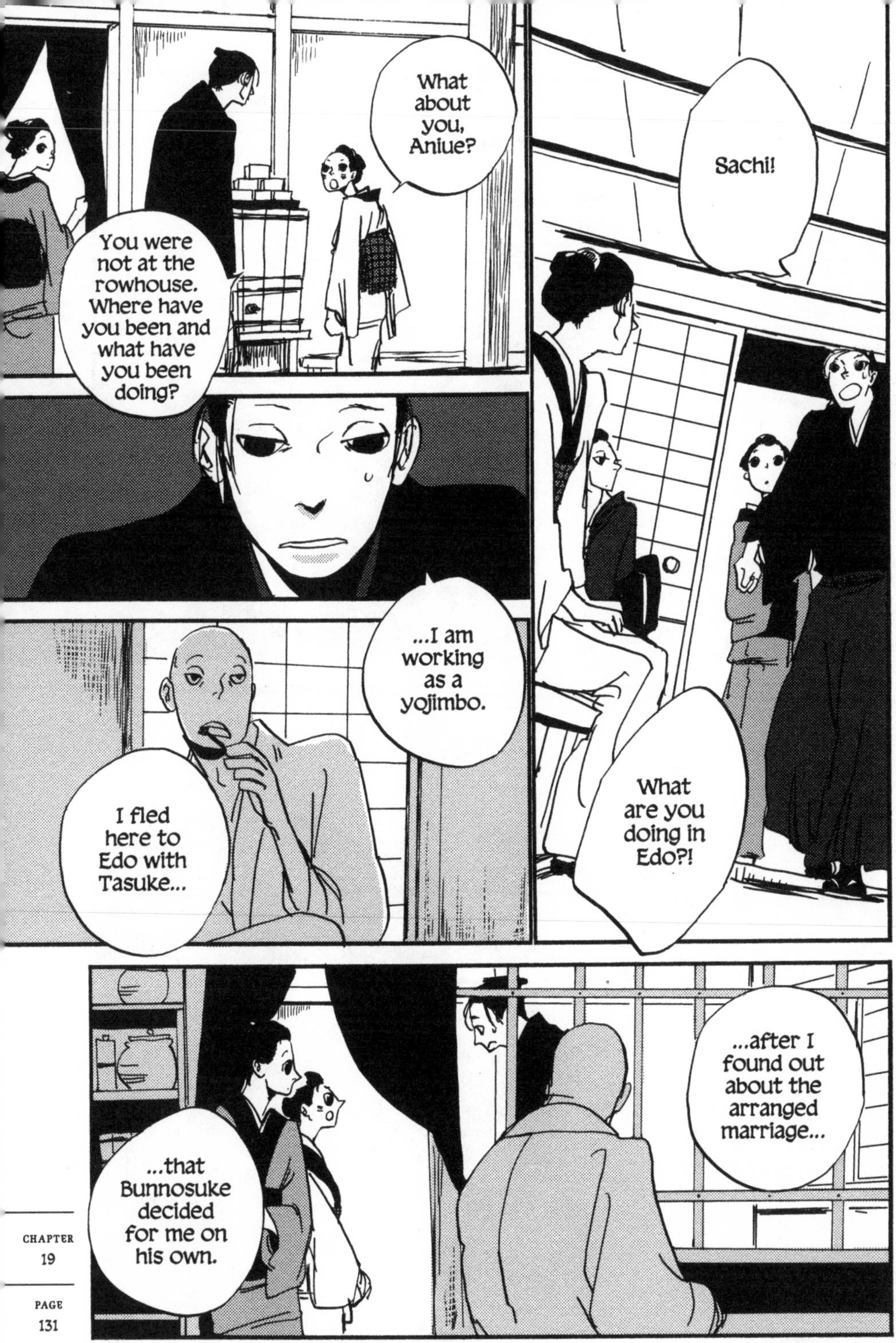
Sachi!
What are you doing in Edo?!
What about you, Aniue?
You were not at the rowhouse. Where have you been and what have you been doing?
...I am working as a yojimbo.
I fled here to Edo with Tasuke...
...after I found out about the arranged marriage...
...that Bunnosuke decided for me on his own.

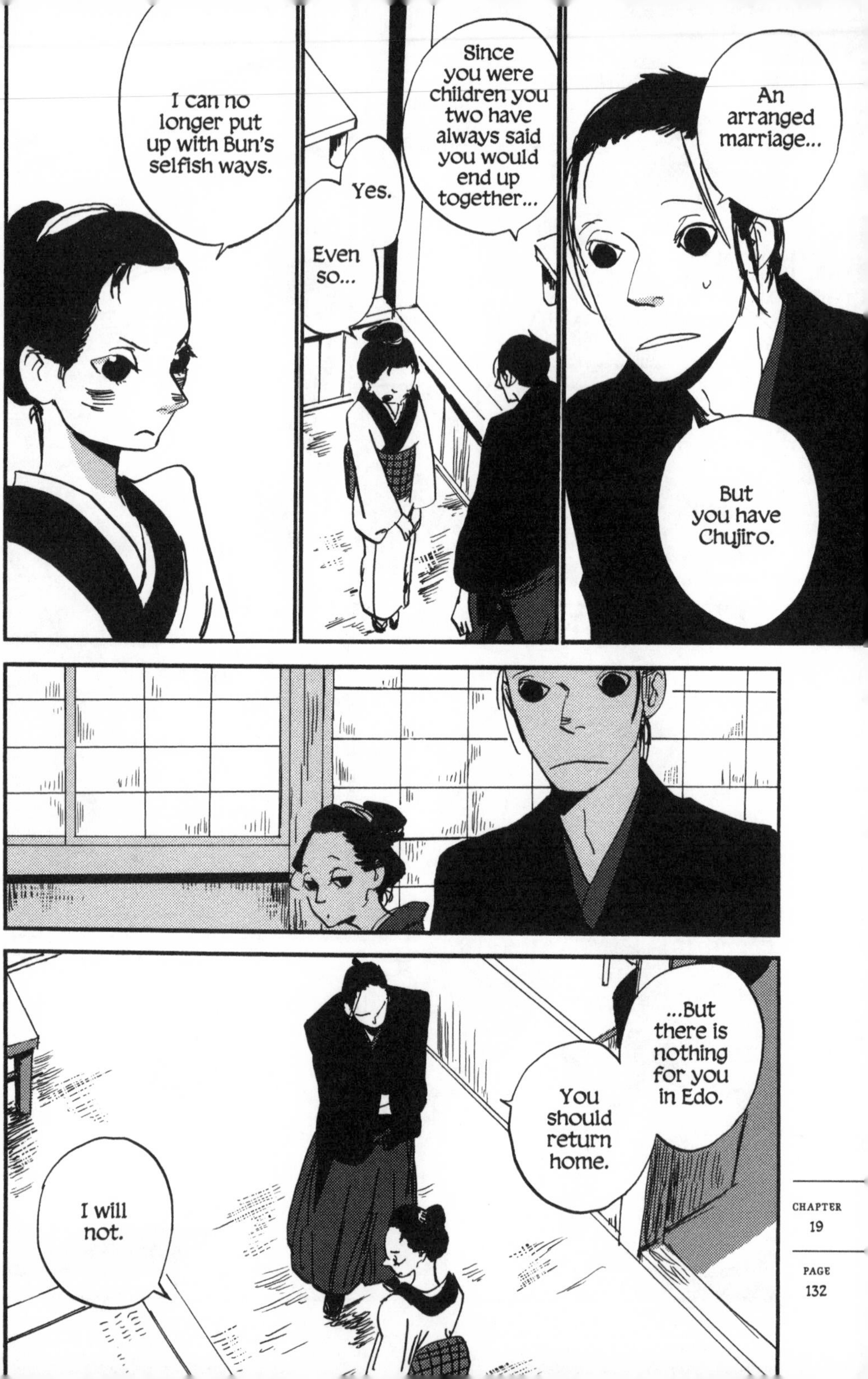
An arranged marriage...
But you have Chujiro.
Since you were children you two have always said you would end up together...
Yes.
Even so...
I can no longer put up with Bun's selfish ways.
...But there is nothing for you in Edo.
You should return home.
I will not.

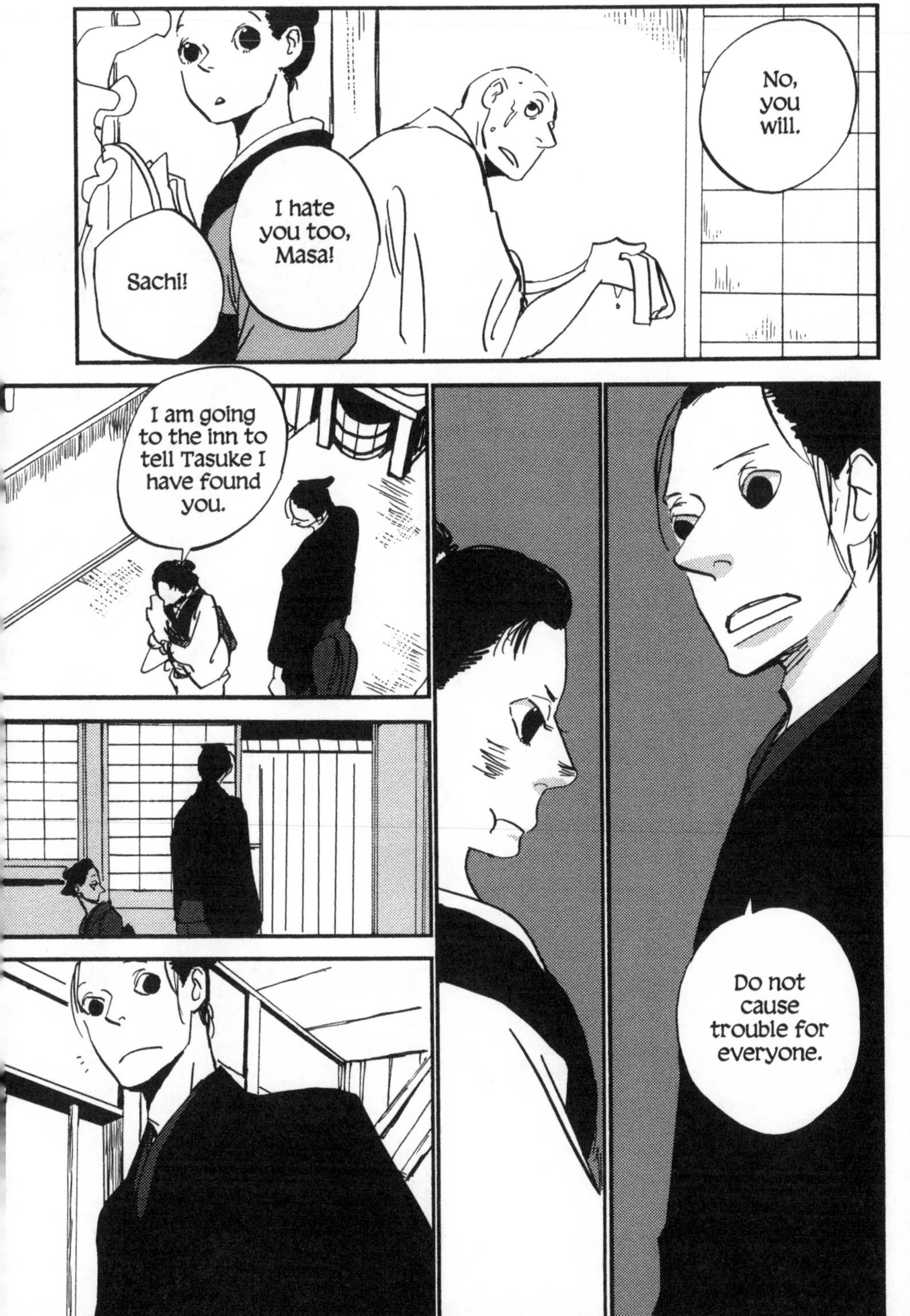
No, you will.
I hate you too, Masa!
Sachi!
Do not cause trouble for everyone.
I am going to the inn to tell Tasuke I have found you.

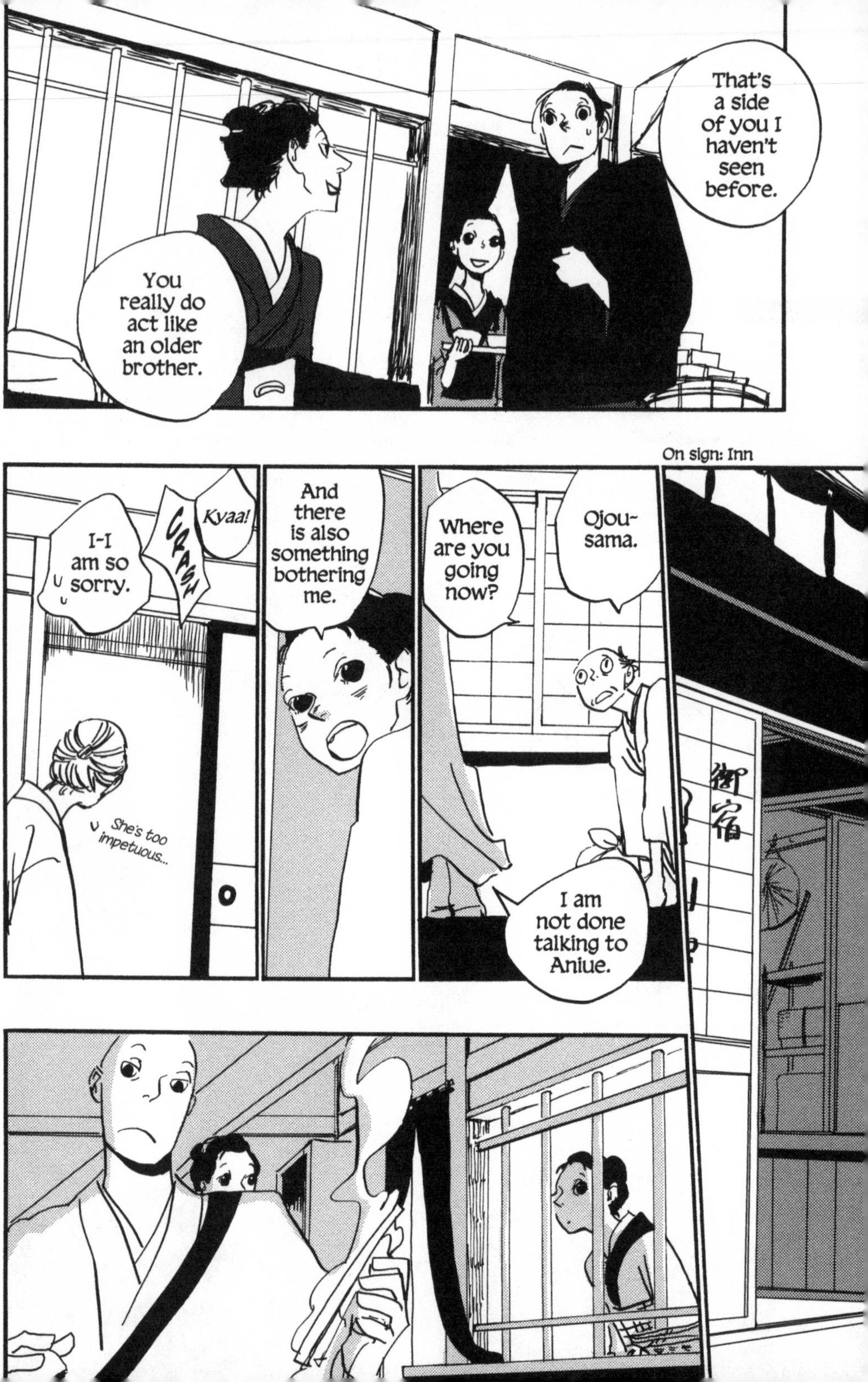
That's a side of you I haven't seen before.
You really do act like an older brother.
On sign: Inn
御宿
Ojou-sama.
Where are you going now?
I am not done talking to Aniue.
And there is also something bothering me.
Kyaa!
CRASH
I-I am so sorry.
She's too impetuous...

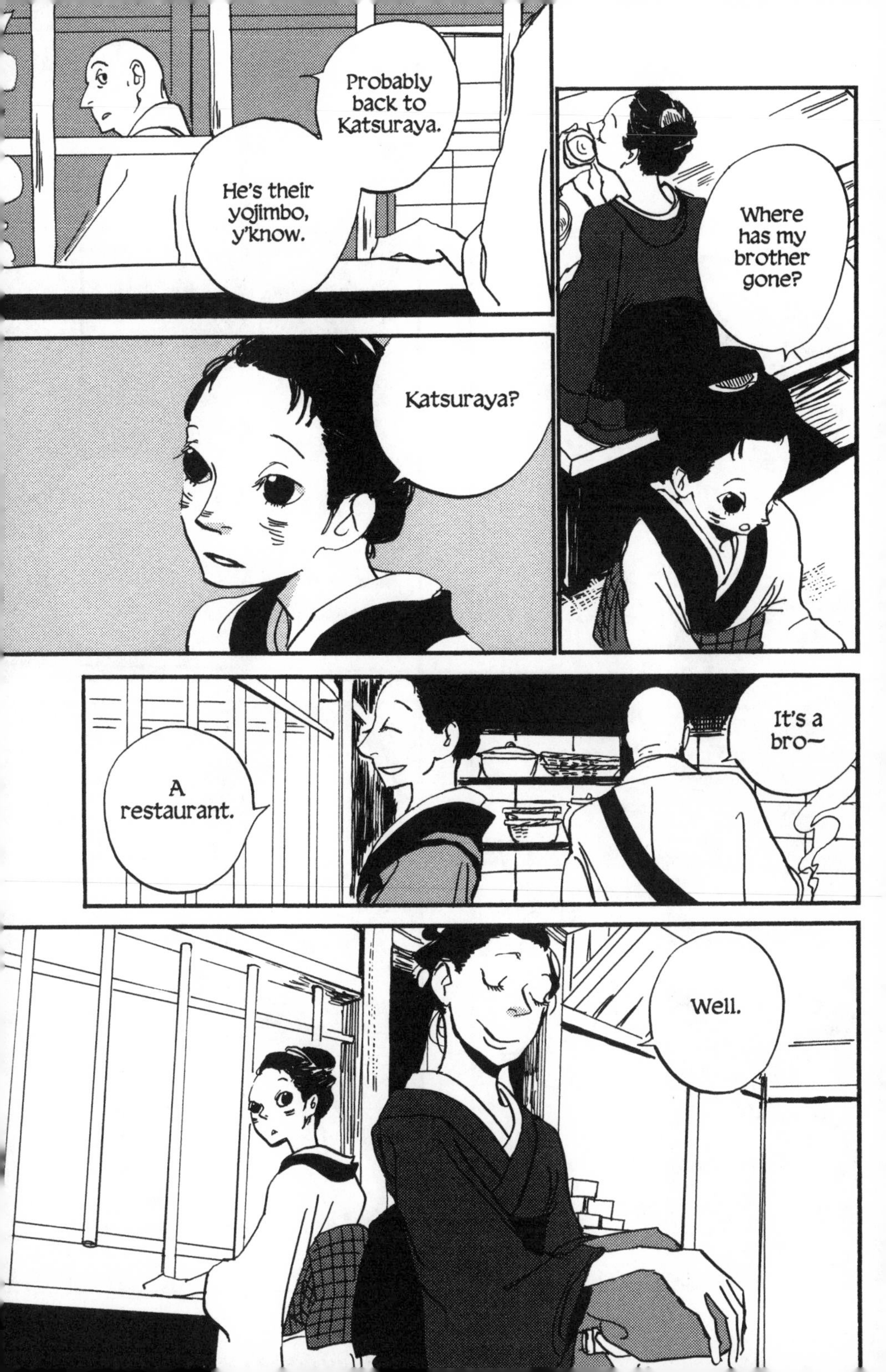
Where has my brother gone?
Probably back to Katsuraya.
He's their yojimbo, y'know.
Katsuraya?
It's a bro~
A restaurant.
Well.

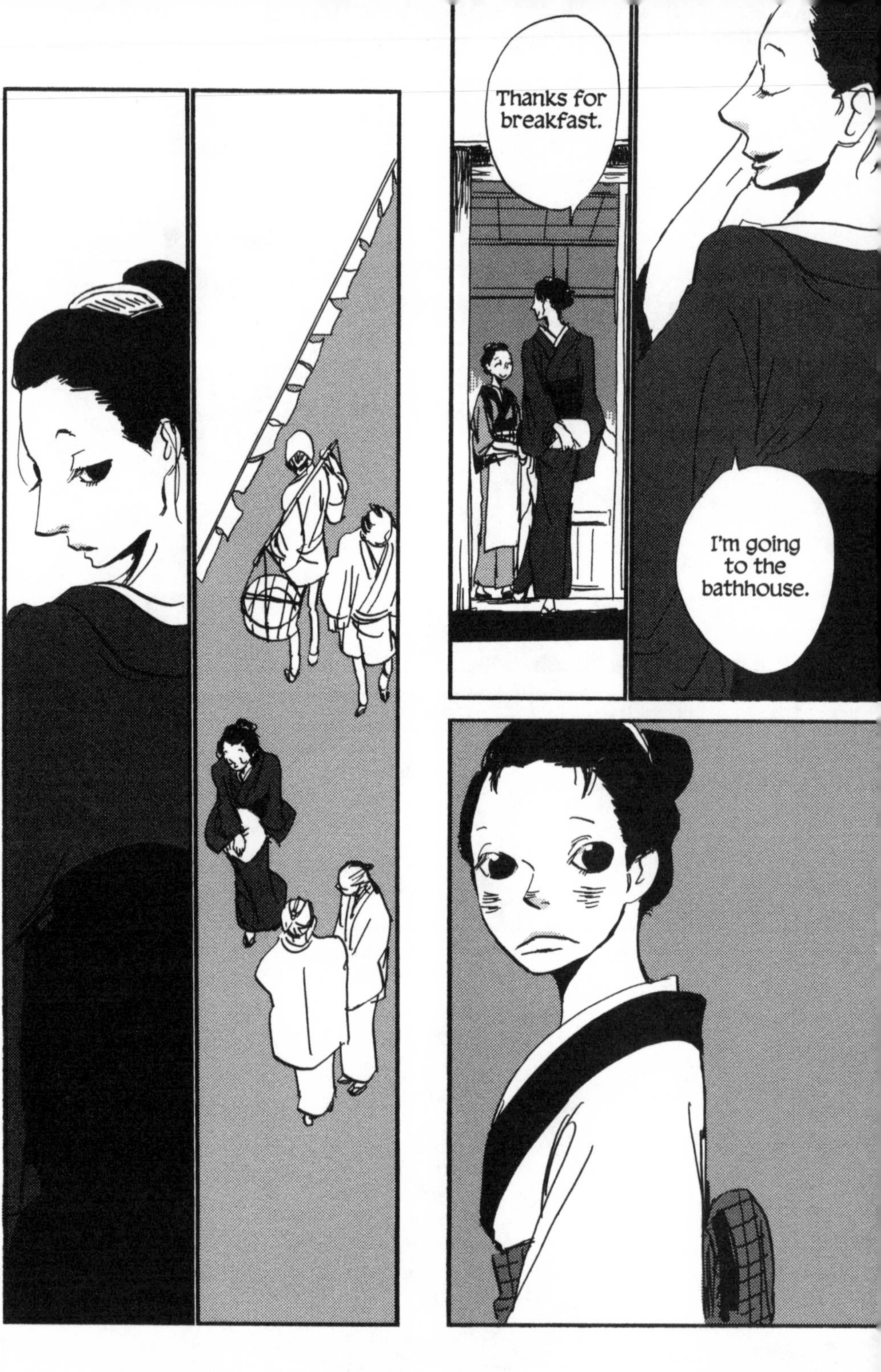
I'm going to the bathhouse.
Thanks for breakfast.

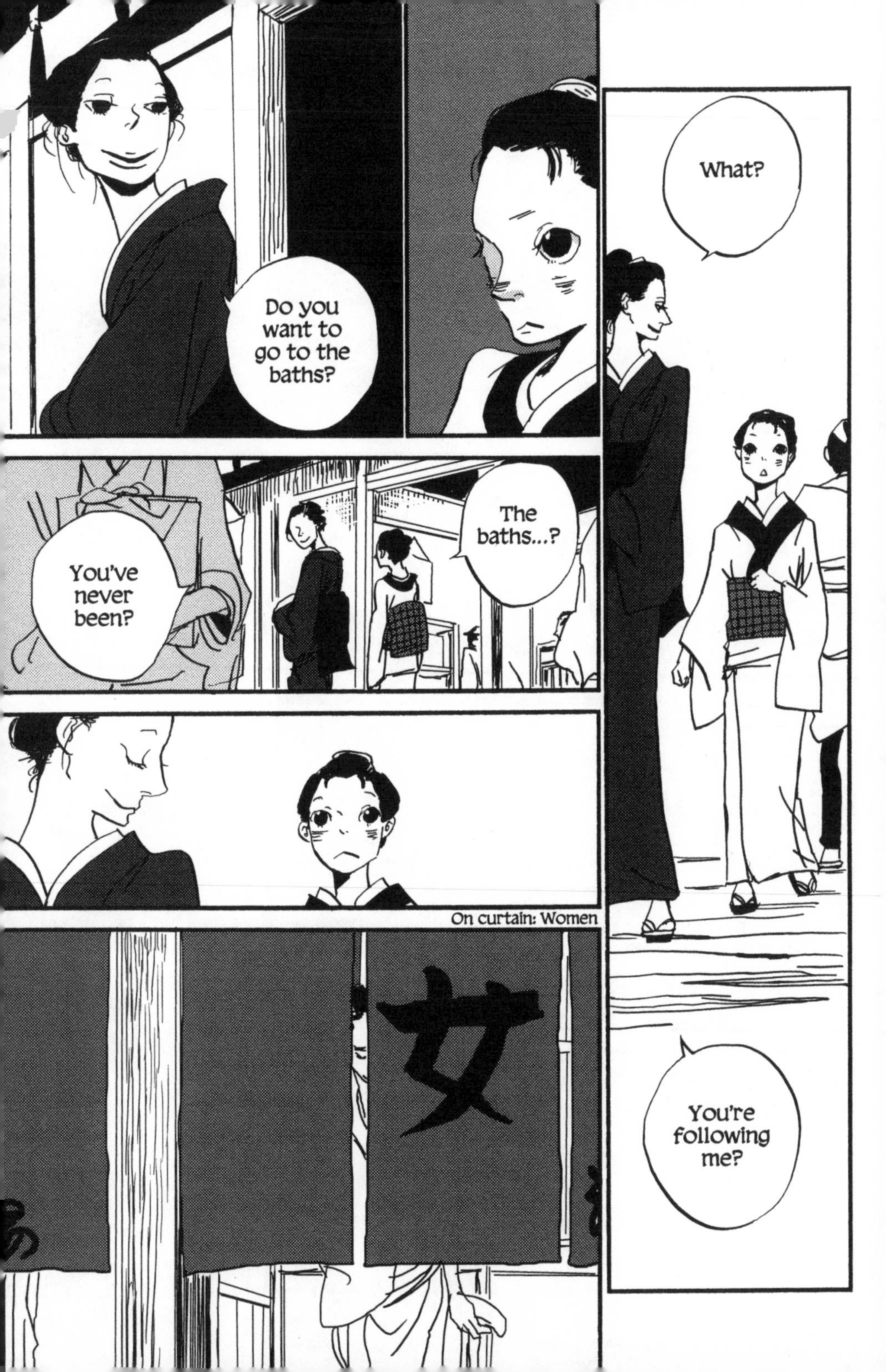
What?
You're following me?
Do you want to go to the baths?
The baths...?
You've never been?
On curtain: Women
女

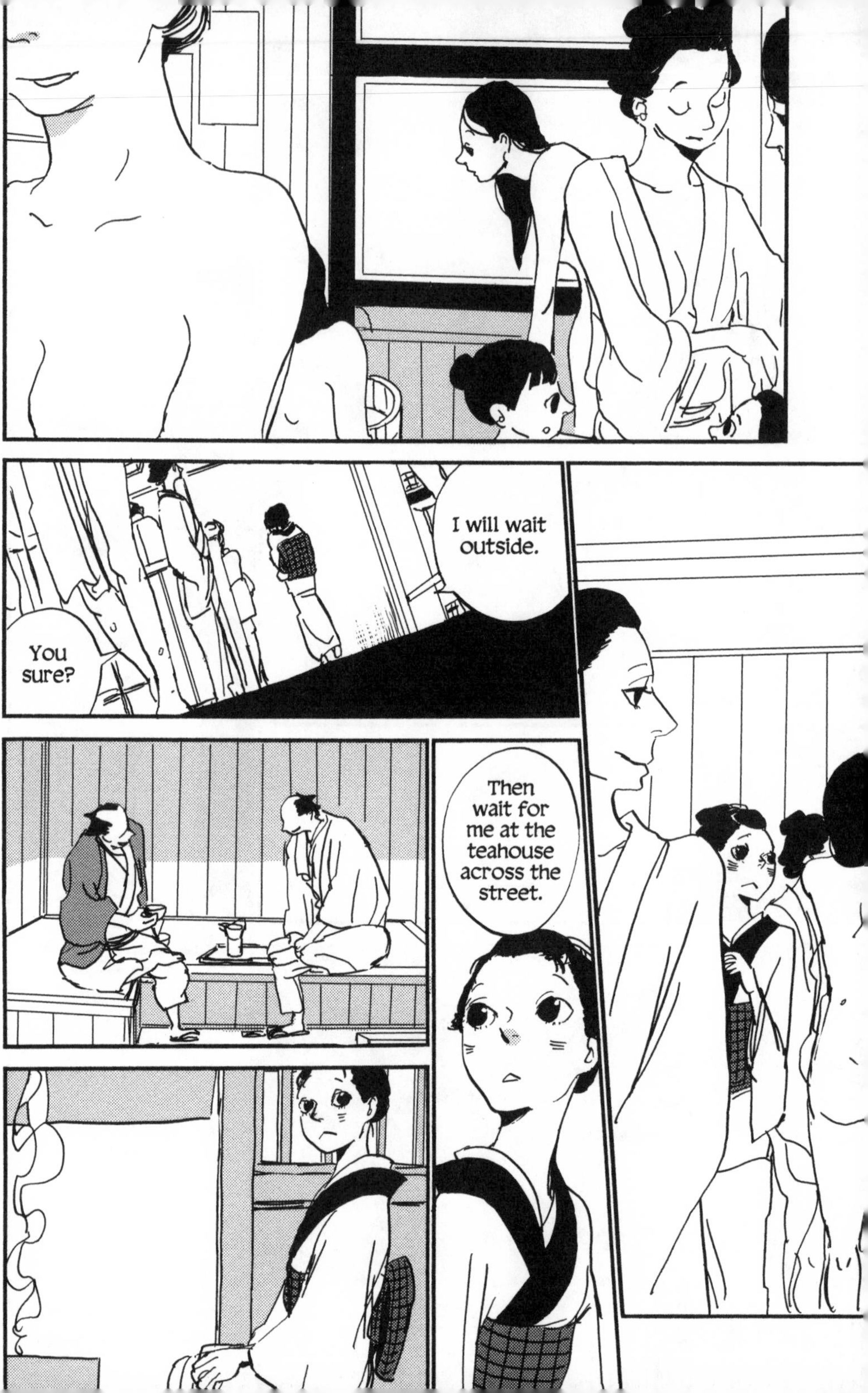
I will wait outside.
You sure?
Then wait for me at the teahouse across the street.

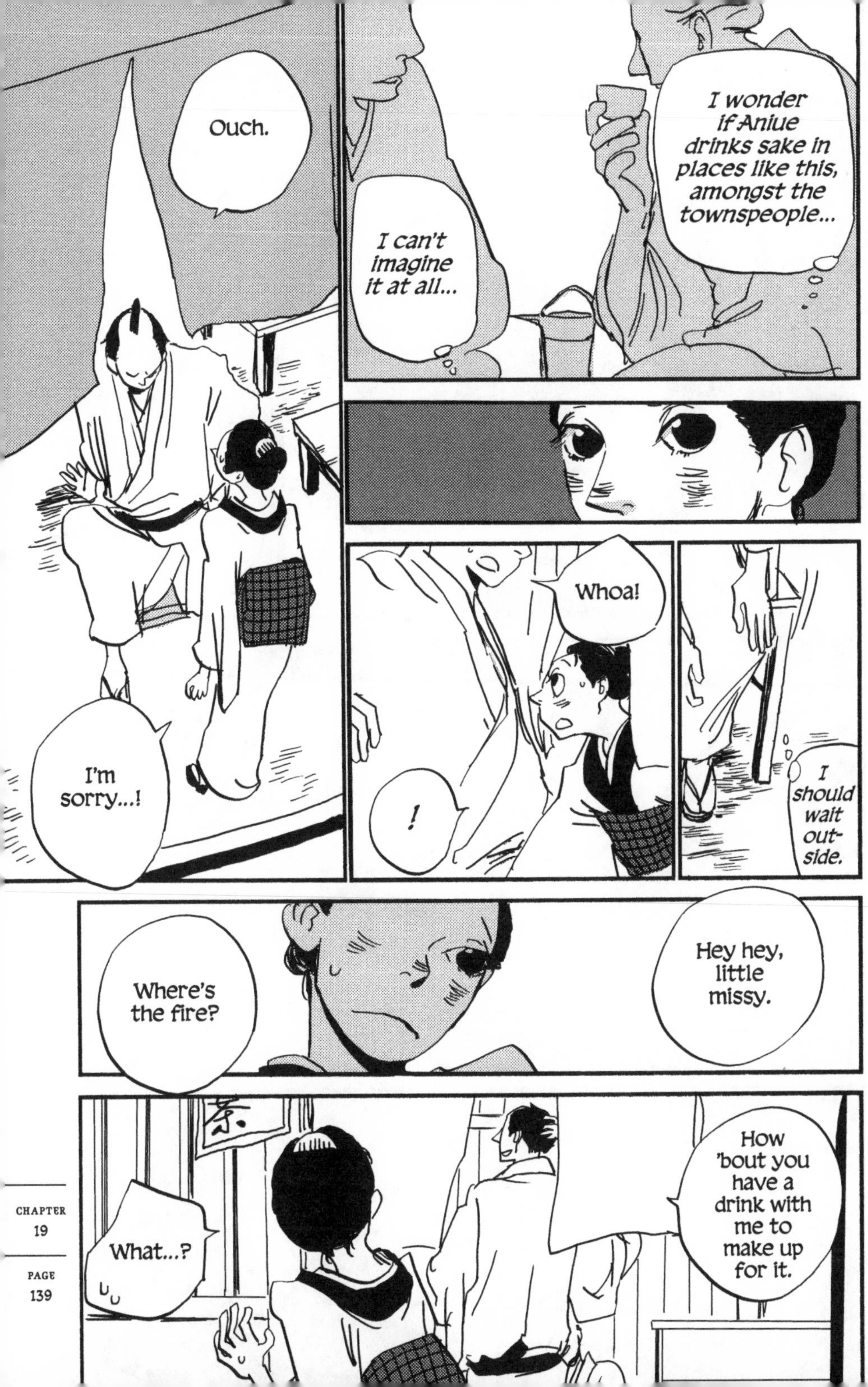
I wonder if Aniue drinks sake in places like this, amongst the townspeople...
I can't imagine it at all...
I should wait outside.
Whoa!
!
Ouch.
I'm sorry...!
Hey hey, little missy.
Where's the fire?
How 'bout you have a drink with me to make up for it.
What...?

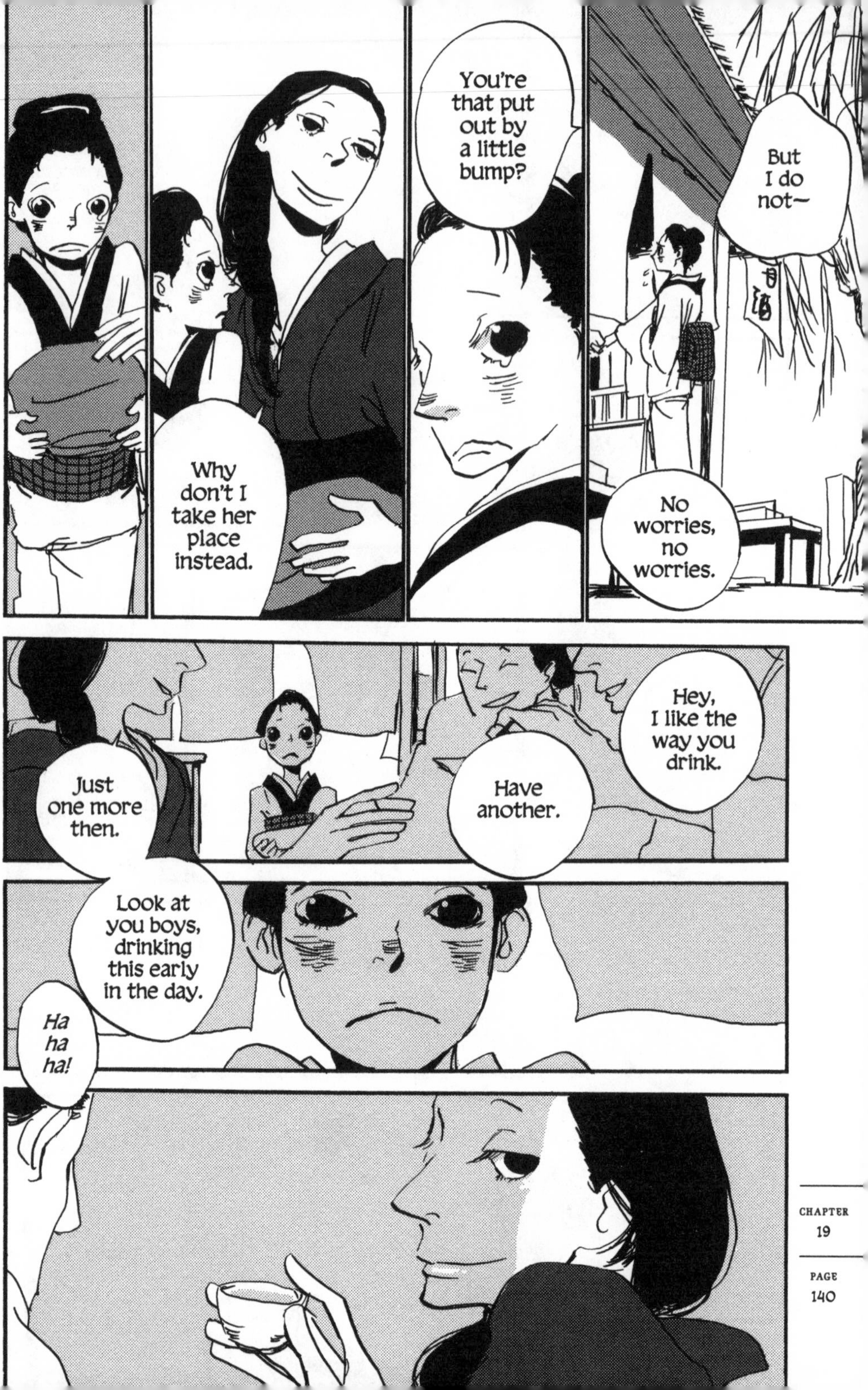

But I do not~
No worries, no worries.
You're that put out by a little bump?
Why don't I take her place instead.
Hey, I like the way you drink.
Have another.
Just one more then.
Look at you boys, drinking this early in the day.
Ha ha ha!

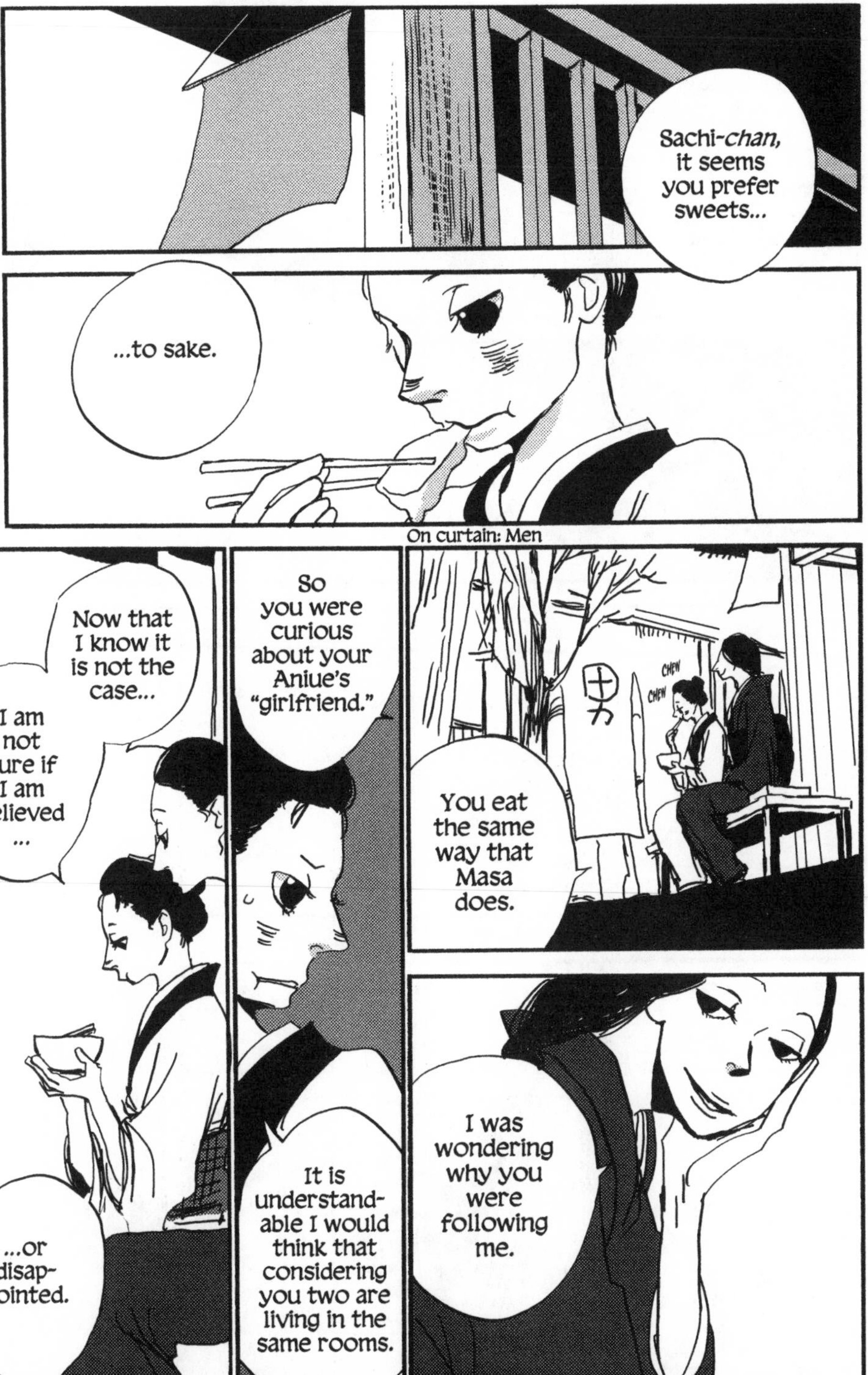
Sachi-*chan*, it seems you prefer sweets...
...to sake.
On curtain: Men
CHEW
CHEW
You eat the same way that Masa does.
I was wondering why you were following me.
So you were curious about your Aniue's "girlfriend."
It is understandable I would think that considering you two are living in the same rooms.
Now that I know it is not the case...
I am not sure if I am relieved ...
...or disappointed.

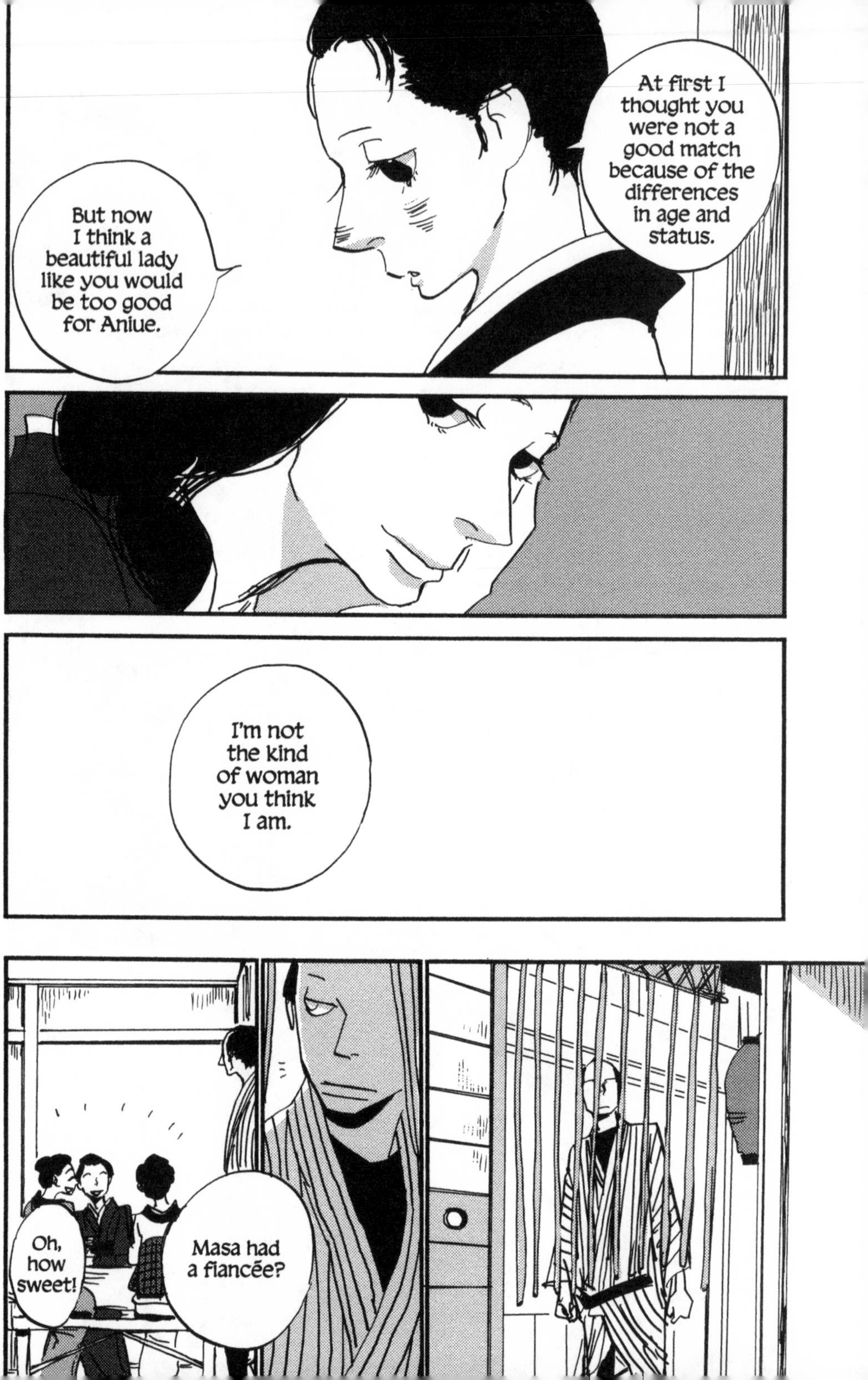
At first I thought you were not a good match because of the differences in age and status.
But now I think a beautiful lady like you would be too good for Aniue.
I'm not the kind of woman you think I am.
Masa had a fiancée?
Oh, how sweet!

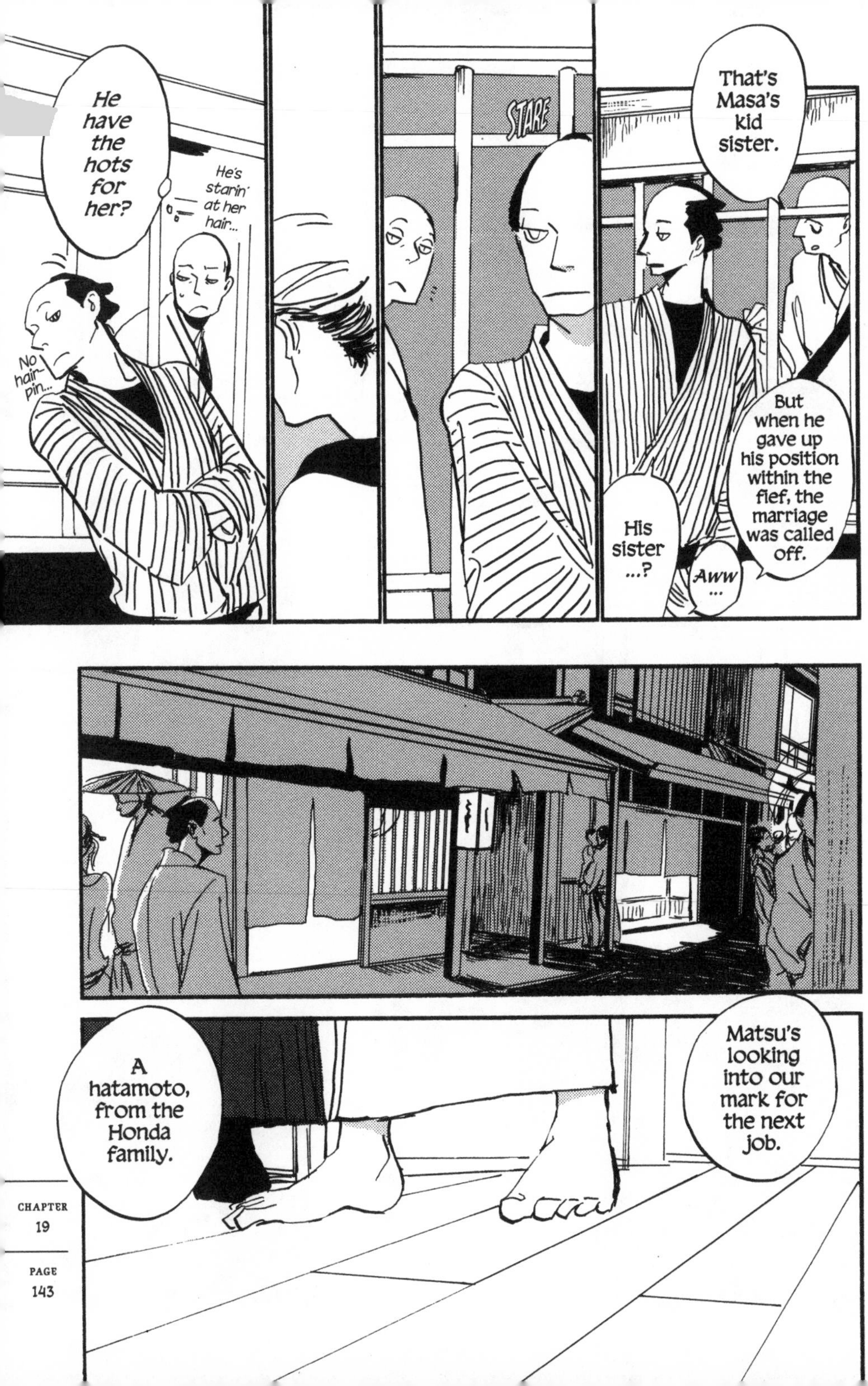
That's Masa's kid sister.
But when he gave up his position within the fief, the marriage was called off.
Aww...
His sister ...?
STARE
He have the hots for her?
He's starin' at her hair...
No hairpin...
Matsu's looking into our mark for the next job.
A hatamoto, from the Honda family.

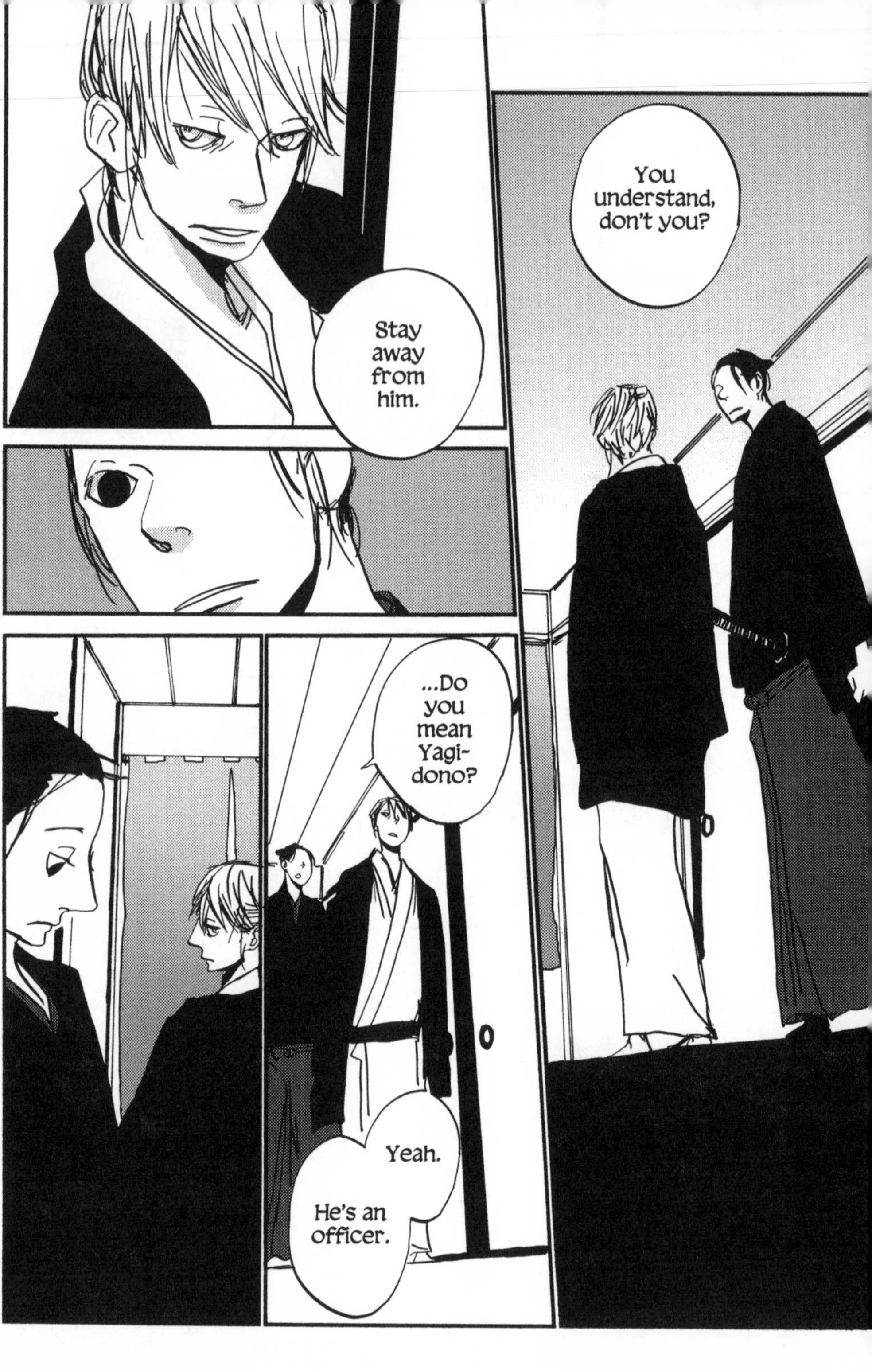
You understand, don't you?
Stay away from him.
...Do you mean Yagi-dono?
Yeah.
He's an officer.

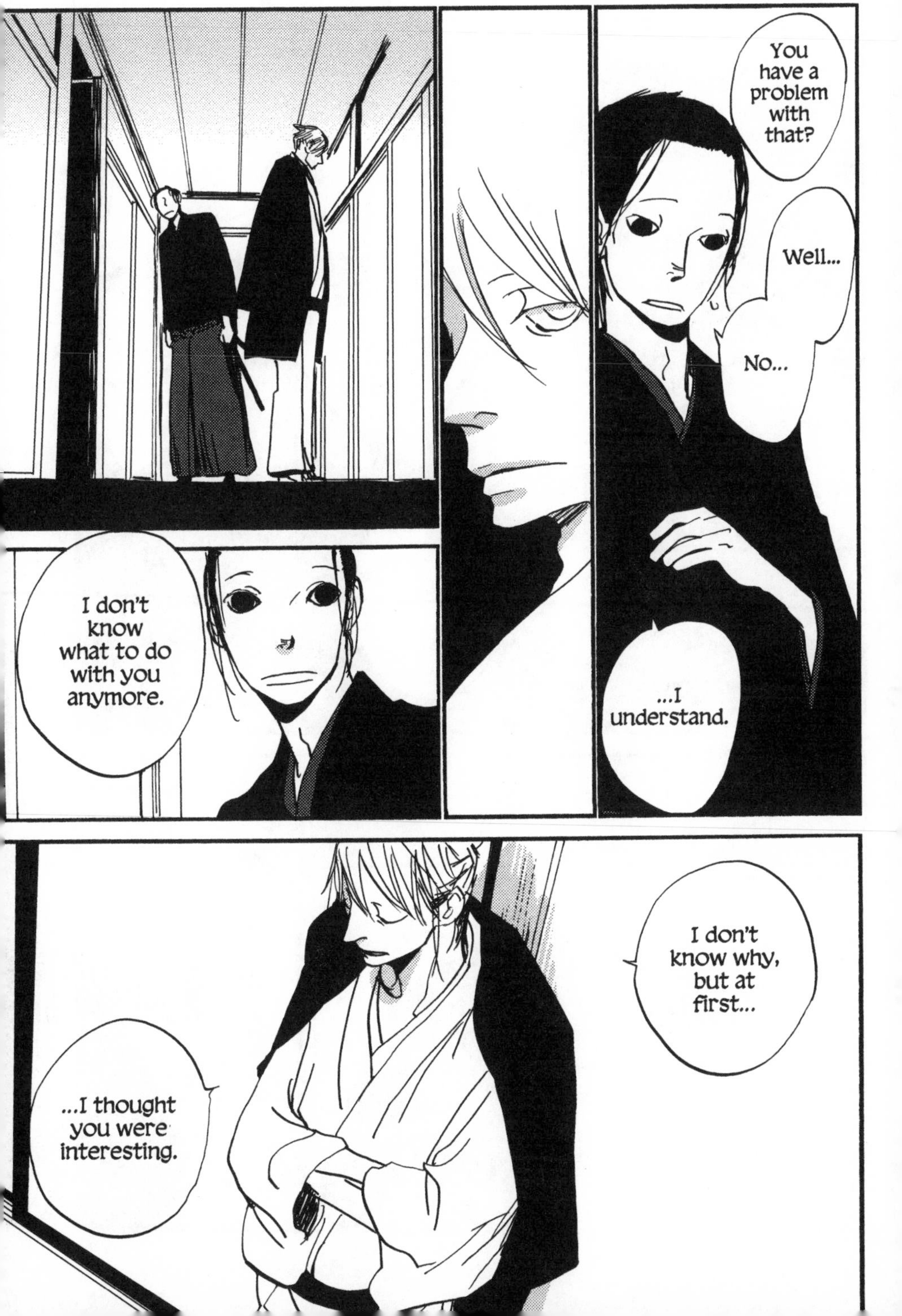
You have a problem with that?
Well...
No...
...I understand.
I don't know what to do with you anymore.
I don't know why, but at first...
...I thought you were interesting.

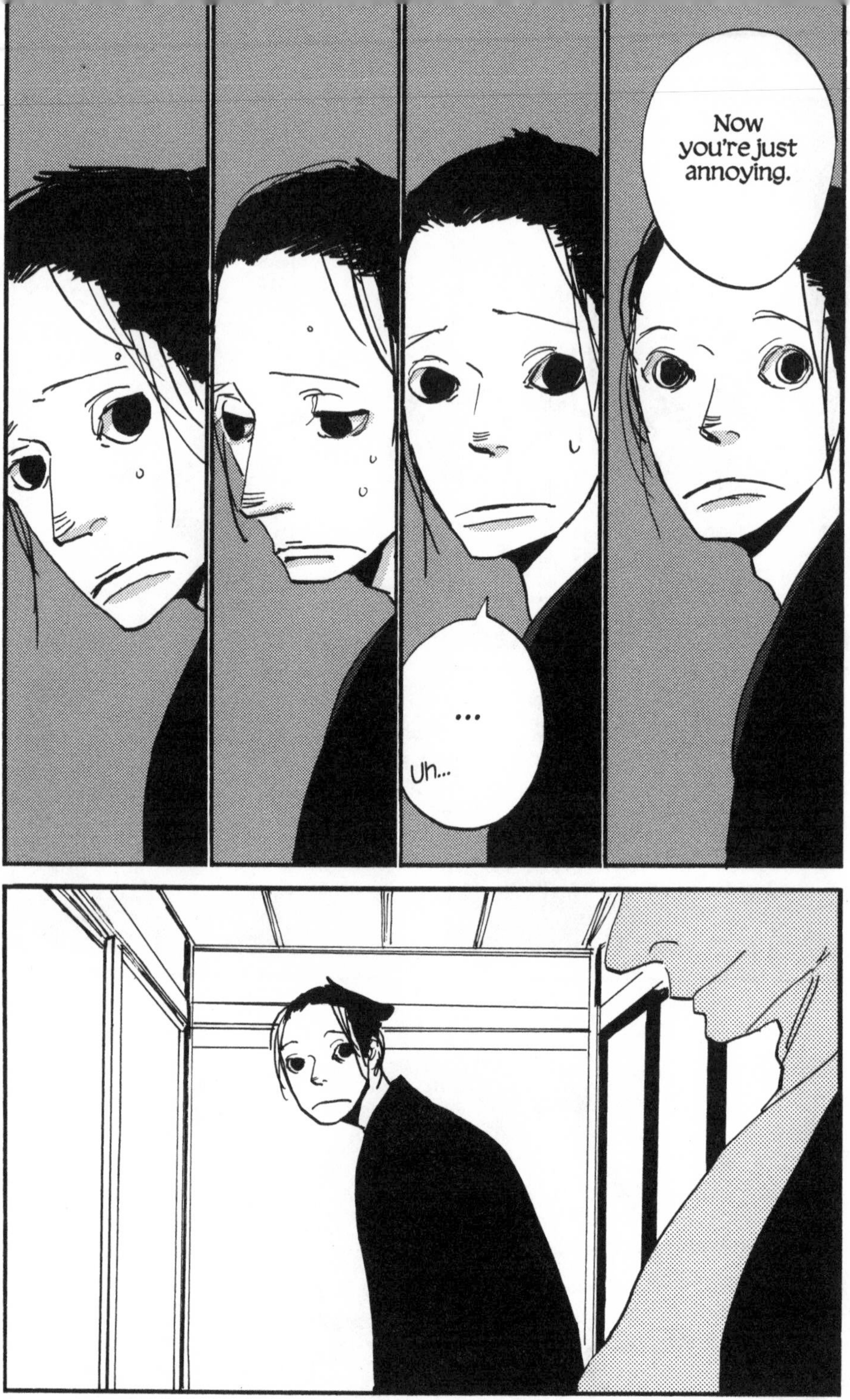
Now you're just annoying.
...
Uh...

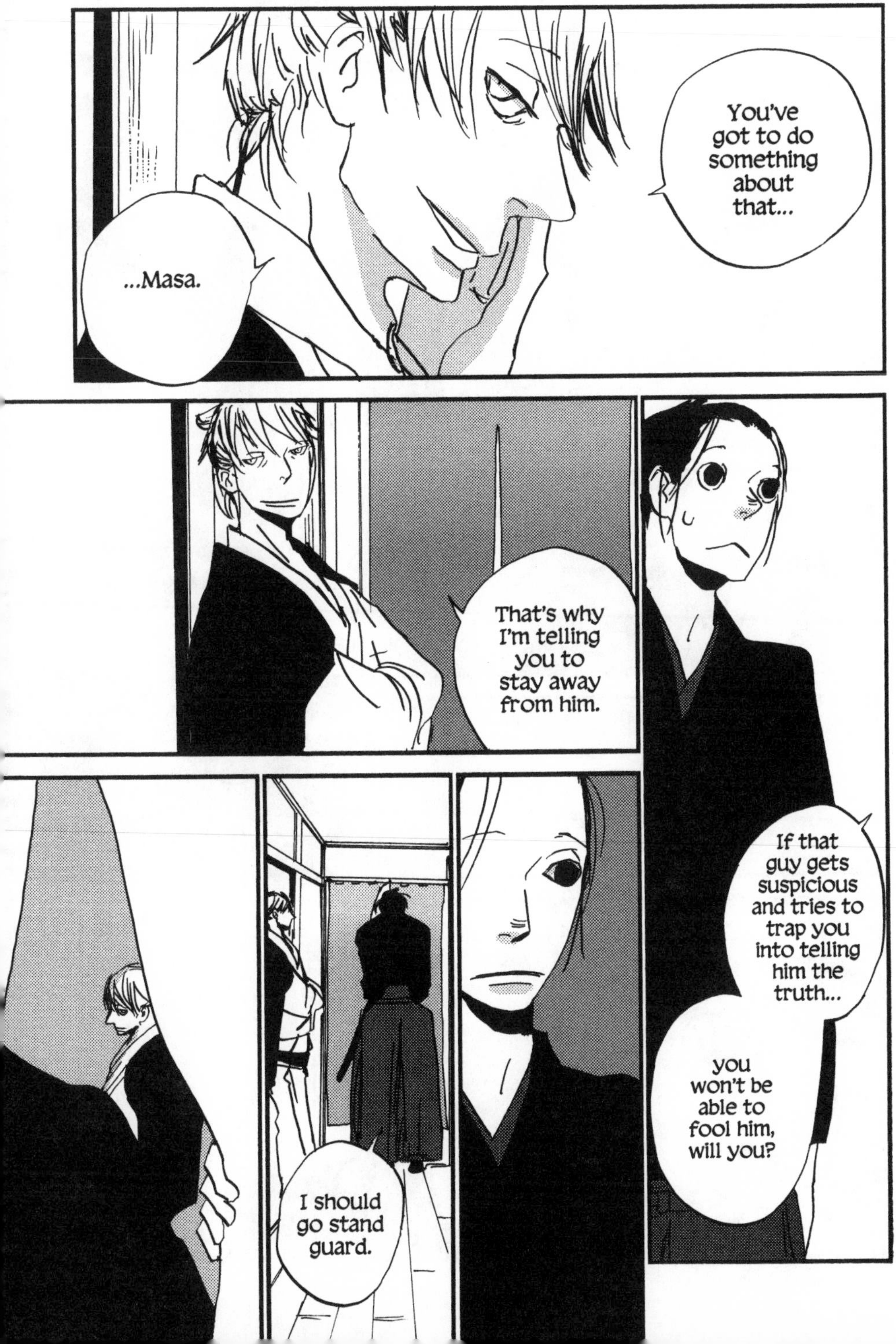
You've got to do something about that...
...Masa.
If that guy gets suspicious and tries to trap you into telling him the truth...
you won't be able to fool him, will you?
That's why I'm telling you to stay away from him.
I should go stand guard.

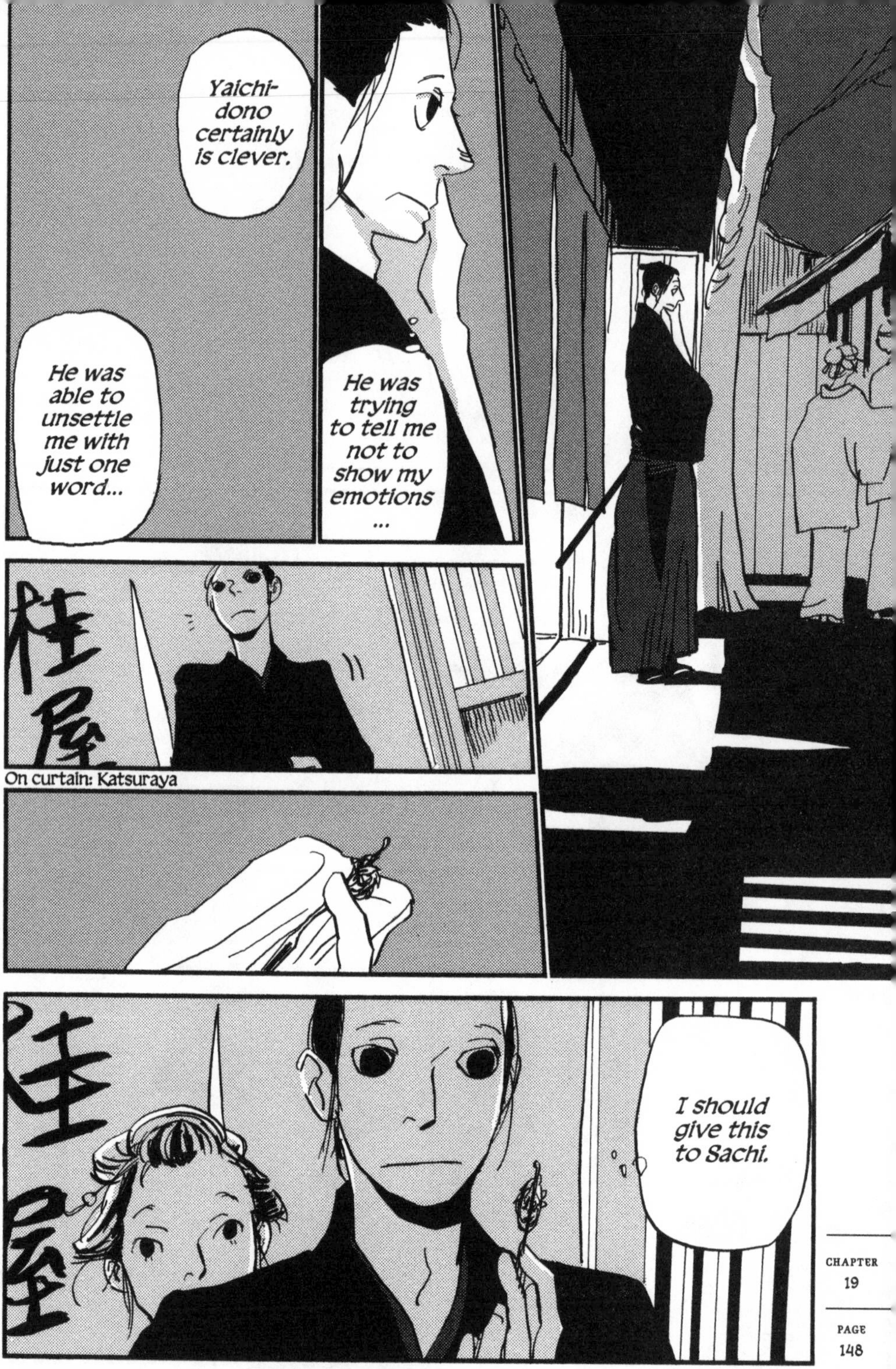
He was trying to tell me not to show my emotions ...
Yaichi-dono certainly is clever.
He was able to unsettle me with just one word...
On curtain: Katsuraya
I should give this to Sachi.

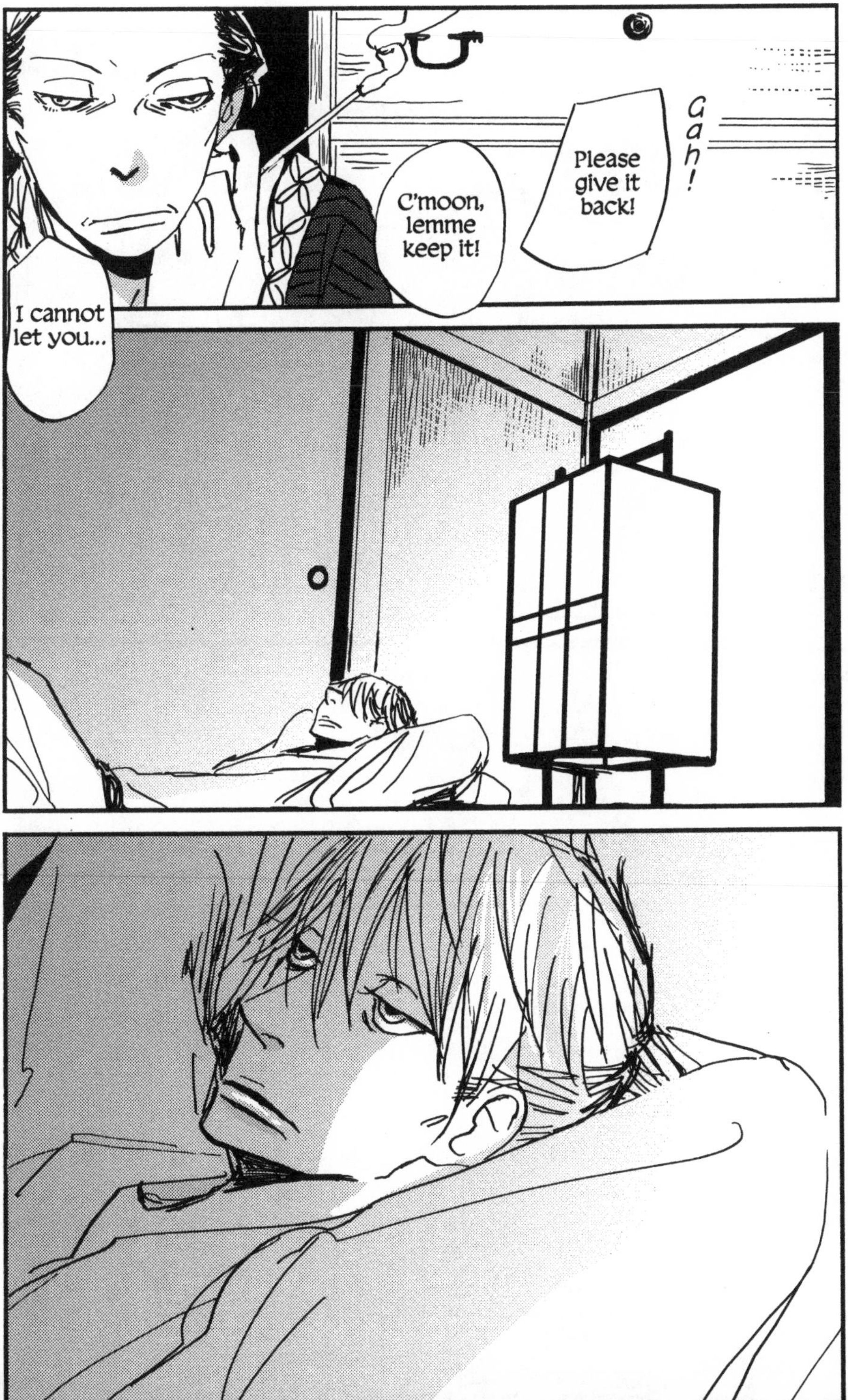
Gah!
Please give it back!
C'moon, lemme keep it!
I cannot let you...

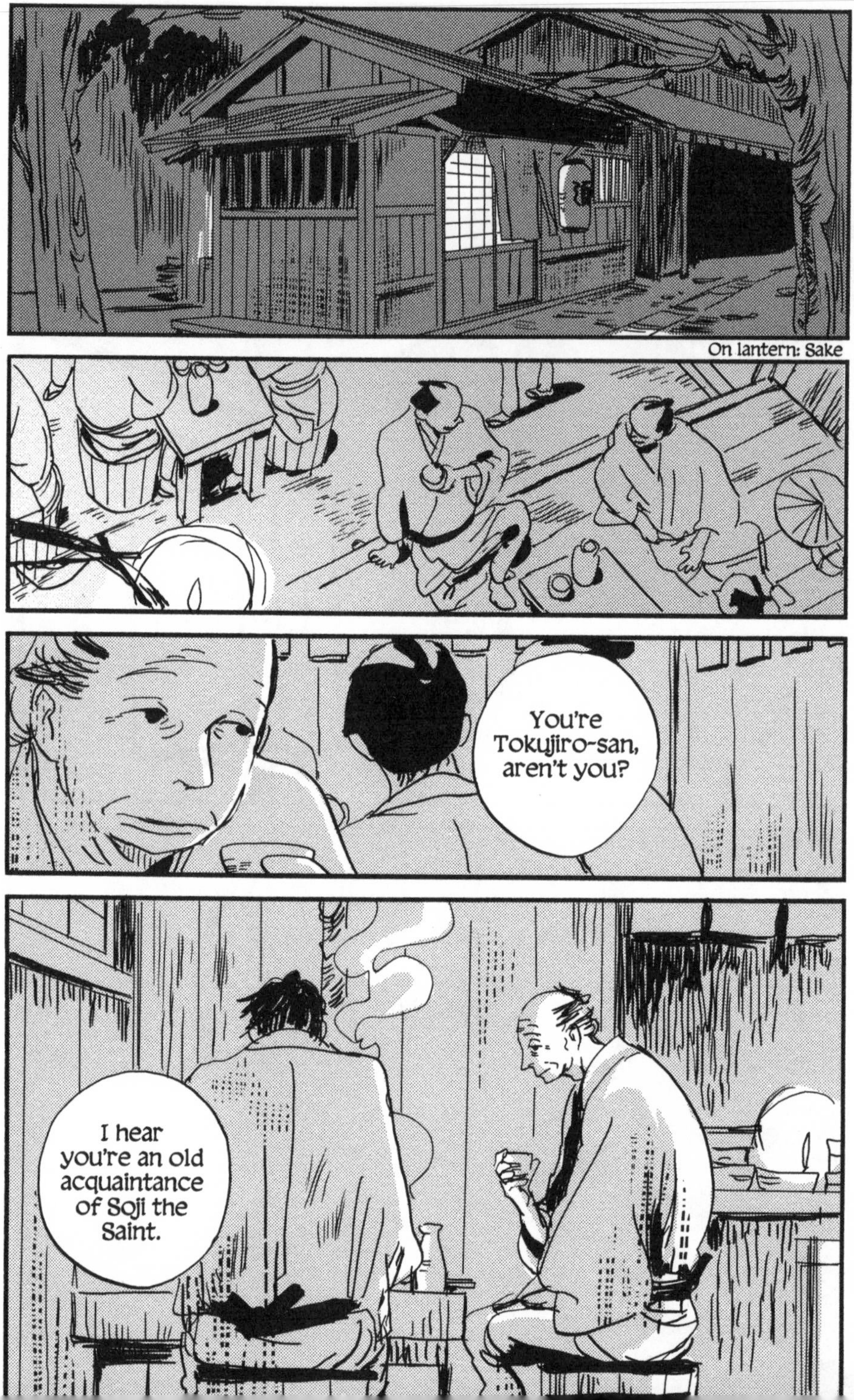
On lantern: Sake
You're Tokujiro-san, aren't you?
I hear you're an old acquaintance of Soji the Saint.

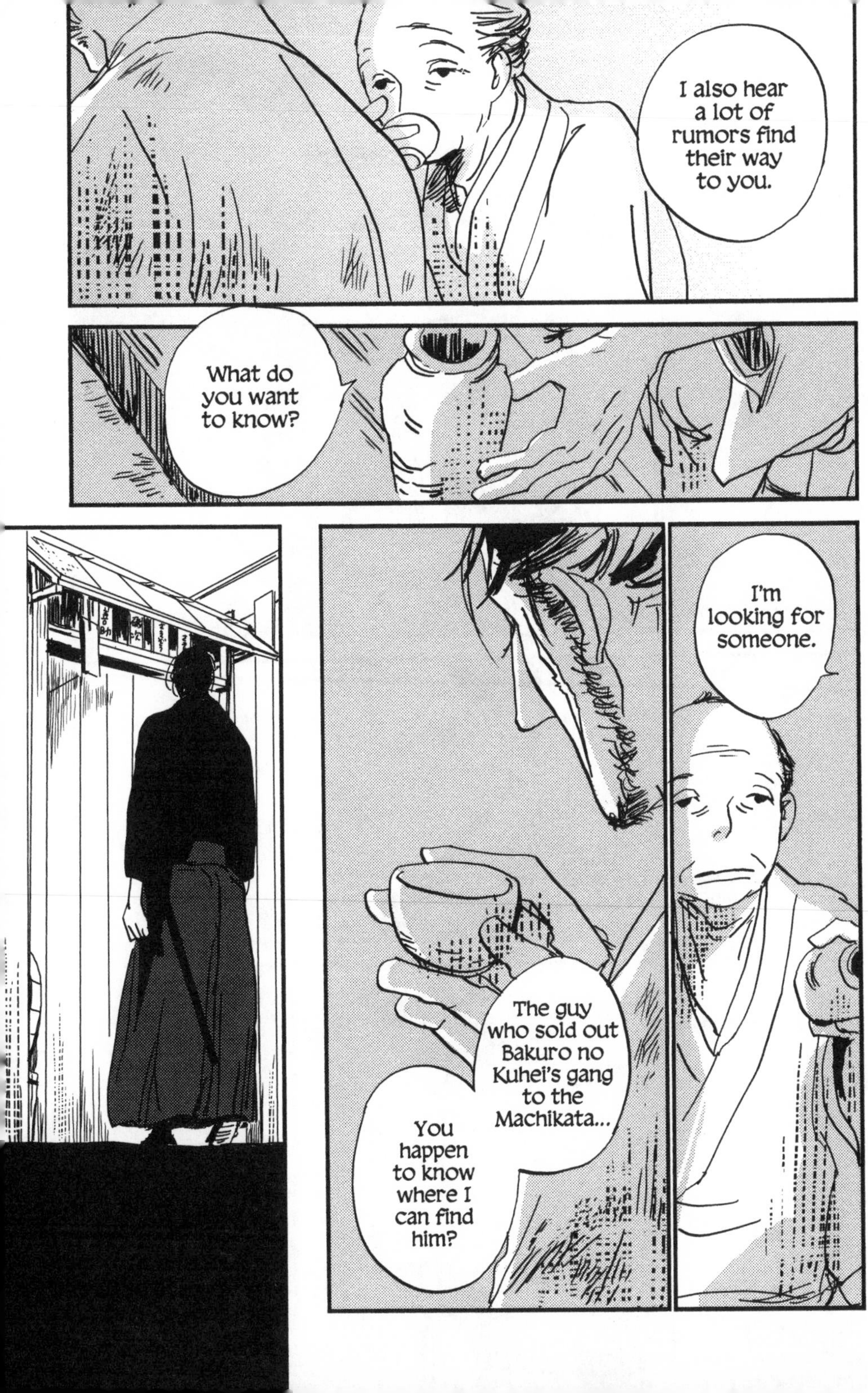
I also hear a lot of rumors find their way to you.
What do you want to know?
I'm looking for someone.
The guy who sold out Bakuro no Kuhei's gang to the Machikata...
You happen to know where I can find him?

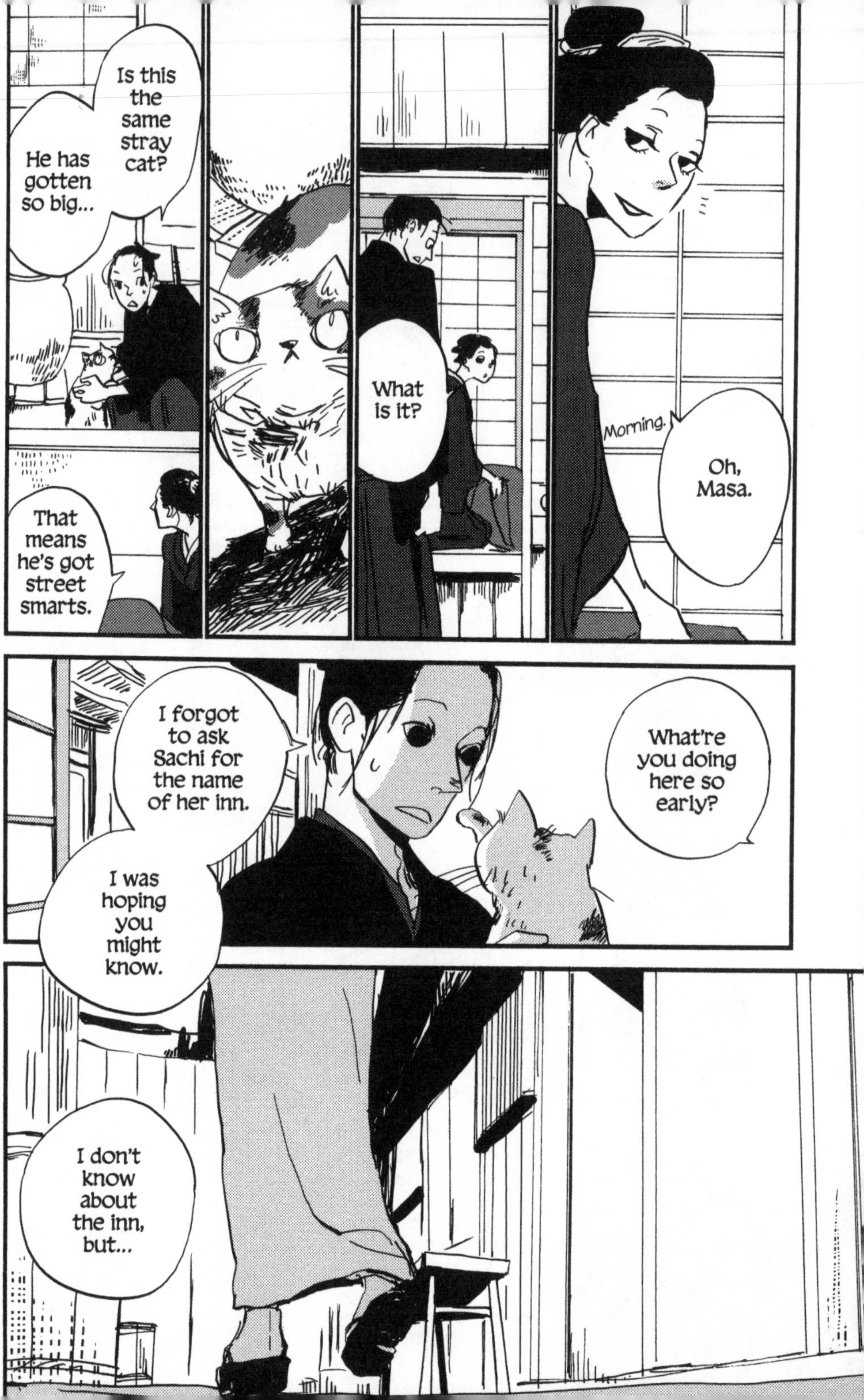
Oh, Masa.
Morning.
What is it?
Is this the same stray cat?
He has gotten so big...
That means he's got street smarts.
What're you doing here so early?
I forgot to ask Sachi for the name of her inn.
I was hoping you might know.
I don't know about the inn, but...

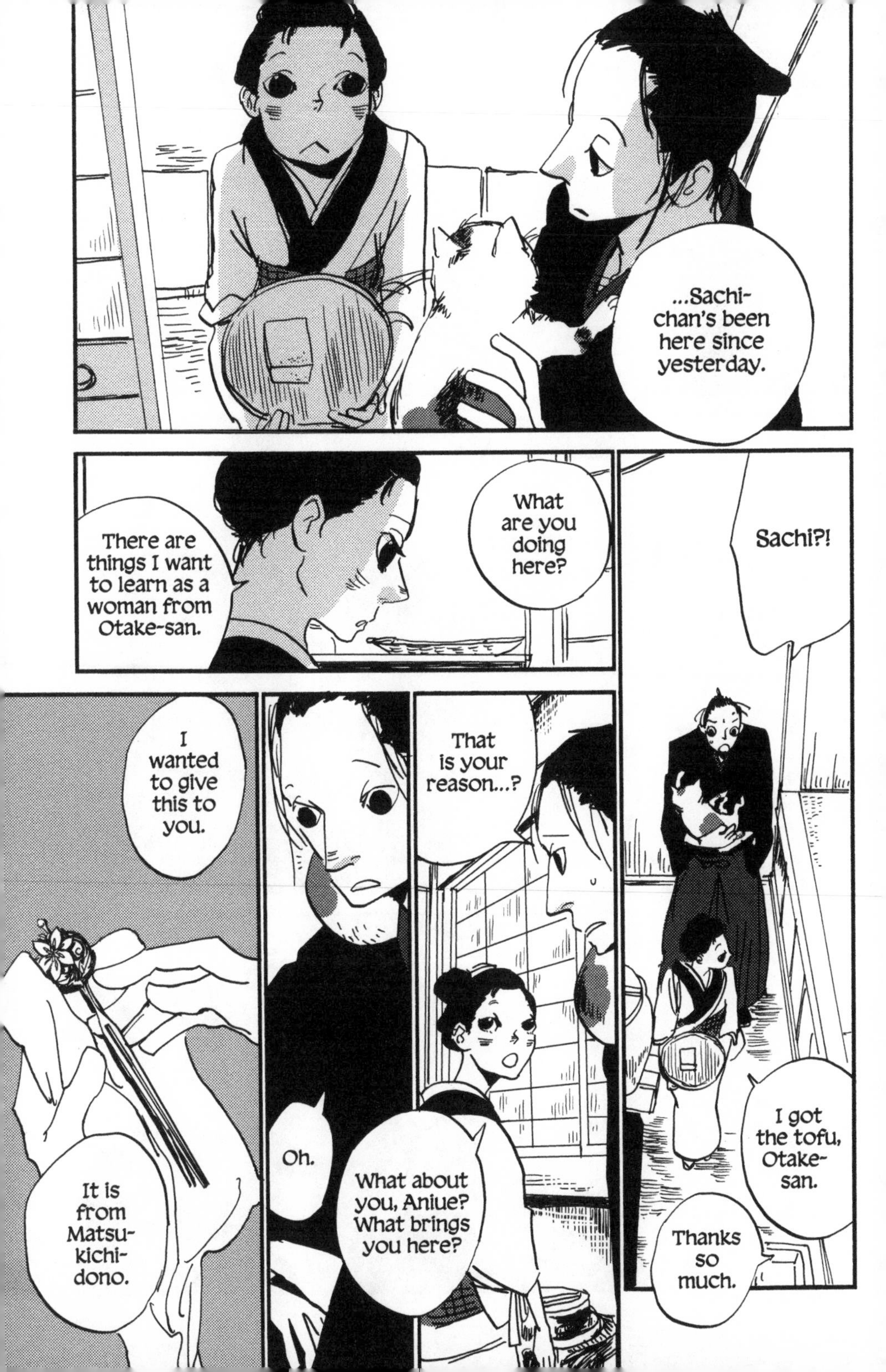
...Sachi-chan's been here since yesterday.
Sachi?!
I got the tofu, Otake-san.
Thanks so much.
What are you doing here?
There are things I want to learn as a woman from Otake-san.
That is your reason...?
Oh.
What about you, Aniue? What brings you here?
I wanted to give this to you.
It is from Matsukichi-dono.

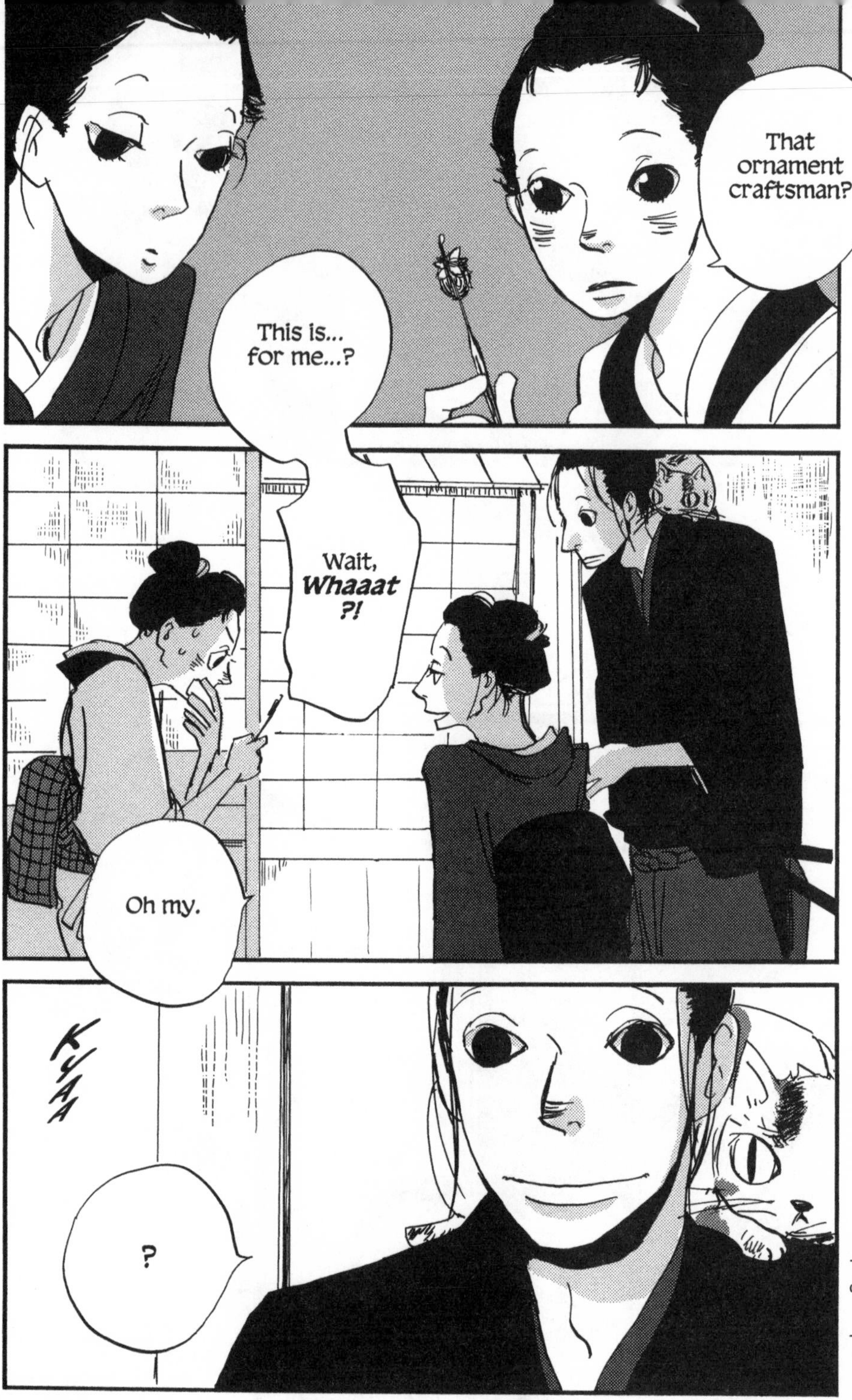
That ornament craftsman?
This is... for me...?
Wait, **Whaaat ?!**
Oh my.
KYAA
?

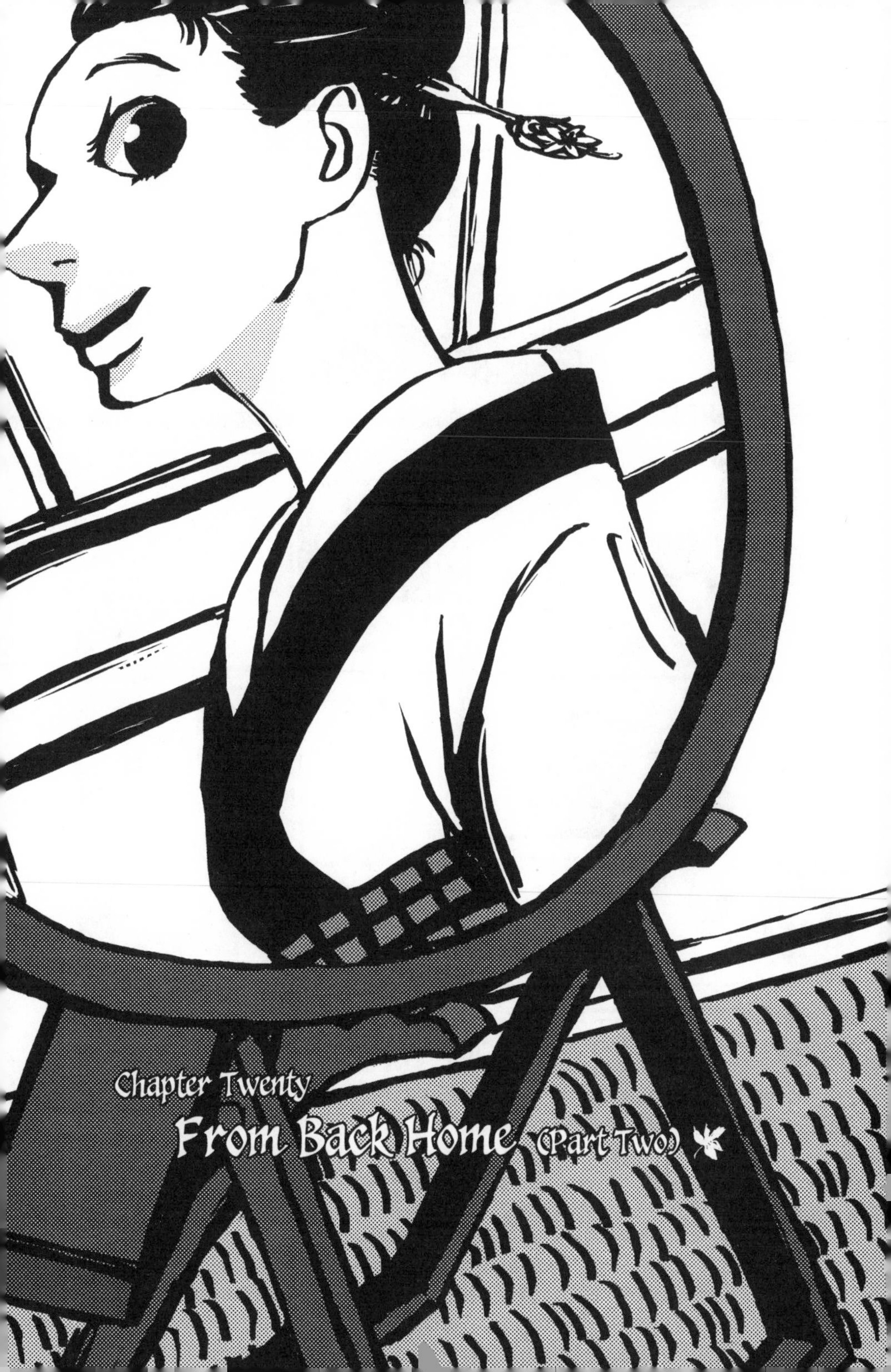
Chapter Twenty
From Back Home (Part Two)

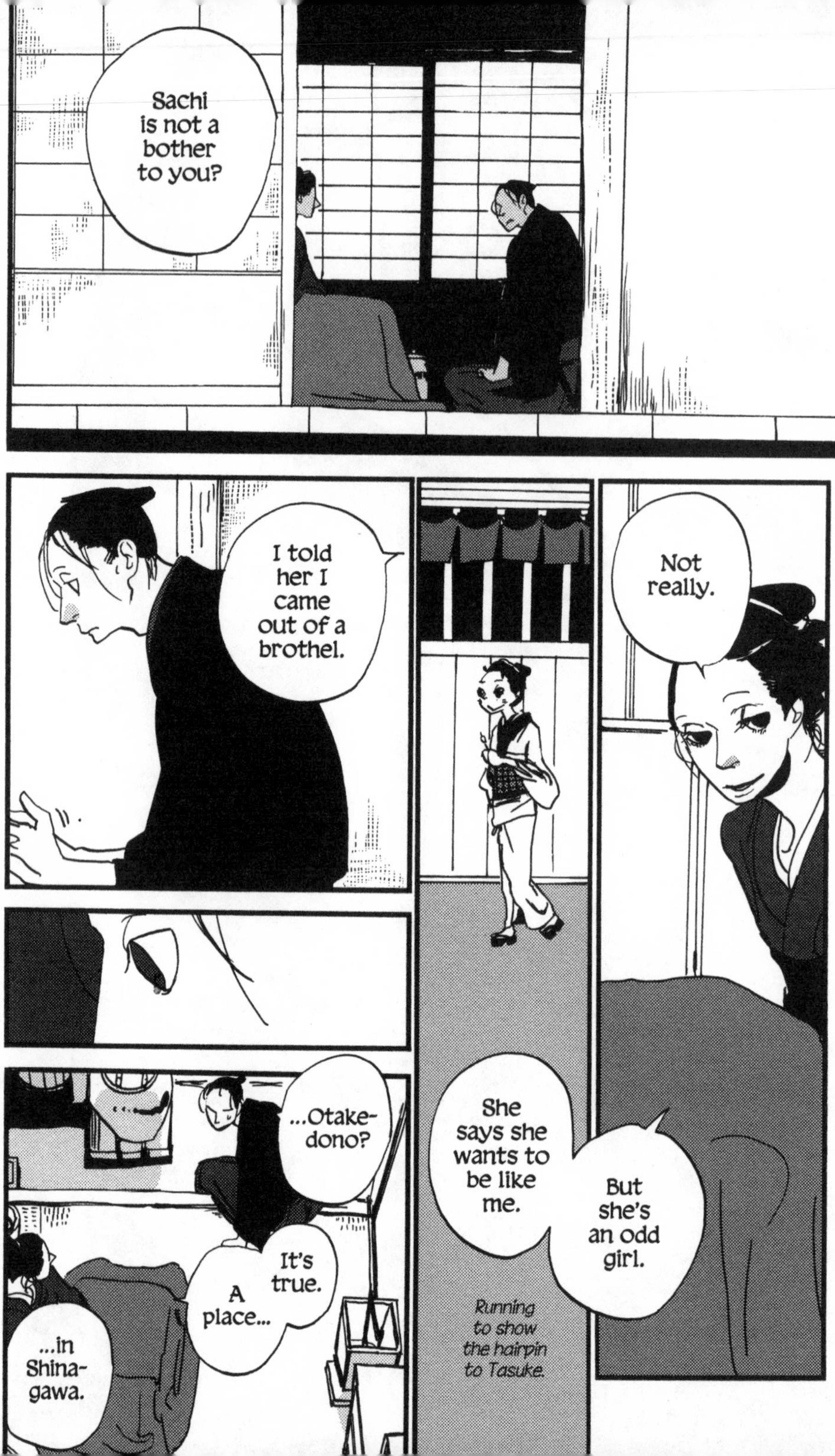
Sachi is not a bother to you?
Not really.
She says she wants to be like me.
But she's an odd girl.
Running to show the hairpin to Tasuke.
I told her I came out of a brothel.
...Otake-dono?
It's true.
A place...
...in Shinagawa.

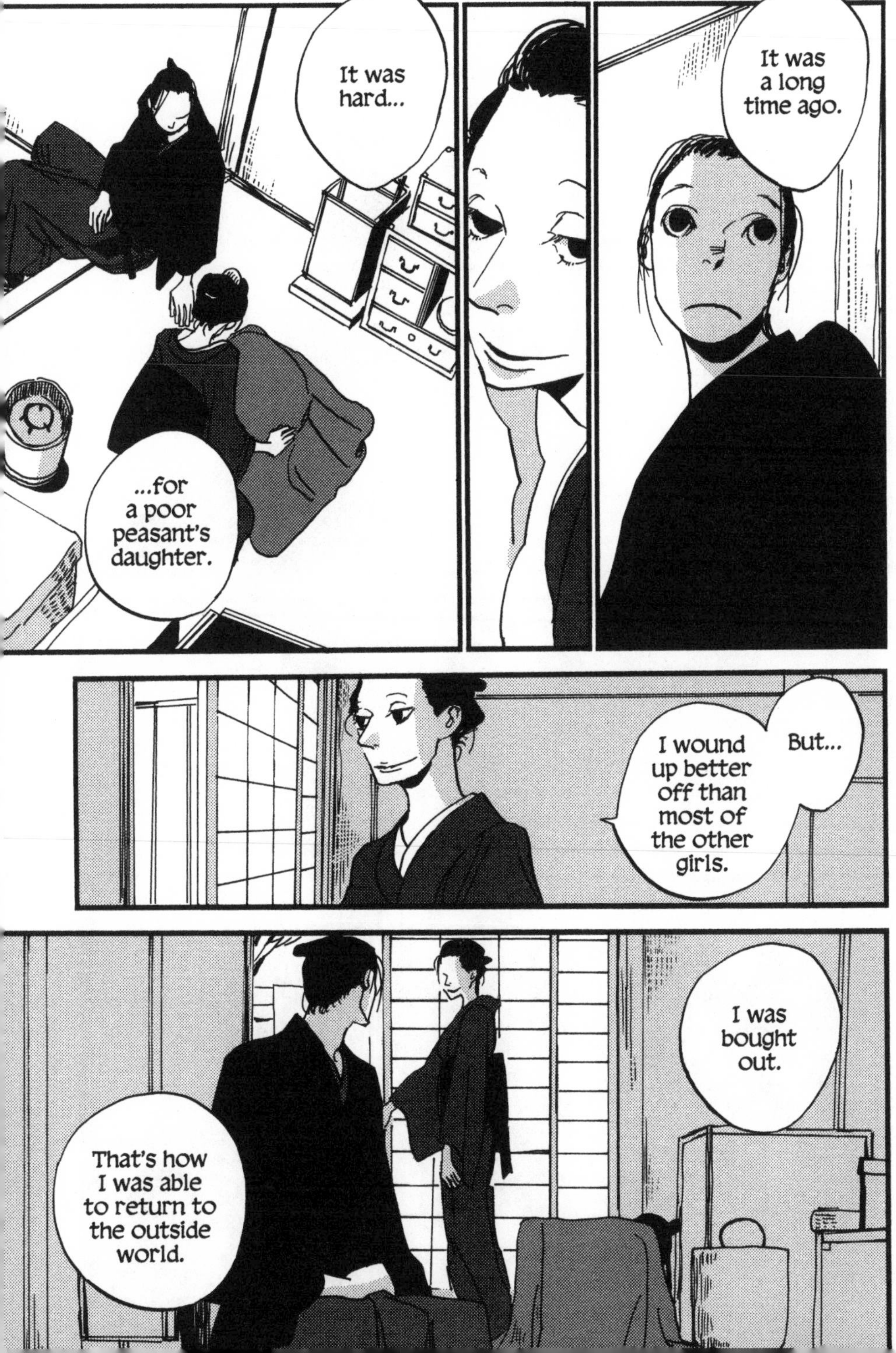
It was a long time ago.
It was hard...
...for a poor peasant's daughter.
But...
I wound up better off than most of the other girls.
I was bought out.
That's how I was able to return to the outside world.

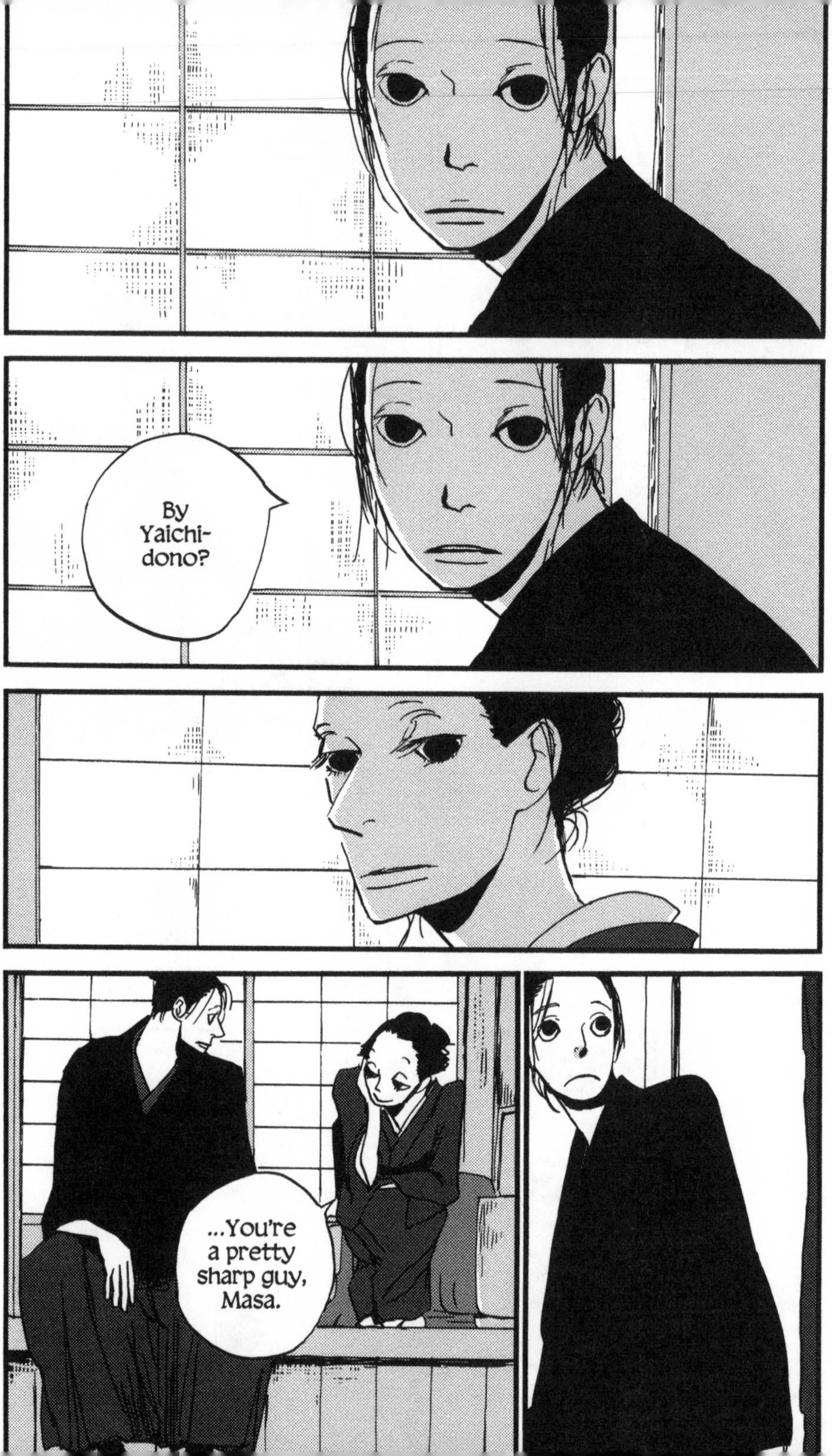
By Yaichi-dono?
...You're a pretty sharp guy, Masa.

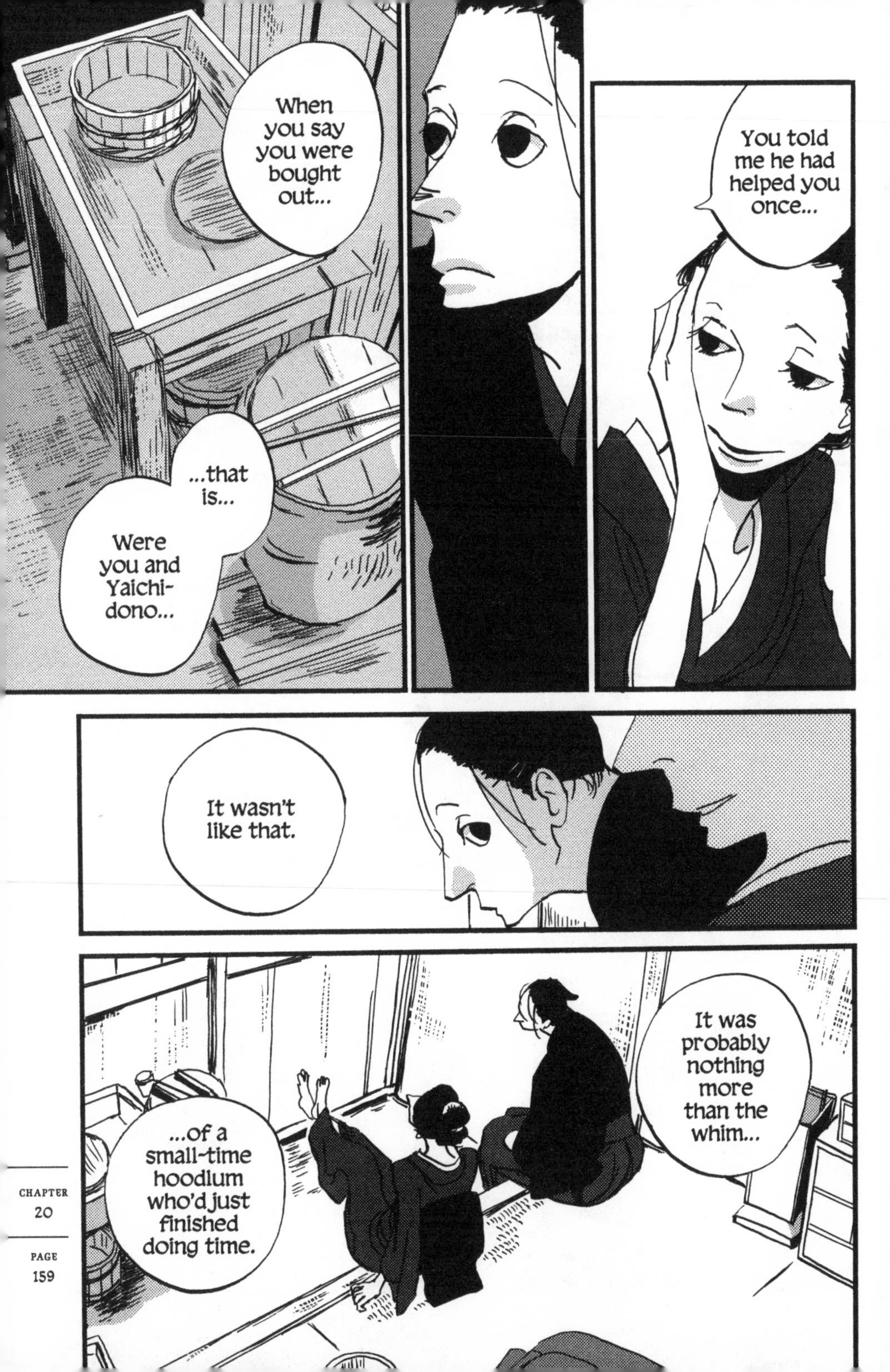
You told me he had helped you once...
When you say you were bought out...
...that is...
Were you and Yaichi-dono...
It wasn't like that.
It was probably nothing more than the whim...
...of a small-time hoodlum who'd just finished doing time.

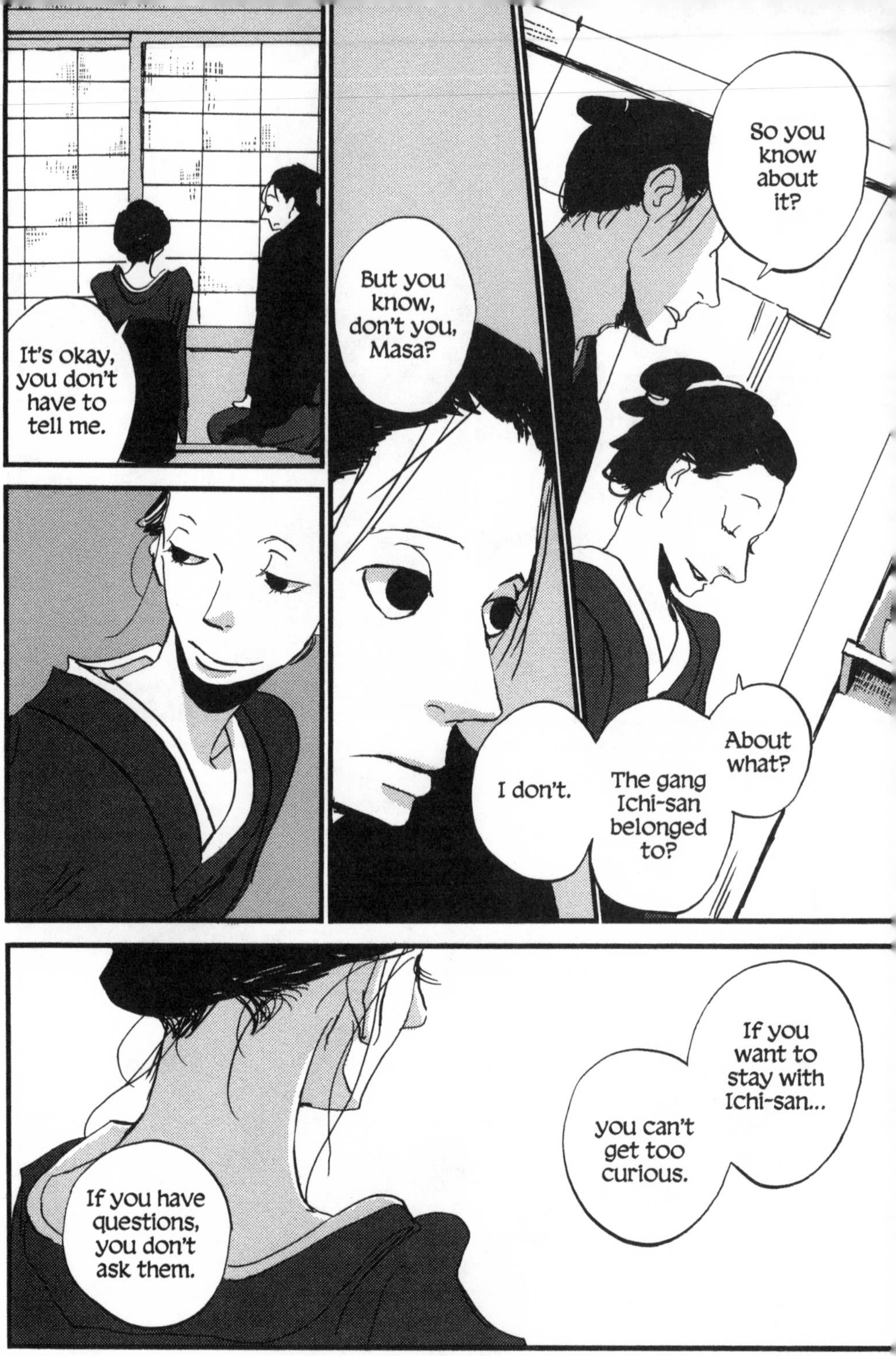
So you know about it?
About what?
The gang Ichi-san belonged to?
I don't.
But you know, don't you, Masa?
It's okay, you don't have to tell me.
If you want to stay with Ichi-san...
you can't get too curious.
If you have questions, you don't ask them.

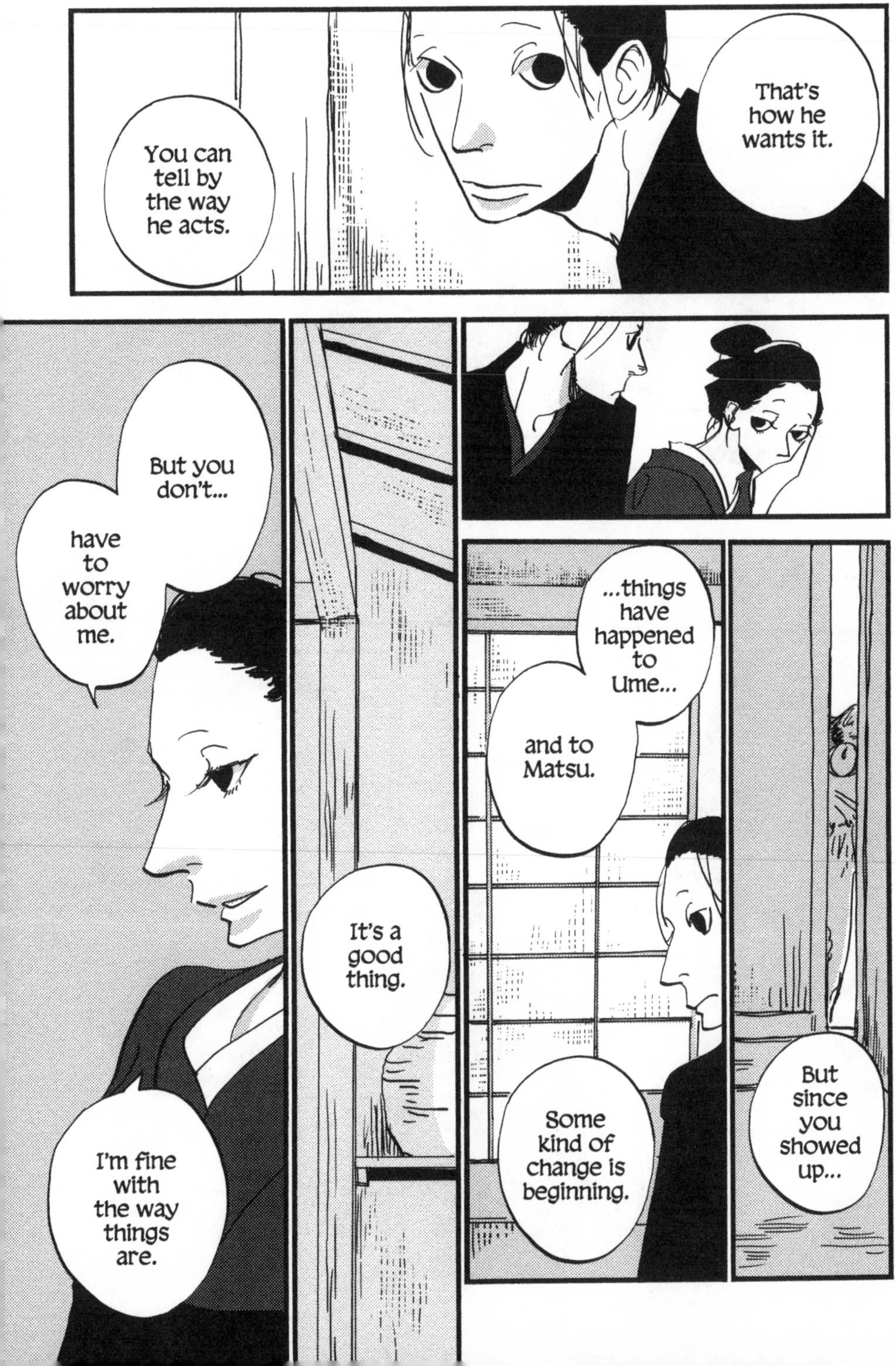
That's how he wants it.
You can tell by the way he acts.
But since you showed up...
...things have happened to Ume...
and to Matsu.
Some kind of change is beginning.
It's a good thing.
But you don't...
have to worry about me.
I'm fine with the way things are.

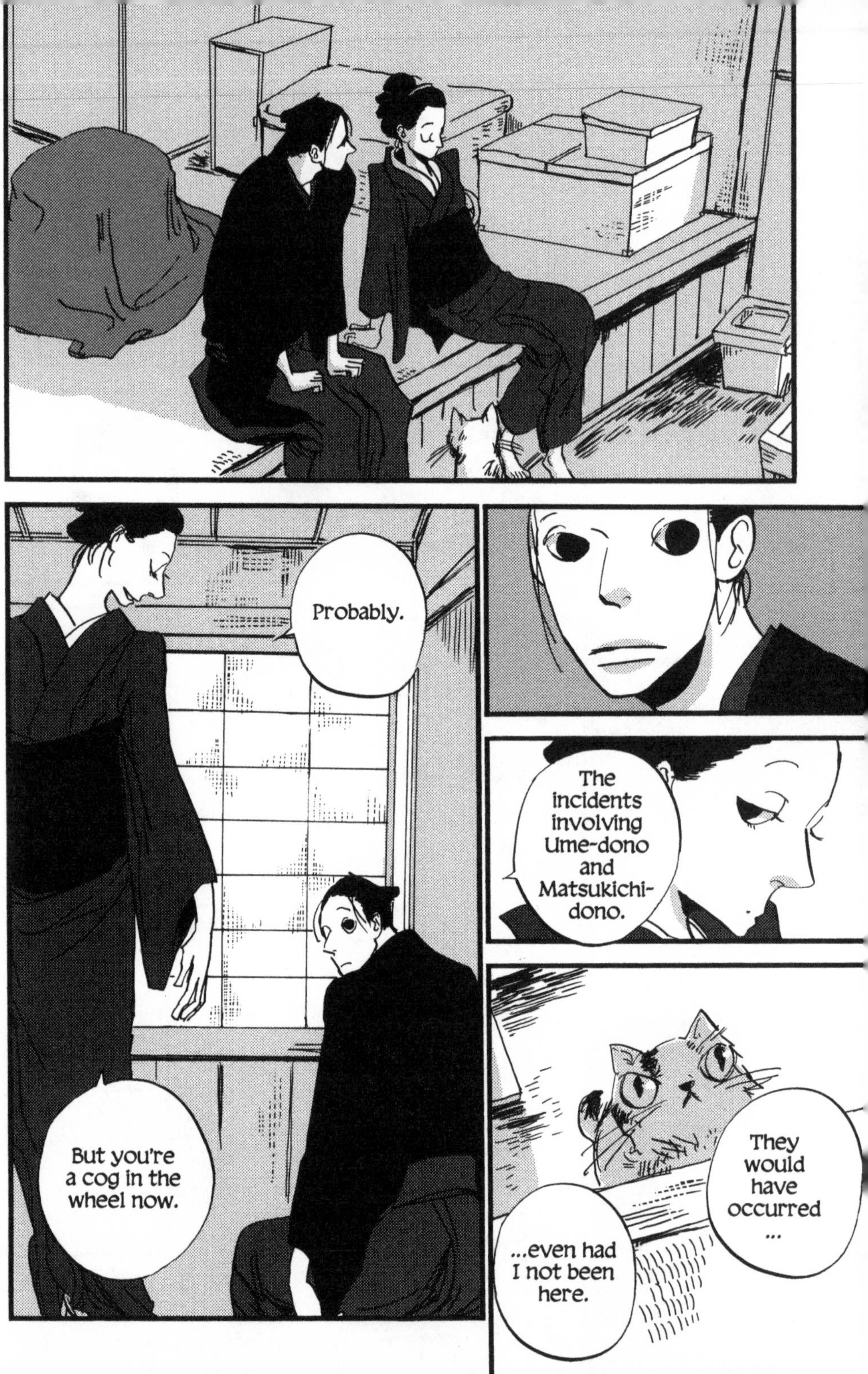
The incidents involving Ume-dono and Matsukichi-dono.
They would have occurred ...
...even had I not been here.
Probably.
But you're a cog in the wheel now.

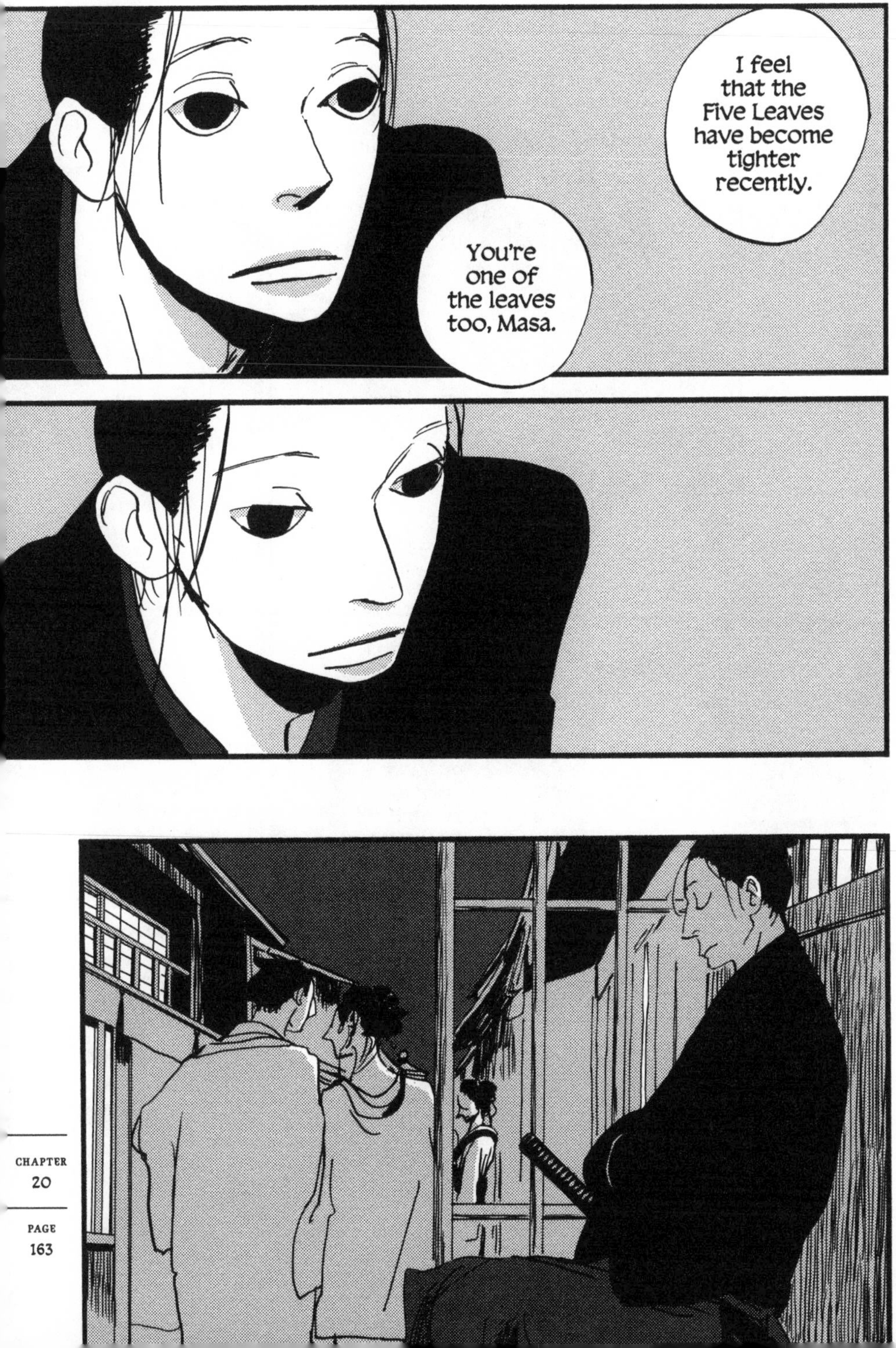
I feel that the Five Leaves have become tighter recently.
You're one of the leaves too, Masa.

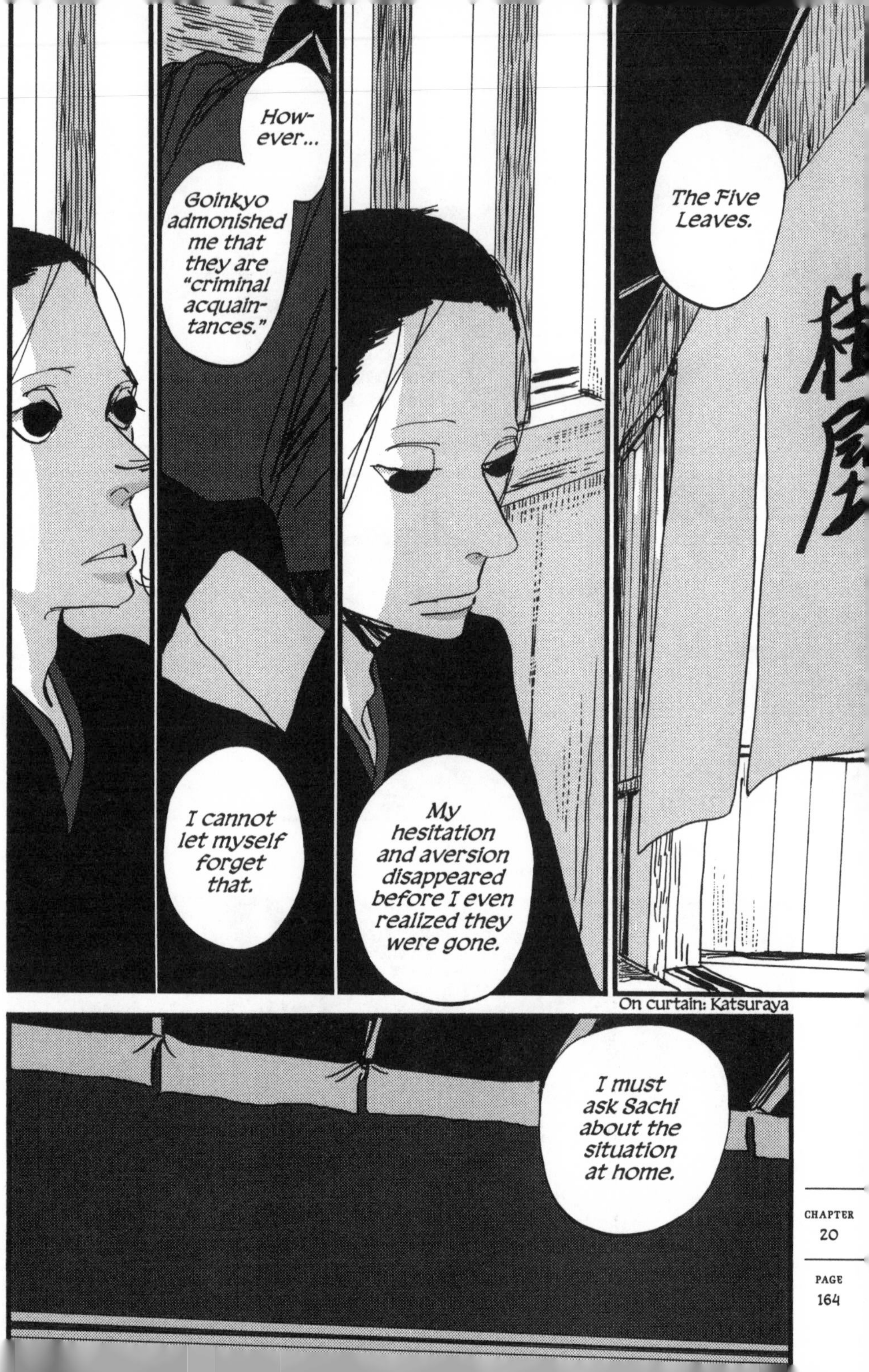
The Five Leaves.
My hesitation and aversion disappeared before I even realized they were gone.
How-ever...
Goinkyo admonished me that they are "criminal acquain-tances."
I cannot let myself forget that.
On curtain: Katsuraya
I must ask Sachi about the situation at home.

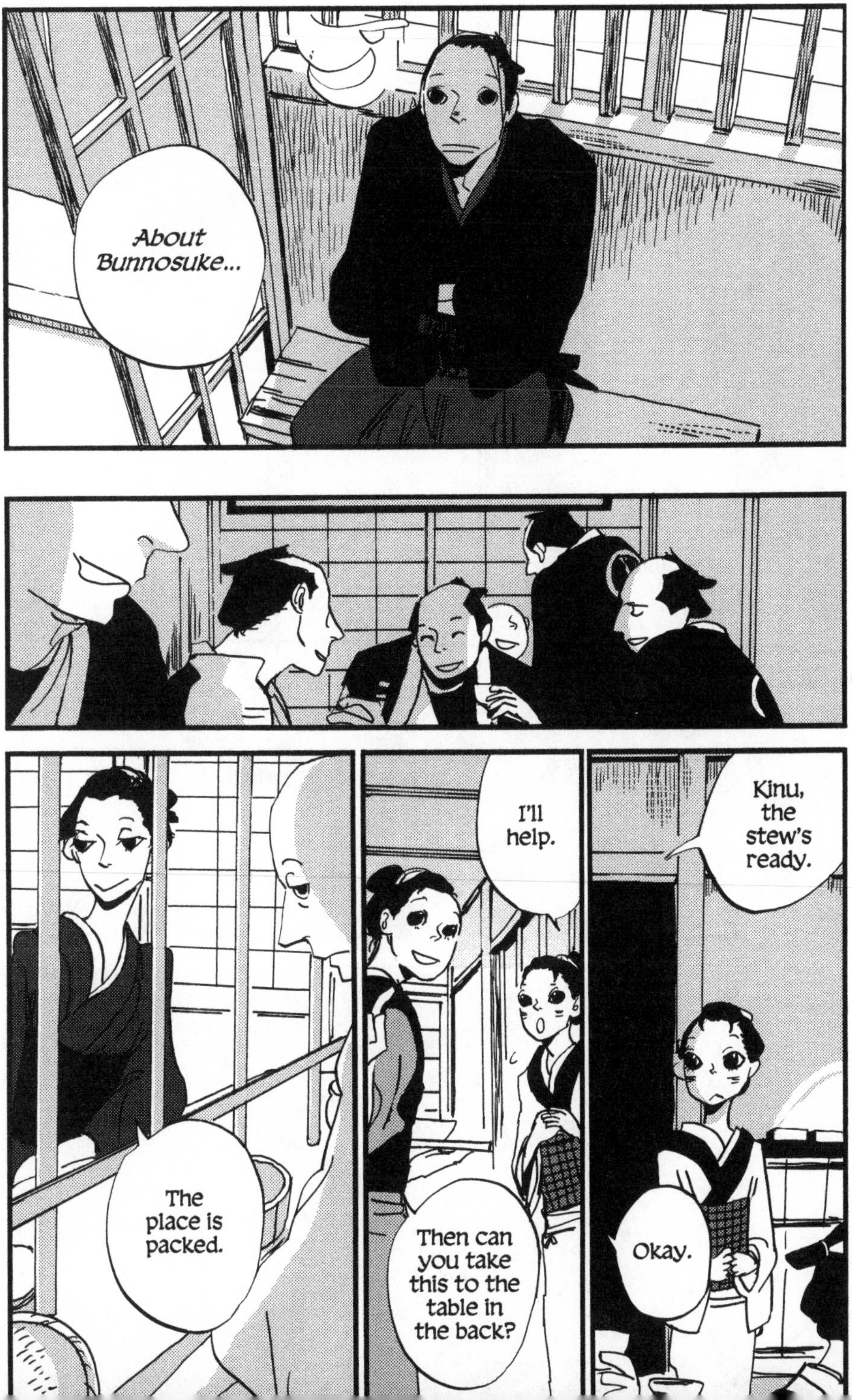
About Bunnosuke...
Kinu, the stew's ready.
Okay.
I'll help.
Then can you take this to the table in the back?
The place is packed.

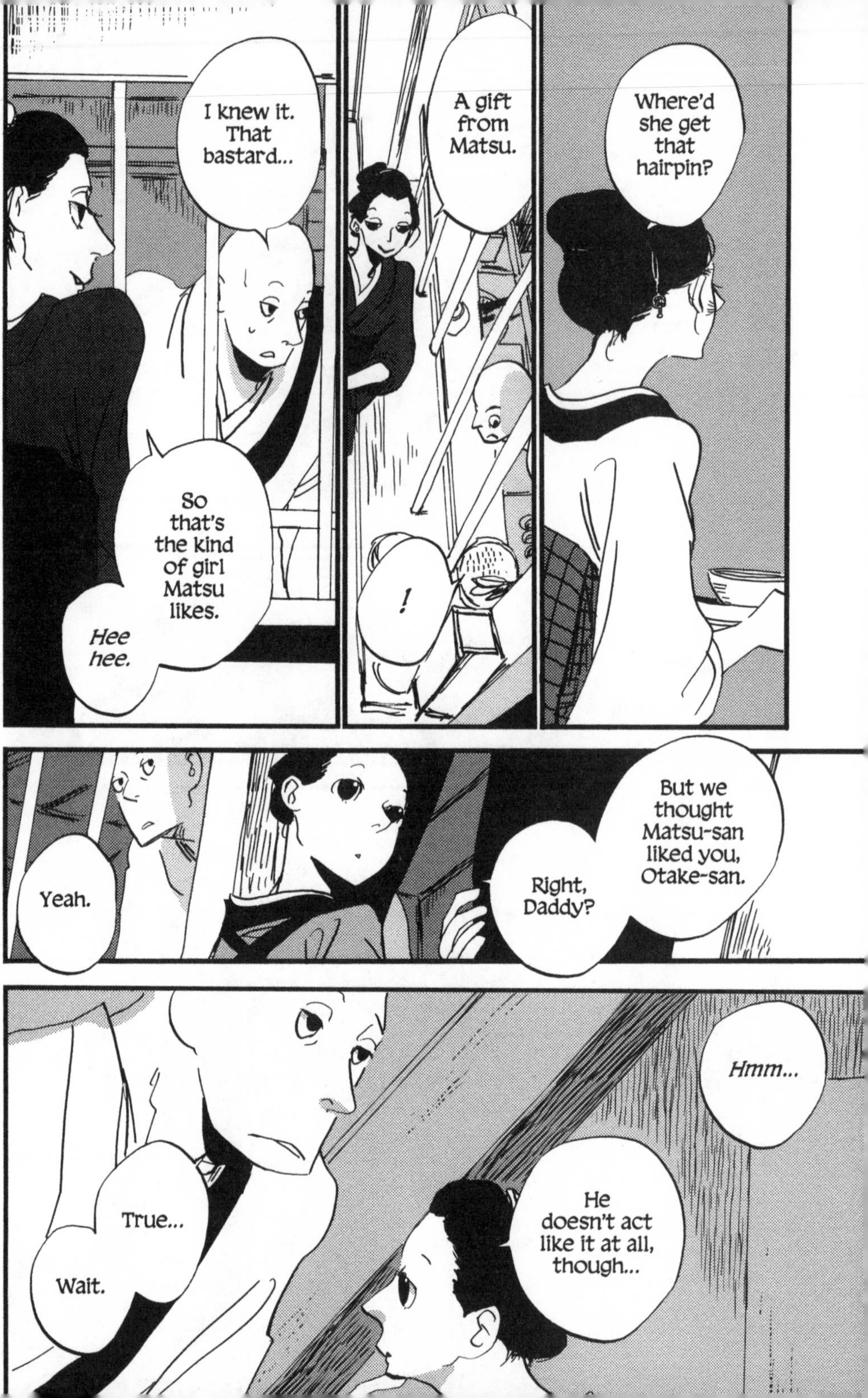
Where'd she get that hairpin?
A gift from Matsu.
!
I knew it. That bastard...
So that's the kind of girl Matsu likes. Hee hee.
But we thought Matsu-san liked you, Otake-san.
Right, Daddy?
Yeah.
Hmm...
He doesn't act like it at all, though...
True...
Wait.

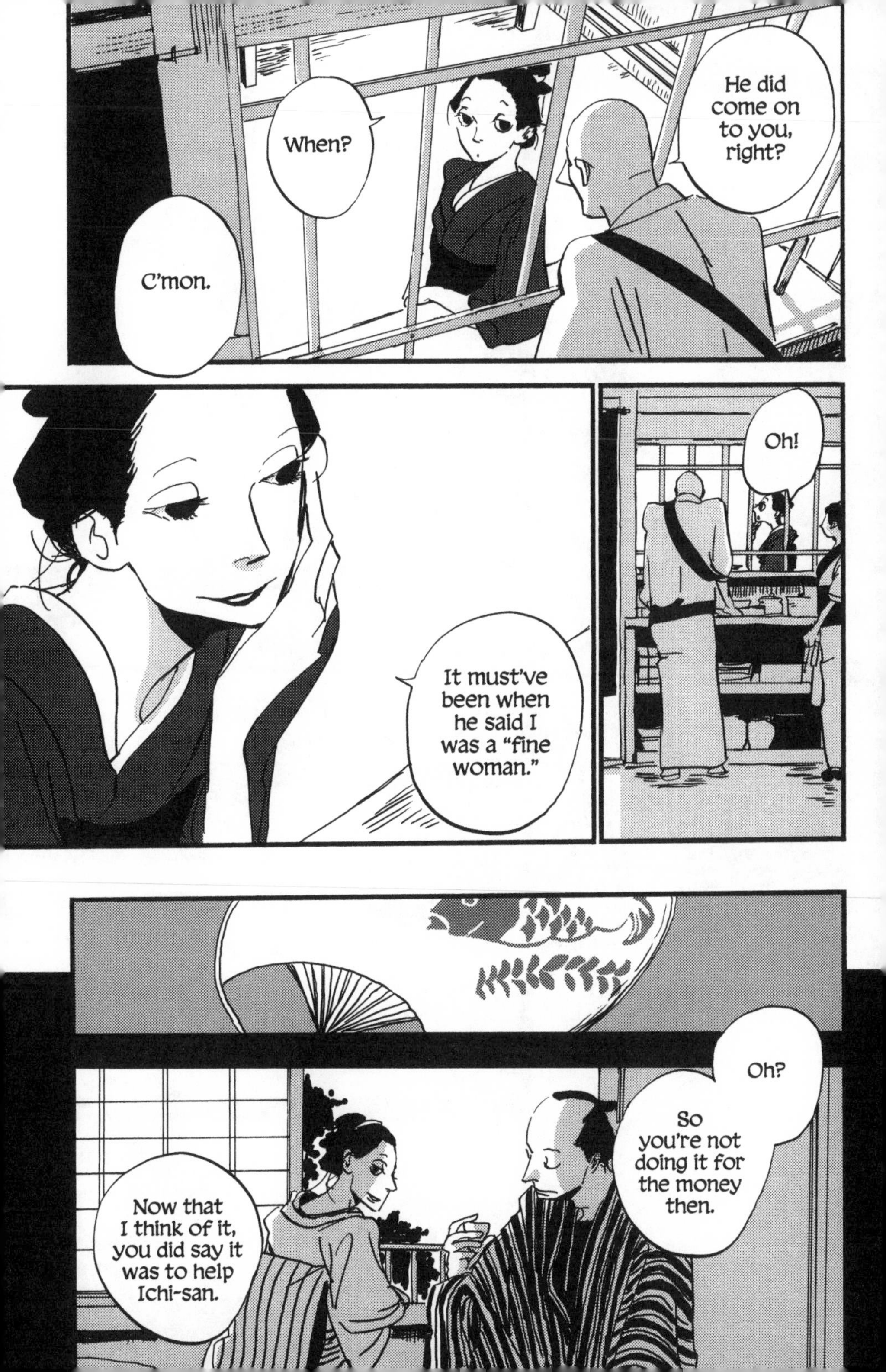
He did come on to you, right?
When?
C'mon.
Oh!
It must've been when he said I was a "fine woman."
Oh?
So you're not doing it for the money then.
Now that I think of it, you did say it was to help Ichi-san.

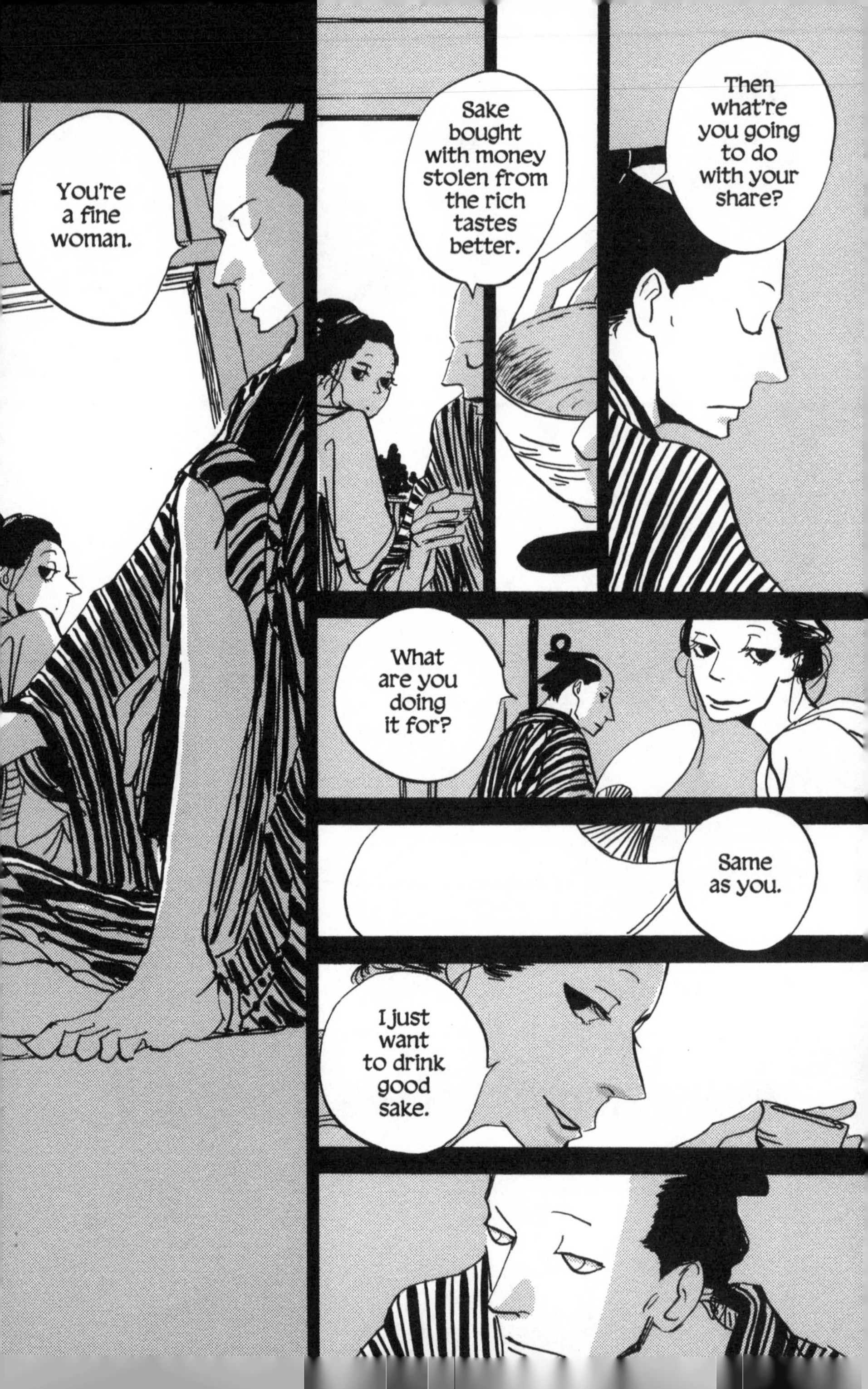
Then what're you going to do with your share?
Sake bought with money stolen from the rich tastes better.
What are you doing it for?
Same as you.
I just want to drink good sake.
You're a fine woman.

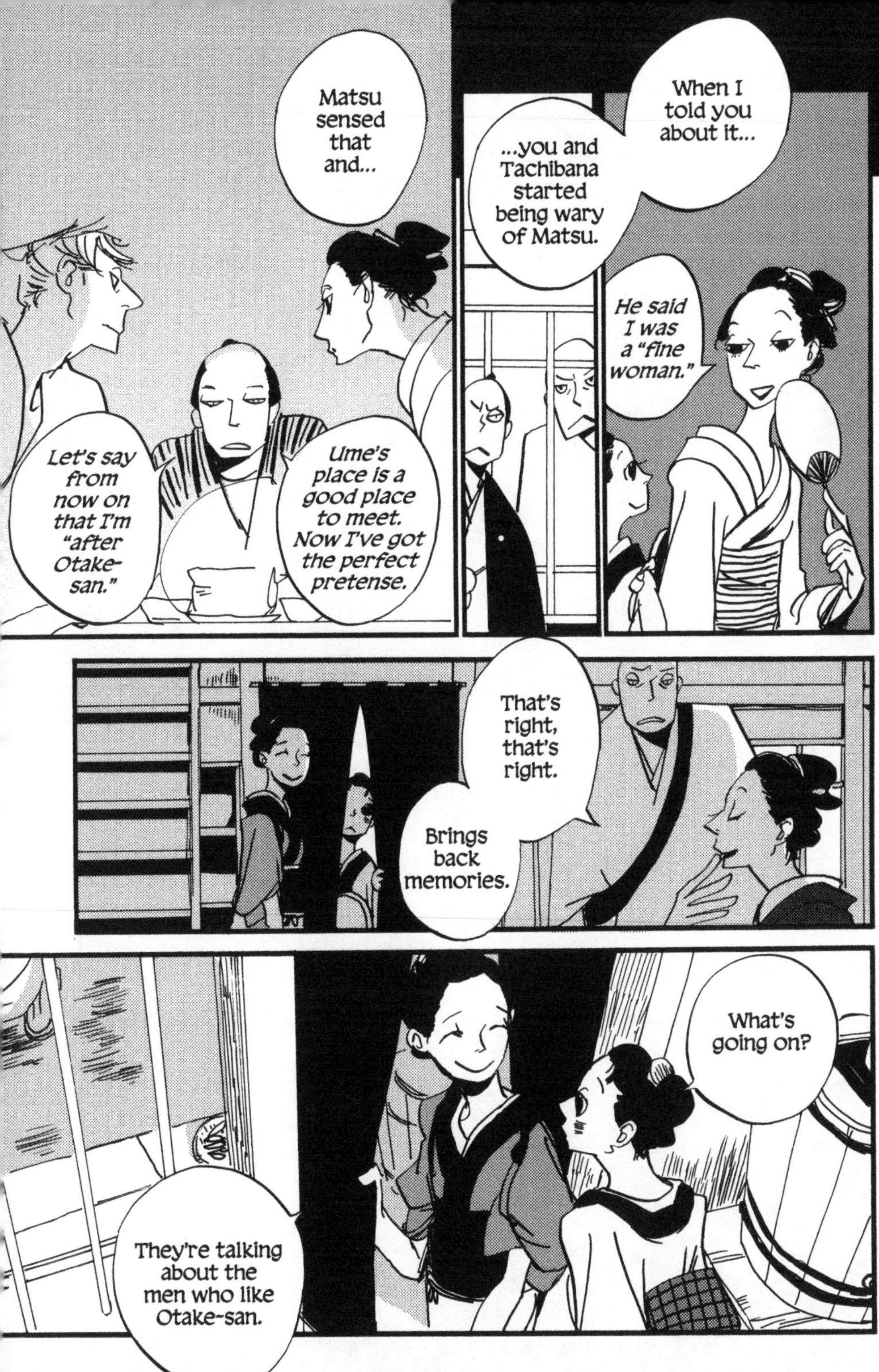
When I told you about it...
...you and Tachibana started being wary of Matsu.
He said I was a "fine woman."
Matsu sensed that and...
Ume's place is a good place to meet. Now I've got the perfect pretense.
Let's say from now on that I'm "after Otake-san."
That's right, that's right.
Brings back memories.
What's going on?
They're talking about the men who like Otake-san.

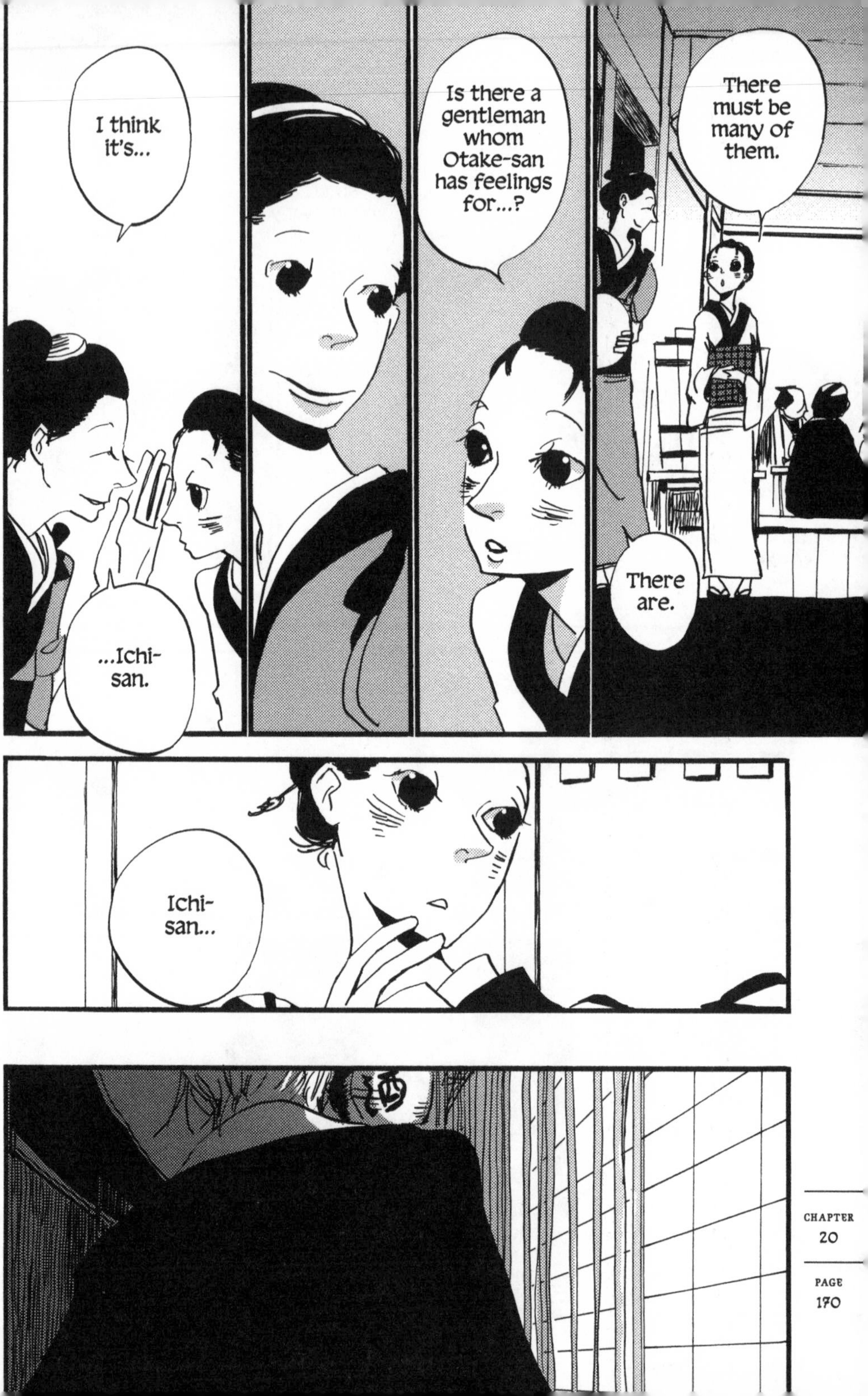
There must be many of them.
There are.
Is there a gentleman whom Otake-san has feelings for...?
I think it's...
...Ichi-san.
Ichi-san...

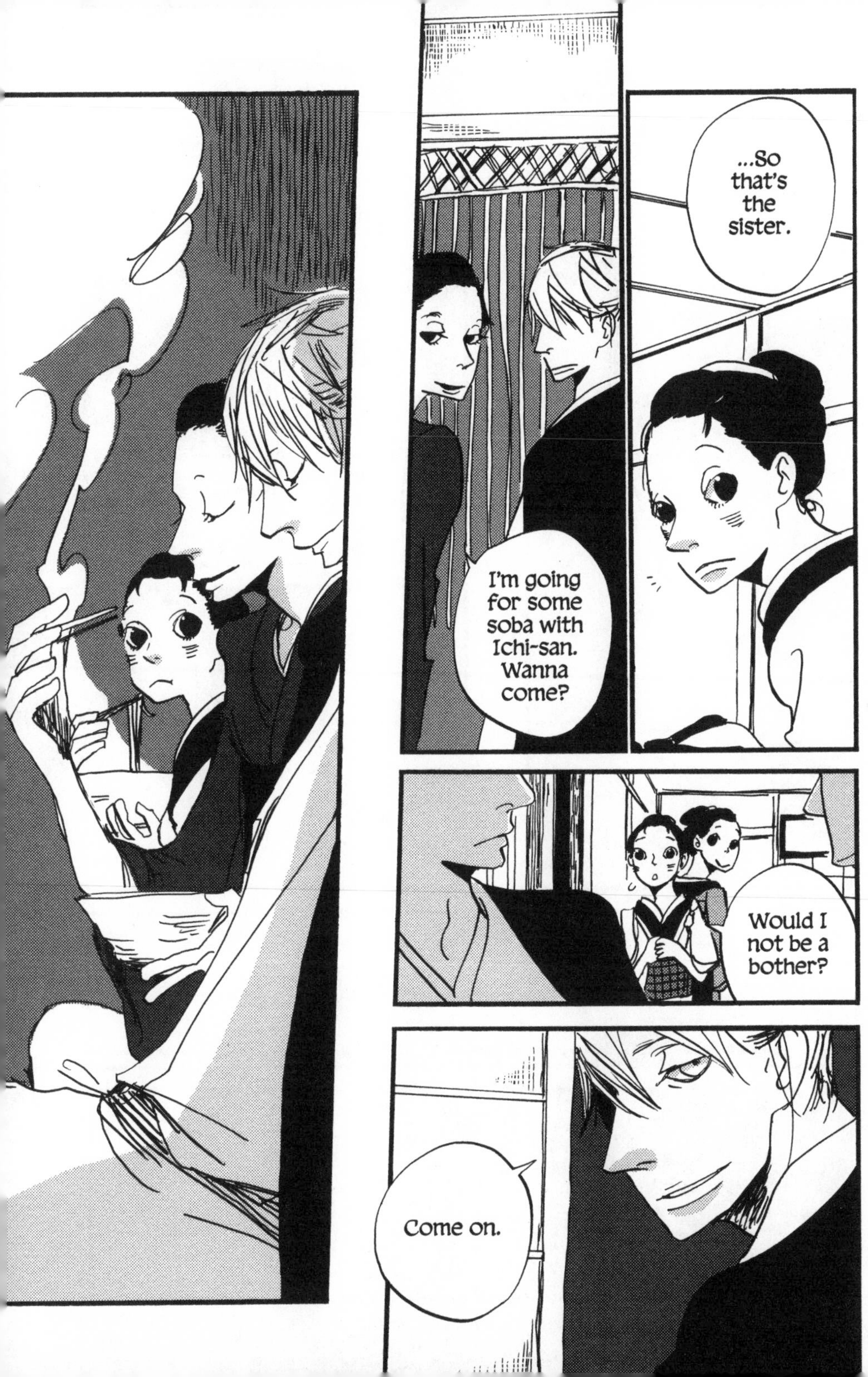
...So that's the sister.
I'm going for some soba with Ichi-san. Wanna come?
Would I not be a bother?
Come on.

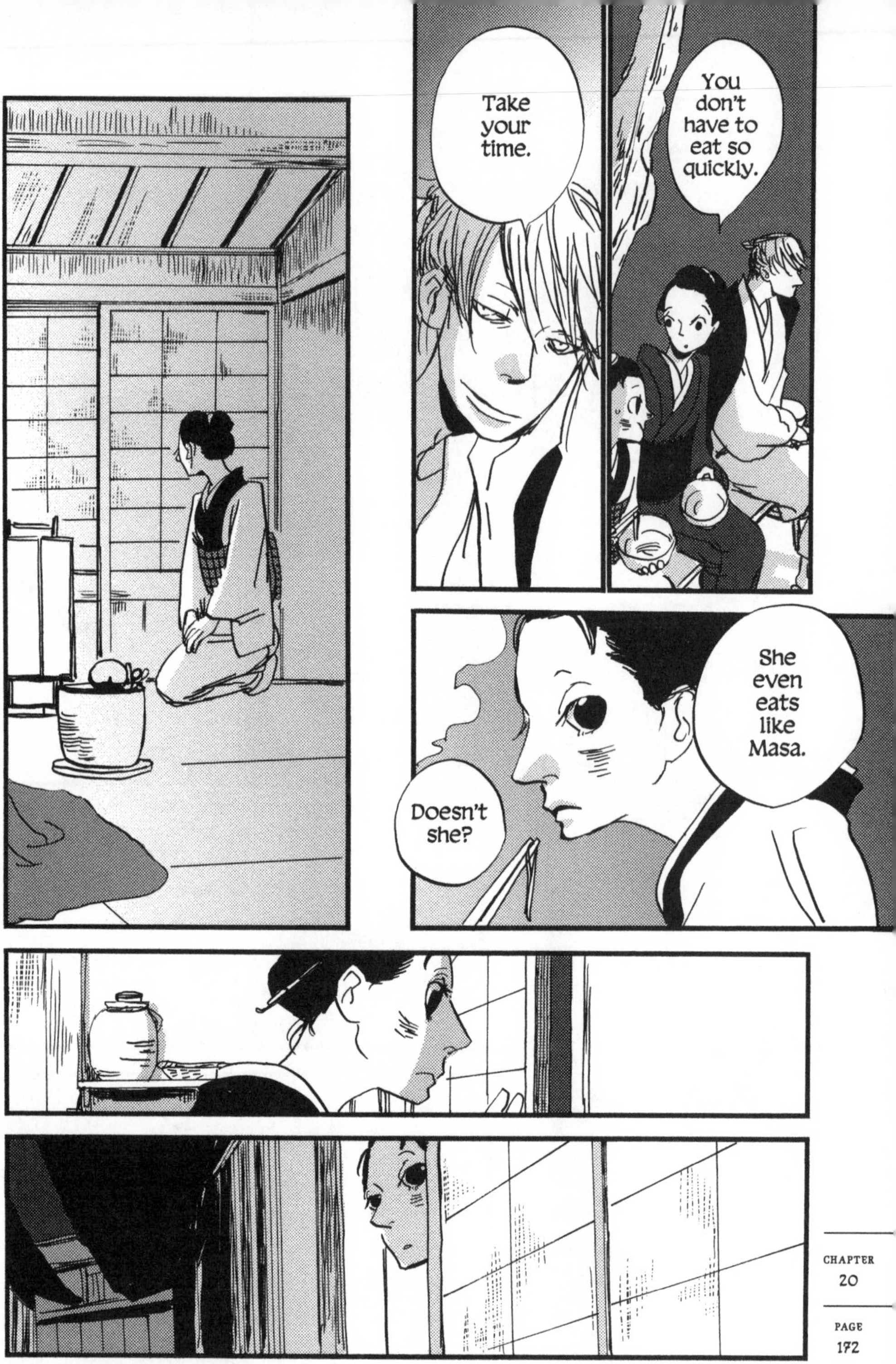
You don't have to eat so quickly.
Take your time.
She even eats like Masa.
Doesn't she?

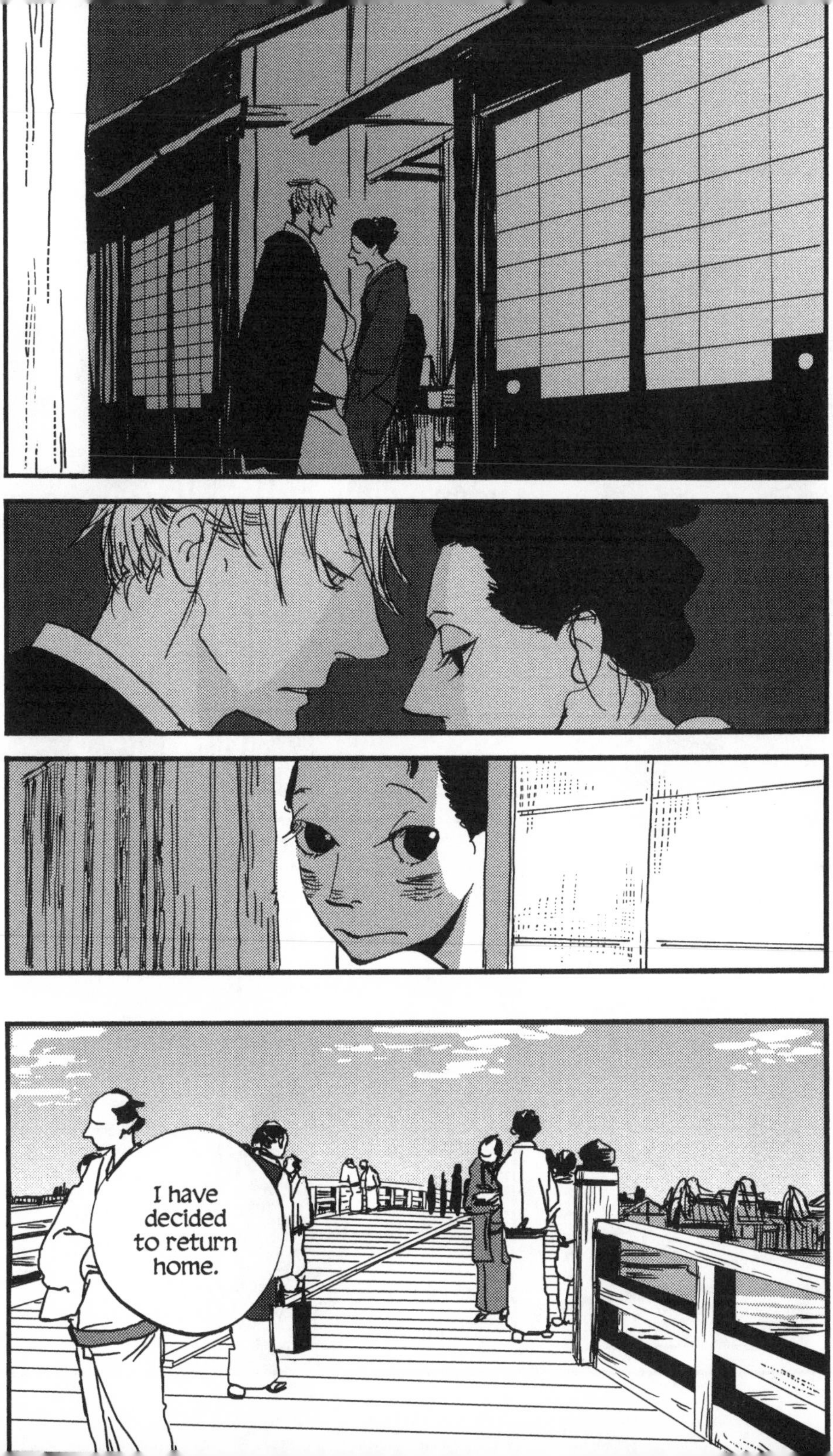
I have decided to return home.

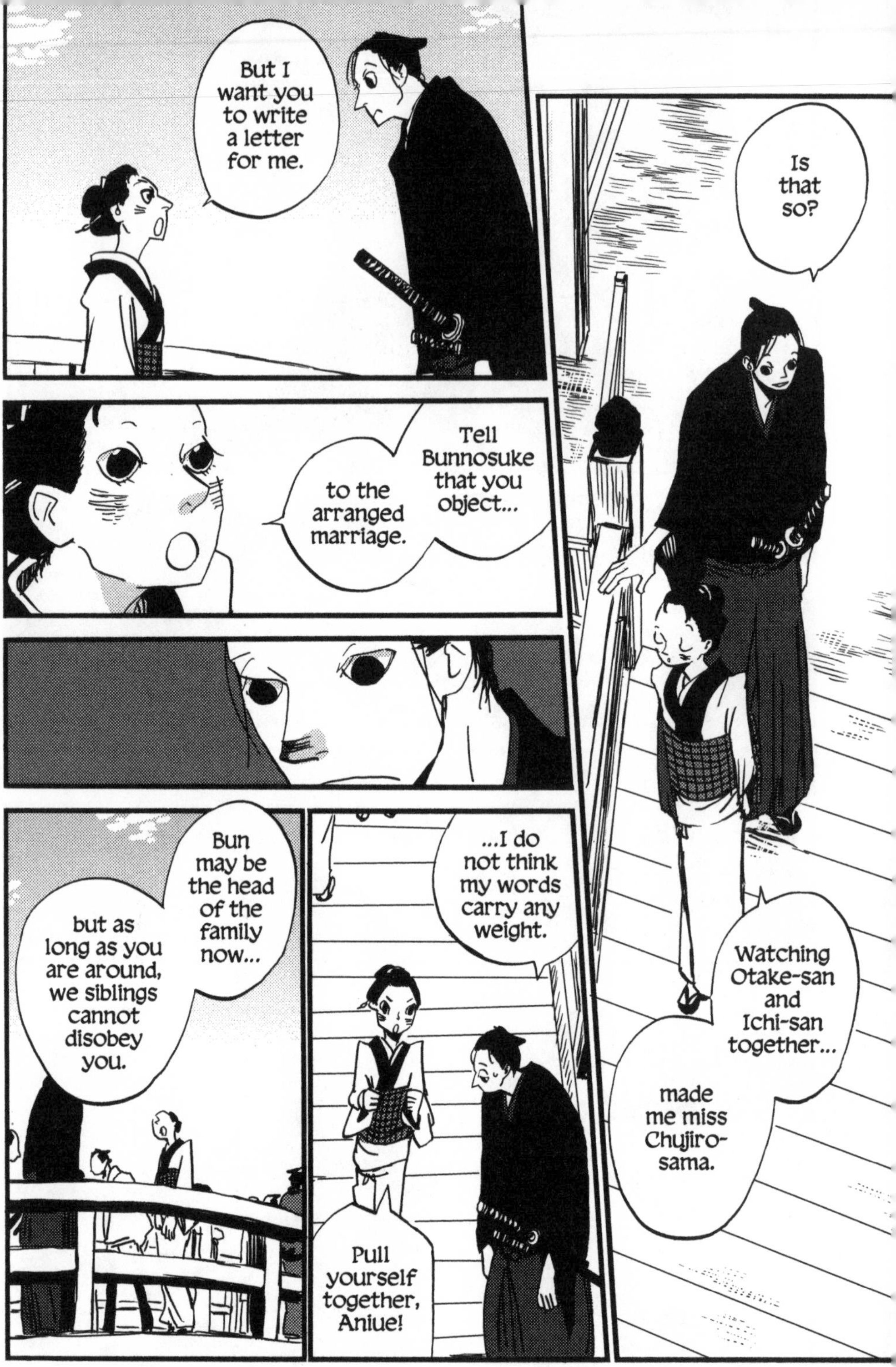
Is that so?
Watching Otake-san and Ichi-san together...
made me miss Chujiro-sama.
But I want you to write a letter for me.
Tell Bunnosuke that you object...
to the arranged marriage.
...I do not think my words carry any weight.
Pull yourself together, Aniue!
Bun may be the head of the family now...
but as long as you are around, we siblings cannot disobey you.

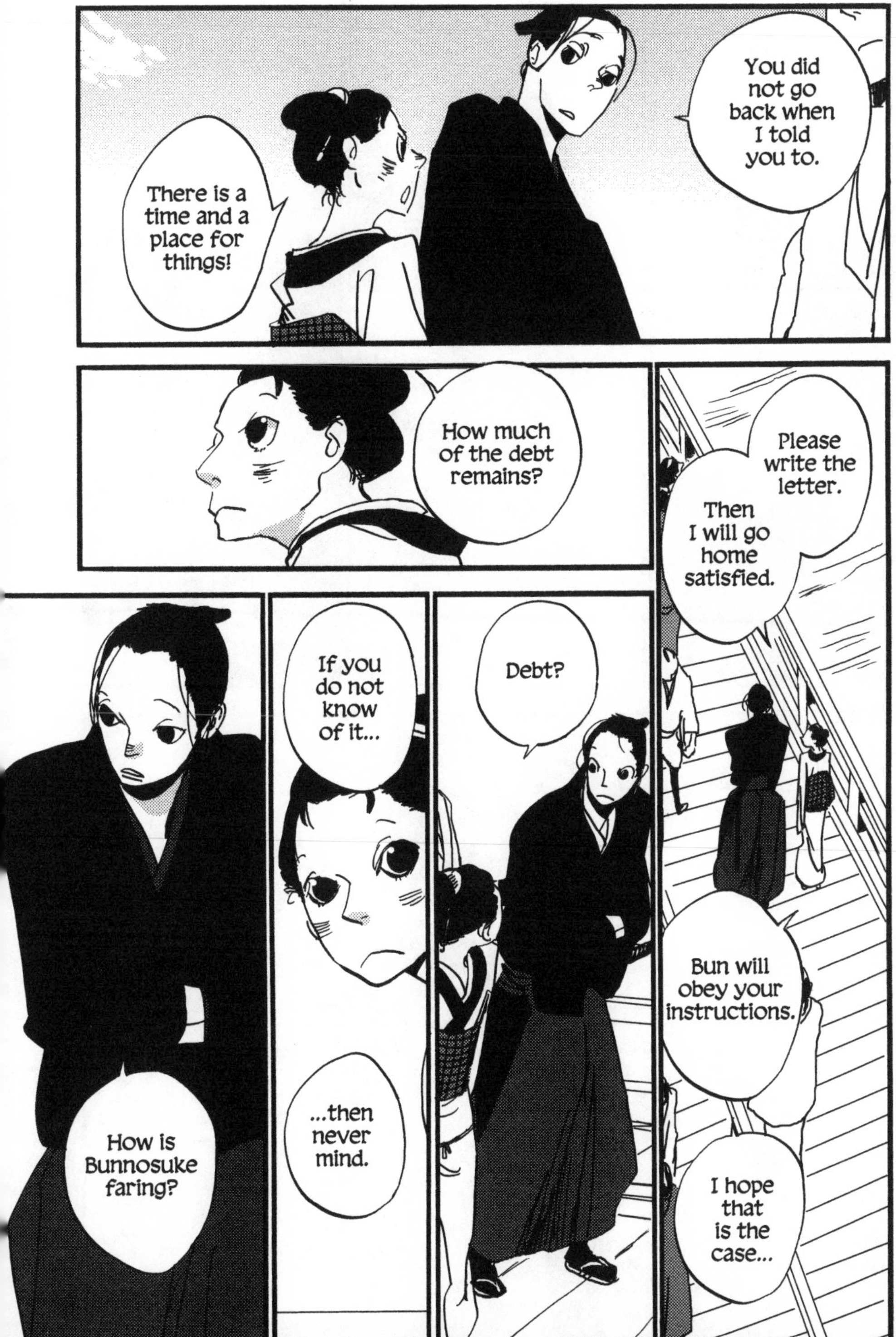
You did not go back when I told you to.
There is a time and a place for things!
Please write the letter.
Then I will go home satisfied.
Bun will obey your instructions.
I hope that is the case...
How much of the debt remains?
Debt?
If you do not know of it...
...then never mind.
How is Bunnosuke faring?

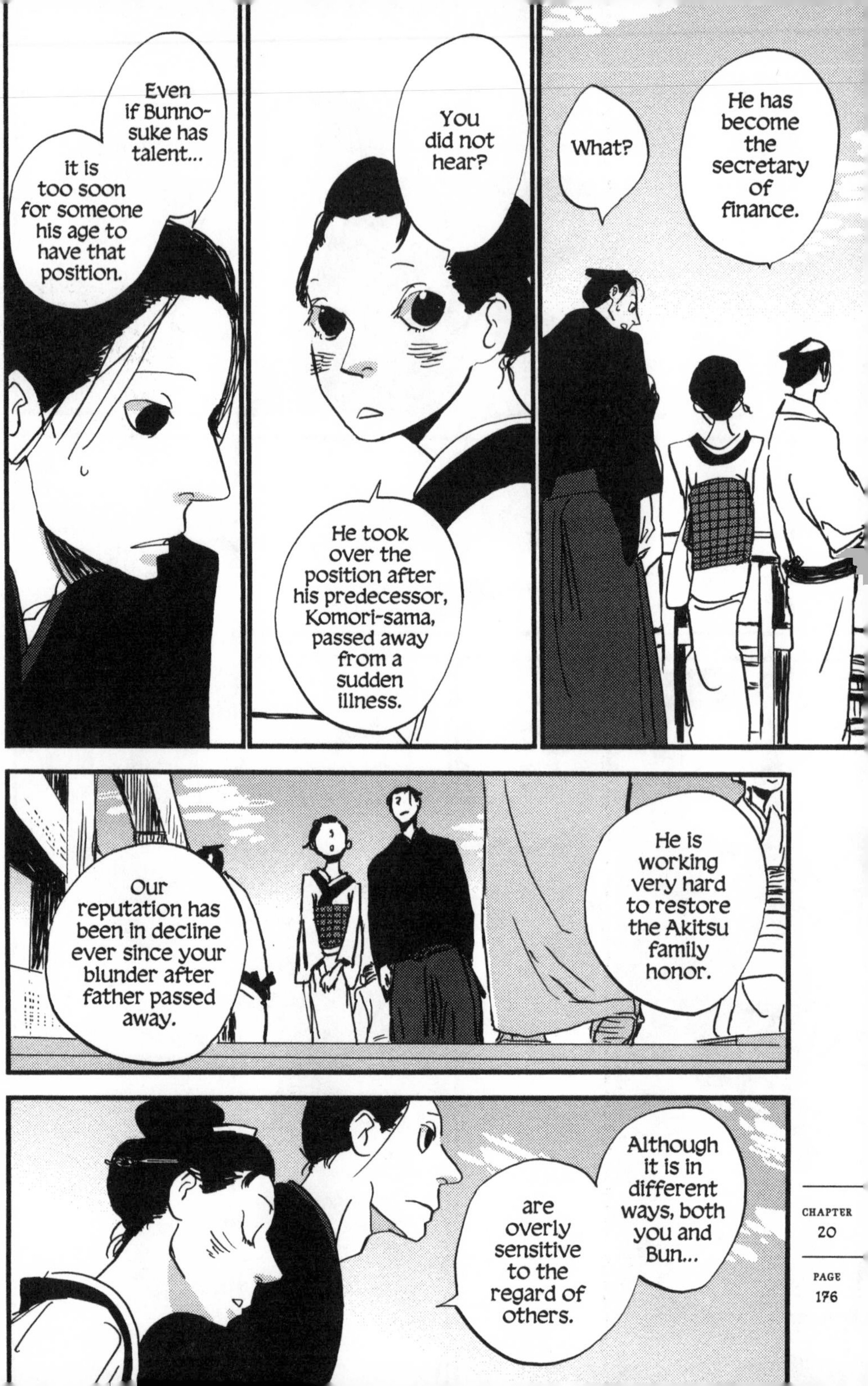
He has become the secretary of finance.
What?
You did not hear?
He took over the position after his predecessor, Komori-sama, passed away from a sudden illness.
Even if Bunnosuke has talent...
it is too soon for someone his age to have that position.
He is working very hard to restore the Akitsu family honor.
Our reputation has been in decline ever since your blunder after father passed away.
Although it is in different ways, both you and Bun...
are overly sensitive to the regard of others.

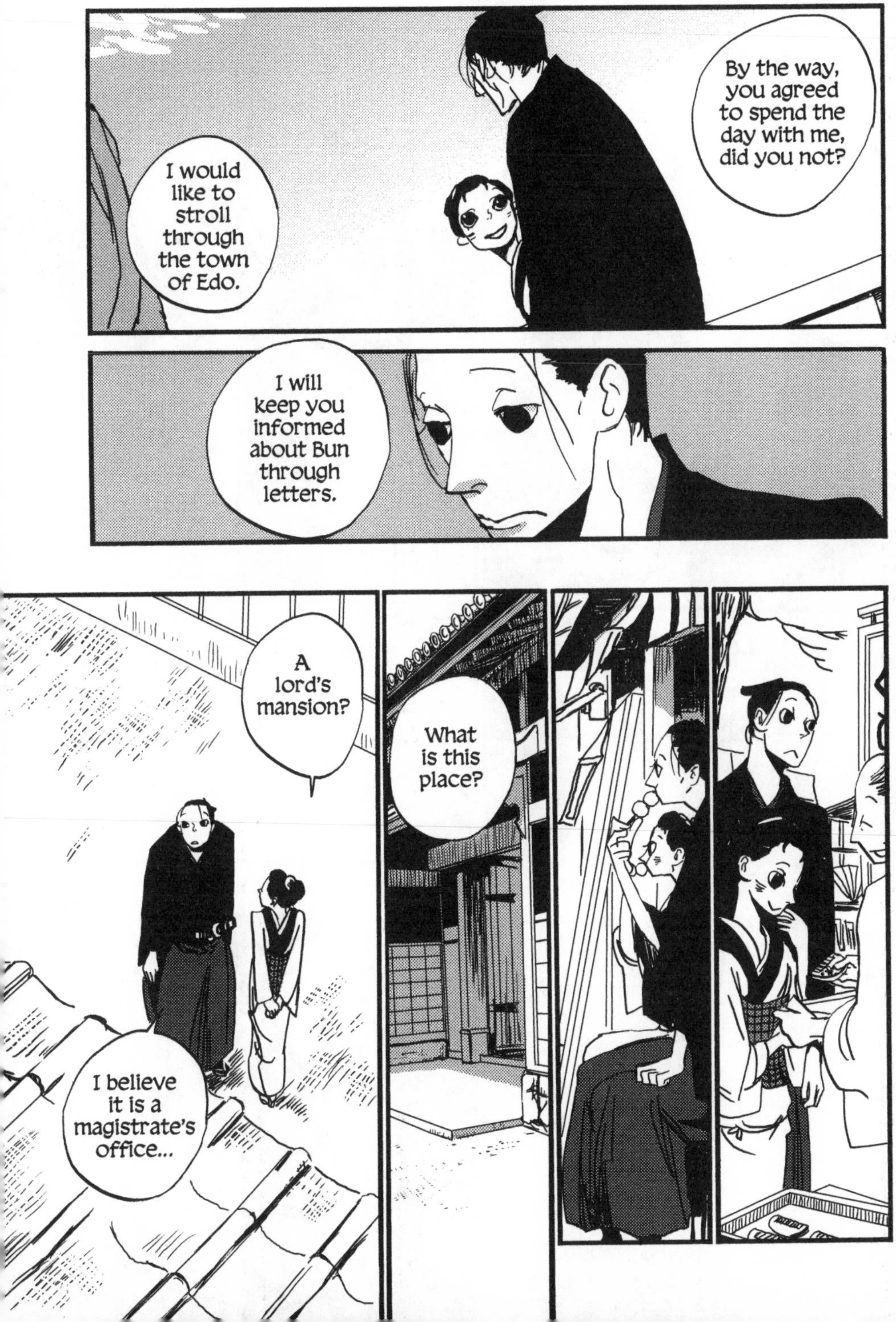
By the way, you agreed to spend the day with me, did you not?
I would like to stroll through the town of Edo.
I will keep you informed about Bun through letters.
What is this place?
A lord's mansion?
I believe it is a magistrate's office...

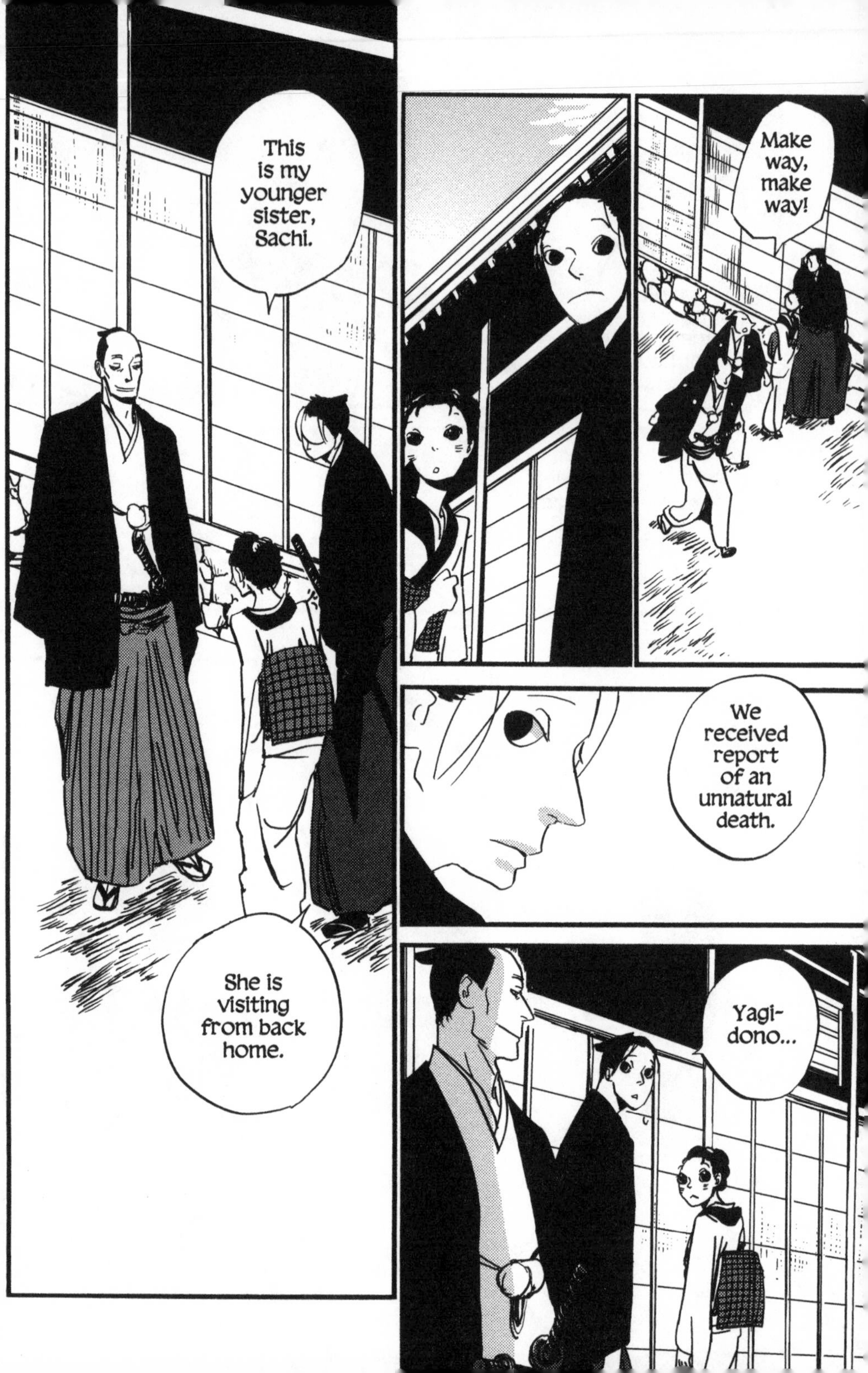
Make way, make way!
We received report of an unnatural death.
Yagi-dono...
This is my younger sister, Sachi.
She is visiting from back home.

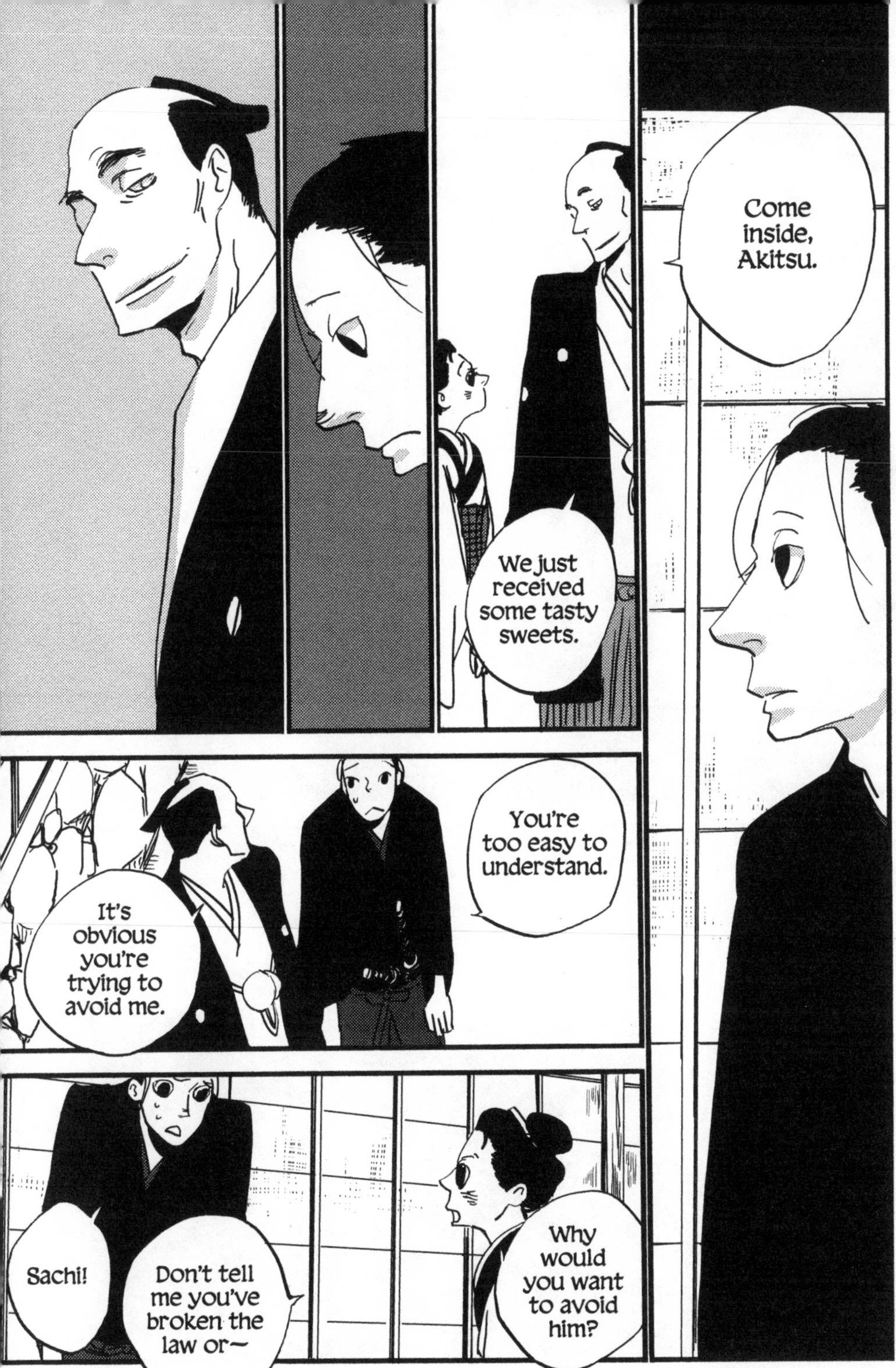
Come inside, Akitsu.
We just received some tasty sweets.
You're too easy to understand.
It's obvious you're trying to avoid me.
Why would you want to avoid him?
Don't tell me you've broken the law or~
Sachi!

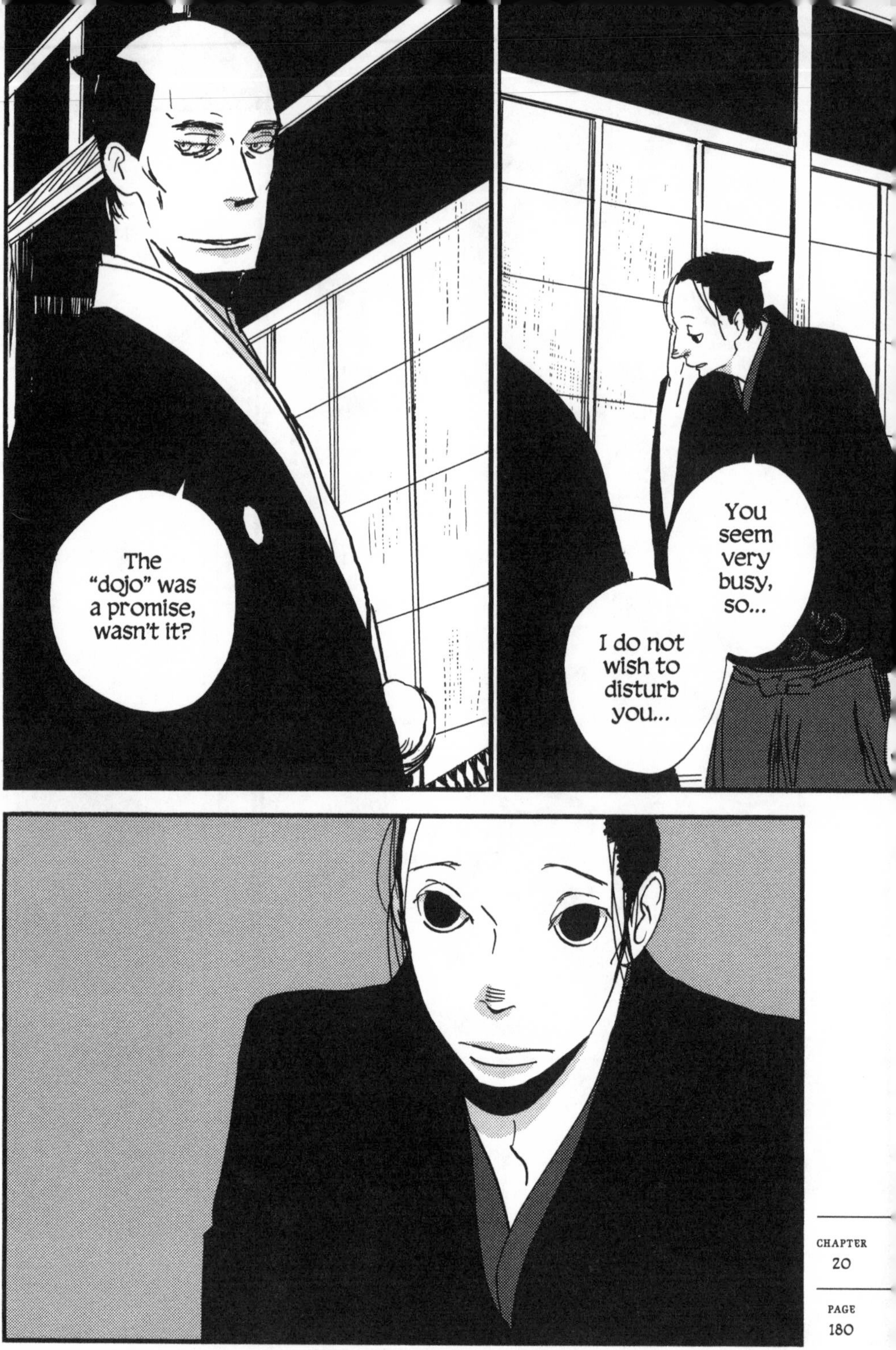
You seem very busy, so...
I do not wish to disturb you...
The "dojo" was a promise, wasn't it?

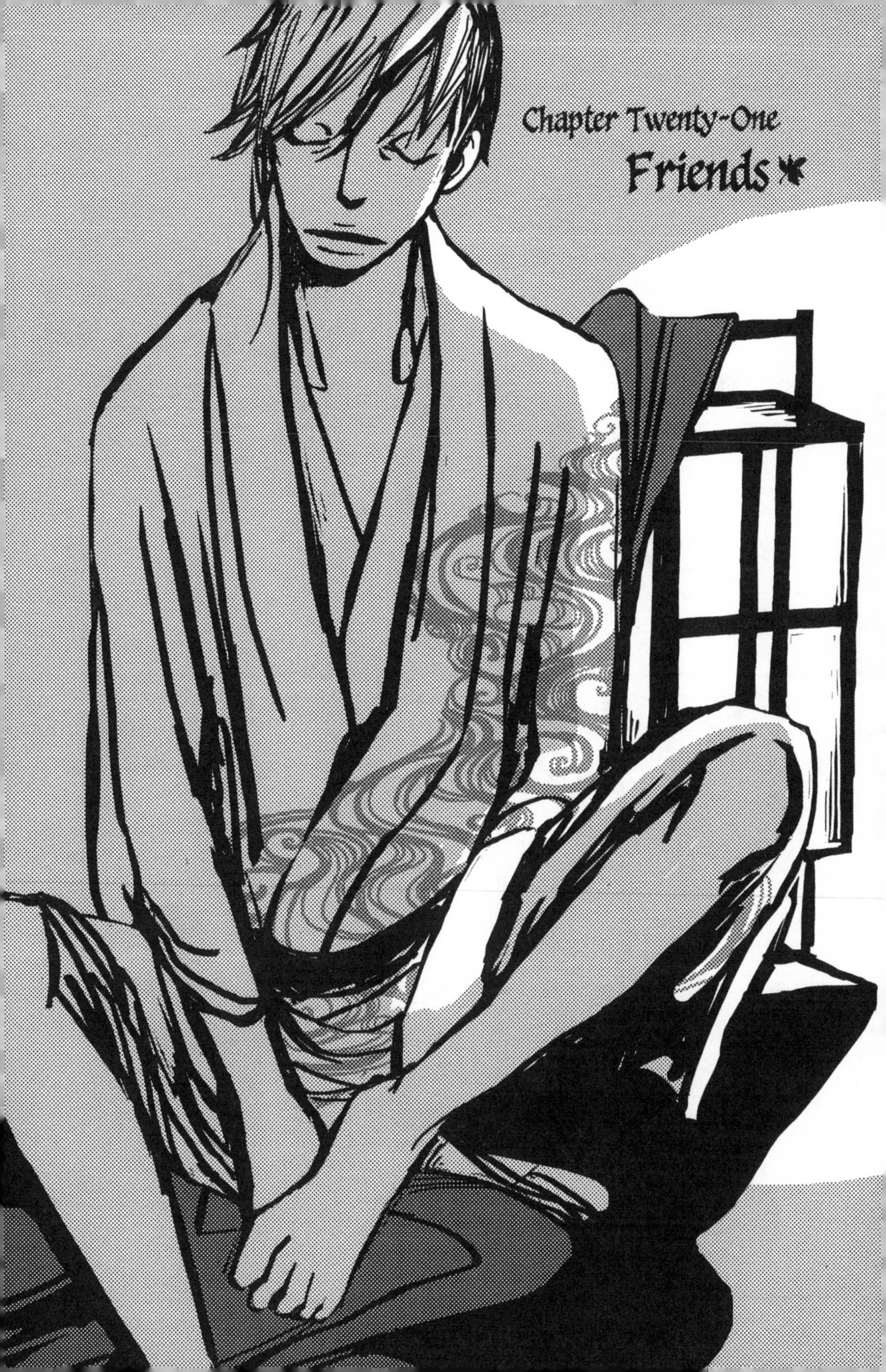
Chapter Twenty-One
Friends

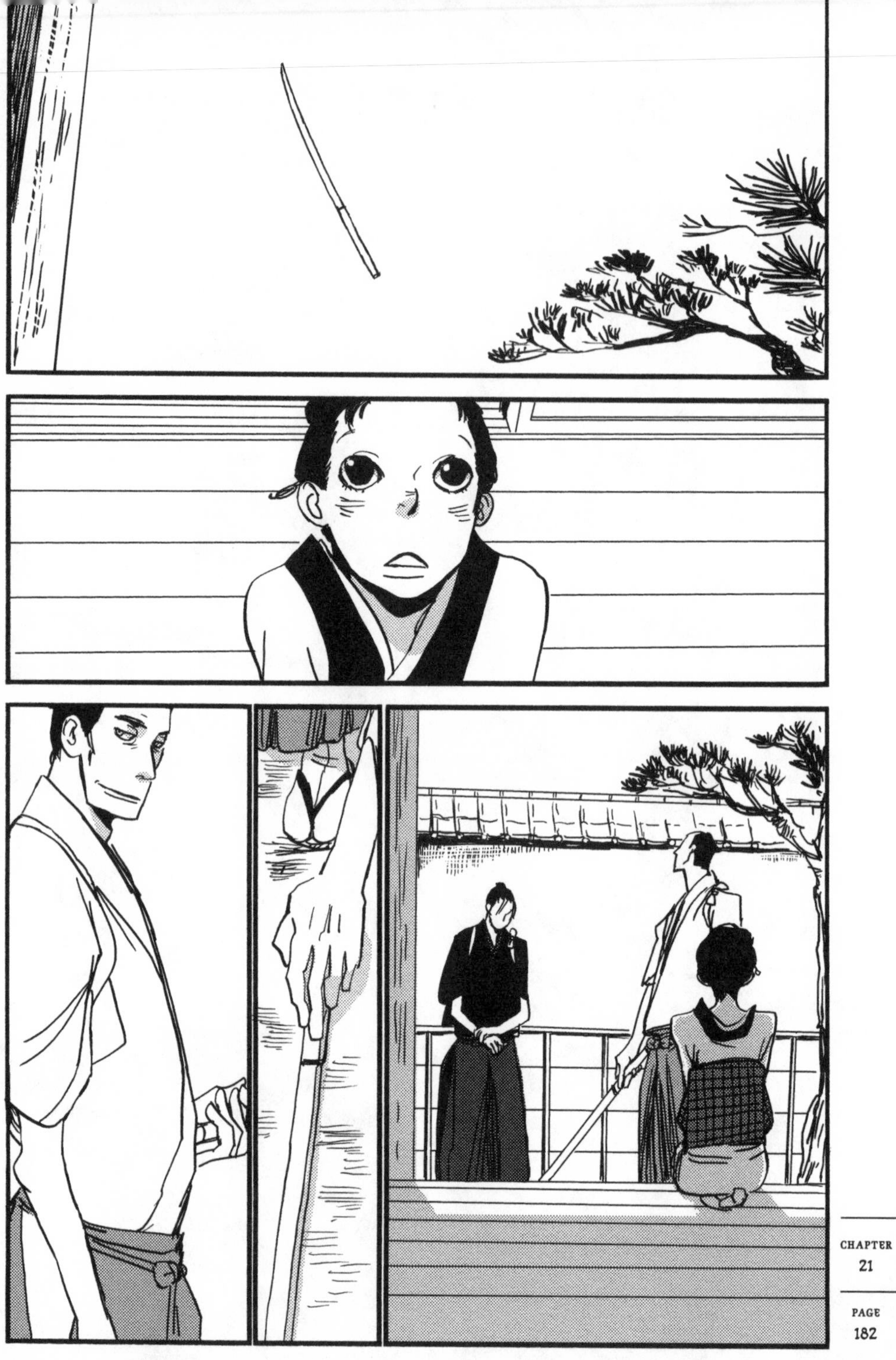

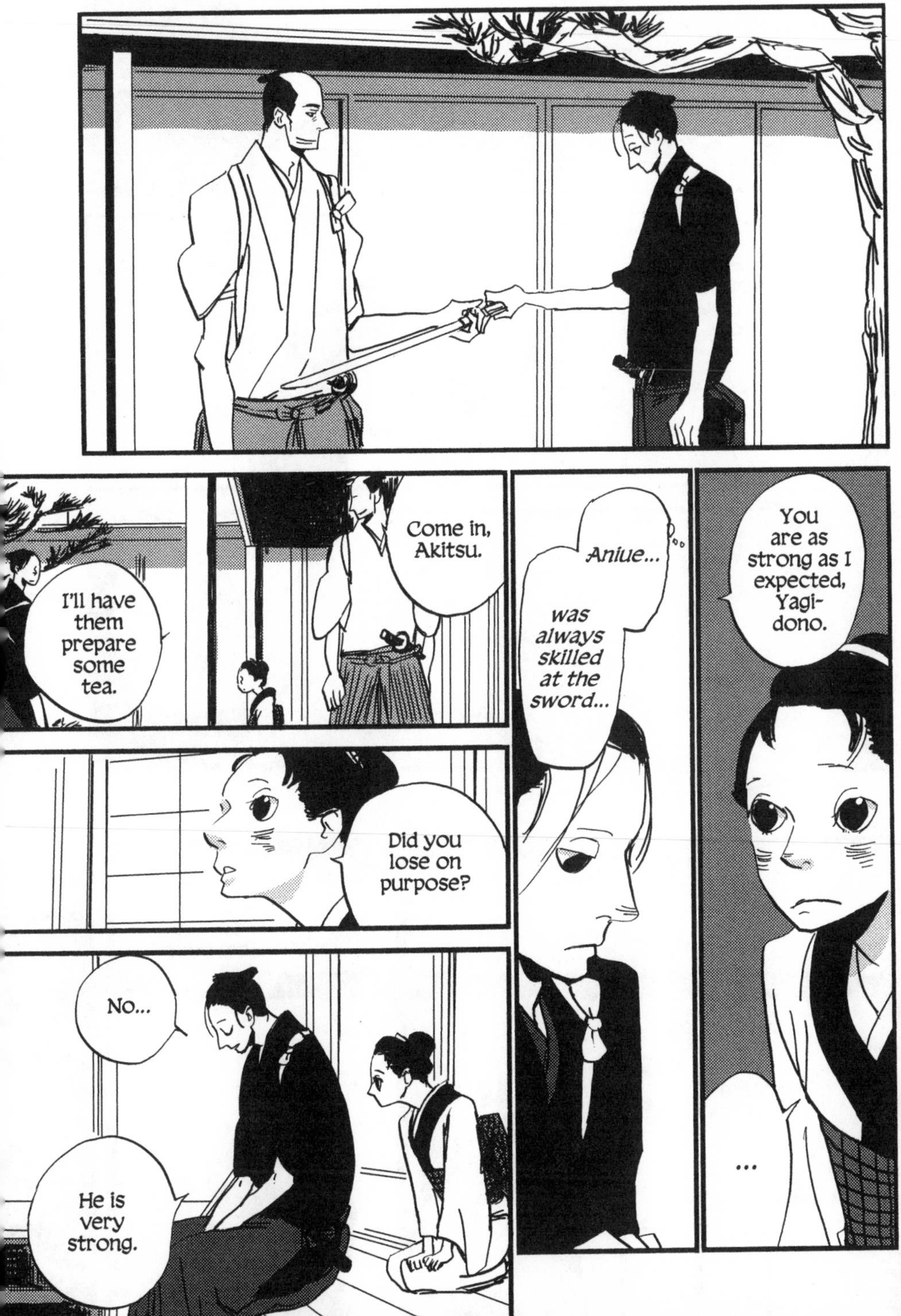
You are as strong as I expected, Yagi-dono.
...
Aniue...
was always skilled at the sword...
Come in, Akitsu.
I'll have them prepare some tea.
Did you lose on purpose?
No...
He is very strong.

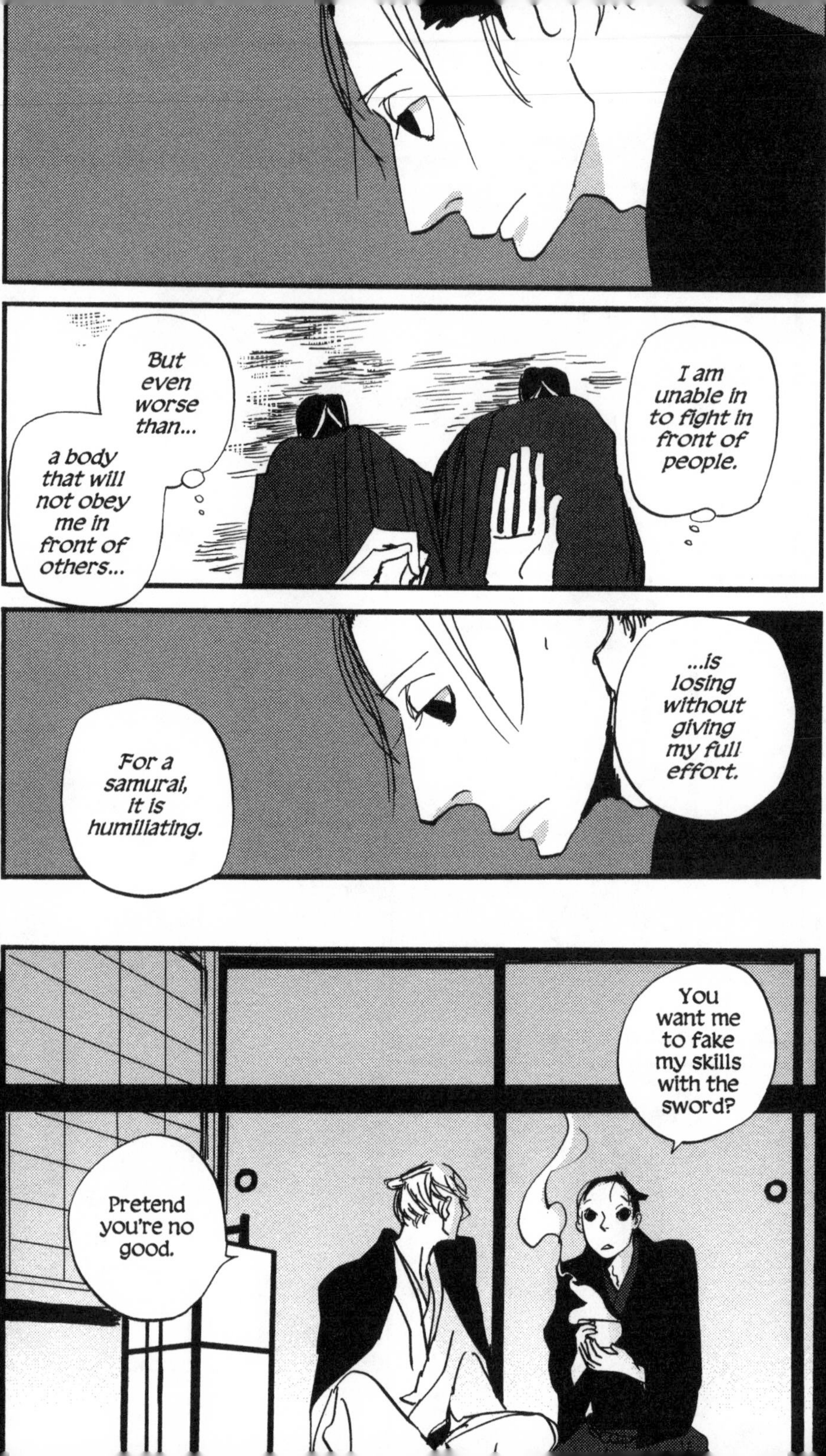
I am unable in to fight in front of people.
But even worse than...
a body that will not obey me in front of others...
...is losing without giving my full effort.
For a samurai, it is humiliating.
You want me to fake my skills with the sword?
Pretend you're no good.

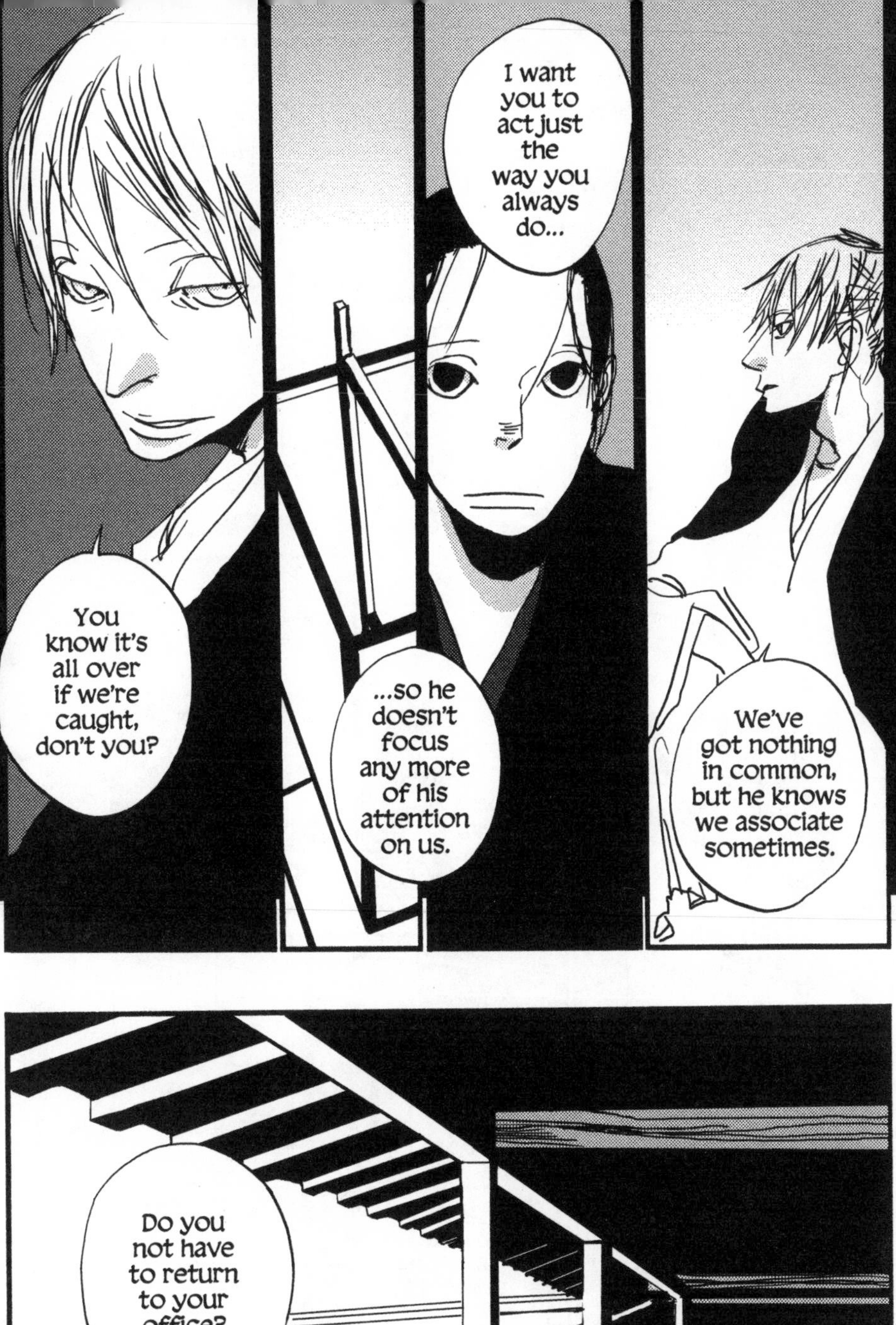
We've got nothing in common, but he knows we associate sometimes.
I want you to act just the way you always do...
...so he doesn't focus any more of his attention on us.
You know it's all over if we're caught, don't you?
Do you not have to return to your office?

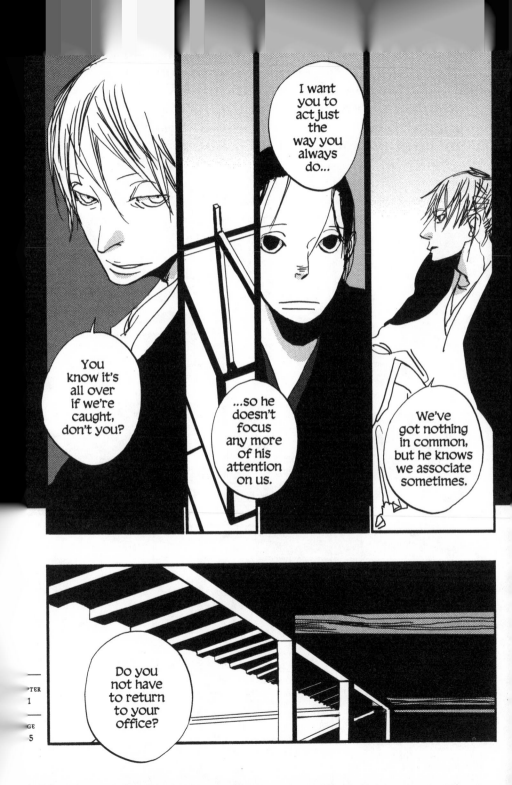

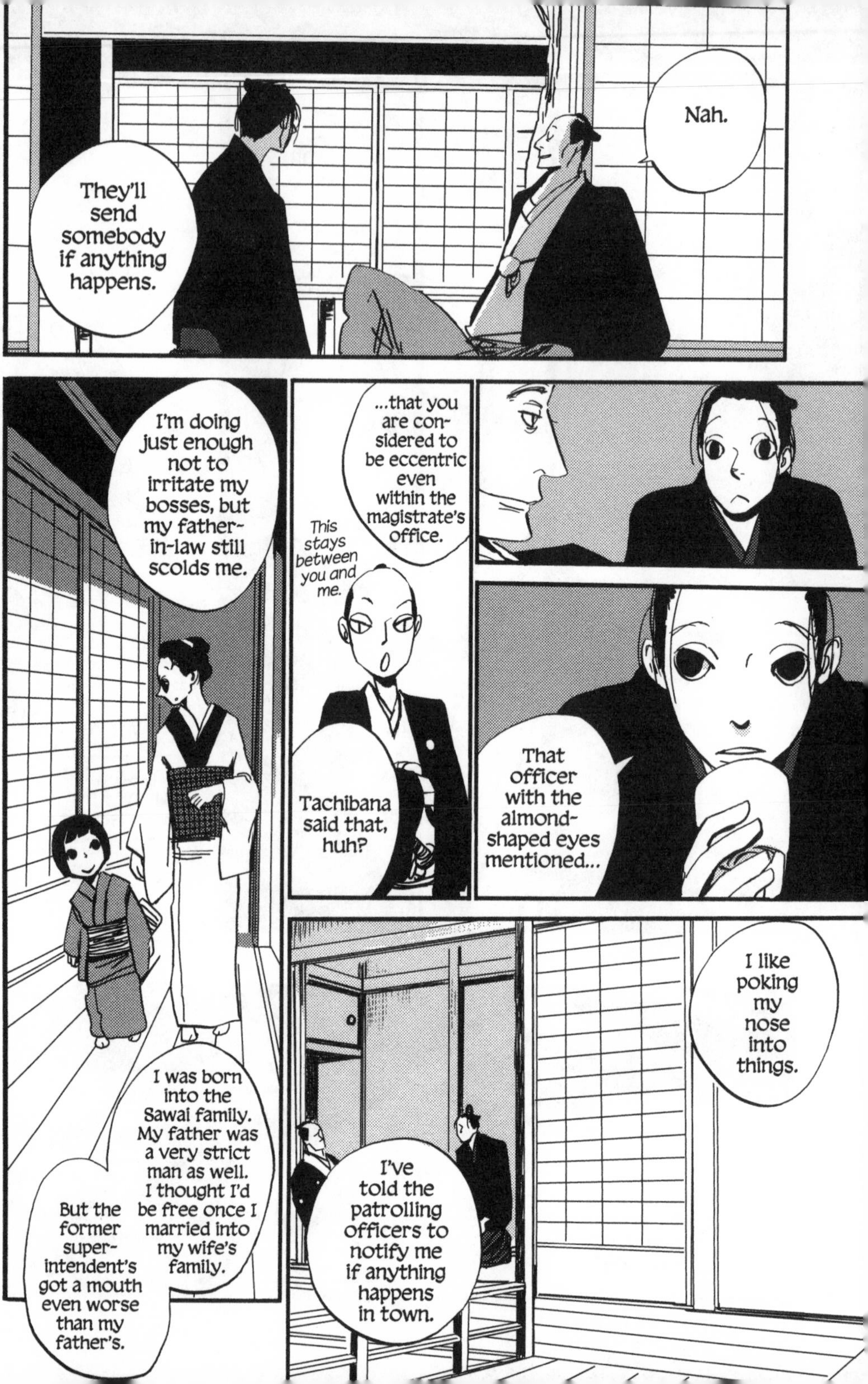
Nah.
They'll send somebody if anything happens.
That officer with the almond-shaped eyes mentioned...
...that you are considered to be eccentric even within the magistrate's office.
This stays between you and me.
Tachibana said that, huh?
I like poking my nose into things.
I've told the patrolling officers to notify me if anything happens in town.
I'm doing just enough not to irritate my bosses, but my father-in-law still scolds me.
I was born into the Sawai family. My father was a very strict man as well. I thought I'd be free once I married into my wife's family.
But the former super-intendent's got a mouth even worse than my father's.

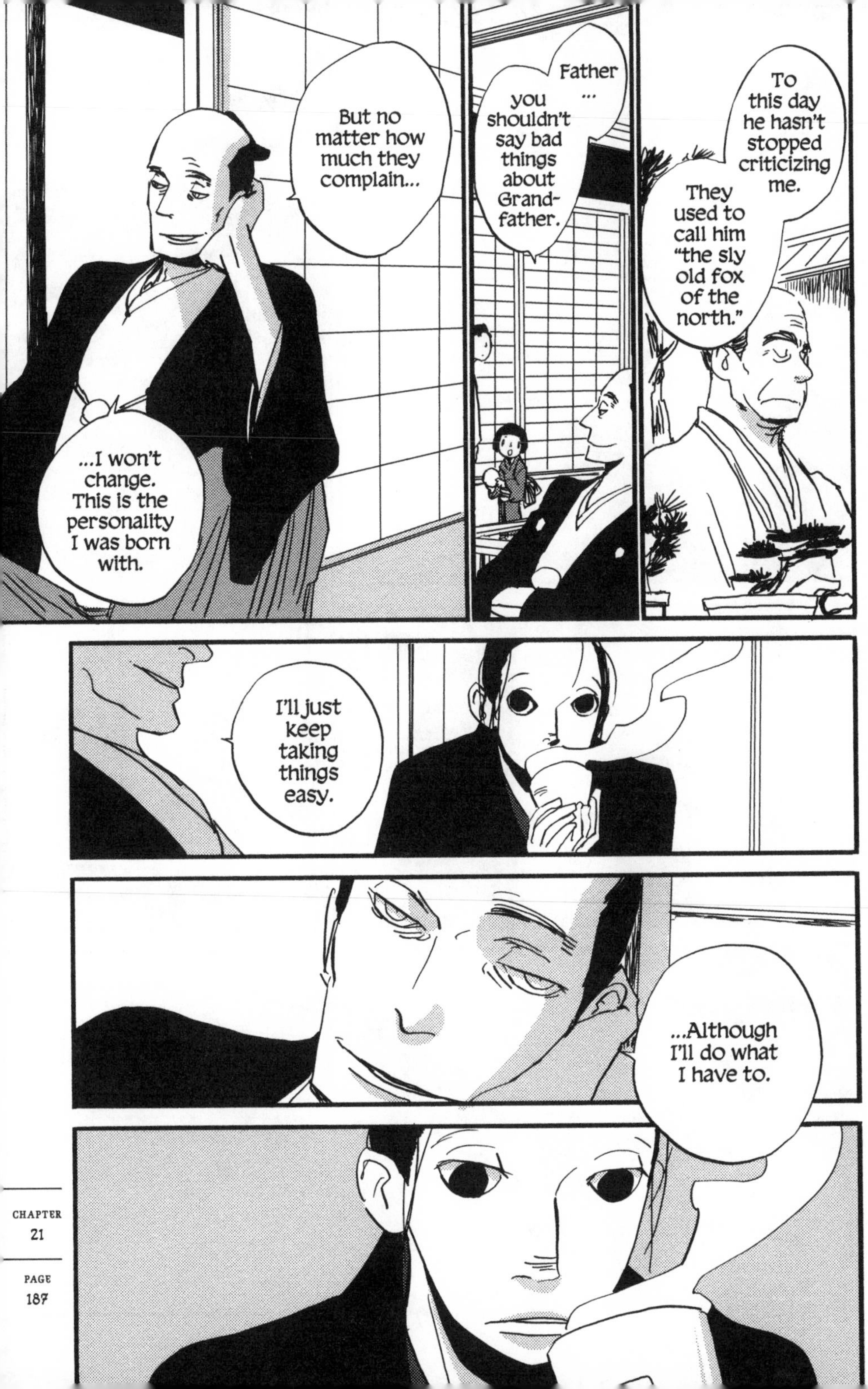
To this day he hasn't stopped criticizing me.
They used to call him "the sly old fox of the north."
Father...
you shouldn't say bad things about Grand-father.
But no matter how much they complain...
...I won't change. This is the personality I was born with.
I'll just keep taking things easy.
...Although I'll do what I have to.

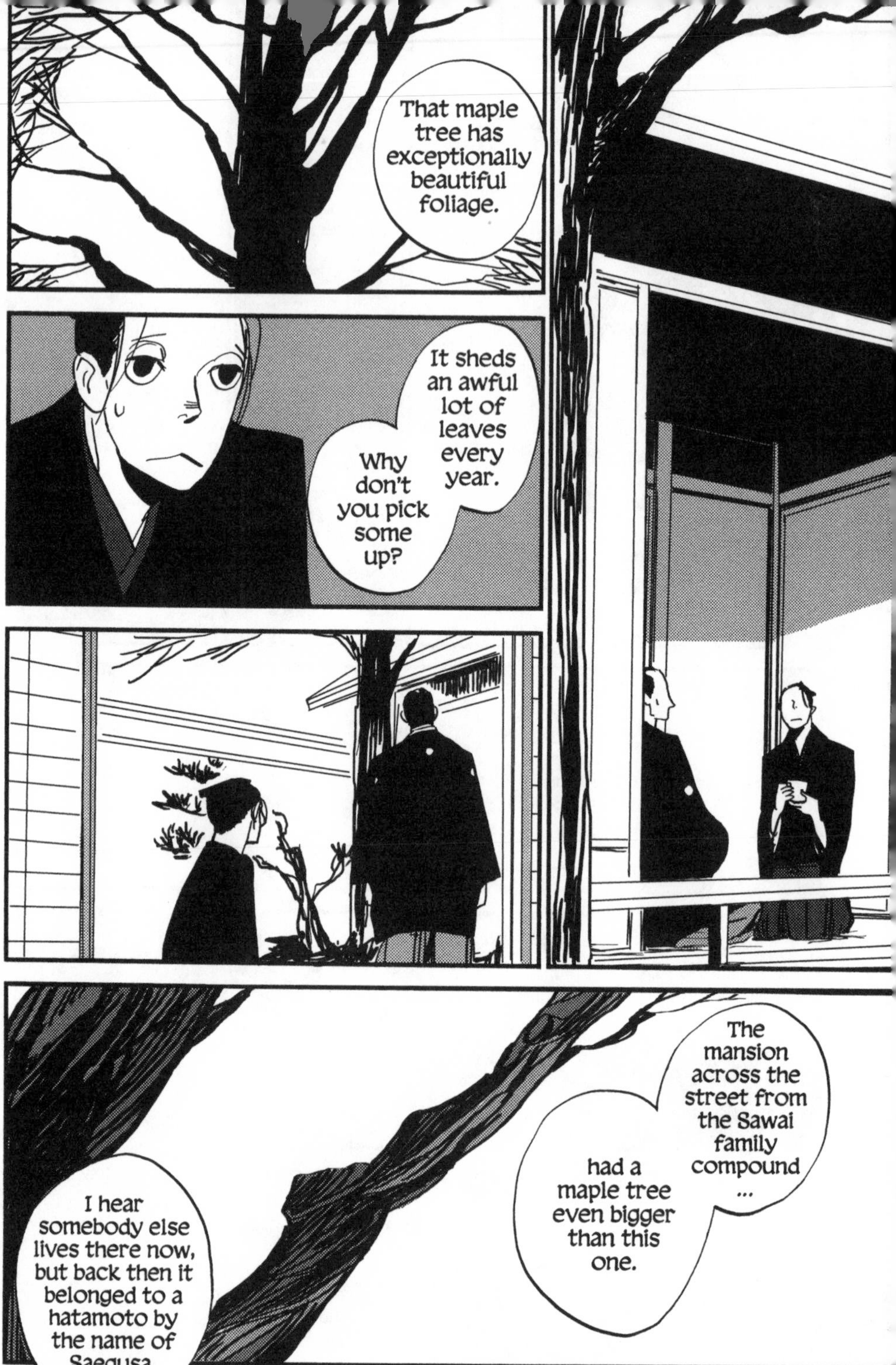
That maple tree has exceptionally beautiful foliage.
It sheds an awful lot of leaves every year.
Why don't you pick some up?
The mansion across the street from the Sawai family compound ...
had a maple tree even bigger than this one.
I hear somebody else lives there now, but back then it belonged to a hatamoto by the name of Saegusa.

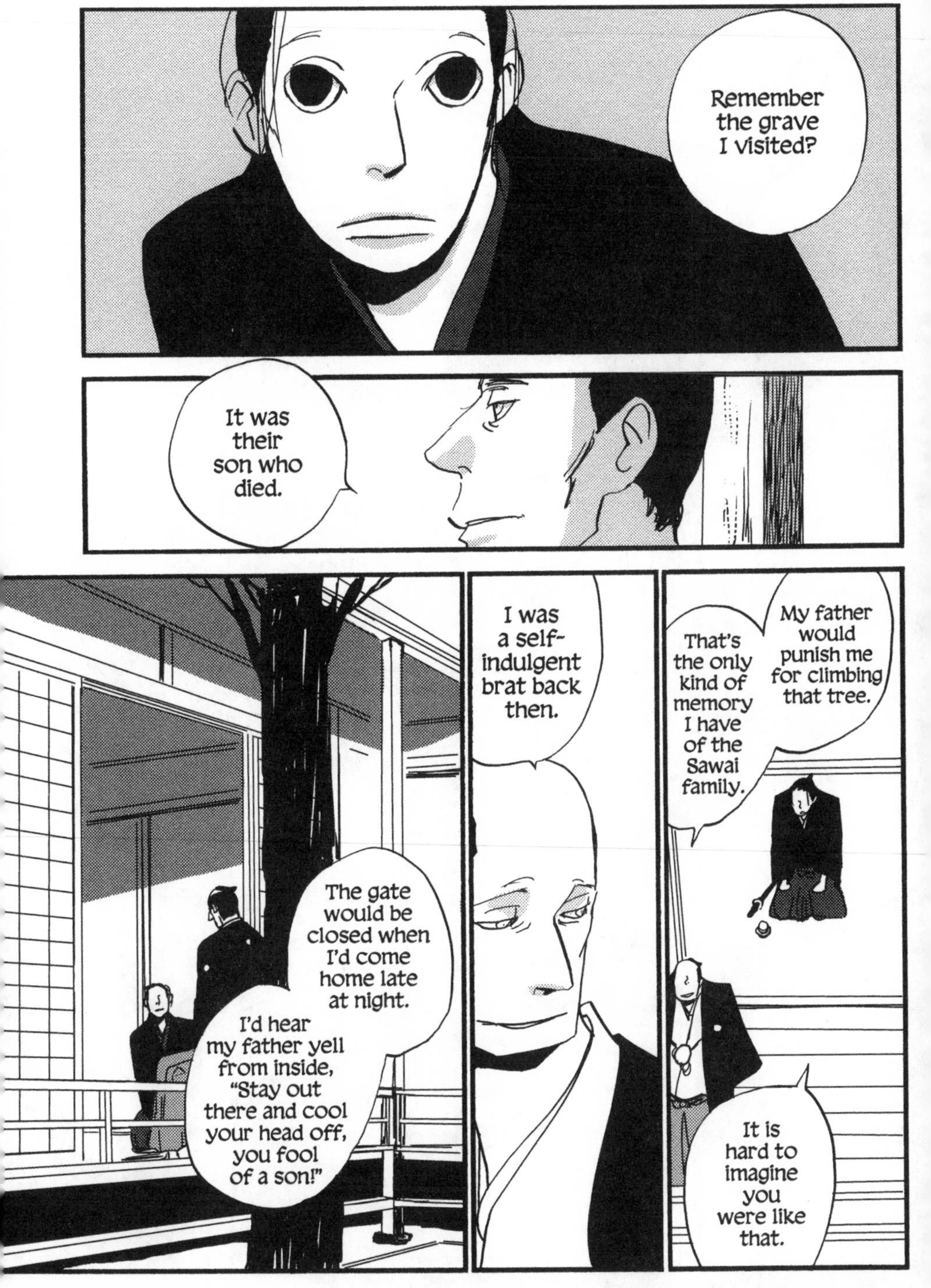
Remember the grave I visited?
It was their son who died.
My father would punish me for climbing that tree.
That's the only kind of memory I have of the Sawai family.
It is hard to imagine you were like that.
I was a self-indulgent brat back then.
The gate would be closed when I'd come home late at night.
I'd hear my father yell from inside, "Stay out there and cool your head off, you fool of a son!"

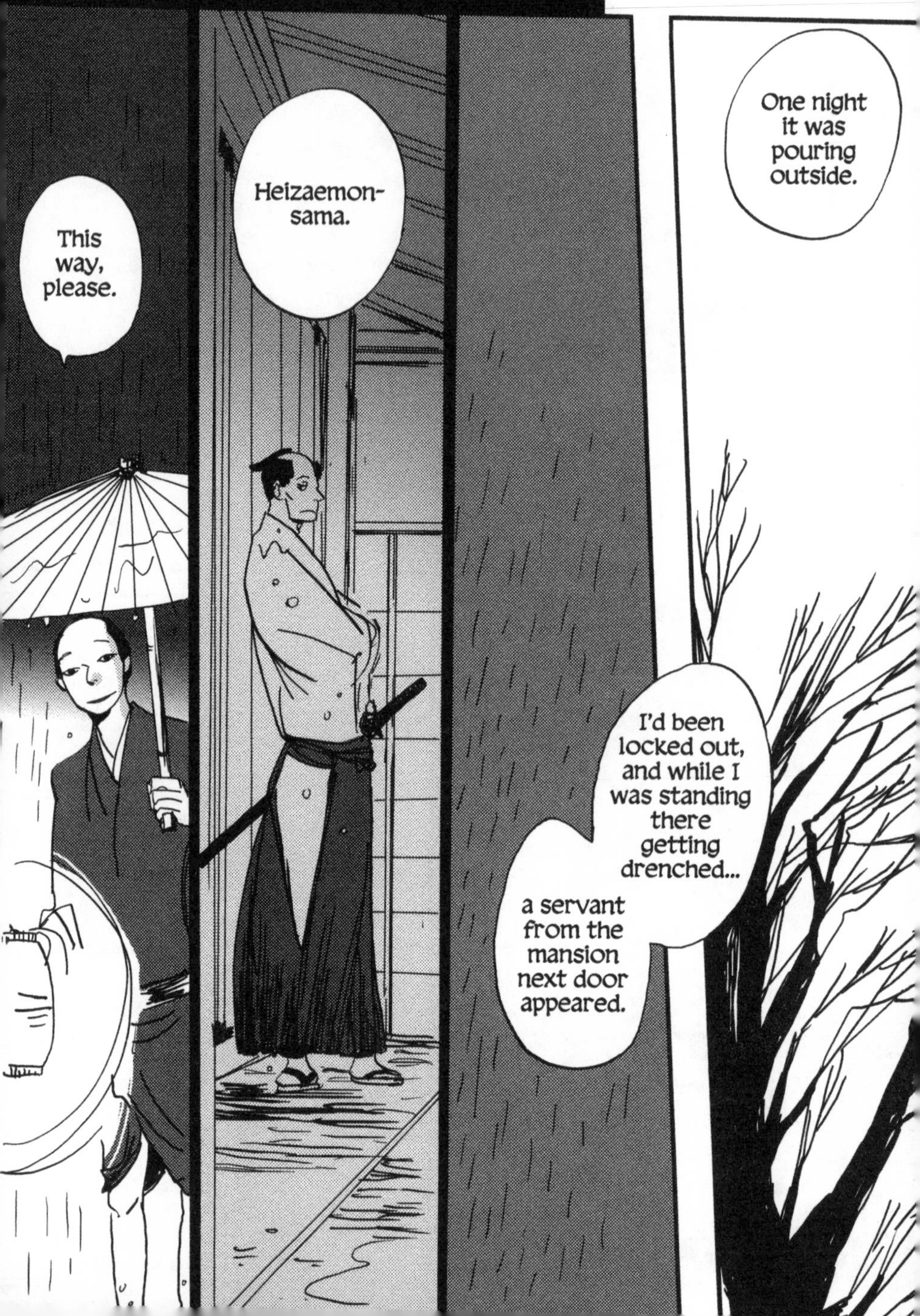
One night it was pouring outside.
I'd been locked out, and while I was standing there getting drenched...
a servant from the mansion next door appeared.
Heizaemon-sama.
This way, please.

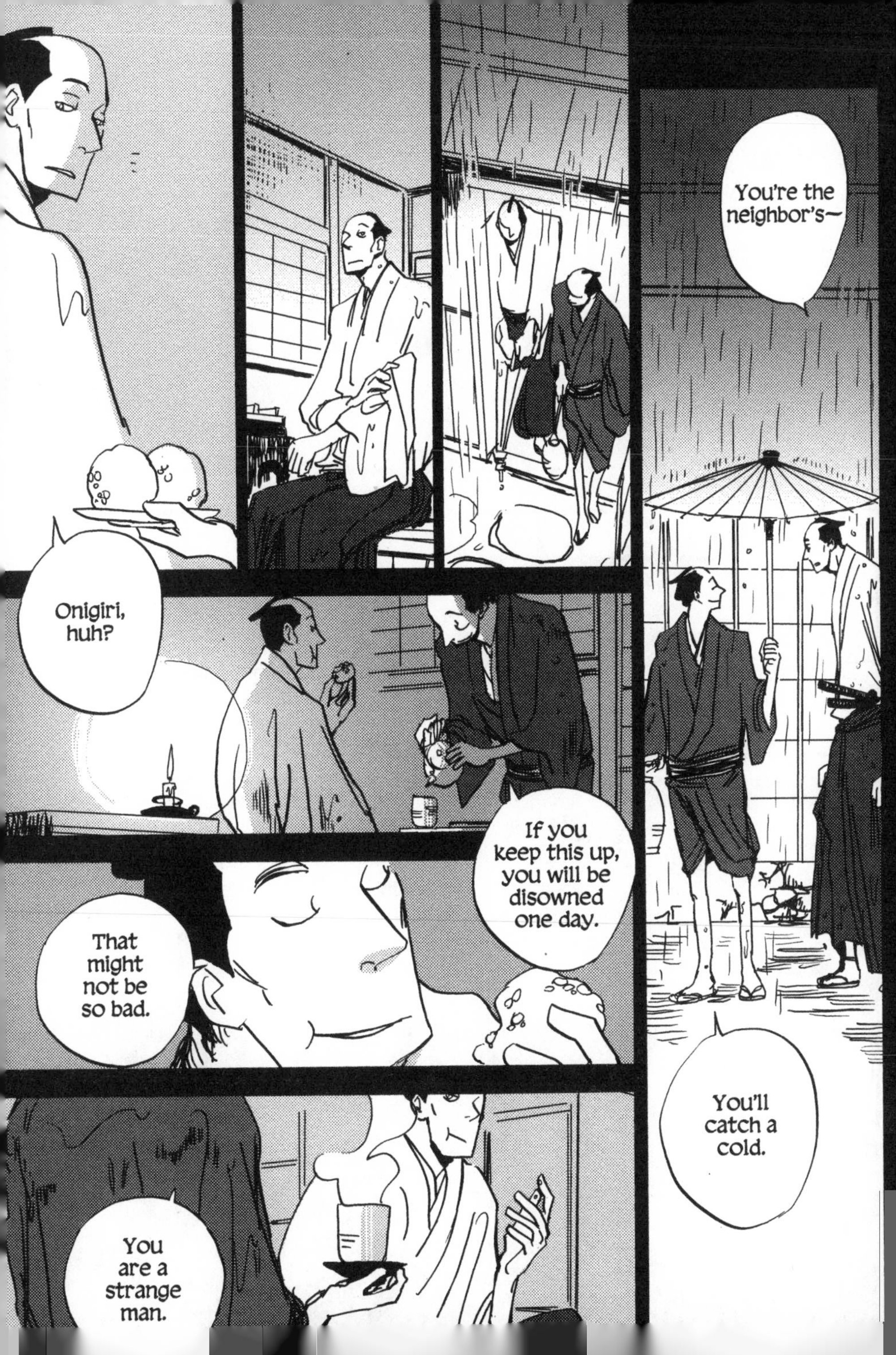
You're the neighbor's~
You'll catch a cold.
Onigiri, huh?
If you keep this up, you will be disowned one day.
That might not be so bad.
You are a strange man.

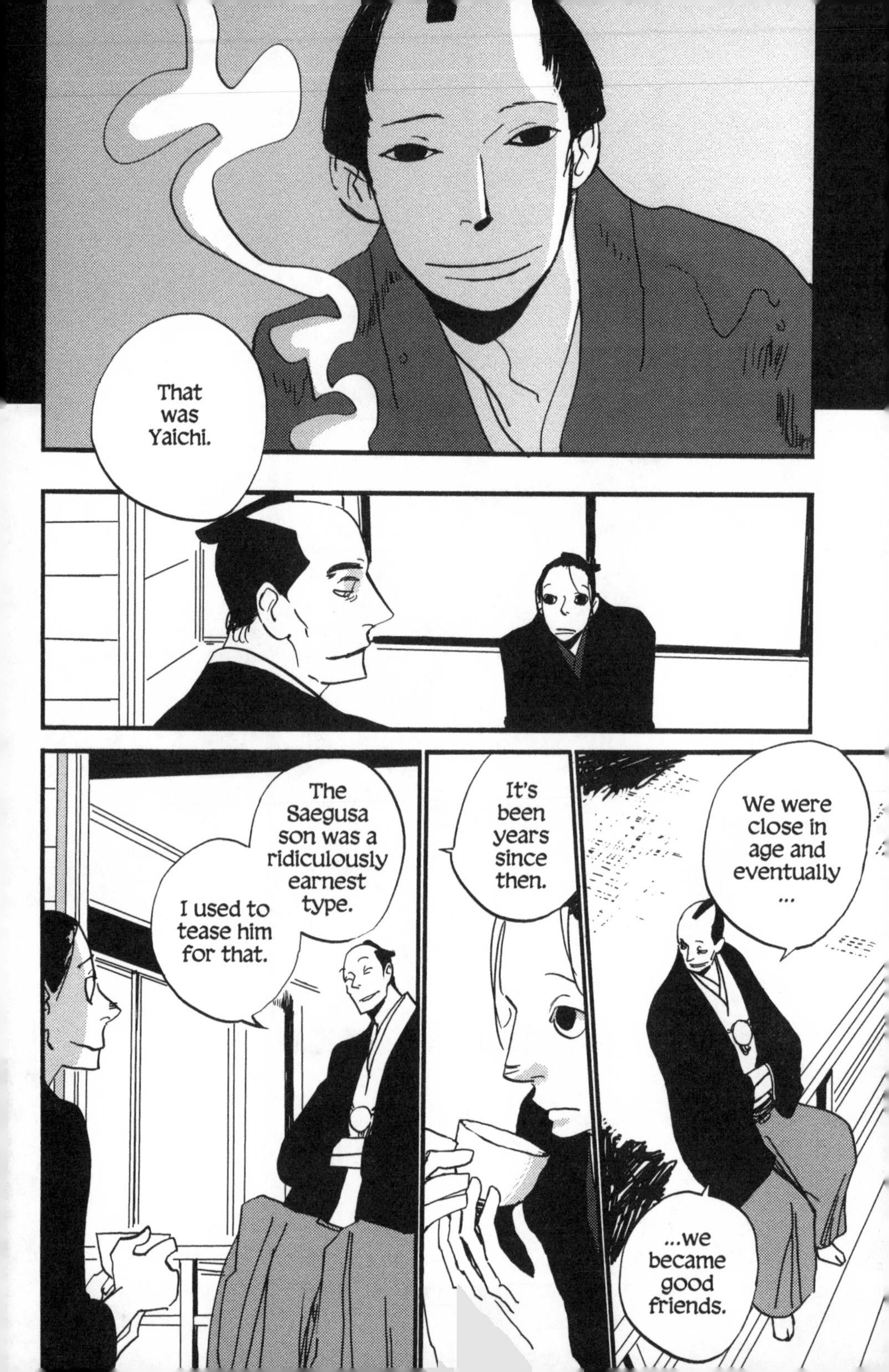
That was Yaichi.
We were close in age and eventually ...
...we became good friends.
It's been years since then.
The Saegusa son was a ridiculously earnest type.
I used to tease him for that.

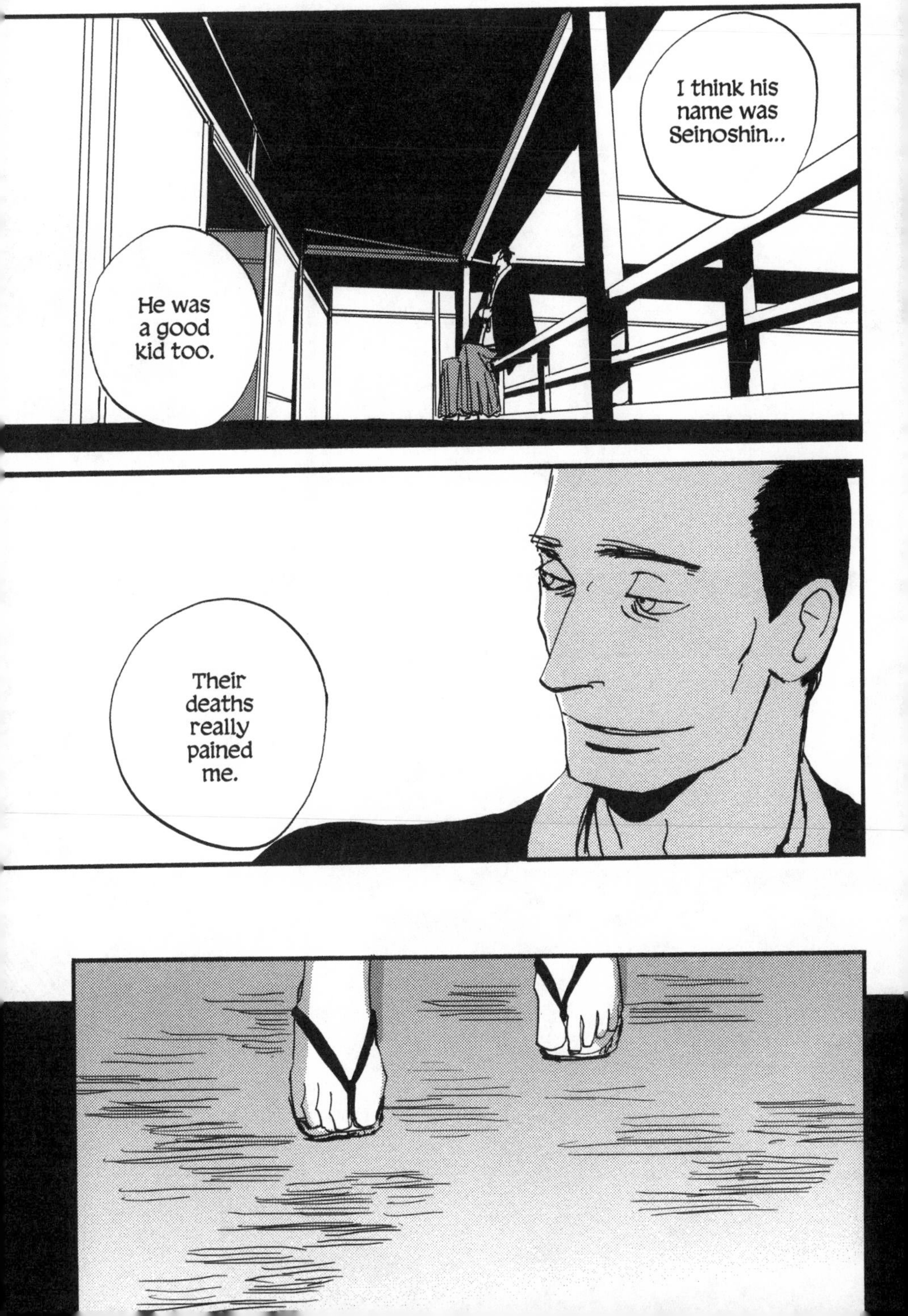
I think his name was Seinoshin...
He was a good kid too.
Their deaths really pained me.

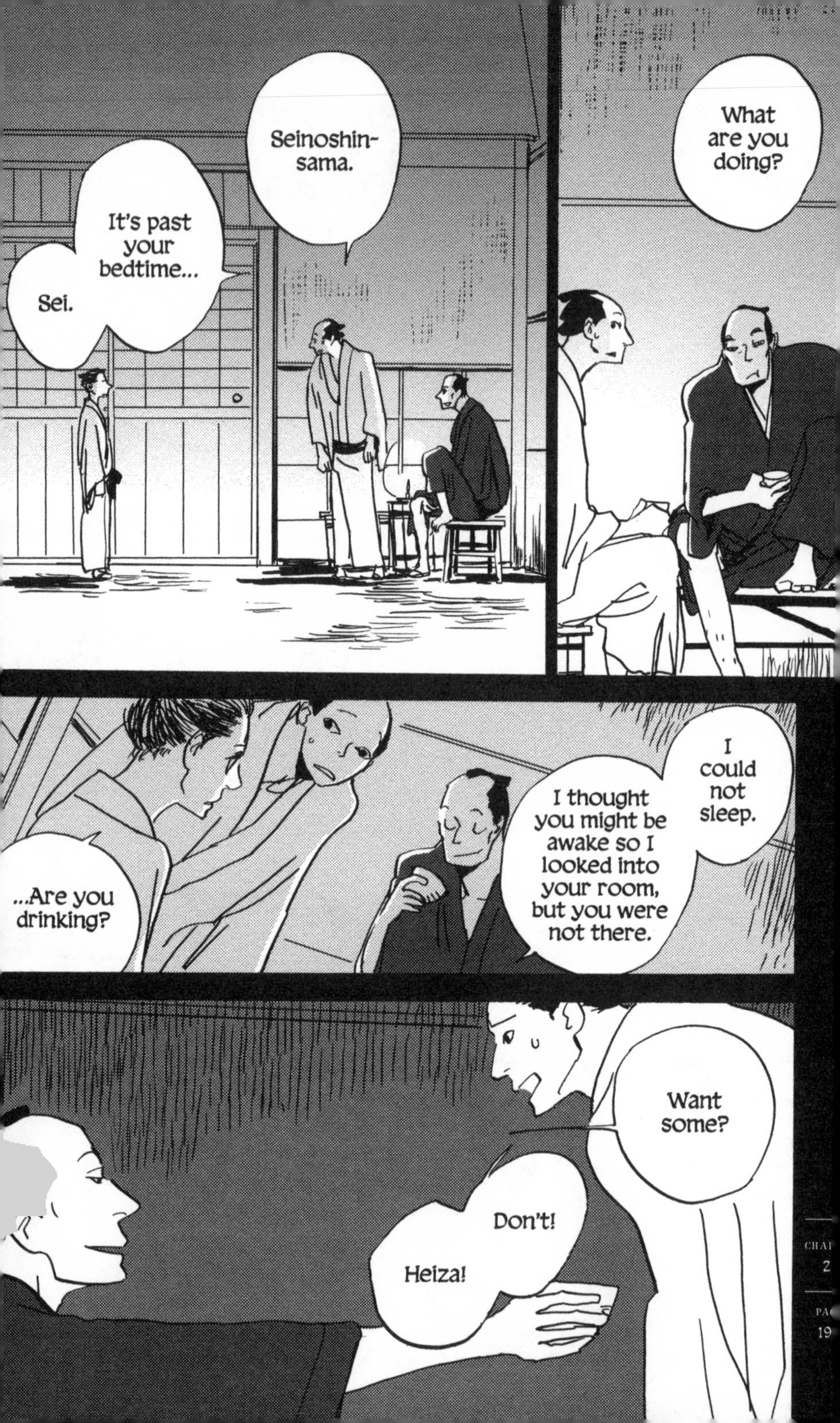
What are you doing?
Seinoshin-sama.
It's past your bedtime...
Sei.
I could not sleep.
I thought you might be awake so I looked into your room, but you were not there.
...Are you drinking?
Want some?
Don't!
Heiza!

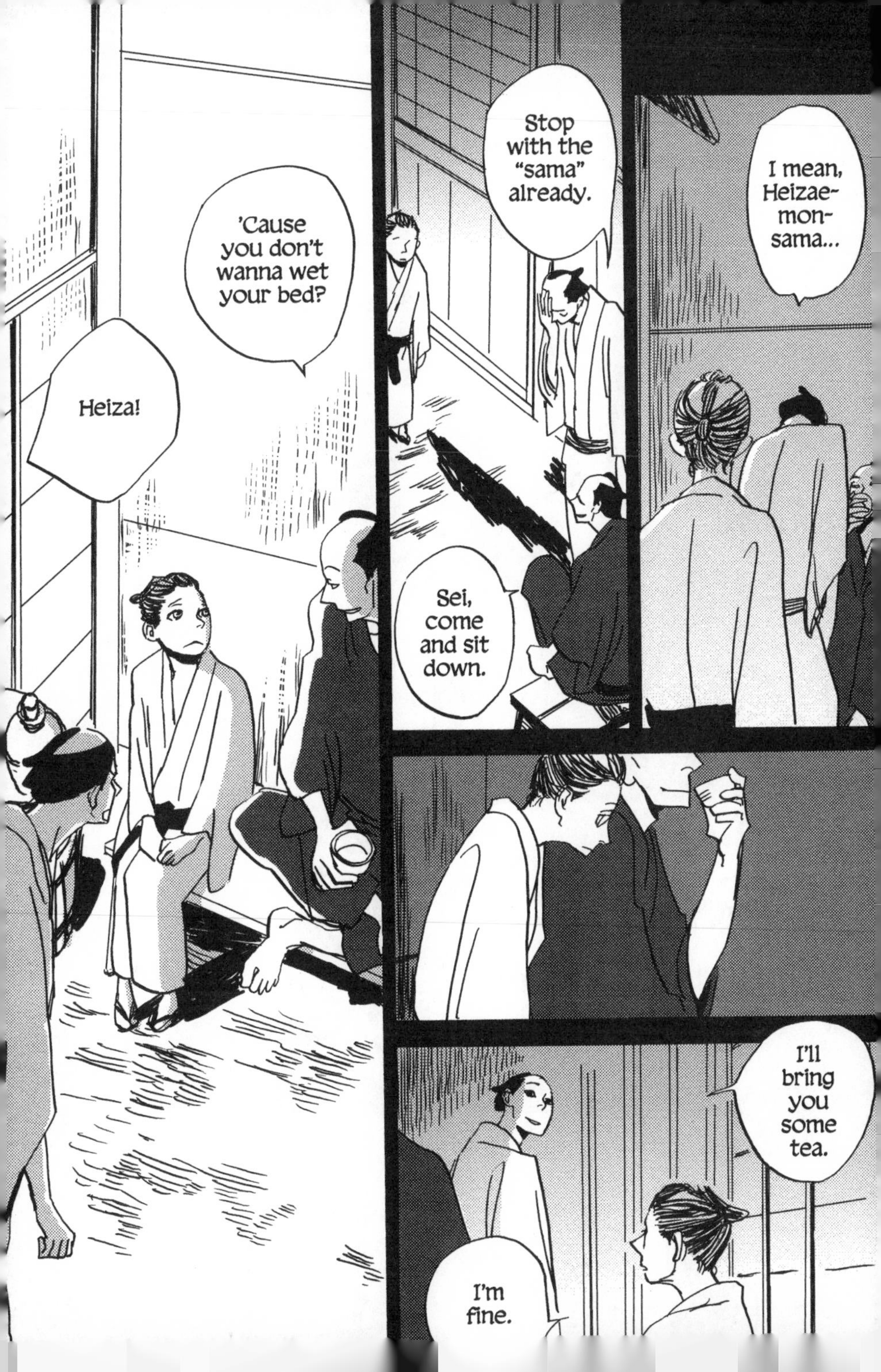
I mean, Heizaemon-sama...
Stop with the "sama" already.
Sei, come and sit down.
I'll bring you some tea.
I'm fine.
'Cause you don't wanna wet your bed?
Heiza!

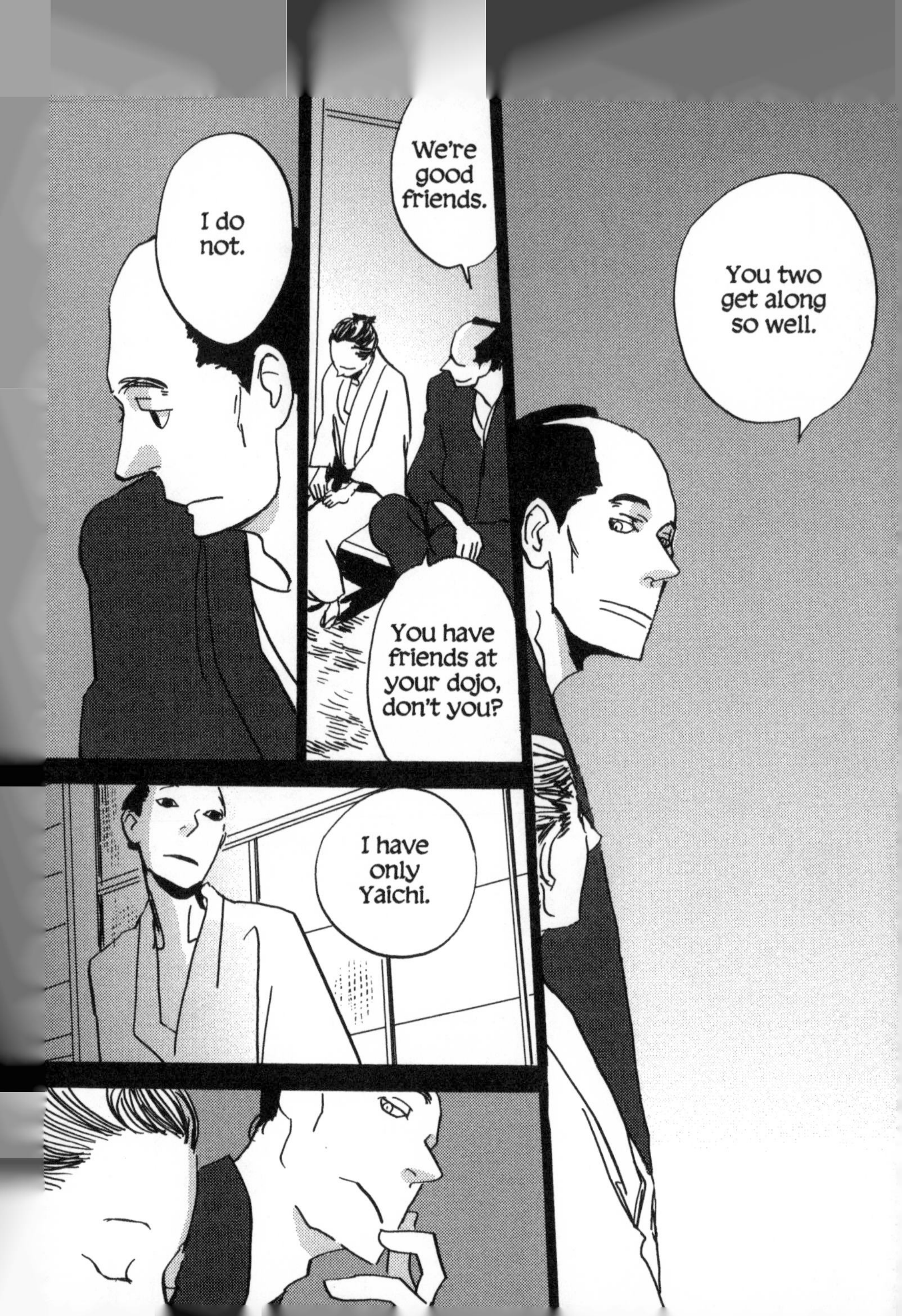
You two get along so well.
We're good friends.
You have friends at your dojo, don't you?
I do not.
I have only Yaichi.

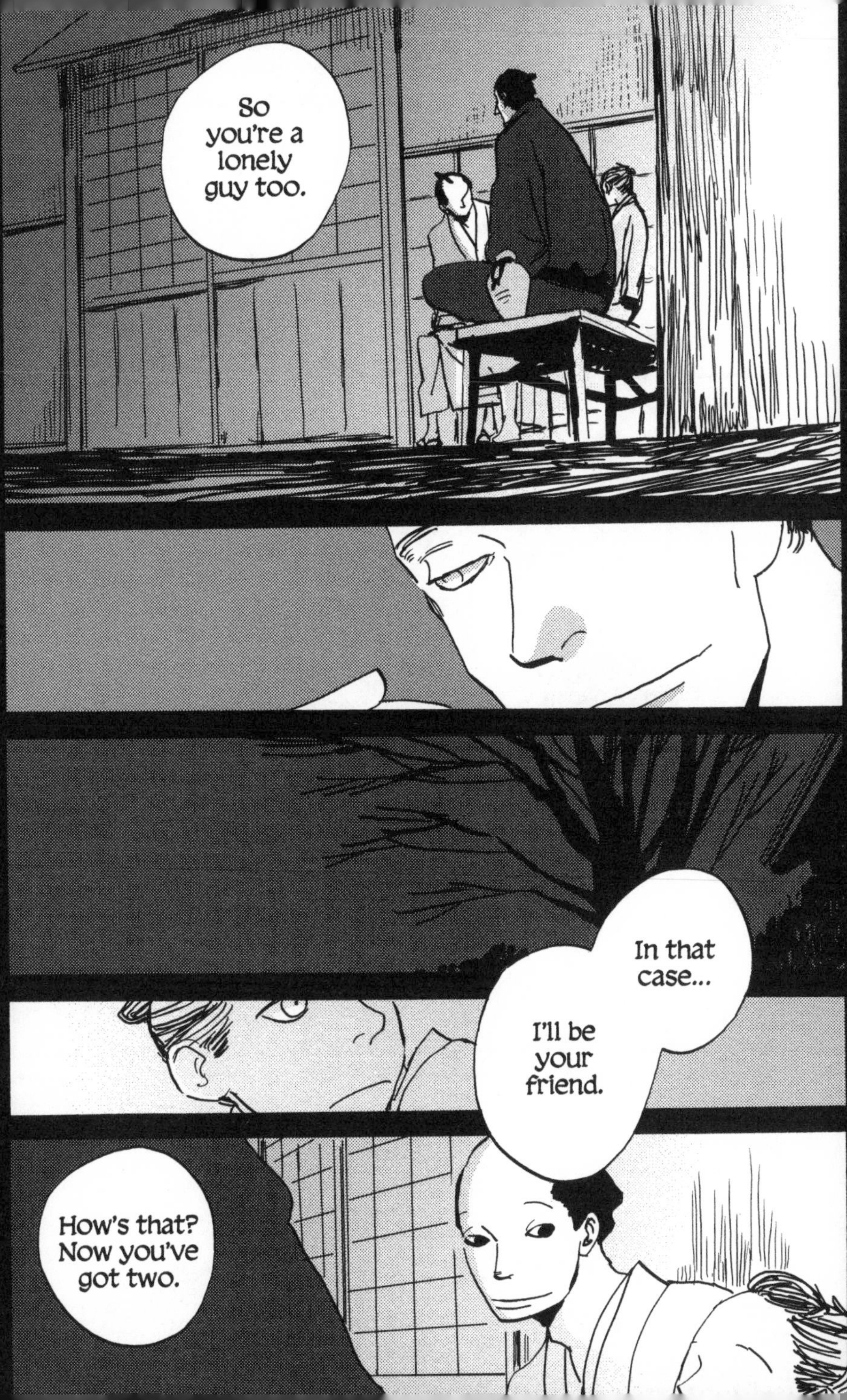
So you're a lonely guy too.
In that case...
I'll be your friend.
How's that? Now you've got two.

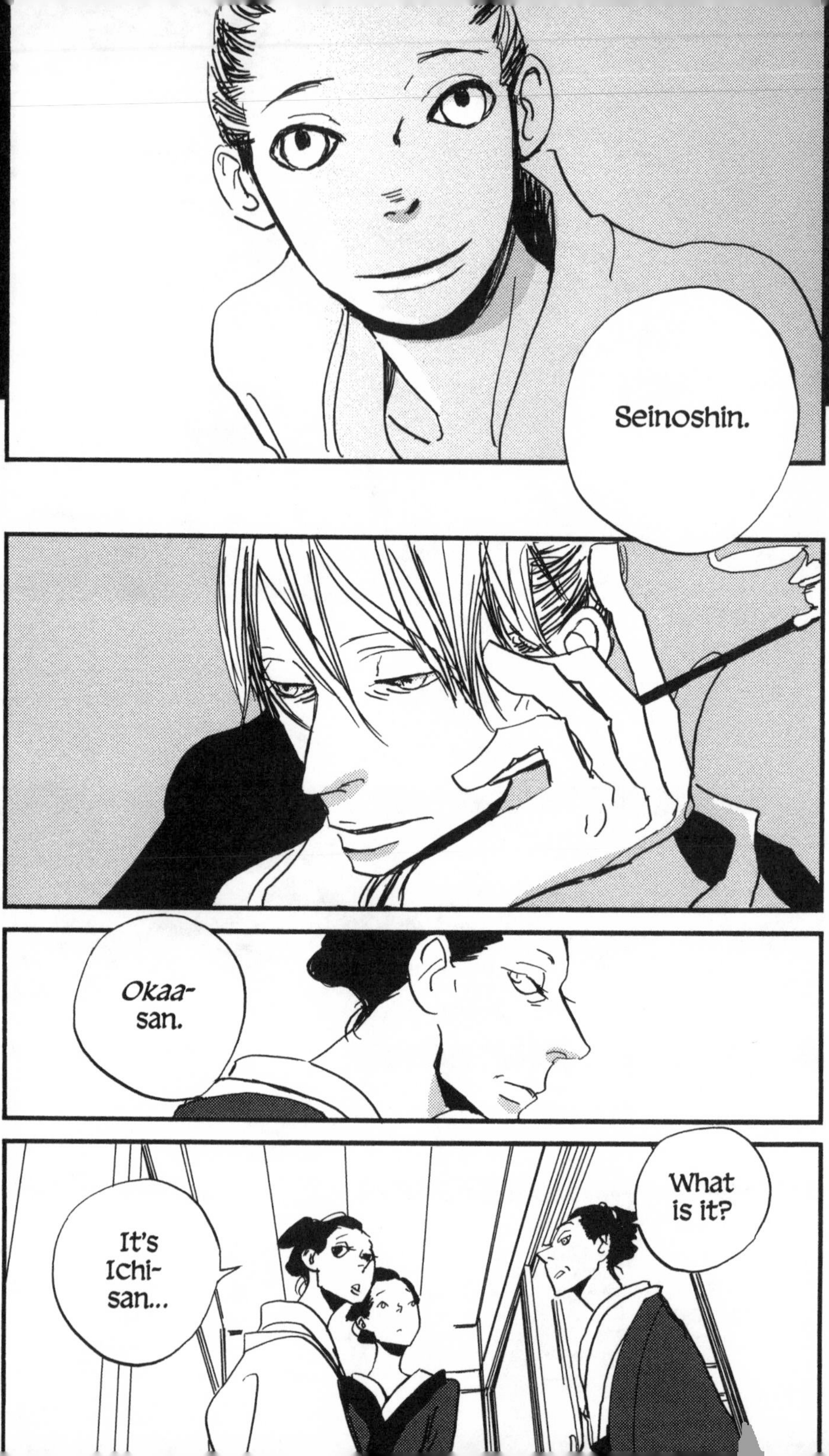
Seinoshin.
Okaa-san.
What is it?
It's Ichi-san...

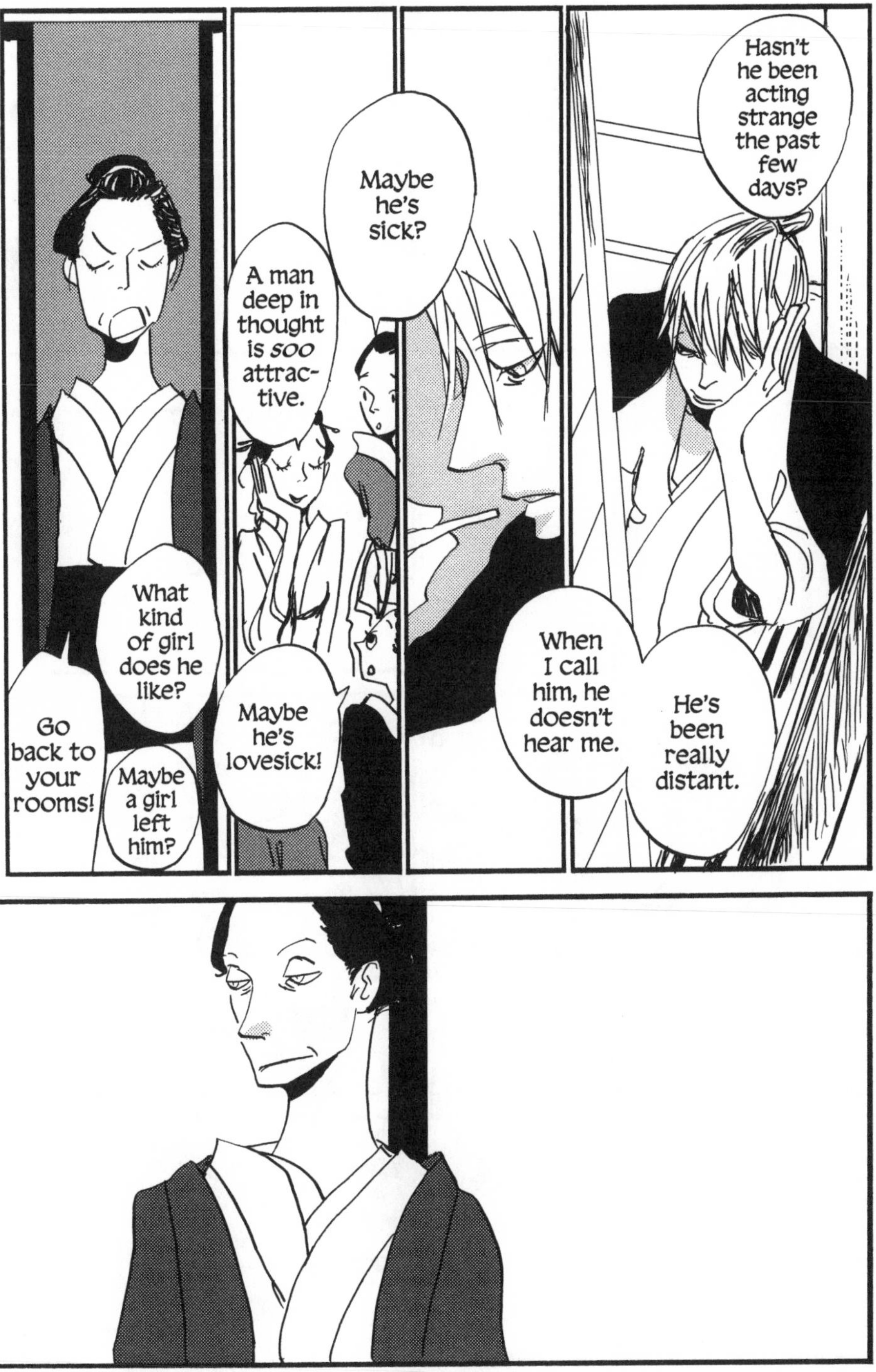
Hasn't he been acting strange the past few days?
He's been really distant.
When I call him, he doesn't hear me.
Maybe he's sick?
A man deep in thought is *soo* attractive.
Maybe he's lovesick!
What kind of girl does he like?
Maybe a girl left him?
Go back to your rooms!

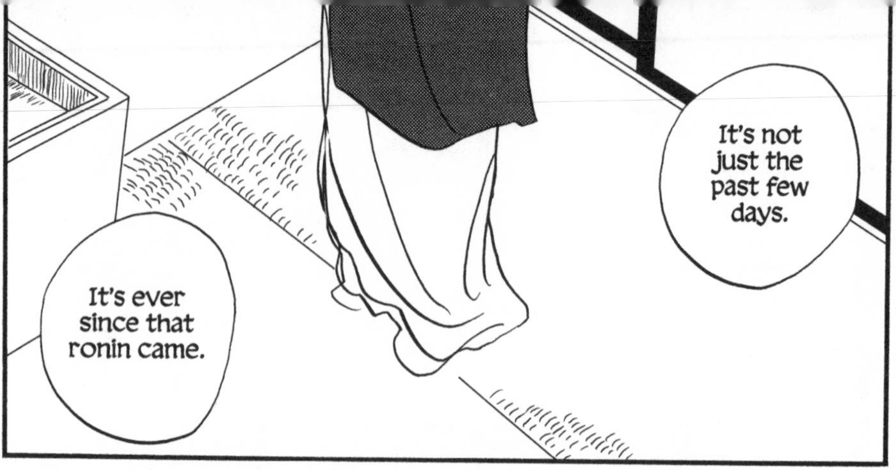
It's not just the past few days.
It's ever since that ronin came.

On sign: Ornament Maker

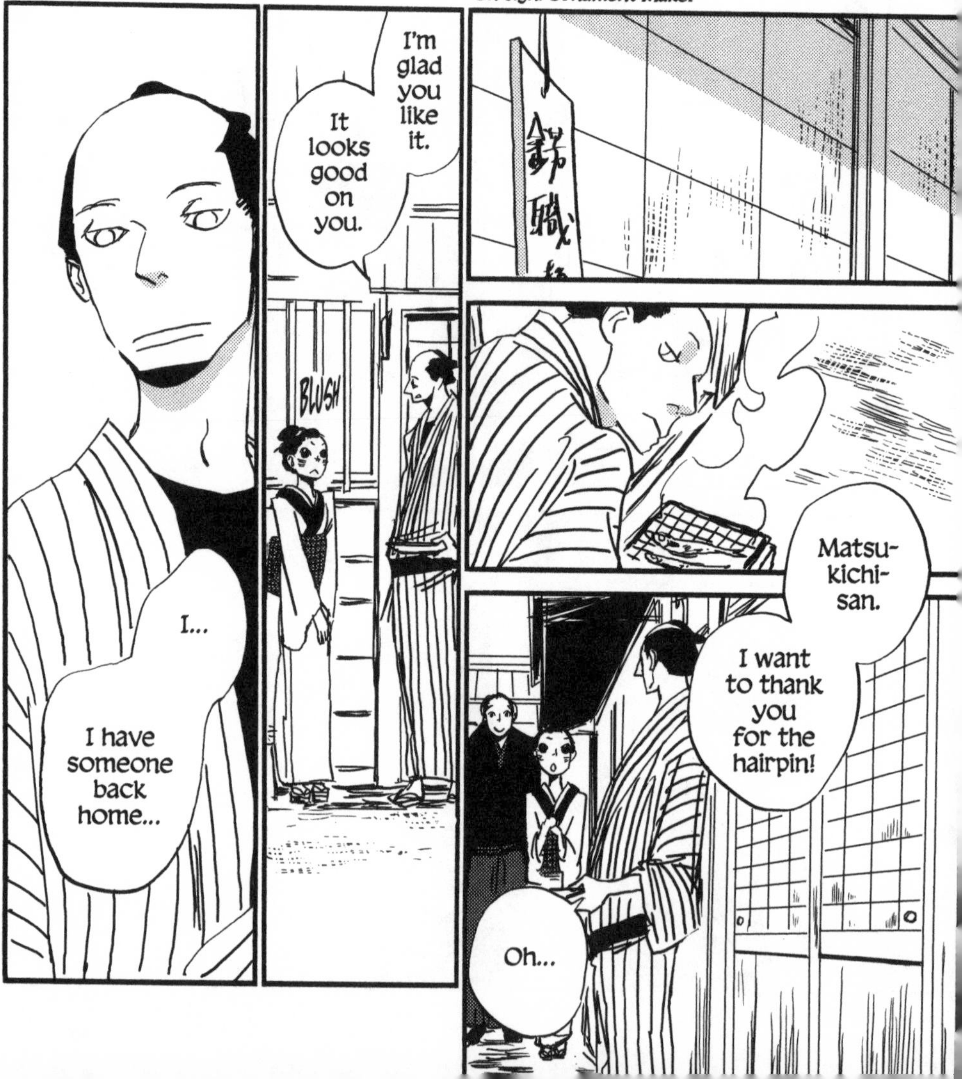
錺職
Matsu-kichi-san.
I want to thank you for the hairpin!
Oh...
I'm glad you like it.
It looks good on you.
BLUSH
I...
I have someone back home...

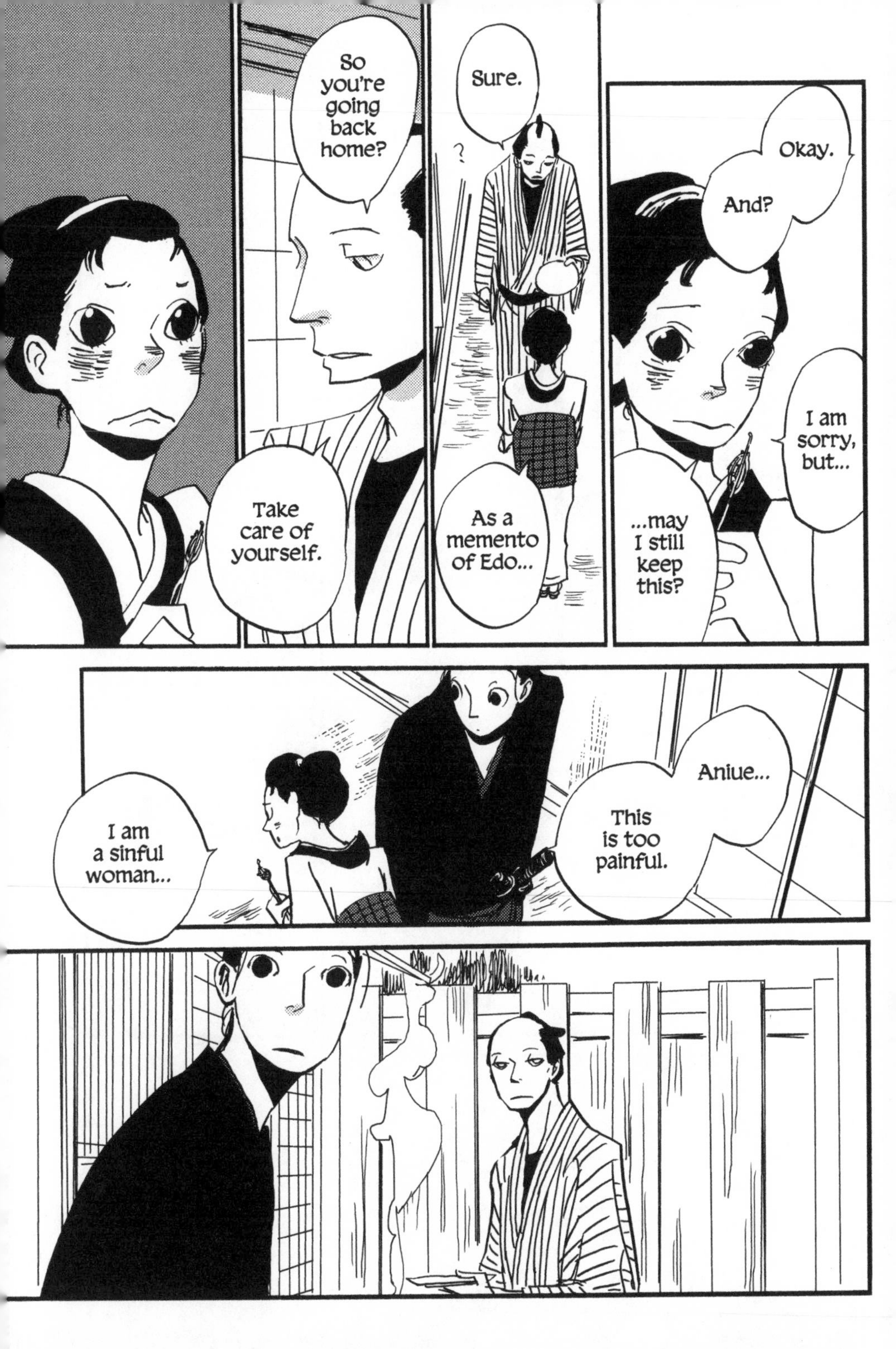
Okay.
And?
I am sorry, but...
...may I still keep this?
Sure.
?
As a memento of Edo...
So you're going back home?
Take care of yourself.
Aniue...
This is too painful.
I am a sinful woman...

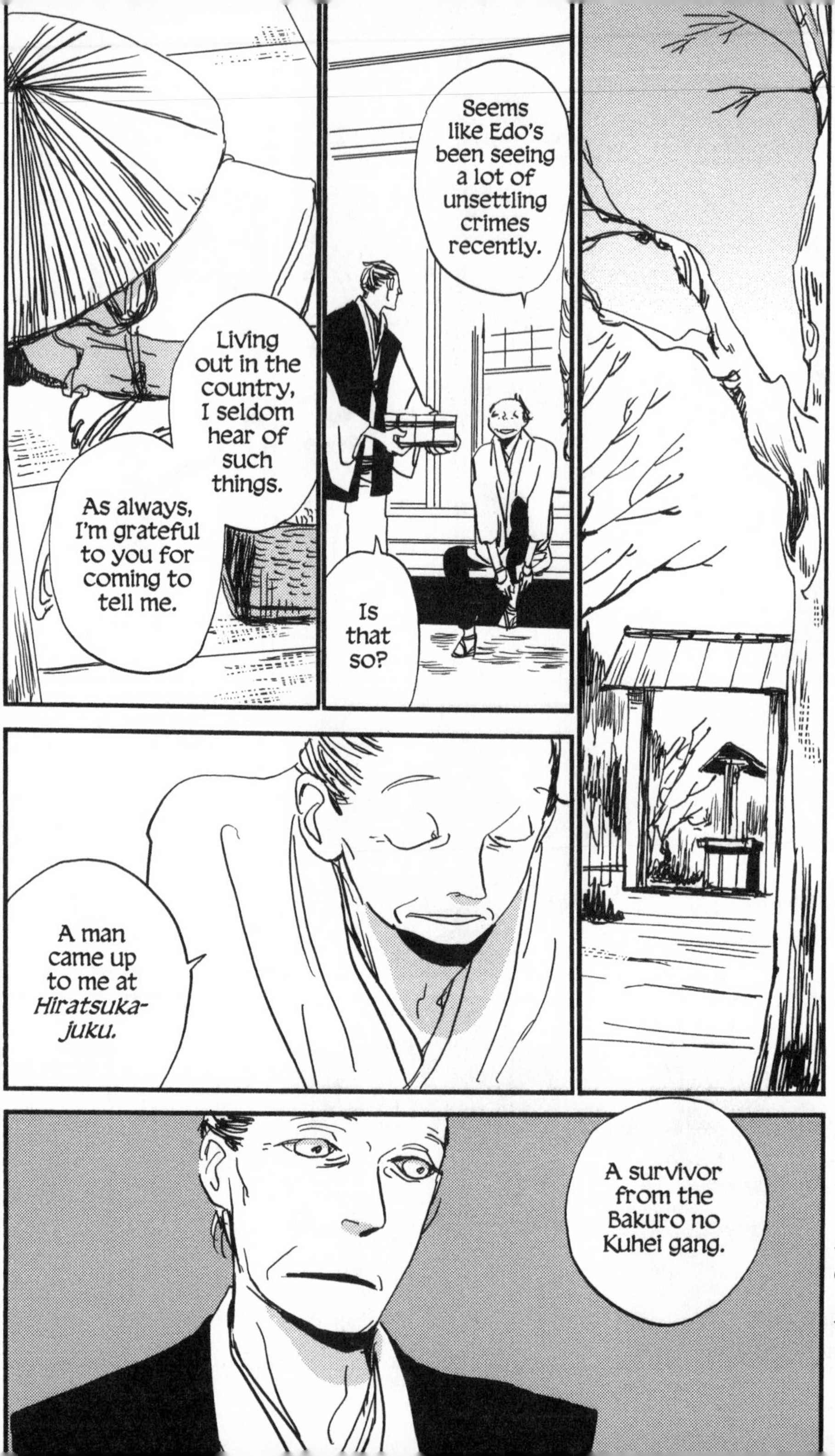
Seems like Edo's been seeing a lot of unsettling crimes recently.
Is that so?
Living out in the country, I seldom hear of such things.
As always, I'm grateful to you for coming to tell me.
A man came up to me at *Hiratsuka-juku.*
A survivor from the Bakuro no Kuhei gang.

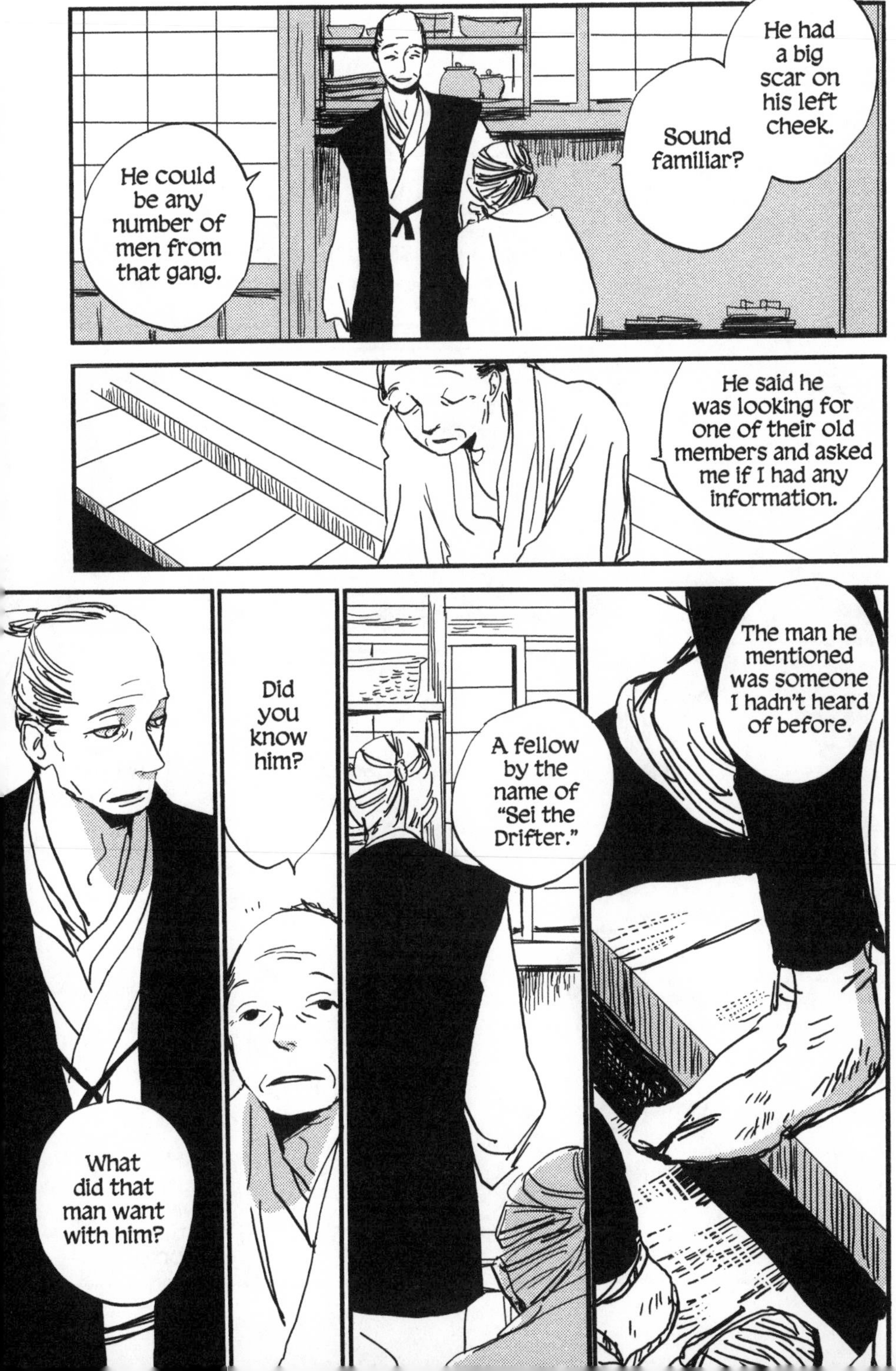
He had a big scar on his left cheek.
Sound familiar?
He could be any number of men from that gang.
He said he was looking for one of their old members and asked me if I had any information.
The man he mentioned was someone I hadn't heard of before.
A fellow by the name of "Sei the Drifter."
Did you know him?
What did that man want with him?

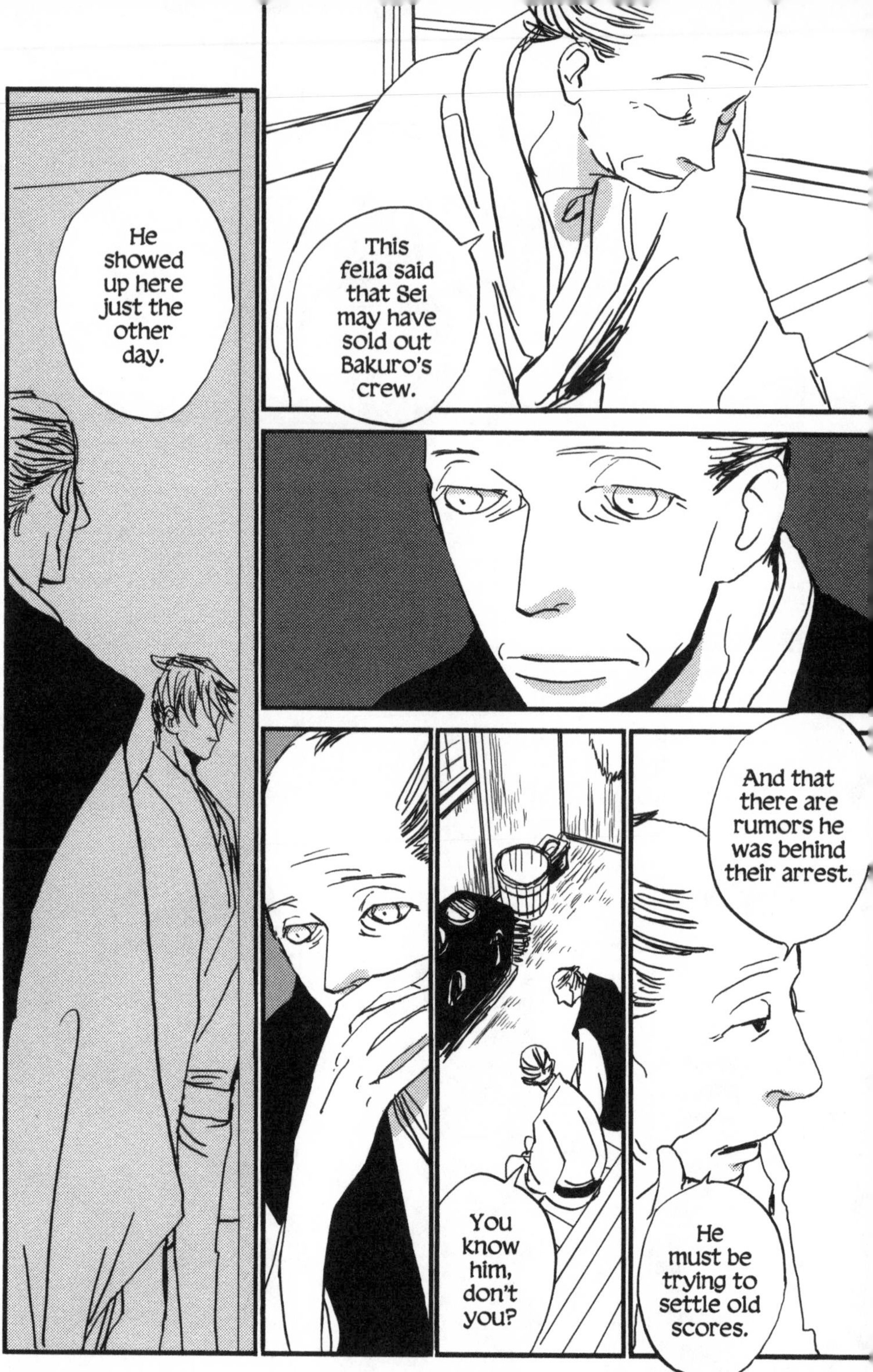
This fella said that Sei may have sold out Bakuro's crew.
And that there are rumors he was behind their arrest.
He must be trying to settle old scores.
You know him, don't you?
He showed up here just the other day.

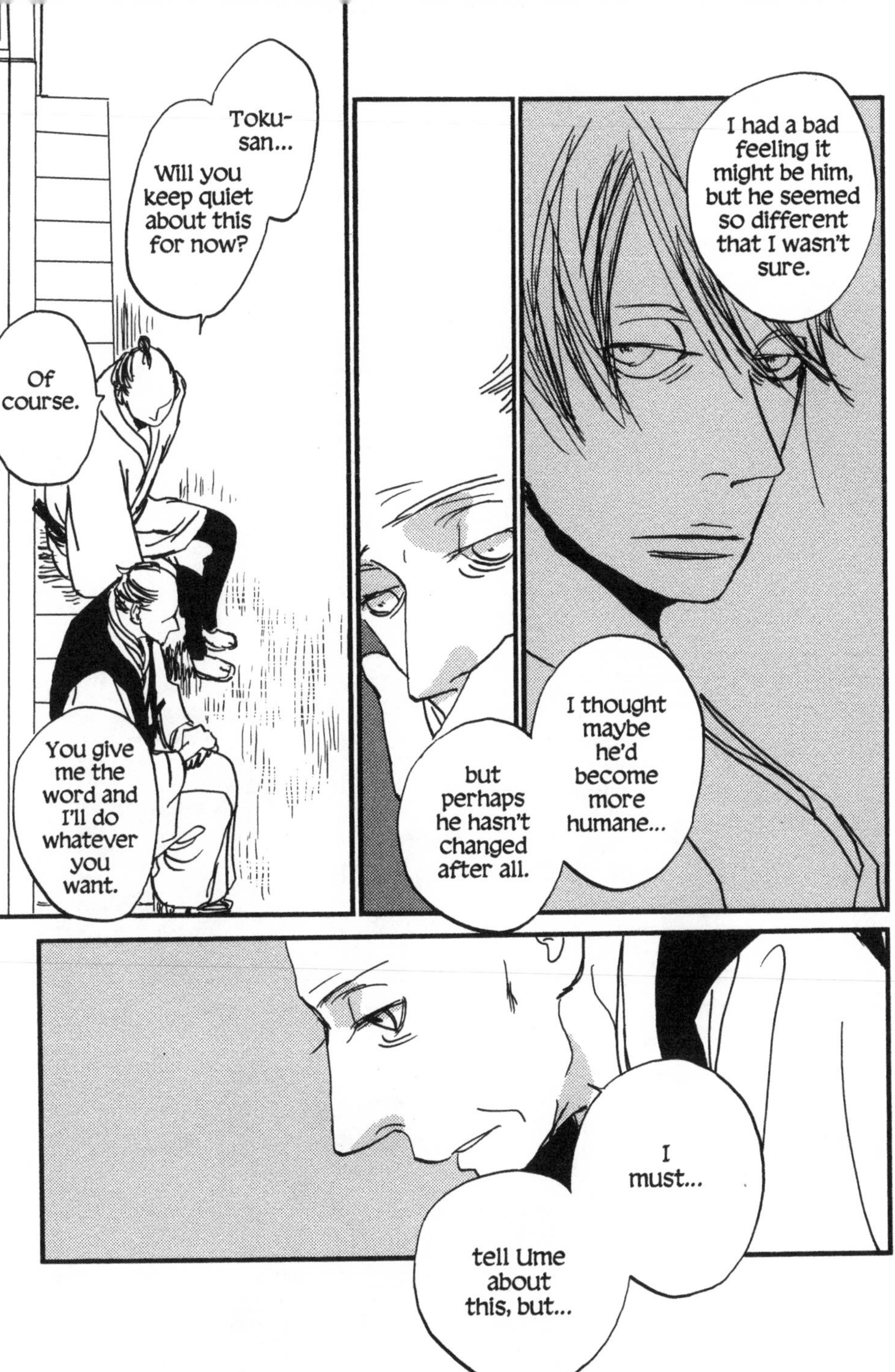
I had a bad feeling it might be him, but he seemed so different that I wasn't sure.
I thought maybe he'd become more humane...
but perhaps he hasn't changed after all.
Toku-san... Will you keep quiet about this for now?
Of course.
You give me the word and I'll do whatever you want.
I must...
tell Ume about this, but...

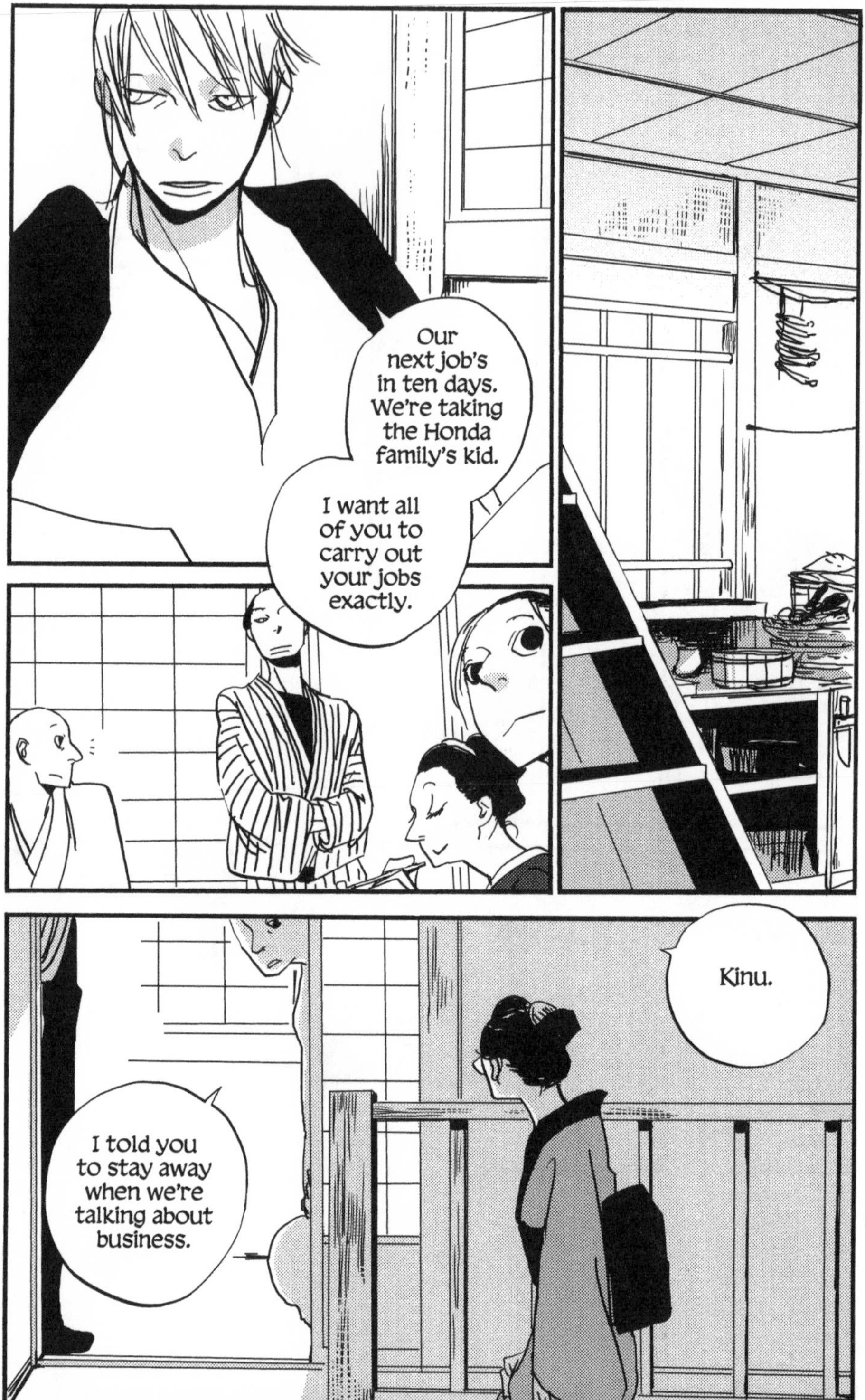
Our next job's in ten days. We're taking the Honda family's kid.
I want all of you to carry out your jobs exactly.
Kinu.
I told you to stay away when we're talking about business.

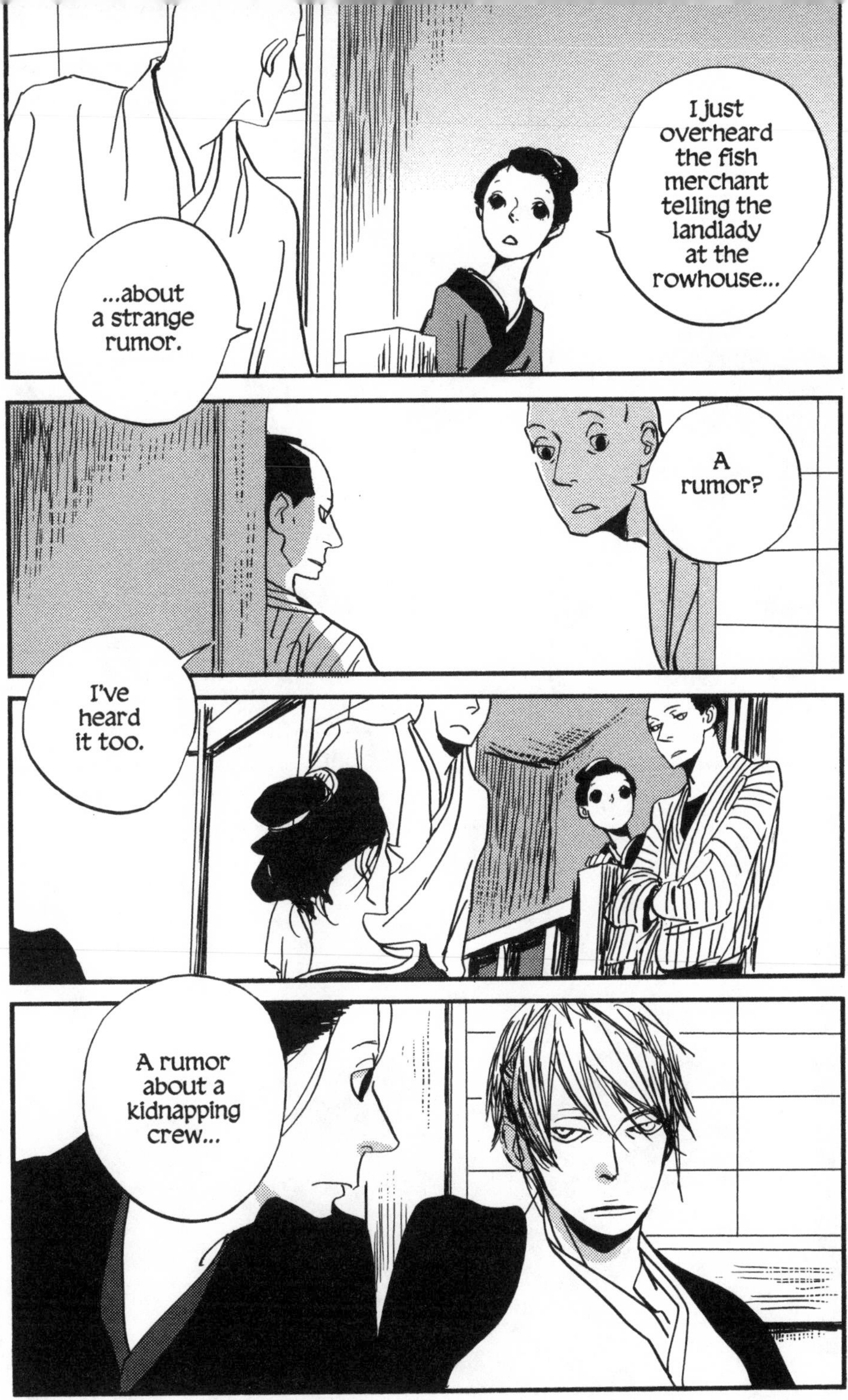
I just overheard the fish merchant telling the landlady at the rowhouse...
...about a strange rumor.
A rumor?
I've heard it too.
A rumor about a kidnapping crew...

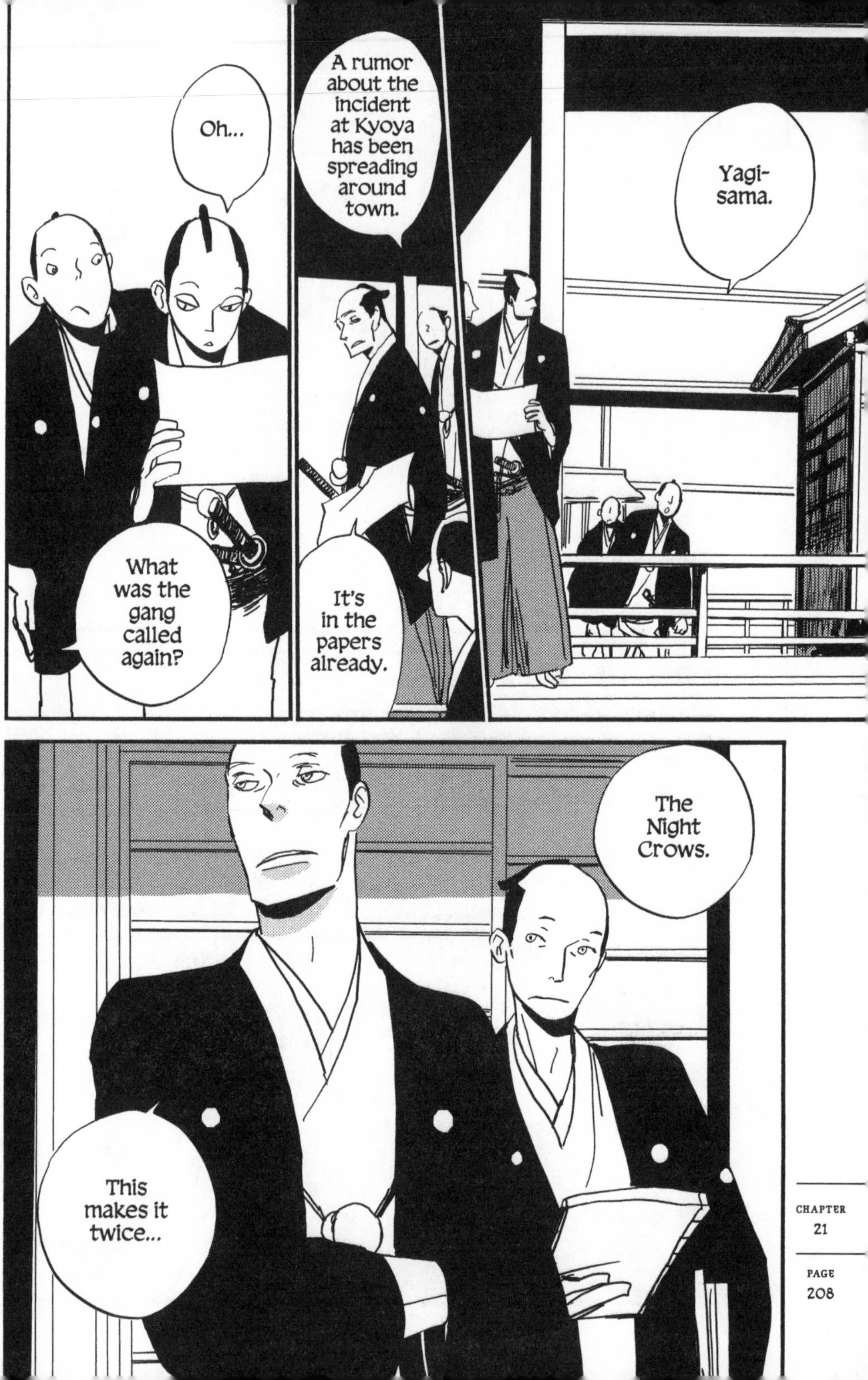
Yagi-sama.
A rumor about the incident at Kyoya has been spreading around town.
It's in the papers already.
Oh...
What was the gang called again?
The Night Crows.
This makes it twice...

On curtains: Food, Sake

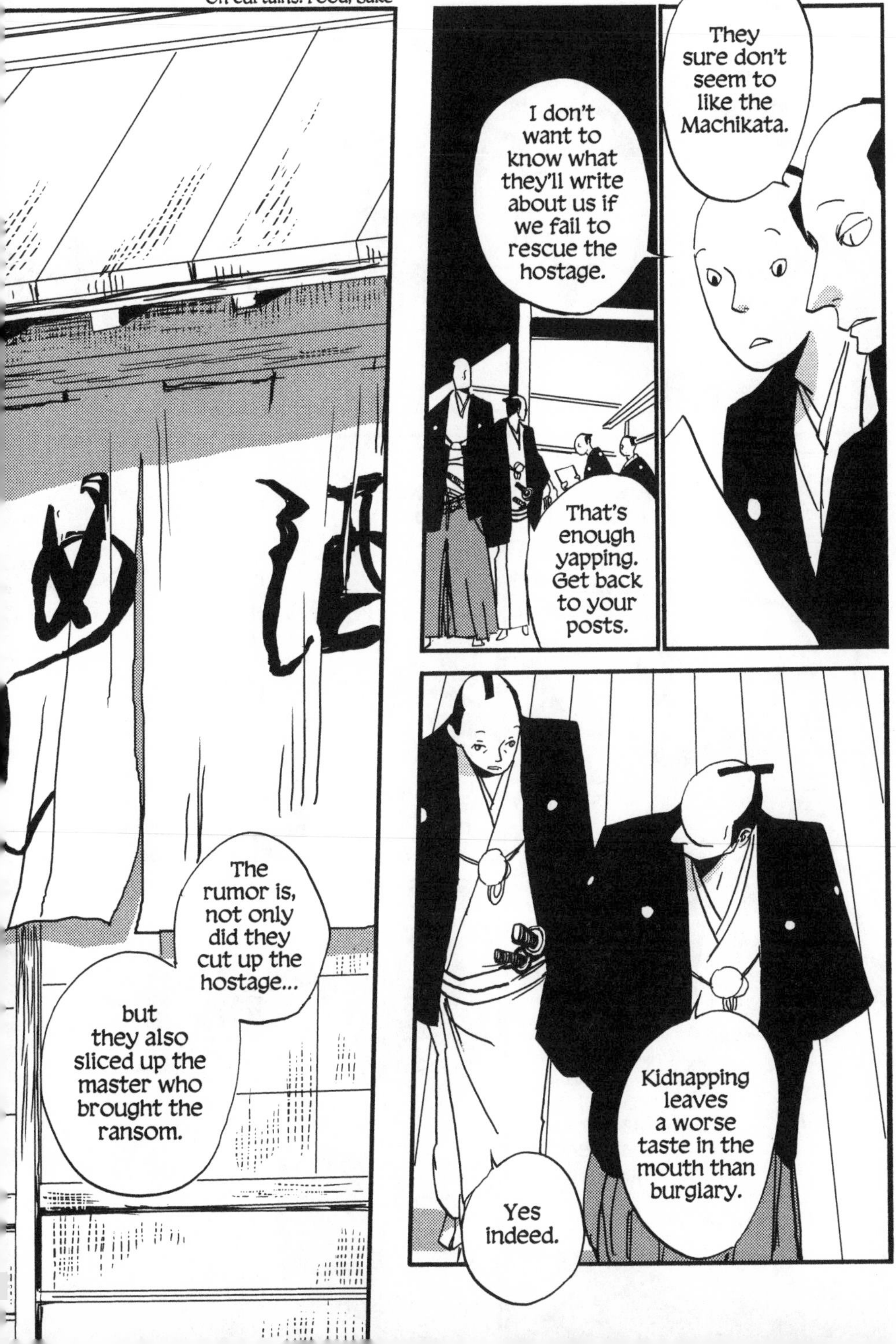
They sure don't seem to like the Machikata.
I don't want to know what they'll write about us if we fail to rescue the hostage.
That's enough yapping. Get back to your posts.
Kidnapping leaves a worse taste in the mouth than burglary.
Yes indeed.
The rumor is, not only did they cut up the hostage...
but they also sliced up the master who brought the ransom.

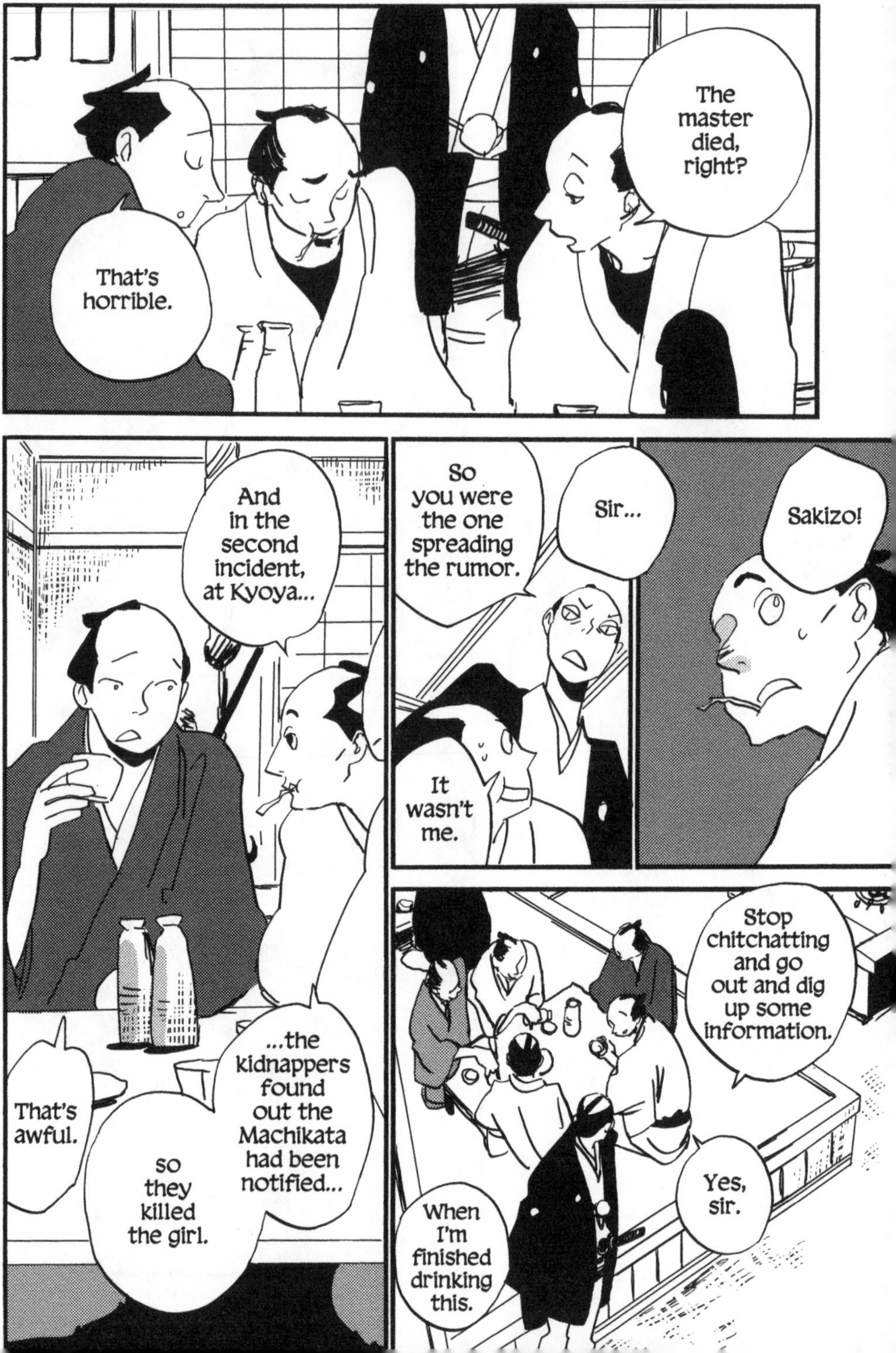
The master died, right?
That's horrible.
Sakizo!
Sir...
So you were the one spreading the rumor.
It wasn't me.
Stop chitchatting and go out and dig up some information.
Yes, sir.
When I'm finished drinking this.
And in the second incident, at Kyoya...
...the kidnappers found out the Machikata had been notified...
so they killed the girl.
That's awful.

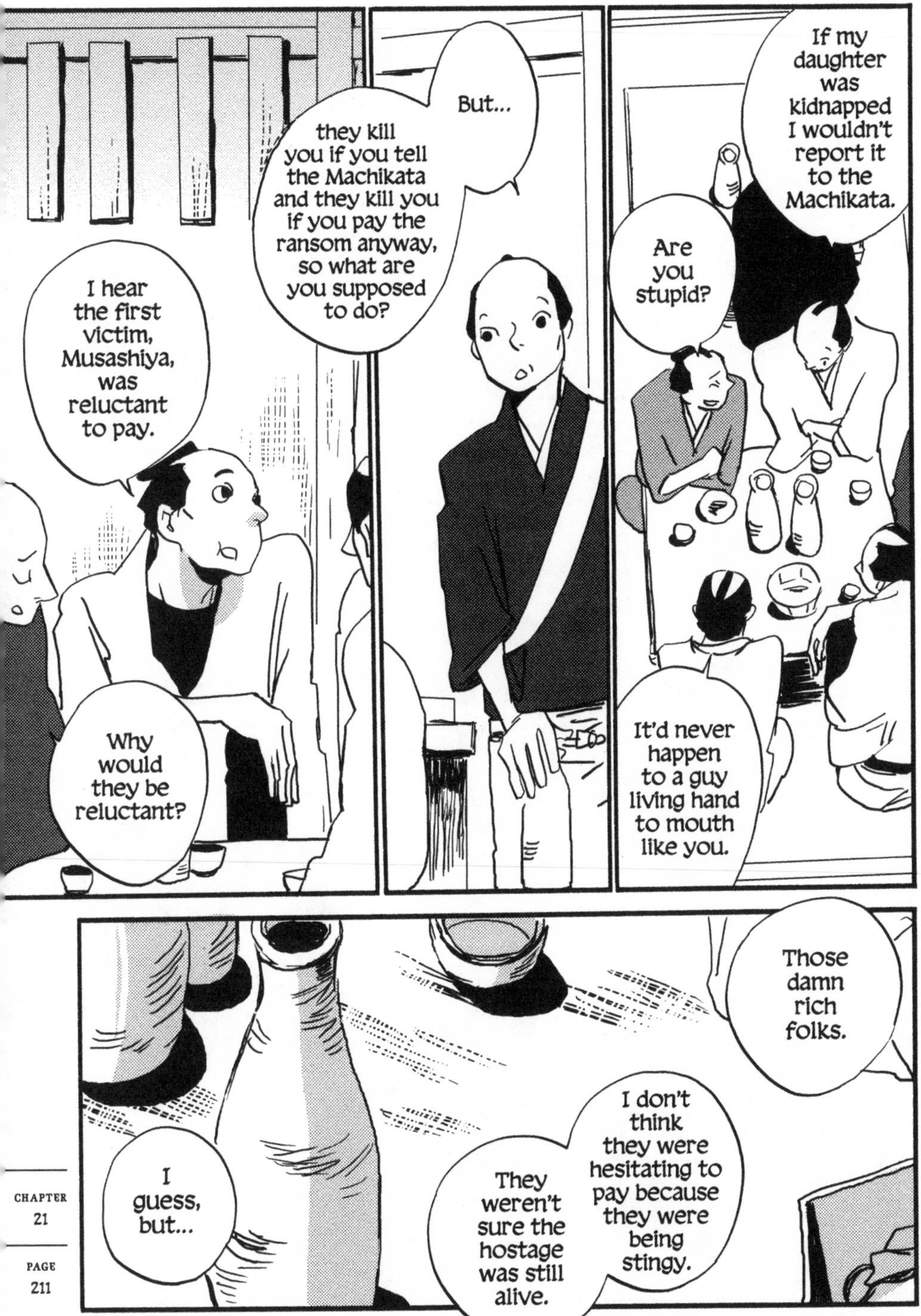
If my daughter was kidnapped I wouldn't report it to the Machikata.
Are you stupid?
It'd never happen to a guy living hand to mouth like you.
But...
they kill you if you tell the Machikata and they kill you if you pay the ransom anyway, so what are you supposed to do?
I hear the first victim, Musashiya, was reluctant to pay.
Why would they be reluctant?
Those damn rich folks.
I don't think they were hesitating to pay because they were being stingy.
They weren't sure the hostage was still alive.
I guess, but...

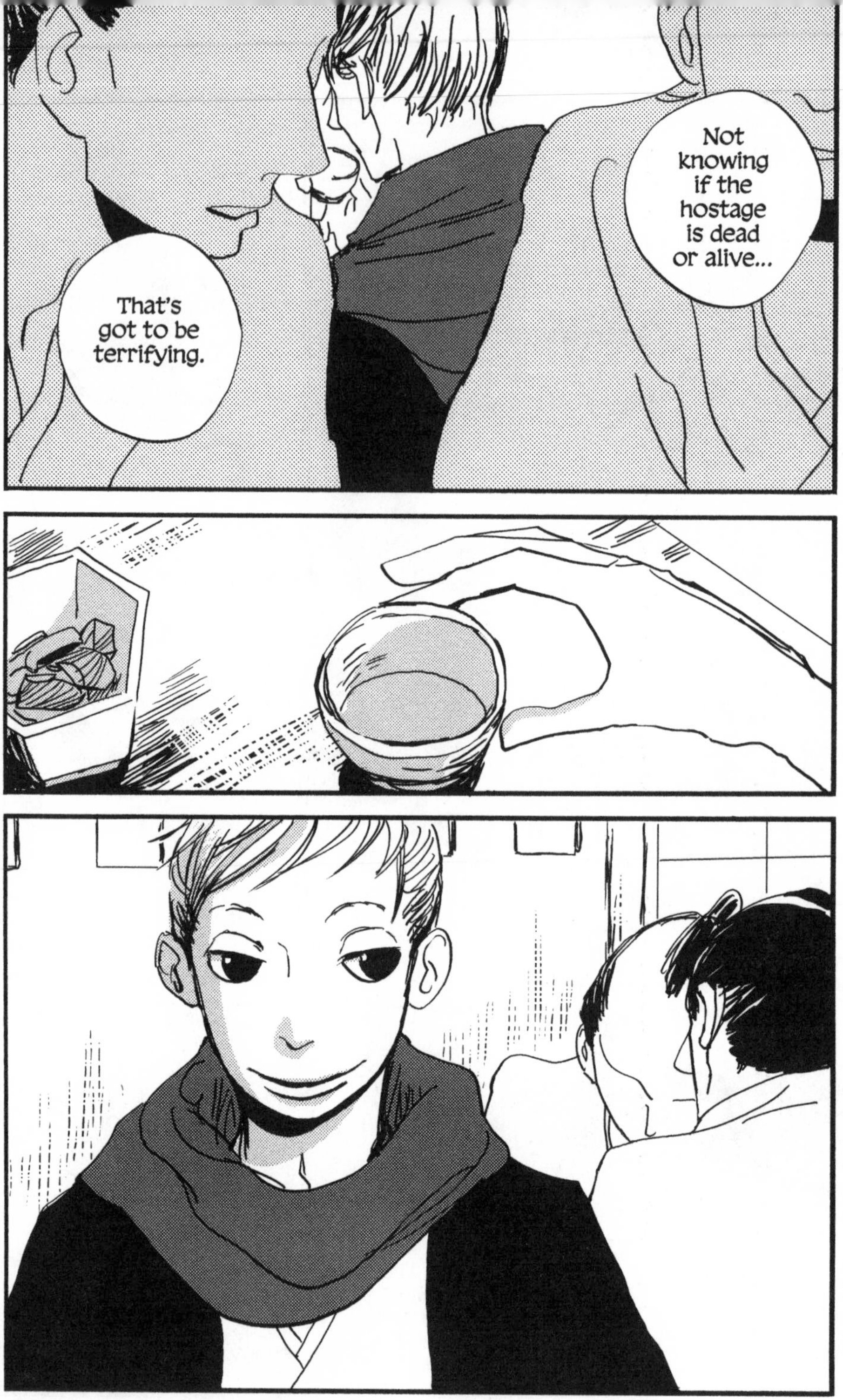
Not knowing if the hostage is dead or alive...
That's got to be terrifying.

END

House of Five Leaves

VOLUME **3**

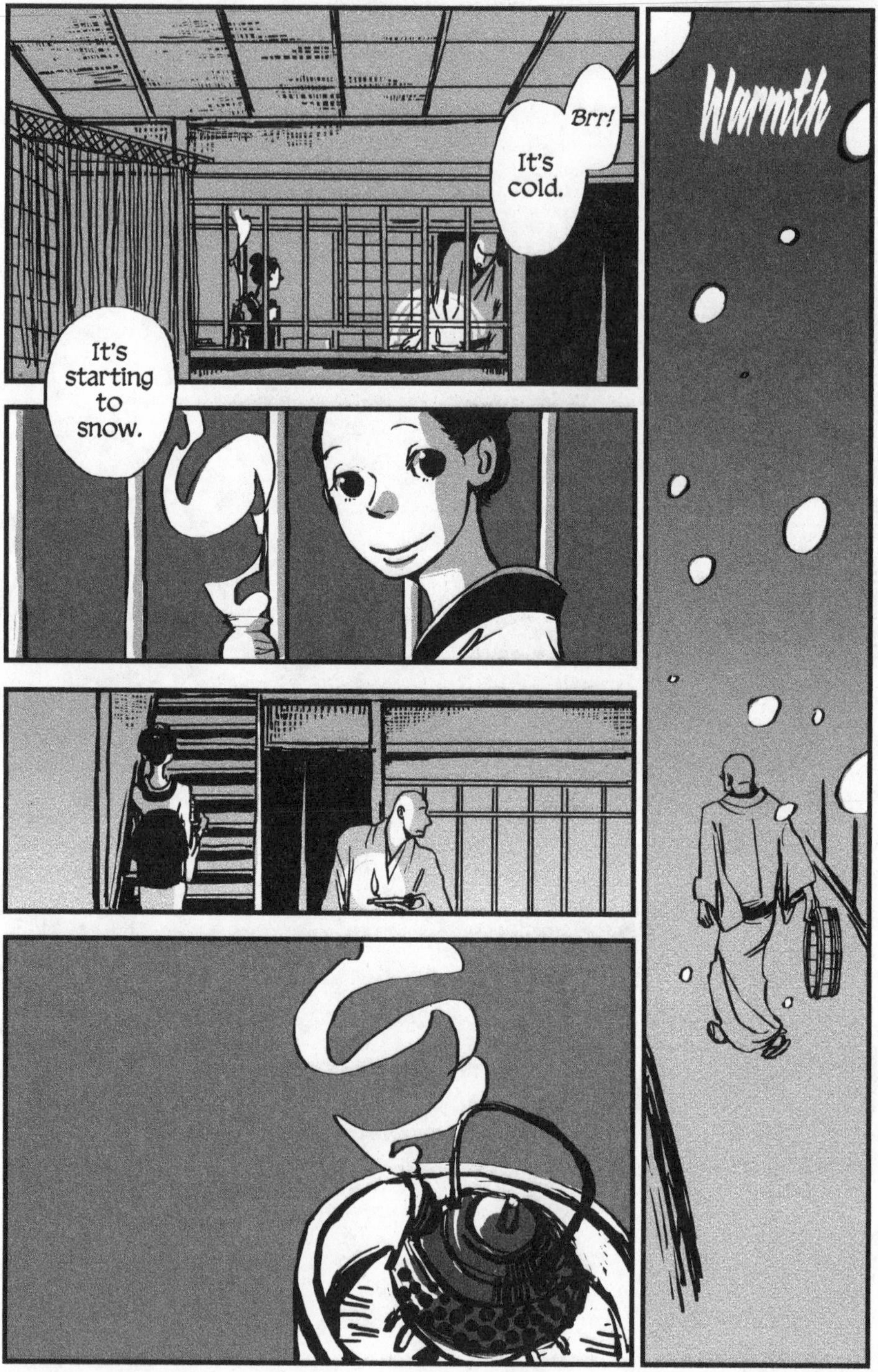
Warmth
Brr!
It's cold.
It's starting to snow.

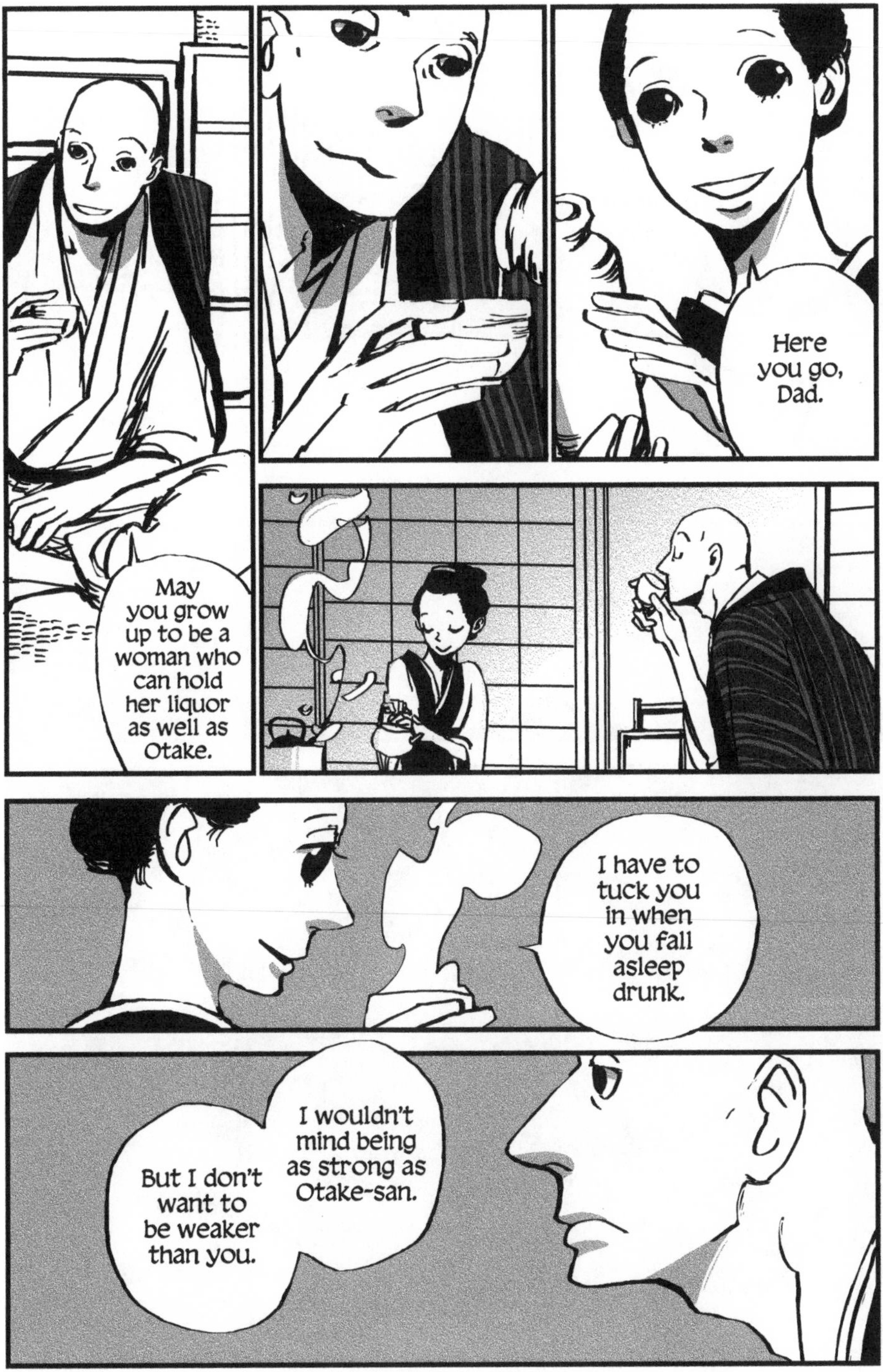
Here you go, Dad.
May you grow up to be a woman who can hold her liquor as well as Otake.
I have to tuck you in when you fall asleep drunk.
I wouldn't mind being as strong as Otake-san.
But I don't want to be weaker than you.

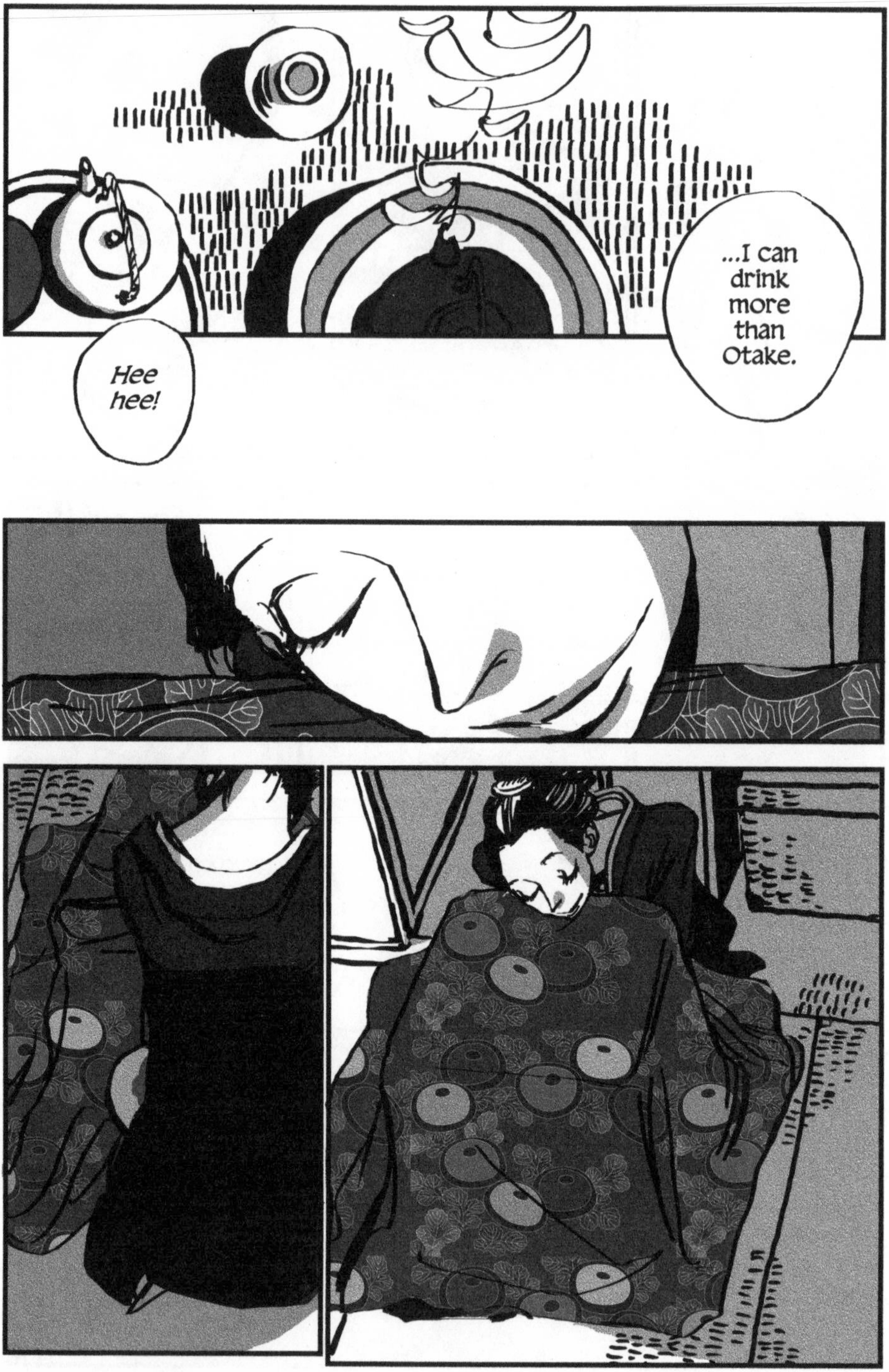
...I can drink more than Otake.
Hee hee!

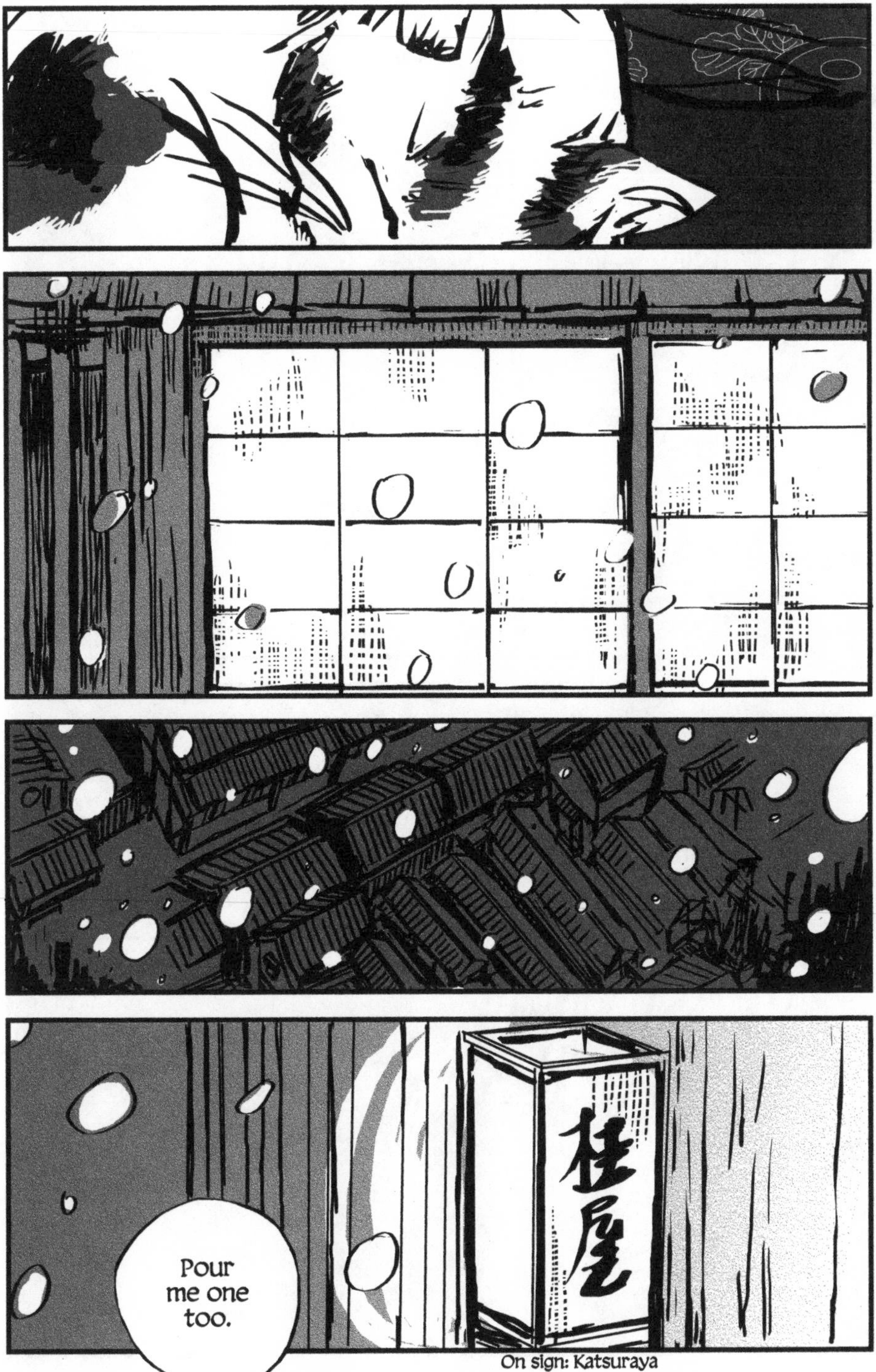
Pour me one too.

On sign: Katsuraya

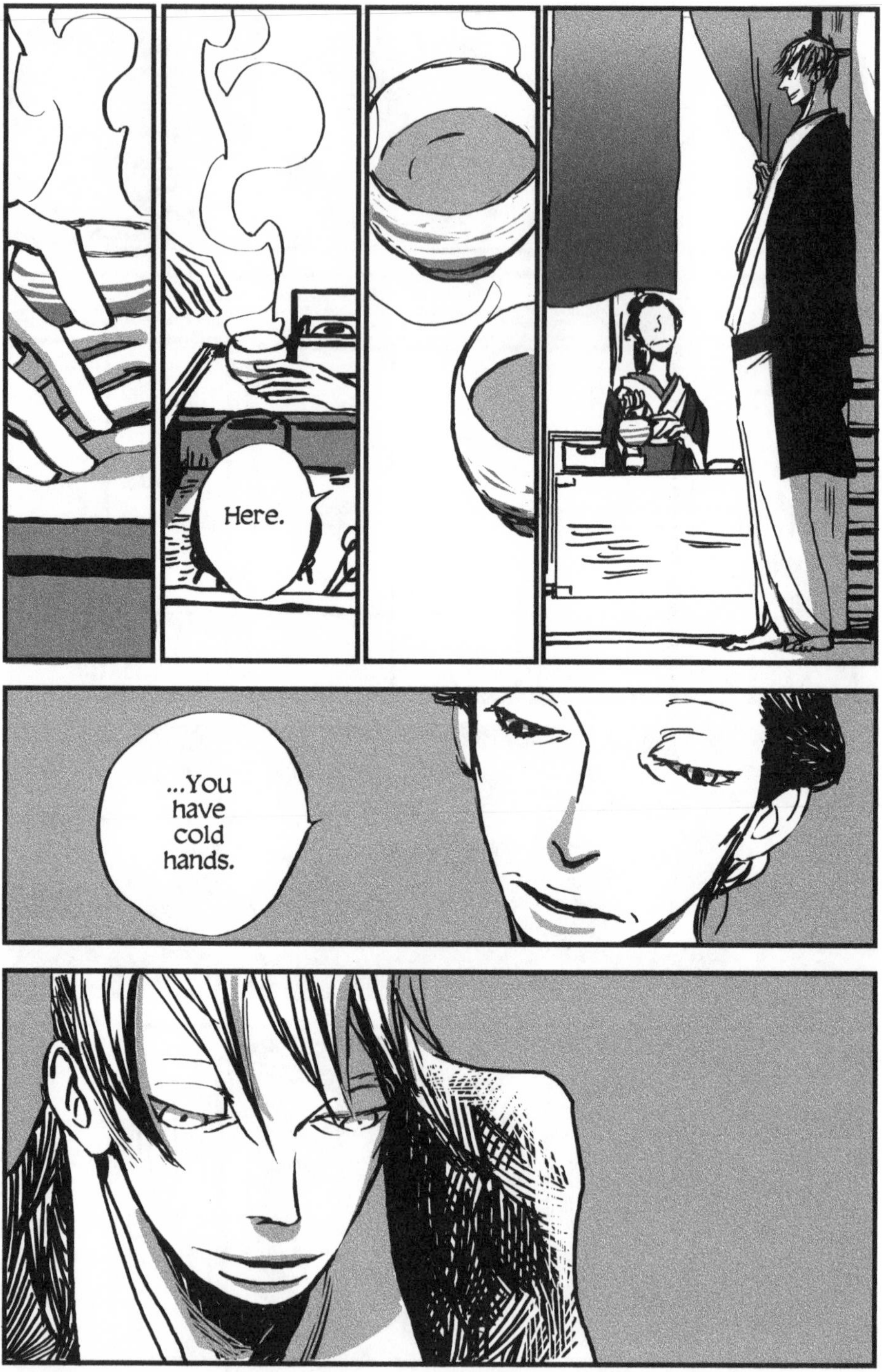
Here.
...You have cold hands.

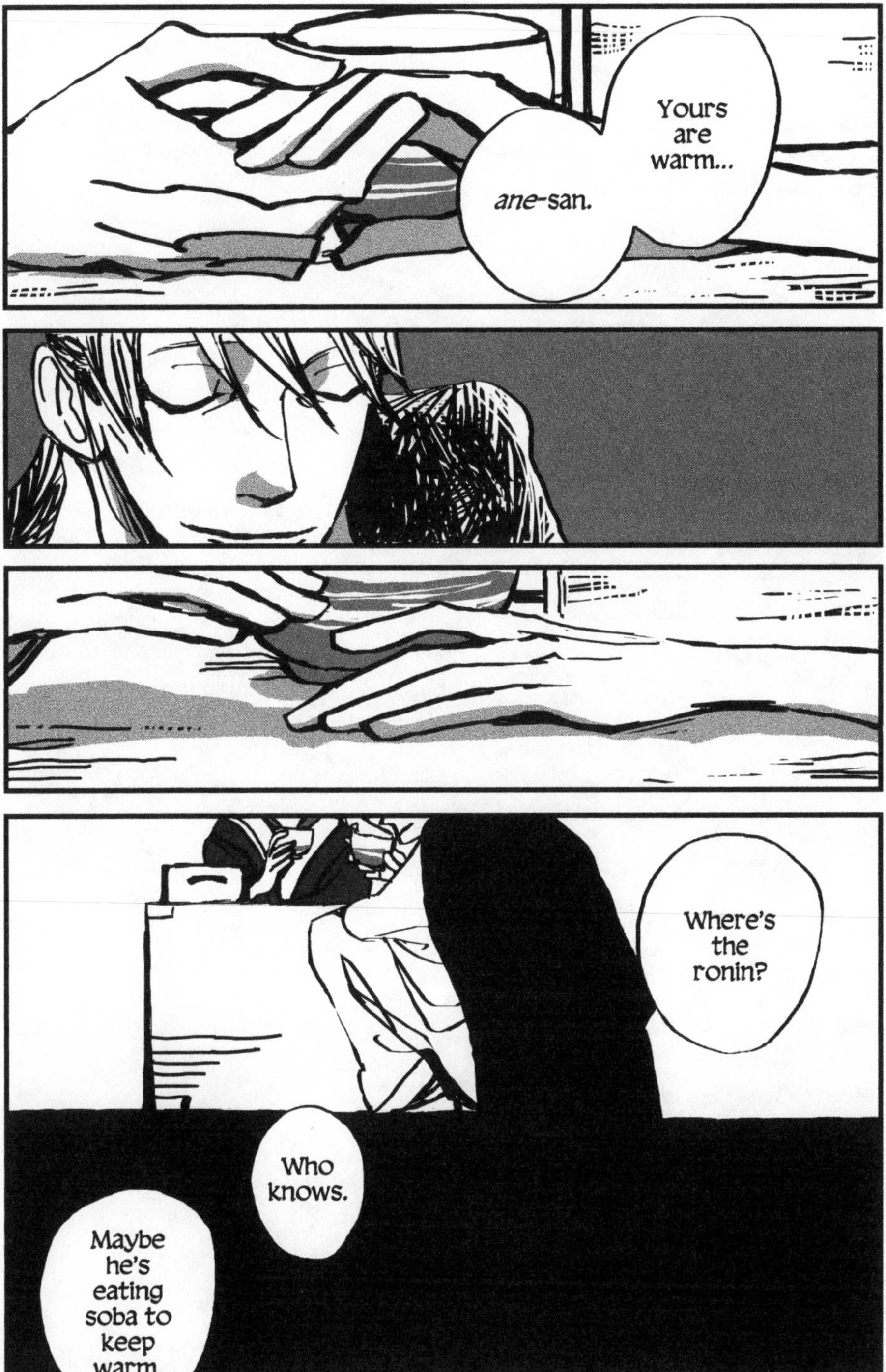
Yours are warm...
ane-san.
Where's the ronin?
Who knows.
Maybe he's eating soba to keep warm.

In this volume the Japanese name order of surname
first, then given name, has been retained. So, for
example, "Akitsu" is Akitsu Masanosuke's surname,
and "Masanosuke" is his first. Many characters are
referred to simply by their surnames or aliases.

The names of several of the members of the Five
Leaves incorporate kanji (writing characters)
that are also the names of trees. The *matsu* in
"Matsukichi" is pine, the *take* in "Otake" is
bamboo, and the *ume* in "Umezou" is plum.
These three kanji may also be read respectively
as *sho*, *chiku*, and *bai*. The grouping of these
three trees, the *Shochikubai*, is considered to
be a symbol of happiness and good fortune.

Additionally, the name of the character Yagi is
written with the kanji for "eight" and "tree."

GLOSSARY

ANE. Literally means "elder sister" but is used as a general term of respect for women older than the speaker. PAGE 219

ANIUE. A respectful term used by younger siblings when addressing the eldest brother in the family. A bit archaic in flavor, it is no longer commonly used. PAGE 123

CHAN. An honorific suffix used as an endearment when the speaker-is talking to a person (usually a girl) younger and lower in status. PAGE 141

DAIMYO. A feudal lord, the ruler of a domain (or *han*, in Japanese) under the shogunate. PAGE 20

DANGO. Rice-flour dumplings threaded onto a skewer and frequently topped with sweet syrups or pastes. PAGE 30

DANNA. An honorific term that carries the meanings "master," "husband," "gentleman," or "sir." It is also used specifically to refer to a geisha's patron. PAGE 19

DONO. An honorific suffix that's the equivalent of "sir" or "lady." A very formal term, it's not commonly used these days. PAGE 10

GOINKYO. The word is made up of the honorific prefix "go" and the characters for "retirement" or "retiree." In Japanese, individuals are not uncommonly referred to by their occupation or social position, as is the case here. *Goinkyo*—as opposed to *taishokusha*, the regular word for "retiree"—is applied particularly to a master or someone who held a position of authority. PAGE 5

HATAMOTO. In the Edo period, men bearing the title of *hatamoto* served directly under the shogun. PAGE 16

HIRATSUKA-JUKU. One of the fifty-three way stations along the Tokaido road, the main travel route between Edo and Kyoto in the feudal era. PAGE 202

IZAKAYA. A traditional Japanese pub that serves liquor and simple dishes. PAGE 122

KORYOURI. Literally means "small cuisine."

Koryouriya were informal places to get a modest meal, filling roughly the same role as contemporary diners. PAGE 105

MACHIKATA. The Edo-era analogue of a uniformed municipal police force, it was staffed mainly by low-ranking samurai. PAGE 81

OJOU. A respectful term used to address females higher in status than the speaker. Roughly equivalent to "Miss" or "Mademoiselle." PAGE 122

OKAA-SAN. Literally means "mother" but is also used by geisha to refer to the madam of their house. PAGE 198

ONIGIRI. A common snack item, *onigiri* are made by pressing cooked rice into a ball or other form that can easily be held in the hand. They are frequently wrapped in *nori* seaweed and can contain fillings such as bits of fish or pickles. PAGE 114

RONIN. A masterless or unemployed samurai. PAGE 103

SAMA. An honorific suffix used when addressing someone higher in status, or when the speaker wants to emphasize the respect in which he or she holds the person being addressed. PAGE 21

SAN. An honorific suffix that functions roughly like "Mr." or "Ms." in English. It is the most status-neutral and common way of addressing others in Japanese. PAGE 11

SENSEI. Although *sensei* literally means "teacher," it is a title often used to indicate respect when addressing someone who is accomplished in a certain field. In this case the man is referred to as "sensei" because of his position as a yojimbo and his presumed skill as a swordsman. PAGE 28

SOBA. Buckwheat noodles served either warm in soup or chilled with dipping sauce. PAGE 47

YOJIMBO. An individual employed as a personal bodyguard or protector, or as a guard or security patrol for an establishment. PAGE 48

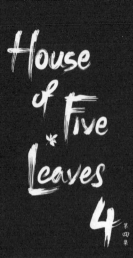

House of Five Leaves 4

第四集

IN THE NEXT VOLUME...

With Masa having joined the crew, the fragile bonds between the members of the Five Leaves begin to change. Further changes are promised by the arrival of Ginta, a self-styled "negotiator" who learns of the existence of the Five Leaves and offers them his services. Meanwhile, the pressure on Yaichi increases as the members of his old gang continue to track him down. Burdened by the weight of his hidden past, his impervious façade begins to crack.

AVAILABLE SEPTEMBER 2011

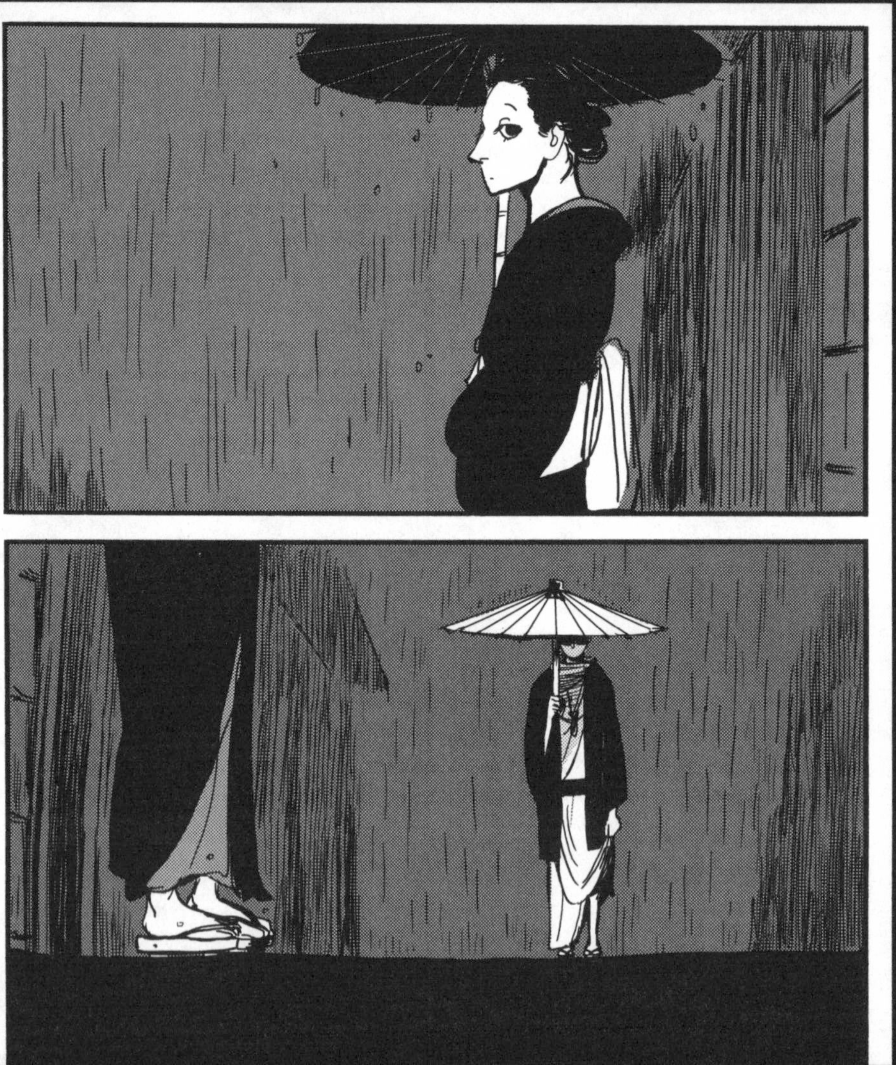

HOUSE OF FIVE LEAVES
Volume Three

VIZ Signature Edition

STORY & ART BY NATSUME ONO

Original Japanese edition "SARAIYA GOYOU" published by SHOGAKUKAN Inc.

Original Japanese cover design by Atsuhiro YAMAMOTO

TRANSLATION Joe Yamazaki
TOUCH-UP ART & LETTERING Gia Cam Luc
DESIGN Courtney Utt, Fawn Lau
EDITOR Leyla Aker

Printed in Canada

Published by VIZ Media, LLC
P.O. Box 77010
San Francisco, CA 94107

10 9 8 7 6 5 4 3 2 1
First printing, April 2011

VIZ SIGNATURE
WWW.SIGIKKI.COM

PARENTAL ADVISORY
HOUSE OF FIVE LEAVES is rated T+ for Older Teen and is recommended for ages 16 and up.

RATED T+ FOR OLDER TEEN
ratings.viz.com

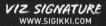

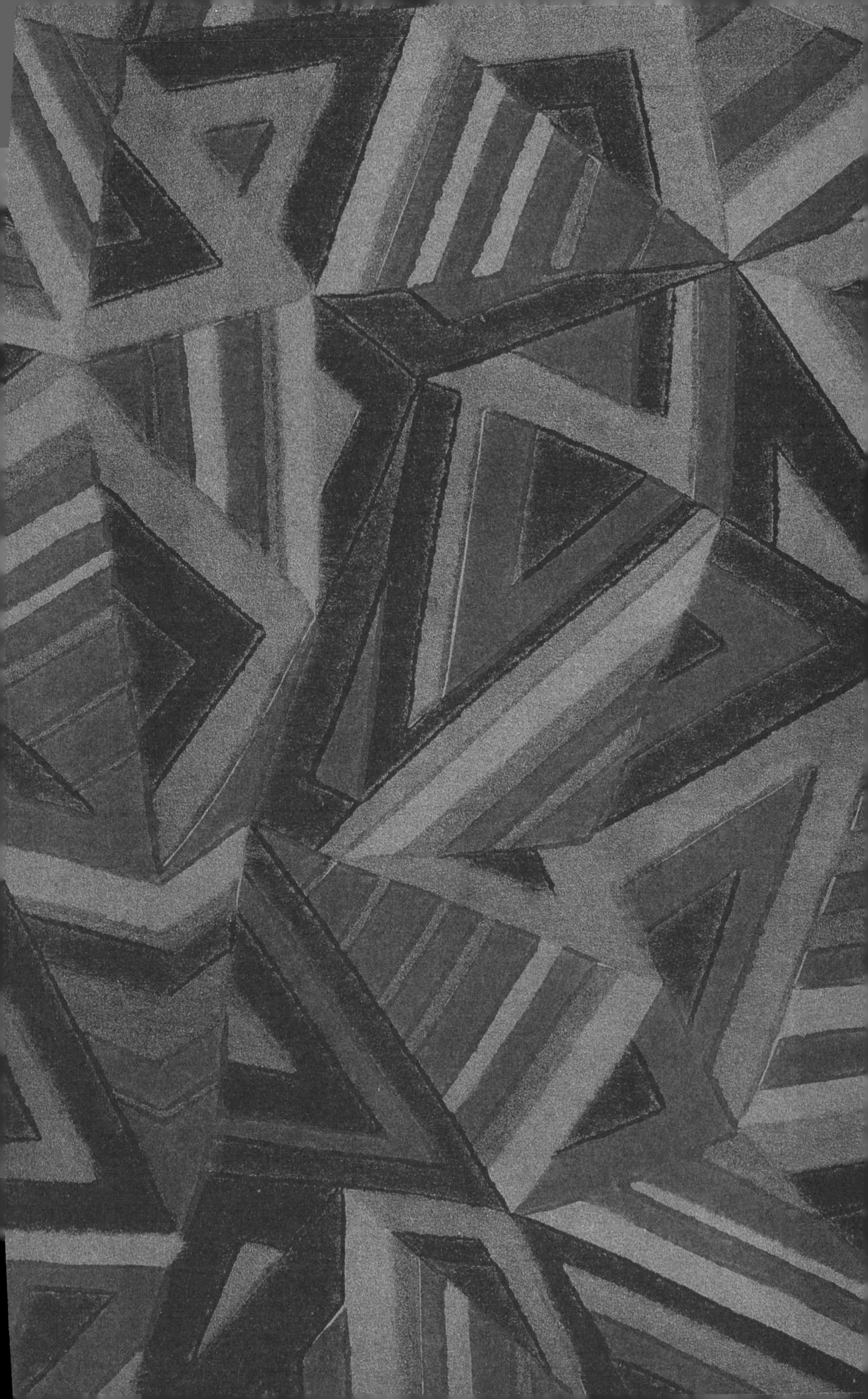